WITHD
D1562044

Forsyth Library

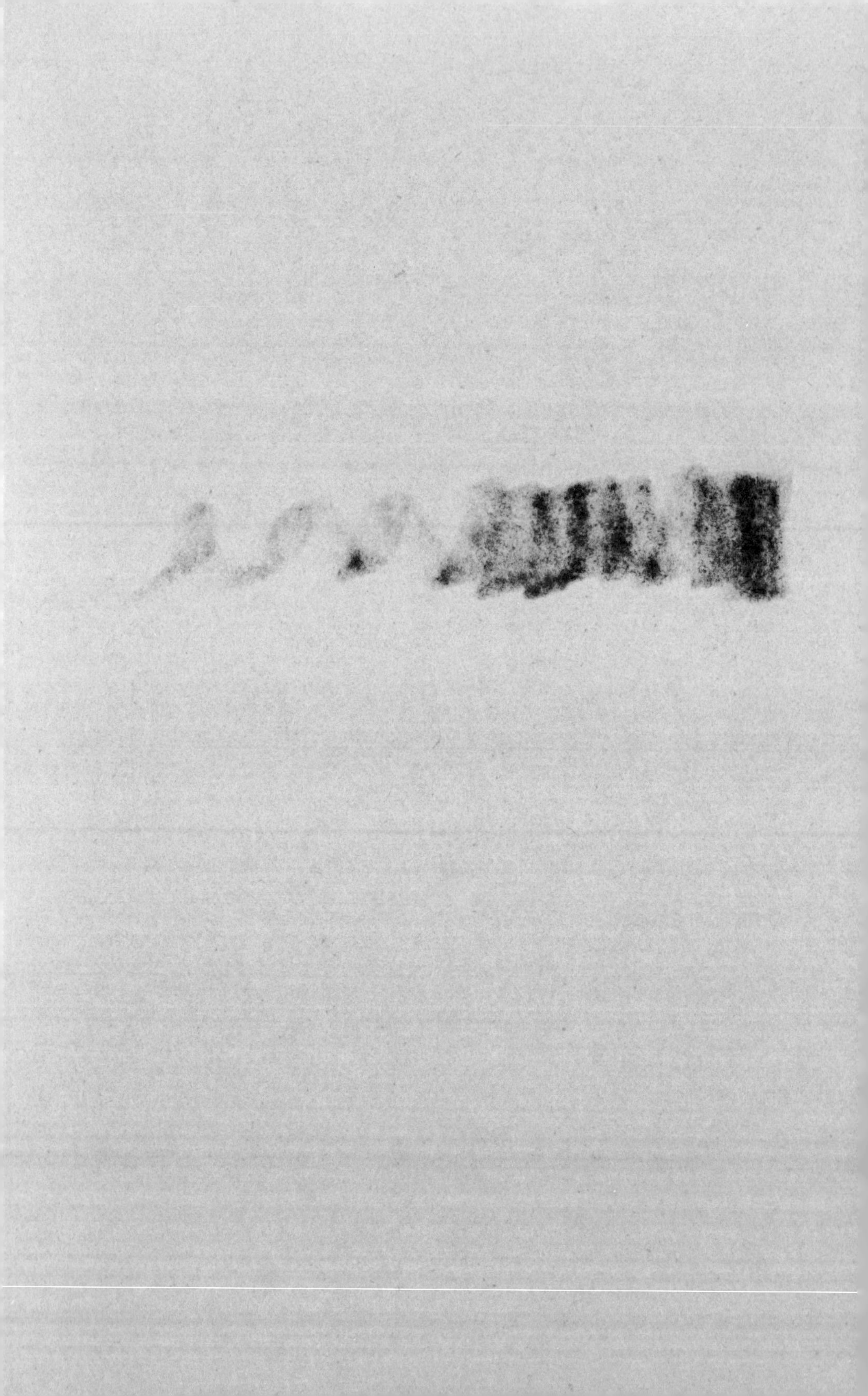

U.S. Foreign Policy and the Shah

U.S. Foreign Policy and the Shah

BUILDING A CLIENT STATE IN IRAN

Mark J. Gasiorowski

Cornell University Press

Ithaca and London

First published 1991 by Cornell University Press.

International Standard Book Number 0-8014-2412-7
Library of Congress Catalog Card Number 90-55919
Printed in the United States of America
Librarians: Library of Congress cataloging information appears on the last page of the book.

♾ The paper in this book meets the minimum requirements of the American National Standard for Information Sciences—Permanence of Paper for Printed Library Materials, ANSI Z39.48-1984.

To John and Abby,
for all they've given me

Contents

Tables and Figure

FIGURE

. . . the shah's regime reflected American interests as faithfully as Vidkun Quisling's puppet government in Norway reflected the interests of Nazi Germany in World War II. The shah's defense program, his industrial and economic transactions, and his oil policy were all considered by most Iranians to be faithful executions of American instructions. Ultimately, the United States was blamed for the thousands killed during the last year by the Iranian army, which was trained, equipped, and seemingly controlled by Washington. Virtually every wall in Iran carried a slogan demanding the death of the "American shah."

—Richard Cottam, "Goodbye to America's Shah," *Foreign Policy* 34 (Spring 1979)

Preface

The Iranian revolution of 1978–79 was a baffling spectacle for most observers. Since the early 1960s, Iran had enjoyed high rates of economic growth and had undergone a thorough "revolution from above" that seemed to have thrust it into the vanguard of modernizing countries. A major land reform program had been carried out, and industrialization had been rapid, providing employment and economic improvement for virtually all elements of Iranian society. Very little popular unrest had surfaced for nearly two decades. A new breed of Western-educated technocrats had been installed in the top positions of government and industry, providing Iran with potentially effective, pragmatic leaders. Iran had become a major regional power and an important actor in world affairs. The country's autocratic ruler, Mohammad Reza Pahlavi, the late shah, had held lavish celebrations of progress and boasted that Iran would become a major world power by the end of the century. Experts and casual observers alike, both inside Iran and in other countries, were bewildered that a revolution could occur so quickly under these circumstances.

The baffling character of the Iranian revolution has made it the subject of many analytic studies. Many of these studies have traced the origins of the revolution to preexisting economic conditions, including widespread poverty and inequality, economic dislocations associated with the high growth rates of the 1960s and 1970s, and the mild recession that followed the oil boom of the early 1970s. Others have taken a political economy approach, examining the consequences of rapid economic development before the revolution for Iran's social structure and consequently for the nature of its domestic politics. Still others have stressed the unique ability of Iran's radical Shi'i clergy to mobilize the Iranian people into a revolutionary movement capable of overthrowing the shah.

Each of these approaches to understanding the causes of the Iranian revolution implicitly suggests a more fundamental cause: the Iranian state had attained a high degree of autonomy under the shah in the sense that it had grown unresponsive to societal pressures and its policies had become divorced from the interests and needs of society. The state's autonomy enabled it to pursue economic policies that were often grossly ill suited to Iran's economic conditions. Poverty and inequality therefore persisted, and the oil boom of the early 1970s was badly mismanaged. Similarly, the state's autonomy enabled it to resist the mounting pressure for social, economic, and political change being voiced by the middle- and lower-class groups that had been spawned by several decades of rapid economic growth. The failure of the state to address the concerns of these groups left them increasingly alienated and susceptible to the appeals of the radical Shi'i clergy. Consequently, while adverse economic conditions and political pressures associated with socioeconomic change and the Shi'i clergy were important determinants of the Iranian revolution, at a more fundamental level it was the character of the Iranian state in the prerevolutionary era that created these conditions and thus precipitated the revolution.

A thorough understanding of the origins of the Iranian revolution must therefore begin with an analysis of the conditions that made the Iranian state highly autonomous in the prerevolutionary period. Although such an analysis is implicit in many works on the subject, very few examine the prerevolutionary Iranian state in much detail and link its character explicitly to the revolution. For those authors who do undertake such an analysis, the most important determinant of the state's high degree of autonomy was its extensive oil income. Oil revenue, which accrues directly to the state in Iran and in most other contemporary oil-producing countries, reduces the state's dependence on society for tax revenue and enables it to co-opt societal groups through public-sector employment and spending on development projects, social services, and other popular programs. Political activists are therefore likely to have a hard time mobilizing public opposition to a state with high oil income, and the state will therefore enjoy some degree of autonomy.

This argument has considerable merit in the case of Iran. But although oil revenue undoubtedly enhanced the autonomy of the Iranian state in the late 1960s and 1970s, when Iran's oil income was very large, it cannot have had much of an effect in the 1950s and early 1960s, when Iran's oil income was much more modest. As Chapters 5 and 6 will show, the shah succeeded in establishing an authoritarian regime during this later period under which the Iranian state achieved a very high degree of autonomy. The state's extensive oil revenue in the late 1960s and 1970s therefore helps to explain the persistence of its high degree of autonomy in this period but not the initial emergence of a highly autonomous state.

Other writers have focused on Iran's relationship with the United States before the revolution as an important factor in Iranian domestic politics. In 1953 the United States sponsored a covert coup d'état that overthrew the pluralistic regime of Prime Minister Mohammad Mosaddeq and permitted the shah to establish an authoritarian regime; it subsequently provided extensive economic aid and security assistance to the shah which enabled him to consolidate this regime. Indeed, before the revolution many Iranians were acutely aware of the U.S. role in establishing and strengthening the shah's regime, leading them to describe their monarch as "America's shah" and giving the revolution a highly anti-American character. But neither studies of the causes of the Iranian revolution nor studies of U.S. foreign policy toward Iran have concretely analyzed the impact of U.S.-Iranian relations on Iran's domestic politics.

This book undertakes such an analysis. The first chapter draws on literature in the fields of international politics and political sociology to develop a theoretical framework for examining how international cliency relationships (such as the one that existed between the United States and Iran before the revolution) can affect the domestic politics of client countries. International cliency relationships are established by patron powers with strategically important client countries mainly to promote political stability in these countries. This is usually done by giving large amounts of economic aid and security assistance to the governments of the client countries. This book's main argument is that assistance of this kind can enable the client state to become more autonomous in the sense that it can more easily resist political pressures from domestic societal groups. Because highly autonomous states lack societal constraint, the policies of client states may increasingly diverge from the interests and needs of society. Serious unrest and instability may eventually result and even lead to revolution. A relationship initially designed to promote political stability in the client country may therefore promote instability in the long run, threatening the patron's strategic interests.

The theoretical framework developed in Chapter 1 guides the subsequent analysis of U.S. policy toward Iran and its impact on Iranian domestic politics in the era before the revolution. Chapter 2 serves as a prologue to this analysis, examining the forces that shaped Iranian domestic politics before the United States first became deeply involved in Iran. Chapter 3 covers the period from May 1951 through August 1953, when U.S. involvement in Iran grew rapidly. This period ended when the CIA sponsored the coup that overthrew Mosaddeq, an event that marked both the beginning of the U.S. cliency relationship with Iran and the establishment of an authoritarian regime there. Chapter 4 examines the specific activities that marked the U.S.-Iran cliency relationship and their implications for state-society relations in Iran. Chapters 5 and 6 examine Iranian domestic politics between the 1953 coup and the revolution, focusing especially on the importance of the U.S.-Iran cliency relationship relative to the other structural factors that affected Iranian politics. Finally, Chapter 7 examines the policies undertaken by the Iranian state in certain issue areas in the 1960s and 1970s, emphasizing how these policies contributed to the 1978–79 revolution.

This book attempts to provide insight both into the forces that shape domestic politics in certain Third World countries and into the problems posed by political unrest in client countries for U.S. national security. Since patron powers tend to establish cliency relationships with countries that can advance their security interests, the ideas developed here are likely to be more relevant to countries located in strategically important regions of the world, such as Central America, the Middle East, Eastern Europe, east Asia and Southeast Asia, than to countries located in regions of less strategic importance, such as South America, Africa, and southern Asia. If the main argument advanced here is reasonably correct, then the widely used superpower strategy of maintaining client states in the Third World is inherently flawed. In the conclusion I make some recommendations for alternative strategies which may enable U.S. policy makers to achieve the short-term goals that lead them to establish cliency relationships while avoiding the undesirable long-term consequences of cliency identified here.

A few important methodological notes are in order. I obtained much of the most crucial material in Chapters 3 through 5 in personal interviews with retired U.S., Iranian, and British officials. Although relying on interviews for source material poses obvious problems of reliability, this approach was inevitable because many key documents on U.S.-Iranian relations remain inaccessible to researchers and many important details were never recorded to begin with. Moreover, most of these interviews were necessarily carried out on a strictly confidential basis, making it impossible for me to identify here the sources of much of the material I obtained in this way.

To minimize the problem of reliability, I have taken great pains to cross-check and verify the material I obtained in these interviews. Several interviewees provided information that conflicted significantly with information I obtained from other sources that I judged to be more reliable; in these cases, I discarded all information provided by the unreliable interviewee. Most of the interview material presented in Chapters 3 through 5 was corroborated by at least one additional source. Material obtained from a single interviewee that could not be corroborated is either qualified in the text or identified in the notes as the product of a single source. In defense of this methodology, I should note that textual sources such as government documents, memoirs, and secondary sources are often quite biased as well. Indeed, it is my general impression that the textual material I have used is considerably less reliable than the material I obtained in personal interviews.

The primary documents used here were drawn from a wide variety of sources. The following conventions are employed in chapter notes to identify them. Documents from the Dwight D. Eisenhower Library, the John F. Kennedy Library, and the Agency for International Development Library are identified with "DDE Library," "JFK Library," or "AID Library" respectively. Documents with an identification code such as "FO/371/104565" are from the British Public Records Office in London. Documents with a code such as "Record Group 59, Box 4110" are from the Diplomatic Records Branch of the U.S. National Archives in Washington. Except where noted, all documents from the U.S. National Security Council, Joint Chiefs of Staff, and State-War-Navy Coordinating Committee are from the Military Records Branch of the National Archives. Documents identified as being from the "Iran White Paper" are from the Information and Privacy Staff of the U.S. Department of State. This white paper was compiled in 1979 by the State Department in conjunction with other U.S. government agencies and subsequently released to various researchers under the Freedom of Information Act (FOIA). It contains both text, which I refer to by section number (e.g., "sec. III.B"), and supporting documents, which I refer to by document number (e.g., "doc. I.B-45"). Documents identified with "*Declass. Docs.*" are from the Declassified Documents Reference System. Except where noted, all other primary documents cited in the notes were obtained under the FOIA from the relevant government agencies.

I owe an enormous debt to Enrique Baloyra, without whom this book simply would never have been written. I have also benefited considerably from the advice and suggestions of Abdel-Monem Al-Mashat, Carol Bargeron, Richard Cottam, Ted Hotchkiss, Earnest Oney, and Mohammad Said. Many other people were exceedingly helpful in illuminating for me the intricacies of U.S. foreign policy and Iranian politics or in otherwise facilitating my research efforts. In particular, I would like to thank Ahmad Anvari, Sasan Ardalan, Peter Avery, Edward Azar, Shahpour Bakhtiar, Abol-Hassan Bani-Sadr, James Bill, John Bowling, Henry Byroade, Shahin Fatemi, Fereidun Fesharaki, Alex Gagarine, Fred Halliday, Hormoz Hekmat, Richard Helms, Homa Katouzian, Nikki Keddie, Houshang Keshevarz-Sadr, Abdul-Karim Lahiji, Bruce Laingen, Roger Louis, Ahmad Madani, Martin Manning, Sally Marks, Hedayat Matin-Daftari, Gordon Mattison, Stephen Meade, Roy Melbourne, Sir George

Middleton, Chung-in Moon, Paul Nitze, Nasser Pakdaman, Eric Pollard, Ibrahim Pourhadi, Mohammad Hossein Qashqai, Nowzar Razmara, Thomas Ricks, Stuart Rockwell, Kim Roosevelt, William Rountree, Mimi Salamat, Andrew Scott, Shahin Shahin, Khosrow Shakeri, Eva Silverfine, Leo Soucek, Phillips Talbott, John Taylor, John Waller, Donald Wilber, Fraser Wilkins, Christopher Montague Woodhouse, Sir Dennis Wright, and Ardeshir Zahedi. I am also grateful to many other people who must remain unnamed here because of their close involvement in some of the events described below.

I would like to express my gratitude to the following institutions for providing me with financial assistance: the National Science Foundation, the R. J. Reynolds Foundation, the University of North Carolina, and Louisiana State University. Earlier versions of Chapters 3 and 4 have appeared in the *International Journal of Middle East Studies* (August 1987; copyright © 1987 by Cambridge University Press; used with the permission of Cambridge University Press), and in Nikki Keddie and Mark J. Gasiorowski, editors, *Neither East Nor West: Iran, the Soviet Union, and the United States* (New Haven, Conn.: Yale University Press, 1990).

MARK J. GASIOROWSKI

Baton Rouge, Louisiana

U.S. Foreign Policy and the Shah

1

International Cliency Relationships and the Politics of Client States

The close relationship between the United States and Iran during the reign of the late shah is a fairly typical example of an international cliency relationship, a familar feature of contemporary world politics. Cliency relationships have figured prominently in most of the major superpower confrontations of the post–World War II era, from the early Cold War disputes over Eastern Europe and Greece and Turkey to the more recent conflicts in the Middle East and Central America. At various times and to varying degrees, many Third World countries have been involved in such relationships, especially countries in Central America, the Middle East, Eastern Europe, east Asia, and Southeast Asia.

Most observers agree that international cliency relationships can affect the domestic politics of client countries. For example, prior to their recent collapse it had been common in the United States to view the Soviet client states in Eastern Europe, Cuba, and Vietnam as mere surrogates of the Soviet Union. Similarly, critics of U.S. foreign policy have often referred to the "banana republics" of Central America or to the U.S. "puppet governments" in South Vietnam and the Philippines. These characterizations often imply not only that the policies of client governments are heavily influenced by their patrons but also that their entire domestic political systems are somehow affected by their cliency relationships. Unfortunately, most discussions of the domestic political effects of cliency are highly polemical and yield little insight into how it can affect a client's politics. A coherent theoretical framework is needed to understand more precisely the domestic political effects of cliency.

International Cliency Relationships

An international cliency relationship is a mutually beneficial, security-oriented relationship between the governments of two countries that differ greatly in size, wealth, and power. Cliency relationships differ substantially in their specifics, but all involve reciprocal exchanges of goods and services that are intended to enhance the security of the patron and the client and generally cannot be obtained by them from other sources. The importance of these goods and services to the security of the two countries binds their governments together in a cooperative, mutually beneficial relationship.[1] Thus an exchange of goods and services is the principal embodiment of a cliency relationship.

The patron typically provides the client with economic aid, including loans, grants, technical advice, and indirect transfers such as import quotas and commodity assistance; security assistance, including training, liaison, and equipment for the client's military, police, and intelligence forces; security agreements, such as treaties, alliances, and informal commitments of support; and often overt or covert intervention in the client's domestic politics. Because of their critical role in cliency, these goods and services are referred to below as cliency instruments. In return, the client typically provides services that enhance the patron's security: it may agree to serve as a regional policeman on the patron's behalf; it may carry out joint military or intelligence operations with the patron; or it may permit the patron to establish military bases or intelligence-gathering facilities on its territory.

The primary motive for a cliency relationship is the desire of both governments to obtain these goods and services. Patrons generally seek cliency relationships with strategically important countries, including countries located near their own borders or the borders of their principal allies and adversaries, countries that control access to vital shipping lanes, and countries that are major sources of vital raw materials. A client government typically enters a cliency relationship to obtain economic aid, security assistance, and protection against domestic or foreign adversaries. Various secondary motives may also exist. A patron may seek to

[1]This definition draws on Christopher C. Shoemaker and John Spanier, *Patron-Client State Relationships: Multilateral Crises in the Nuclear Age* (New York: Praeger, 1984), chap. 2, and Klaus Knorr, *The Power of Nations* (New York: Basic Books, 1975), 24–26. For a good collection of studies on a similar topic see Jan F. Triska, ed., *Dominant Powers and Subordinate States: The United States in Latin America and the Soviet Union in Eastern Europe* (Durham, N.C.: Duke University Press, 1986). The term *cliency* is used in a different context in the literature on clientelist politics. For an overview of this literature see S. N. Eisenstadt and Rene Lemarchand, eds., *Political Clientelism, Patronage, and Development* (Beverly Hills, Calif.: Sage, 1981).

spread its ideological views or expand its base of support in international forums such as the United Nations. A client may seek increased commercial ties with the patron or the prestige of being associated with it.

As a cliency relationship evolves, other kinds of interactions may result. The security provided by the relationship may lead businessmen in the patron country to invest in the client country. Personal contacts made through the relationship may lead to greater commercial, educational, or cultural ties between the two countries. These subsidiary interactions may foster other relationships that parallel the cliency relationship, such as economic dependence or cultural penetration. These parallel relationships may reinforce public awareness of the cliency relationship in the client country, often with harmful consequences. They can also affect social and political conditions in the client country in their own right, often making it hard to distinguish their domestic political effects from the effects of the cliency relationship itself.[2]

If the goods and services exchanged are of greater value to one participant in the cliency relationship than to the other, they may enable the government that benefits less to exert influence over the government that benefits more.[3] Because economic aid and other cliency instruments are often crucial to the survival of a client government, such influence usually accrues to the patron; under certain circumstances, however, it may accrue to the client instead.[4] This influence can be used to change the distribution of benefits in the cliency relationship, as when a patron seeks to expand a military base or a client seeks a higher aid allocation, or to coerce, as when a patron seeks major changes in a client's domestic policies or tries to influence the selection of officials in the client government.

One aspect of cliency requires particular emphasis here. Because a patron's security interests often dictate a high reliance on certain strategically important client countries, maintaining political stability in these countries is usually vital to the patron and therefore the main focus of its relationships with them. Patrons try to reduce political instability by providing client states with goods and services that enhance their ability to repress or co-opt unrest; indeed, economic aid, security assistance, and intervention are often used solely for this purpose. Furthermore, if a

[2]For an exhaustive discussion of other kinds of relationships that can emerge in this context see Marshall R. Singer, *Weak States in a World of Powers: The Dynamics of International Relationships* (New York: Free Press, 1972).

[3]On influence in this context see Jeffrey L. Hughes, "On Bargaining," in Triska, *Dominant Powers and Subordinate States*, 168–199, and Joan M. Nelson, *Aid, Influence, and Foreign Policy* (New York: Macmillan, 1968).

[4]See Robert O. Keohane, "The Big Influence of Small Allies," *Foreign Policy* 2 (Spring 1971), 161–82.

patron can exert influence over a client, this influence can be used to encourage the client government to take steps to reduce unrest, such as arresting opposition leaders or carrying out reforms. When a client is vital to its security, a patron will usually provide whatever goods and services are necessary to maintain political stability, including emergency economic aid and even military intervention. Cliency relationships are thus tailored to particular circumstances: the cliency instruments used depend on the security needs of the patron and client governments and on the context of the relationship, including the domestic political climate in the client country.

State and Society

Before examining the domestic political effects of cliency, it is necessary first to discuss what is meant here by the state and to examine the complex relationship between the state and society. The state an administrative body that exercises compulsory authority over a particular territory, based, ultimately, on its claim to a monopoly over the legitimate use of force in that territory.[5] The state exercises its authority through a variety of apparatuses: military, police, and intelligence forces; agencies that allocate goods and services; the economics and planning ministries; and agencies that deal with socialization and culture. The state's activities are directed by a group of people who are collectively known as "the government." The terms *state* and *government*, often used interchangeably, differ in that the government consists of decision makers who hold office temporarily and are empowered to formulate and implement public policy, whereas the state encompasses both the government and the agencies through which public policy is implemented.

The state's authority can be directed toward many goals, both legitimate and illegitimate. For our purposes the most important of these goals involve the organization and maintenance of the social system, including the maintenance of a healthy economy, the preservation of public order and national security, and the regulation of social and cultural affairs. Because its efforts to achieve these goals have so great an impact on society, the state is inevitably the object of intense pressure from competing societal groups. Furthermore, to achieve its goals, the state generally

[5]This definition is based mainly on Max Weber, *Economy and Society* (New York: Bedminster, 1968), 54–56 and chaps. 9–11. Two useful sources on the state are Bertrand Badie and Pierre Birnbaum, *The Sociology of the State* (Chicago: University of Chicago Press, 1983), and Martin Carnoy, *The State and Political Theory* (Princeton, N.J.: Princeton University Press, 1984).

needs cooperation from certain groups: the upper and middle classes must provide it with tax revenue; technocrats and businessmen must help it run the economy; military officers must help maintain order; and intellectuals and leaders of popular organizations may be needed to help legitimate the state. The state's need for cooperation from these groups generally makes it dependent upon them and gives them some influence over it. Hence the state does not exist independently of society. Rather, it is caught in a complex web of reciprocal relations with a broad spectrum of societal groups which it is dependent upon in certain ways and which attempt to influence its policies.

How do societal groups influence the state? There are several schools of thought on this question. Pluralists such as David Truman and Robert Dahl view state policy as the resultant of diverse pressures exerted by competing groups in society. These pressures are manifested through political participation,[6] which can take five basic forms: electoral activity, organizational activity, lobbying (including demonstrations), contacting, and violence.[7] A group's ability to influence the state through these forms of participation depends on how powerful it is, both absolutely and relative to other groups. Truman identifies three main sources of group power: (1) strategic position in society, including social status, membership among state officials, and usefulness to the state; (2) internal group characteristics, such as size, wealth, organization, leadership, cohesion, and level of mobilization; and (3) certain characteristics of state institutions, such as their operating structure and group life.[8] A group's political power enables it not only to influence state policy directly, through political participation, but also to influence it indirectly by influencing other societal groups or societal institutions in ways that favorably affect state policy. For example, businessmen may pressure labor unions to lobby the state on their behalf, or they may use the news media to influence public opinion, and hence state policy. Pluralists argue that variations in group power, overlapping group memberships, and variable group participation rates create a rough parity in group influence over the state. Implicit in the pluralist model is the idea that societies possess a homeostatic mechanism that maximizes their general welfare. This mechanism operates much like the familiar "hidden hand" of Adam Smith: because state policy is entirely determined by group pressures in a pluralistic society, and because all societal groups have nearly equal influence, state policy reflects the inter-

[6]David B. Truman, *The Governmental Process* (New York: Knopf, 1951); Robert A. Dahl, *Who Governs?* (New Haven, Conn.: Yale University Press, 1961).

[7]Samuel P. Huntington and Joan M. Nelson, *No Easy Choice: Political Participation in Developing Countries* (Cambridge: Harvard University Press, 1976), 12–13.

[8]Truman, *Governmental Process*, 506–7.

ests of each societal group in rough proportion to its size and therefore maximizes the collective good.[9]

The pluralist view has, of course, been widely criticized, mainly on the grounds that power is unevenly distributed in society and that societal influence over the state is therefore highly concentrated. Elite theorists such as C. Wright Mills argue that only politicians, businessmen, military officers, celebrities, and the very rich have significant influence over the state and that these groups are inordinately powerful because of their wealth, occupations, superior education, and social connections.[10] Marxists argue that a group's power, and hence its influence over the state, depends on its relationship to the means of production. The capitalist class is extremely powerful because its ownership of the means of production gives it extensive financial resources and enables it to foster or frustrate state policies and the activities of other classes. By contrast, the working class must rely for influence on strikes and revolutionary activity; it is hampered by a lack of cohesion, by corrupt leadership, and by socialization that reinforces the ideology and beliefs of the capitalist class.[11]

These criticisms of pluralist theory bring out an important point about state-society relations: there *is* substantial variation in group power and therefore in group influence. Upper-class groups are wealthier and better educated, have better social connections and higher membership among state officials, are more useful to the state, and are often better mobilized and more cohesive than lower- and middle-class groups. These sources of power enable upper-class groups to exert extensive influence over the state both directly, through organizational activity, lobbying, contacting, and certain kinds of electoral activity, and indirectly, by pressuring other societal groups and influencing societal institutions. The main source of power for middle- and lower-class groups is their size, which enables them to participate through collective action, including voting, demonstrations, and mass violence. Their reliance on collective action makes it extremely important for middle- and lower-class groups to work through political organizations such as parties and labor unions to influence the state. Thus leadership skills and organizational ability are important determinants of middle- and lower-class political power. To gain influence over the state, middle- and lower-class groups often establish formal or informal coalitions with other groups, including broad-based political parties, multi-

[9]For a good discussion of this issue see Alfred Stepan, *The State and Society: Peru in Comparative Perspective* (Princeton, N.J.: Princeton University Press, 1978), 7–10.

[10]C. Wright Mills, *The Power Elite* (New York: Oxford University Press, 1957).

[11]See, e.g., Ralph Miliband, *The State in Capitalist Society* (New York: Basic Books, 1969). Miliband is the leading proponent of what has come to be known as the instrumental Marxist view of the state.

party coalitions, and patronage bonds of various kinds. Participants in these coalitions must inevitably make large compromises, diluting their influence over the state. This is particularly so for lower-class groups, which are usually the weakest members of these coalitions.

Political power is most visible when groups actively use it to influence state policy, as in lobbying, elections, and revolutionary activity. But as Truman emphasizes, political power is also embodied in the character of state institutions and practices. For example, to the extent that they are representative, institutions such as elections and legislatures largely embody the political power of middle-class groups. The mere existence of these institutions ensures that state policy will reflect the interests of these groups even when they are not actively trying to influence the state. Similarly, because fostering a healthy economy is one of the state's primary preoccupations, it must maintain the confidence of key economic elites. This ensures that state policy will reflect the interests of these elites whether or not they actively exert influence.[12] State institutions and practices such as these are themselves usually products of past efforts by societal groups to influence the functioning of states and they therefore broadly reflect the distribution of power in society. Because they are fairly resistant to change, however, these institutions and practices may not closely reflect the contemporary distribution of power in a society undergoing rapid change.

The term *political regime* refers to the character of the institutions and practices that govern state-society relations in a particular country.[13] Because these institutions and practices embody the political power of societal groups, political regimes also broadly reflect the distribution of power in society. Democratic regimes contain effective, well-established institutions and practices that permit all societal groups to have some influence over the state. Because lower- and middle-class groups must rely for their influence primarily on collective action, democratic regimes inevitably contain mechanisms that encourage mass participation, such as political parties and free elections. Authoritarian regimes lack such institutions and practices; and the state generally uses a mixture of repression and co-optation to prevent certain middle- and lower-class groups from engaging in political participation under an authoritarian regime.[14] Democratic regimes generally exist where the distribution of political

[12]Fred Block, "The Ruling Class Does Not Rule: Notes on the Marxist Theory of the State," *Socialist Revolution* 7 (May–June 1977), 6–28.

[13]This definition is adapted from Roy C. Macridis, *Modern Political Regimes* (Boston: Little, Brown, 1986), 2.

[14]For more thorough definitions of democracy and authoritarianism see Juan J. Linz, "Totalitarian and Authoritarian Regimes," in Fred I. Greenstein and Nelson W. Polsby, eds., *Handbook of Political Science, vol. 3* (Reading, Mass.: Addison-Wesley, 1975).

power has enabled certain middle class groups to impose representative institutions and practices upon the dominant groups in society. Authoritarian regimes exist where political power is so concentrated that the dominant groups in society have been able to resist the demands of other groups for representation. In practice, most political regimes contain both democratic and authoritarian features, reflecting power distributions that lie somewhere between these two characterizations.

A state often becomes closely identified with one or more of the most powerful groups in society, which then become known as its social base of support. The relationship between the state and its social base of support is reciprocal: the state pursues policies that serve the interests of the groups in its base of support, and these groups respond by helping the state. The state's base of support in many contemporary Third World countries consists of a narrow stratum of wealthy businessmen, top bureaucrats, and military officers. When middle- and lower-class groups have become fairly powerful, some Third World states have developed a base of support among these groups and thus taken on a populist character.[15] Marxists often refer to the groups that constitute the state's social base of support as the "hegemonic groups" in society.[16] Since most political parties and organizations are supported by, and represent the interests of, one or more distinct societal groups, the term *base of support* can also refer to the groups represented by a particular political organization.

The Politics of the Autonomous State

The pluralist view of the state, modified to account for some of the criticisms of elite theorists and Marxists, depicts state policy as the resultant of pressures exerted by a broad spectrum of societal groups with varying abilities to influence the state. Yet the state is not simply a passive target of societal influence; it can do much to shape the interests of societal groups and deflect societal pressure. State policy making is also inevitably affected by the whims and personal priorities of state officials and by considerations such as resource shortages, cultural conditions, and aspects of the international environment. The relationship between the state and society is therefore complex and often rather distant: the state may enjoy considerable independence from societal pressures, and many other factors can affect state policy making.

[15]On populism see Robert H. Dix, "Populism: Authoritarian and Democratic," *Latin American Research Review* 20 (1985), 29–52.

[16]This term has its origins in the work of Antonio Gramsci; see Carnoy, *State and Political Theory*, chap. 3.

The idea that the state can be autonomous in this sense was first clearly expressed in the Marxist debate over the nature of the capitalist state. Nicos Poulantzas, the main proponent of what has come to be known as the structural Marxist view of the state, argued that the capitalist state is not simply an instrument of the capitalist class or "a committee for managing the affairs of the whole bourgeoisie," as stated by Marx and Engels and implied in the work of instrumental Marxists such as Ralph Miliband.[17] Rather, the state often acts with considerable autonomy vis-à-vis the capitalist class in order to maintain the viability of the capitalist system, according to Poulantzas. Autonomy of this sort is exemplified in actions such as the state's willingness to enact social welfare programs and tolerate labor unions, which conflict with the immediate interests of the capitalist class but strengthen the capitalist system in the long term by helping to co-opt the working class. Non-Marxists such as Eric Nordlinger use the concept of state autonomy more broadly to refer to the state's ability to formulate and implement policy independently of pressures exerted by any societal group.[18] Other writers describe the state as "strong" or "weak," depending on whether or not it can act independently of societal pressures.[19]

One of the central theoretical issues posed by the concept of state autonomy is the question of what makes the state more or less autonomous. Most writers working in this area either implicitly or explicitly have addressed this issue and identified two broad categories of determinants. Some writers have focused on the characteristics and capabilities of societal groups or of the state itself which affect state autonomy. Others have focused on broad, structural features of societies, including certain aspects of their international relations, which affect state autonomy by altering the characteristics and capabilities of societal groups or the state. Figure 1

[17]Poulantzas's critique is directed mainly at Miliband and is stated most clearly in the articles by these two authors reprinted in Robin Blackburn, ed., *Ideology in Social Science* (New York: Random House, Vintage, 1973); see also Nicos Poulantzas, *Political Power and Social Classes* (London: New Left, 1973). For discussions of related literature see David A. Gold, Clarence Y. H. Lo, and Erik Olin Wright, "Recent Developments in Marxist Theories of the Capitalist State," *Monthly Review* 27 (October 1975), 29–43, and (November 1975), 36–51; Carnoy, *State and Political Theory*; and Theda Skocpol, "Bringing the State Back In: Strategies of Analysis in Current Research," in Peter B. Evans, Dietrich Rueschemeyer, and Theda Skocpol, eds., *Bringing the State Back In* (Cambridge: Cambridge University Press, 1985), 3–37. The quotation here is from Karl Marx and Frederick Engels, *The Communist Manifesto* (New York: Appleton-Century-Crofts, 1955), 12.

[18]Eric Nordlinger, *On the Autonomy of the Democratic State* (Cambridge: Harvard University Press, 1981).

[19]Peter J. Katzenstein, "International Relations and Domestic Structures: Foreign Economic Policies of Advanced Industrial States," *International Organization* 30 (Winter 1976), 1–46; Stephen D. Krasner, *Defending the National Interest* (Princeton, N.J.: Princeton University Press, 1978).

Figure 1. The determinants of state autonomy

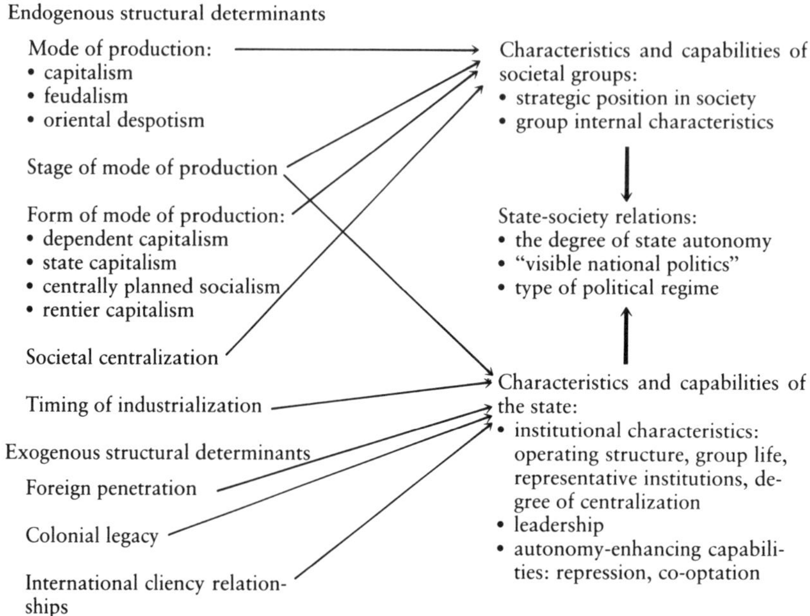

depicts how the structural determinants of state autonomy affect the characteristics and capabilities of societal groups and the state.

The most obvious determinants of state autonomy are the characteristics and capabilities of societal groups that affect their degree of political power. According to pluralists, a group's political power depends on its strategic position in society, its internal characteristics, and certain characteristics of state institutions; and it is manifested through political participation, including electoral and organizational activity, lobbying, contacting, and violence. Obviously, the state is less independent from relatively powerful groups than from relatively weak ones. Group power also affects the degree to which the state is independent from society as a whole: a society in which many groups are relatively powerful because they are well-educated, well-organized, or highly mobilized will have more aggregate influence over the state than one in which most groups are relatively weak.

State autonomy also depends on certain characteristics and capabilities of the state itself. As discussed above, pluralists argue that group power is partly determined by the characteristics of state institutions, including their operating structure and group life. In particular, characteristics of state institutions that bear on the nature of the political regime, such as the degree to which elections and legislatures are representative, can have a considerable effect on state autonomy. Peter Katzenstein argues that highly centralized states can formulate and implement policy more effectively than decentralized states, making them more autonomous.[20] Similarly, state officials who exercise strong leadership can increase the effectiveness of state policy making by forcing state agencies to coordinate their activities more closely or by gaining the cooperation of key societal groups, again increasing the state's autonomy.

Another characteristic of the state that affects its autonomy is its use of "autonomy-enhancing capabilities" to reduce society's influence over it.[21] The state's most obvious autonomy-enhancing capability is its repressive apparatus, which is especially effective against middle- and lower-class groups because they rely mainly on collective action for their influence. States also usually have a variety of co-optative mechanisms that can enhance their autonomy. Through their economic and development planning ministries and social service agencies, states can selectively allocate goods and services as a means of co-optation. They can also co-opt societal groups through corporatist institutions, which are state-controlled, hierarchically organized mechanisms of interest representation which afford their members limited influence in exchange for the observance of certain restrictions on interest articulation.[22] Although corporatist institutions and other co-optative mechanisms are generally aimed at middle- and lower-class groups, they can also be used to increase the state's independence from upper-class groups.

The interaction between the characteristics and capabilities of societal groups and those of the state (Fig. 1) is what determines the character of state-society relations, including the state's degree of autonomy. In practice, much of this interaction involves what can be called "visible national politics," where individuals and organizations representing societal groups and coalitions compete for influence over the state and where state officials manipulate these individuals and organizations in order to carry out policies and enhance their own power. This visible national politics consists of activities such as elections, demonstrations, violence, repres-

[20]Peter J. Katzenstein, "Conclusion: Domestic Structures and Strategies of Foreign Economic Policy," in idem, ed., *Between Power and Plenty: Foreign Economic Policies of Advanced Industrial States* (Madison: University of Wisconsin Press, 1978), 323–32.

[21]Nordlinger, *On the Autonomy of the Democratic State*, 90–98, 109–15, and 128–34.

[22]This definition is adapted from Phillippe C. Schmitter, "Still the Century of Corporatism?" *Review of Politics* 36 (1974), 85–131.

sion, and state efforts to implement policies; it is what we usually refer to when we use the term *politics*. Much less visible, however, are aspects of state-society relations such as organizational activity, lobbying, and contacting, as well as most of the state's internal decision making. The type of political regime is also determined by the way the characteristics and capabilities of societal groups interact with those of the state (Fig. 1).

The characteristics and capabilities of societal groups and those of the state are affected by certain structural factors (Fig. 1), which therefore constitute higher-level determinants of state autonomy. Two main types of structural determinants can be distinguished: endogenous structural determinants, which are features of a society itself, and exogenous structural determinants, which are aspects of a society's involvement in the international system which affect its domestic politics. Because they affect the characteristics and capabilities of societal groups and those of the state, these structural factors shape and constrain the options available to political actors and thus affect state-society relations, including the degree of state autonomy. Structural factors do not, however, force political actors to pursue certain strategies; they therefore do not fully "determine" the degree of state autonomy but merely shape the broad contours of state-society relations.[23]

The most widely studied endogenous structural determinant of state autonomy is the mode of production, which affects state autonomy by determining the class structure of society and shaping the distribution of power among social classes. The capitalist class is inherently powerful under capitalism because it controls the means of production. The working class can exert some influence over the state under capitalism through "class struggle," a euphemism for the various forms of participation available to this class. The state's autonomy is determined by the balance between these competing class forces, according to structural Marxists.[24] Non-Marxists would emphasize that the mode of production is not the only structural determinant of class power and that nonclass groups play important roles in state-society relations as well. Society is also divided into classes under precapitalist modes of production, such as feudalism and oriental despotism (which existed in Iran until the early twentieth century). While the landlord class is usually extremely powerful under

[23]For a fuller discussion of this issue in a related context, see Adam Przeworski, "Some Problems in the Study of the Transition to Democracy," in Guillermo O'Donnell, Phillippe C. Schmitter, and Laurence Whitehead, eds., *Transitions from Authoritarian Rule: Comparative Perspectives* (Baltimore: Johns Hopkins University Press, 1986), 47–50.

[24]See esp. Block, "Ruling Class Does Not Rule." For a critical analysis and application of Block's ideas see Theda Skocpol, "Political Response to Capitalist Crisis: Neo-Marxist Theories of the State and the Case of the New Deal," *Politics and Society* 10 (1980), 155–201.

feudalism (though not under oriental despotism), some state autonomy can presumably occur as a result of class struggle by the peasantry.

Several writers stress as endogenous structural determinants not only the mode of production but also its stage of development, which also affects the distribution of power among social classes. Ellen Kay Trimberger argues that the decline of feudalism in late nineteenth-century Ottoman Turkey and Tokugawa Japan weakened the landowning classes and enabled the state to become more autonomous.[25] Poulantzas argues that relatively autonomous, fascist states emerged in Europe in the 1920s and 1930s during periods of transition between stages of capitalism. The state became relatively autonomous because the dominant class fraction of the declining stage of capitalism had grown weak and the dominant class fraction of the emerging stage had not yet become powerful enough to control the state.[26] Similarly, Nora Hamilton argues that the state was able to become autonomous in Mexico in the 1930s because capitalism was not yet firmly established, leaving the capitalist class still relatively weak.[27] Both Poulantzas and Hamilton use Marx's notion of the "Bonapartist state" to describe the high degree of state autonomy during periods of transition between modes of production or between stages of capitalism.[28] In the classic description of Bonapartism, the bourgeoisie "exchange the right to rule for the right to make money."

A closely related endogenous structural determinant is the particular form the mode of production takes. Hamilton argues that state autonomy in Mexico was heightened by the world depression of the 1930s, which weakened foreign economic interests that had previously exercised great influence over the Mexican state.[29] Her implication is that the social structure of dependent capitalism includes powerful foreign actors who may also constrain the state. Stephen Krasner argues that state autonomy is higher in countries where the state has extensive, direct control over the economy through mechanisms such as publicly owned enterprises or powerful regulatory agencies—a condition that occurs under state capitalism or centrally planned socialism. A state that enjoys extensive control over the economy through mechanisms such as these will have less need for cooperation from private economic actors and will therefore be

[25]Ellen Kay Trimberger, *Revolution from Above* (New Brunswick, N.J.: Transaction Books, 1977), 61–65.

[26]Nicos Poulantzas, *Fascism and Dictatorship* (London: New Left, 1974).

[27]Nora Hamilton, *The Limits of State Autonomy: Post-revolutionary Mexico* (Princeton, N.J.: Princeton University Press, 1982), 8–25.

[28]This concept is developed in Karl Marx, *The Eighteenth Brumaire of Louis Bonaparte* (New York: International Publishers, 1963).

[29]Hamilton, *Limits of State Autonomy.*

more autonomous.[30] Similarly, Theda Skocpol argues that states which control large amounts of wealth, such as the rentier capitalist states in oil-producing countries like modern Iran, are likely to be less dependent on society for revenue and cooperation and therefore more autonomous.[31]

These writers focus on economic structure as an endogenous structural determinant. Katzenstein takes a different approach, emphasizing the degree of centralization of societal groups and state institutions. Relatively heterogeneous societies like the United States experience more intergroup conflict than homogeneous ones like Japan. In the former, the state is subject to more frequent pressures from more groups, reducing its autonomy. State institutions are also much less centralized in the United States than in Japan, according to Katzenstein, and are therefore less independent from societal pressures. Following Barrington Moore, Katzenstein attributes the difference mainly to the timing of industrialization in these countries: the United States began to industrialize much earlier and therefore did not need to develop the extensive bureaucracy that made industrialization possible in Japan.[32]

A variety of exogenous structural factors can also affect state autonomy. Economic dependence introduces powerful foreign actors into a society, reducing the state's autonomy. Trimberger argues that the threat of foreign economic and military penetration in Ottoman Turkey and Tokugawa Japan resulted in the establishment of Western-oriented schools and the recruitment of bureaucrats on the basis of ability rather than personal connections, which reduced the power of the dominant landowning classes and made the state more autonomous.[33] Similarly, Hamza Alavi argues that colonialism left a strong state bureaucracy in the remnants of Britain's Indian empire which was relatively independent from foreign capital and from the indigenous landowning and capitalist classes.[34] Finally, I argue in this book that the cliency relationship estab-

[30]Stephen D. Krasner, "Domestic Constraints on International Economic Leverage," in Klaus Knorr and Frank N. Trager, eds., *Economic Issues and National Security* (Lawrence: Regents Press of Kansas, 1977), 160–81. Krasner refers to state strength or weakness rather than state autonomy.

[31]Theda Skocpol, "Rentier State and Shi'a Islam in the Iranian Revolution," *Theory and Society* 11 (May 1982), esp. 269–70. The concept of the rentier state is developed in Hossein Mahdavy, "Patterns and Problems of Economic Development in Rentier States: The Case of Iran," in M. A. Cook, ed., *Studies in the Economic History of the Middle East* (London: Oxford University Press, 1970), 428–67.

[32]Katzenstein, "Conclusion," 323–32; Barrington Moore, *Social Origins of Dictatorship and Democracy: Lord and Peasant in the Making of the Modern World* (Boston: Beacon, 1966).

[33]Trimberger, *Revolution from Above*, 70–72.

[34]Hamza Alavi, "The State in Post-Colonial Societies: Pakistan and Bangladesh," *New Left Review* 74 (July–August 1972), 59–82.

lished in 1953 between the United States and Iran was an exogenous structural factor that greatly increased the autonomy of the Iranian state by strengthening its autonomy-enhancing capabilities.

Of the eight structural determinants of state autonomy identified in Figure 1, three are immutable or slow to change: colonial legacy, societal centralization, and mode of production. These determinants are therefore unlikely to bring about rapid changes in the degree of state autonomy. However, the other five structural determinants *can* change fairly quickly (i.e., within a decade or two) and therefore may indeed produce rapid changes in state autonomy. In particular, the stage and form of the mode of production have changed very rapidly in most Third World countries in the last few decades as a result of economic development. Since these two structural factors affect state-society relations mainly through their effect on the class structure of society, class has become very important in the domestic politics of many Third World countries and especially in Iran, where very rapid economic development occurred between the early 1950s and late 1970s. Class dynamics is therefore central to the empirical analysis in this book.

Changes in the degree of state autonomy often lag well behind changes in these structural determinants. For example, a change in the stage or form of the mode of production may greatly increase the size of a particular societal group, such as the industrial working class, but it may take this group a decade or more to mobilize new members and incorporate them into its political organizations. Moreover, because state institutions and practices often resist change, there may be a considerable delay before changes in the characteristics and capabilities of a societal group bring about changes in the type of political regime. The effects of Iran's cliency relationship with the United States on state autonomy in Iran were not fully manifested until at least a decade after this relationship had begun.

As discussed above, the pluralist model of state-society relations maintains that in pluralistic societies a homeostatic mechanism maximizes the welfare of society as a whole. The converse of this argument underlies the instrumental Marxist view of the state. According to this view, the control the capitalist class exercises over the state amounts to a kind of temporary, class-bound homeostatic mechanism by assuring that state policy serves the interests of this class. But because the working class is excluded under capitalism, it remains mired in misery; when its misery becomes intolerable, it erupts in revolution, destroying the capitalist system. While the interests of the capitalist class are temporarily served by its control over the state, the absence of an effective, societywide homeostatic mechanism therefore eventually produces a breakdown of the capitalist system.

Criticisms of these ideas lie at the heart of several important studies that emphasize, either implicitly or explicitly, the state's autonomy or lack of autonomy. The first major writer to make such a criticism was Theodore Lowi. In *The End of Liberalism*, Lowi argued that government in the United States has become impotent because of the rise of "interest group liberalism," a public philosophy that encourages societal groups to pursue their interests by seeking to influence state policy.[35] Interest group liberalism disrupts the homeostatic mechanism postulated by pluralists by leaving the state too mired in interest group politics to pursue the welfare of society as a whole. Implicit in Lowi's argument is the idea that the state must be relatively independent from societal pressure in order to serve the collective good. Katzenstein and several other writers make similar arguments in a comparative framework.[36]

Poulantzas makes a corresponding criticism of the instrumental Marxist argument in his analysis of the rise of fascism. He argues that the fascist states that emerged in Europe in the 1920s and 1930s were relatively autonomous because of economic crises associated with the transition between stages of capitalism. Their autonomy enabled these states to carry out the policies necessary to achieve successful transitions and thus to avoid the revolutions that seemed imminent at the time.[37] Trimberger and Skocpol make similar arguments. Trimberger views state autonomy as a necessary precondition for the "revolutions from above" that transformed Turkey and Japan from feudal to capitalist societies. State autonomy emerged in these countries because of the decline of the landowning classes and the emergence of centralized bureaucracies; it enabled the state to transform society and thus to avert revolutions from below.[38] By contrast, Skocpol argues that the state was not sufficiently autonomous in France, Russia, or China to bring about such a transformation, and revolutions therefore occurred.[39]

These arguments modify, rather than negate, the widely held assumption that a homeostatic mechanism operates through political participation. Although participation guarantees that state policy will reflect the interests of participating groups, too much participation leaves the state so caught up in pursuing the short-term interests of these groups that it

[35]Theodore J. Lowi, *The End of Liberalism: Ideology, Policy, and the Crisis of Public Authority* (New York: Norton, 1969). A similar argument is made in Michel Crozier, Samuel P. Huntington, and Joji Watanuki, *The Crisis of Democracy* (New York: New York University Press, 1975).

[36]Katzenstein, *Between Power and Plenty*.

[37]Poulantzas, *Fascism and Dictatorship*.

[38]Trimberger, *Revolution from Above*.

[39]Theda Skocpol, *States and Social Revolutions* (Cambridge: Cambridge University Press, 1979), 47–51.

cannot pursue their long-term, systemic interests. A state with little or no autonomy is therefore unable to pursue the long-term, systemic interests of powerful societal groups or of society as a whole. Social or economic crises may result, creating political unrest and possibly revolution. By contrast, a state that is constrained by societal pressures but still relatively autonomous is better able to pursue the long-term, systemic interests of society and thus prevent crises and political unrest. The homeostatic mechanism implicit in both the pluralist and the instrumental Marxist views therefore operates more effectively when the state has *some* autonomy.

If some degree of state autonomy is necessary for this homeostatic mechanism to operate, what happens if a state becomes highly autonomous—so autonomous that no societal group can exert sustained and effective influence over it? Lacking societal constraint, a highly autonomous state, though it is obviously not mired in too much participation, is also not constrained to act in the long-term, systemic interests of any societal group or of society as a whole. The homeostatic mechanism therefore will not operate, and the state's policies will be determined by other factors. The whims and personal priorities of state officials are likely to have a much greater effect on state policy making. Shortages of resources such as capital or skilled labor may constrain the state's policies. Aspects of the international environment, such as foreign economic ties, diplomatic relationships with other countries, and involvement in war, may have an effect. Even cultural factors such as society's propensity to save and the status of women may affect state policy making. In the absence of societal constraint, policy makers are likely to respond to these influences in ways that diverge from the interests and needs of society. If this divergence persists and becomes acute, political unrest may grow, possibly leading to revolution. A highly autonomous state may therefore generate political unrest and even revolution, much like a state that enjoys little or no autonomy.

The Politics of the Client State

A patron generally tries to promote political stability in a client country by using cliency instruments such as economic aid, security assistance, security agreements, and intervention to increase the ability of the client state to repress and co-opt unrest. By strengthening the client state's autonomy-enhancing capabilities, these cliency instruments not only promote political stability but also make the client state more autonomous, perhaps causing political unrest and even revolution, as occurred in Iran in the late 1970s. To understand how this occurs, it is useful to consider how each of the major types of cliency instruments affects the autonomy-enhancing capabilities of the client state.

Patron powers use economic aid extensively to promote political stability in client countries.[40] Financial assistance in the form of loans, grants, and indirect transfers increases aggregate demand in the recipient's economy, promoting economic growth and thus reducing popular unrest. Financial assistance and technical advice can also improve the recipient's economic and administrative infrastructure, enhancing economic growth and the quality of public services and therefore further reducing unrest. The recipient government can use financial assistance to co-opt particular societal groups by financing transfers to these groups through mechanisms such as commodity or production subsidies, development projects, social services, and corruption. Co-opting these groups reduces their ability to exert influence over the state, enhancing the state's autonomy. Although middle- and lower-class groups are often the main beneficiaries of economic aid and are therefore most likely to be co-opted by it, upper-class groups can also be coopted in this way.

Security assistance can be a crucial means of promoting political stability in a client country when opposition groups are staging strikes and demonstrations or when guerrilla groups are active. Although military matériel is readily available in the international arms market, a patron can provide it on favorable terms and can provide specialized equipment and training unavailable from other sources. Equipment and training for crowd control and counterinsurgency can be particularly important in promoting political stability, as can intelligence training and liaison, which can greatly enhance the effectiveness of the recipient's domestic intelligence forces. Security assistance increases the client state's autonomy by improving the morale and effectiveness of its repressive apparatus and therefore undermining the ability of societal groups to exert influence over it. Security assistance is particularly effective against middle- and lower-class groups, because they must rely mainly on collective action to influence the state.[41]

Intervention can take many forms, including overt military intervention; overt and covert assistance to organizations such as labor unions, political parties, and newspapers; and covert political action, including

[40]On the uses of foreign aid see Hans J. Morgenthau, "Preface to a Political Theory of Foreign Aid," in Robert A. Goldwin, ed., *Why Foreign Aid?* (Chicago: Rand-McNally, 1963), 70–89; Jacob J. Kaplan, *The Challenge of Foreign Aid* (New York: Praeger, 1967); and Nelson, *Aid, Influence, and Foreign Policy.*

[41]For a study of U.S. security assistance that emphasizes its political implications see Michael T. Klare, *American Arms Supermarket* (Austin: University of Texas Press, 1984).

propaganda, assassination, and coups d'état.[42] The explicit goal of intervention is to influence domestic politics in the target country, either by weakening hostile groups or by assisting groups regarded as friendly, thereby strengthening the client government and its domestic political allies. In effect, intervention augments the client state's repressive apparatus, increasing its autonomy by undermining the ability of societal groups to exert influence over it. Although intervention can be used against any societal group, it is particularly effective against middle- and lower-class groups because of their greater reliance on collective action.

In a cliency relationship, security agreements such as treaties and alliances often embody commitments by the patron to intervene on behalf of the client government in the event of domestic unrest. By demonstrating the patron's willingness to assist the client government in this way and by providing an institutional basis for such assistance, a security agreement further augments the client state's repressive apparatus and therefore further increases its autonomy.

In addition to these cliency instruments, the influence accruing to the patron can also affect the autonomy of the client state. Such influence can be used to change the client state's policies or increase its responsiveness to societal pressures. For example, U.S. foreign aid has often been used to encourage Third World governments to act against leftist groups or improve human rights conditions.[43] Because the uses to which it is put depend on the desires of the patron government, it is impossible to say a priori how this influence will affect the client state's autonomy and which societal groups will be most affected. Moreover, under certain circumstances a patron may not be able to exert any influence over a particular client state. For these reasons the main focus in this book is on the effect of the cliency instruments the United States used in Iran rather than on U.S. influence wielded there.

When a particular client country is vital to its security, a patron will take whatever steps are necessary to maintain political stability there, tailoring the cliency relationship to conditions in the client country. Under these circumstances, if a domestic societal group poses a serious challenge to the

[42]For studies that adopt this broad view of intervention see Andrew M. Scott, "Nonintervention and Conditional Intervention," *Journal of International Affairs* 22 (1968), 208–16, and Jan Knippers Black, *United States Penetration of Brazil* (Philadelphia: University of Pennsylvania Press, 1977). On covert action see Roy Godson, ed., *Intelligence Requirements for the 1980's, No. 4, Covert Action* (Washington: National Strategic Information Center, 1981). The best description of covert operations in practice is Philip Agee, *Inside the Company: CIA Diary* (New York: Bantam, 1975).

[43]On the use of U.S. foreign aid to promote human rights in Latin America see Lars Schoultz, *Human Rights and United States Policy toward Latin America* (Princeton, N.J.: Princeton University Press, 1981), esp. chaps. 4–6.

authority of the client government, the patron will provide the client government with whatever cliency instruments it needs to put down this challenge, including emergency economic aid, crowd control or counterinsurgency equipment, and perhaps even military intervention. Although in the long term the patron may be unable to keep the client government in power, in the short term the cliency instruments it provides will prevent societal groups from exerting much influence over the state. The client state is therefore likely to attain considerable autonomy, perhaps even becoming highly autonomous. In general, the domestic political consequences of cliency depend on the intensity of the cliency relationship, which is determined mainly by the strategic importance of the client and by domestic political conditions in the client country.

If a client state does become highly autonomous, then its policies may increasingly diverge from the interests and needs of society, producing growing political unrest and perhaps even a revolution. Cliency relationships can therefore involve a fundamental paradox: although one of its main goals is to promote political stability in the client country, a cliency relationship may instead promote instability by enabling the client state to become highly autonomous. Cliency may in this way undermine rather than enhance the patron's security in the long term by promoting instability in a vitally important client country. Moreover, if a patron becomes too closely identified with a highly autonomous client state, political unrest may be directed at it as well as at the client state, further undermining its security.

It is important to emphasize here that many other structural factors can increase or reduce a client state's autonomy, complementing or offsetting the effect of cliency and often making it difficult to determine how much of an effect cliency has actually had on a particular client state. For example, middle-class groups in advanced capitalist societies are usually powerful enough to limit the state's autonomy. A client state is therefore unlikely to become highly autonomous in an advanced capitalist society, no matter how intense its cliency relationship. This may explain why client states in advanced capitalist societies such as postwar Japan and contemporary Israel have not become highly autonomous. In the case of Iran, a tremendous increase in the state's oil revenue and rapid economic growth thoroughly transformed the mode of production in the 1960s and 1970s, strengthening both the state and certain societal groups. These structural changes occurred at roughly the same time as Iran's cliency relationship with the United States, making it somewhat difficult to determine the precise effect of cliency on state autonomy in Iran.

Inasmuch as promoting democracy has been an important declared objective of U.S. foreign policy toward the Third World,[44] it is useful briefly to consider here how cliency relationships affect political regimes in client countries. Because democratic regimes contain institutions and practices that permit all societal groups to have some influence over the state, state autonomy is fundamentally limited under a democratic regime. Consequently, if cliency or some other structural factor greatly increases the state's autonomy under a democratic regime, the institutions and practices that embody the democratic regime may cease to function effectively. In addition to promoting state autonomy, cliency may therefore also promote authoritarianism in client countries by undermining existing democratic institutions and practices. This can occur most obviously when a patron intervenes in the client's domestic politics, as when the United States staged a coup d'état in Iran in 1953 which ousted a popularly elected prime minister. Similarly, economic aid and security assistance may increase the ability of officials in the client government to co-opt and repress societal groups, leading them to believe that they can rule more effectively through authoritarian methods and thus to suspend democratic institutions and practices.

Although cliency may therefore undermine democracy in client countries, this is not inevitable. As with state autonomy, other structural factors can offset the effect of cliency on a country's political regime. In particular, because advanced capitalist societies have social structures that are very conducive to democracy, cliency will probably not completely destroy democratic institutions and practices in such countries. Furthermore, because the domestic political consequences of cliency depend on the intensity of the cliency relationship, cliency is likely to have a less negative effect on democratic regimes in countries involved in weak cliency relationships. Finally, a patron can use whatever influence accrues to it under a cliency relationship to *promote* democracy and offset the adverse effect of cliency on democratic institutions and practices, as the United States did when it imposed democratic regimes on postwar Germany and Japan.

United States and Soviet Clients in the Postwar Era

In order to illustrate which countries the foregoing ideas can best be applied to, it is useful to identify the main U.S. and Soviet clients of the

[44]See esp. Laurence Whitehead, "International Aspects of Democratization," in O'Donnell, Schmitter, and Whitehead, *Transitions from Authoritarian Rule*, 3–46.

postwar era. Table 1 contains data for 1954 through 1977 on U.S. and Soviet economic aid, military training, and defense agreements, which are three of the most important cliency instruments. These data, when compared with the recipients' government expenditures and number of military personnel (see Table 1), identify the main U.S. and Soviet clients of this era and help to distinguish between strong, moderate, and weak cliency relationships (Table 2).

The first group of possible clients shown in Table 1 are the European countries. Because the Marshall Plan had ended by 1954, none of the major Western European countries received enough U.S. economic aid or military training between 1954 and 1977 to be included in the table. Although three smaller Western European countries (Denmark, Luxembourg, and Norway) are included, none of them received enough U.S. aid to qualify as important U.S. clients. Greece and Turkey received substantially larger amounts of U.S. aid, were members of NATO, and provided the United States with important military bases, making them moderately important U.S. clients (Table 2). The six Warsaw Pact countries shown in the table received surprisingly small amounts of economic aid from the Soviet Union. Nevertheless, the extensive influence the Soviet Union exerted over their domestic politics and the ever-present threat of Soviet military intervention in these countries clearly qualify them as strong Soviet clients in this period.[45]

The United States has provided large amounts of economic aid and military training to the Latin American countries shown in Table 1 and has a treaty with most of them (the Rio Pact). Because of the relatively large amounts of U.S. economic and military aid they received and their close cooperation with the United States on military and intelligence matters, Guatemala, Nicaragua, and Panama stand out as the strongest U.S. clients in the region (Table 2). Most of the remaining countries in Latin America can be considered moderate or weak U.S. clients, although several (e.g., Bolivia, Costa Rica, and El Salvador) might perhaps be classified as strong U.S. clients.[46] Despite the inadequacies of the data, Cuba has been a strong Soviet client since the early 1960s.

[45]On Soviet relations with the Warsaw Pact countries see esp. Christopher D. Jones, *Soviet Influence in Eastern Europe: Political Autonomy and the Warsaw Pact* (New York: Praeger, 1981), and Zbigniew Brzezinski, *The Soviet Bloc* (Cambridge: Harvard University Press, 1976).

[46]I do not classify these countries as strong clients because their relative U.S. aid levels are substantially lower than those of Guatemala, Nicaragua, and Panama and because they have not cooperated with the United States as closely on military and intelligence matters. For a study of U.S. and Soviet cliency relationships in Latin America see Mark J. Gasiorowski, "Dependency and Cliency in Latin America," *Journal of Inter-American Studies and World Affairs* 28 (Fall 1986), 47–65.

Table 1. Major U.S. and Soviet aid recipients and treaty partners, 1954–1977

Country[a]	U.S. economic aid, 1954–77[b] (1)	U.S. military trainees, 1955–77 (2)	U.S. defense treaty, 1965[c] (3)	Soviet economic aid, 1954–77[b] (4)	Soviet military trainees, 1955–77[d] (5)	Soviet defense treaty, 1965[c] (6)	Government expenditures, 1965 (7)	Military personnel, 1965 (8)
Europe:								
Bulgaria	0	0	no	83.0	n.a.	yes	2,667.5	178
Czechoslovakia	0	0	no	.6	n.a.	yes	4,031.3	207
Denmark	2.9	108.6	yes	0	0	no	1,698.3	50
East Germany	.1	0	no	41.3	n.a.	yes	n.a.	205
Greece	37.0	568.5	yes	.3	0	no	1,133.3	190
Hungary	.7	0	no	14.5	n.a.	yes	1,640.2	156
Luxembourg	0	6.5	yes	0	0	no	158.7	2
Norway	17.1	127.5	yes	0	0	no	1,551.6	35
Poland	34.2	0	no	117.3	n.a.	yes	2,889.0	302
Rumania	10.3	0	no	5.1	n.a.	yes	3,719.9	249
Turkey	118.4	729.3	yes	49.2	0	no	1,119.5	490
Latin America:								
Argentina	40.0	174.7	yes	9.2	0	no	2,094.4	155
Bolivia	33.3	192.2	yes	2.5	0	no	45.0	16
Brazil	193.0	375.9	yes	3.7	0	no	1,988.7	320
Chile	74.7	297.8	yes	9.9	0	no	1,240.1	70
Colombia	72.0	311.8	yes	8.8	0	no	544.6	50
Costa Rica	11.2	30.3	yes	.6	0	no	78.4	2
Cuba	125.0	20.5	no	2.7	n.a.	no	n.a.	110
Dom. Republic	29.3	174.3	yes	0	0	no	139.8	17
Ecuador	15.4	219.0	yes	0	0	no	173.9	14
El Salvador	8.0	85.7	yes	0	0	no	89.1	4
Guatemala	20.1	145.0	yes	0	0	no	132.9	10
Haiti	9.4	26.1	yes	0	0	no	28.7	15
Honduras	10.8	130.1	yes	0	0	no	53.6	5

Table 1. Continued

Country[a]	U.S. economic aid, 1954–77[b] (1)	U.S. military trainees, 1955–77 (2)	U.S. defense treaty, 1965[c] (3)	Soviet economic aid, 1954–77[b] (4)	Soviet military trainees, 1955–77[d] (5)	Soviet defense treaty, 1965[c] (6)	Government expenditures, 1965 (7)	Military personnel, 1965 (8)
Nicaragua	13.0	234.5	yes	0	0	no	56.1	6
Panama	22.5	201.0	yes	0	0	no	94.9	4
Paraguay	20.3	81.4	yes	0	0	no	35.9	20
Peru	52.3	339.7	yes	1.1	27.2	no	710.0	70
Trinidad-Tobago	16.1	0	yes	0	0	no	146.3	1
Uruguay	7.5	122.0	yes	2.2	0	no	n.a.	13
Venezuela	24.0	222.2	yes	0	0	no	1,581.8	25
Africa:								
Ethiopia	17.3	169.9	no	4.4	0	no	155.9	60
Guinea	8.1	.2	no	10.1	42.5	no	54.3	9
Liberia	16.0	27.7	yes	0	0	no	56.0	4
Mali	5.5	3.7	no	4.9	19.4	no	37.2	8
Somalia	5.1	0	no	8.6	133.3	no	31.9	12
Zaire	47.1	43.9	no	0	0	no	181.8	25
Middle East:								
Egypt	138.0	0	no	60.0	236.5	no	784.2	205
Iran	82.1	459.9	yes	33.5	14.1	*	986.5	205
Israel	145.8	0	no	0	0	no	998.2	65
Jordan	48.4	66.4	no	1.0	0	no	133.2	55
South Yemen	.4	0	no	3.5	77.3	no	n.a.	n.a.
Syria	17.0	.9	no	21.5	158.7	no	184.7	80
Tunisia	39.8	36.7	no	3.7	0	no	172.0	20
Asia:								
Afghanistan	22.9	20.3	no	52.6	162.0	no	n.a.	97
Cambodia	38.7	2,933.2	*	1.0	1.1	no	106.1	76
Indonesia	115.5	223.5	no	4.8	403.3	no	131.6	351
Japan	105.5	674.1	yes	0	0	no	10,753.7	246

Laos	39.1	1,934.7	*	.2	0	no	43.7	86
Mongolia	0	0	no	67.0	n.a.	no	n.a.	0
North Korea	0	0	no	4.9	n.a.	yes	n.a.	378
North Vietnam	0	0	no	18.9	n.a.	no	n.a.	256
Pakistan	217.7	206.8	yes	27.2	2.1	no	803.0	277
Philippines	80.0	634.1	yes	1.5	0	no	532.6	46
South Korea	268.0	1,384.3	yes	0	0	no	624.0	604
South Vietnam	315.0	2,075.8	no	0	0	no	n.a.	565
Taiwan	105.4	1,007.7	yes	0	0	no	n.a.	524
Thailand	36.4	736.8	yes	0	0	no	572.0	132

Sources: Col. 1: U.S. Agency for International Development, *U.S. Overseas Loans and Grants: Series of Yearly Data,* vols. 1–5 (Washington, 1985); Col. 2: U.S. Department of Defense, Defense Security Assistance Agency, *Fiscal Year Series, 1980* (Washington, 1980); Col. 3: Congressional Quarterly Service, *Global Defense: U.S. Military Commitments Abroad* (Washington, 1969), iv; Col. 4: CIA, National Foreign Assessment Center, *Communist Aid to Less Developed Countries of the Free World, 1977* (Washington, 1978), 5–6; Col. 5: idem, *Handbook of Economic Statistics, 1978* (Washington, 1978), 78; Col. 6: Zafar Imam, "Soviet Treaties with Third World Countries," *Soviet Studies* 35 (Jan. 1983), 53–70; Col. 7: Arthur S. Banks, *Cross-Polity Time-Series Data* (Cambridge: M.I.T. Press, 1971); Col. 8: U.S. Arms Control and Disarmament Agency, *World Military Expenditures and Arms Transfers, 1965–1974* (Washington, 1976).

Notes: Economic aid and government expenditure are in millions of U.S. dollars. Military personnel are in thousands. Aid and military trainee figures are yearly averages for the period indicated. For countries that became independent after 1954, averages are for the postindependence period only.

[a]Most countries included in the table meet two of three conditions: (1) their average yearly level of economic aid from the United States or the Soviet Union between 1954 and 1977 exceeded 10% of their government expenditures in 1965; (2) their average yearly number of military personnel trained by the United States or the Soviet Union between 1955 and 1977 exceeded .1% of their 1965 military personnel level (Col. 8); (3) they had a treaty with the United States or the Soviet Union in 1965. Several countries are included because they seem to have been major U.S. or Soviet clients but either (1) could not be evaluated according to these criteria because of missing data in Col. 7 or 8 (the Warsaw Pact countries, South Yemen, Afghanistan, Mongolia, and North Vietnam) or (2) did not meet these criteria but were nonetheless widely regarded as U.S. or Soviet clients (Israel and Egypt).

[b]The 1954–77 period is the only one for which Soviet aid data are available. To make U.S. economic aid data comparable to Soviet aid data, U.S. government loans (e.g., Export-Import Bank loans) are included. Soviet economic aid data do not include concessionary pricing arrangements, such as the large amounts of subsidized oil provided to Cuba.

[c]Soviet treaties are "friendship and cooperation treaties"; U.S. treaties are multilateral and bilateral defense treaties and defense-oriented executive agreements. See text for explanations of * treaty status.

[d]Data on Soviet military training for communist countries are not available.

Only a few African countries could be considered U.S. or Soviet clients between 1954 and 1977. Liberia and Zaire received moderate amounts of U.S. economic and military aid, and Liberia also had a treaty with the United States,[47] so these two countries can probably be considered moderately important U.S. clients. Similarly, Guinea and Somalia received moderate amounts of Soviet aid and can probably be considered moderately important Soviet clients. Ethiopia and Mali received small amounts of U.S. and Soviet aid (respectively) and therefore can be considered only weak clients.[48]

The Middle East contained many important U.S. and Soviet clients in the 1954–77 period. Iran received moderate amounts of U.S. economic and military aid, had a treaty with the United States,[49] and was the target of a major U.S. covert intervention in 1953, making it a strong U.S. client. Although Israel is clearly the preeminent U.S. client in the Middle East today, the U.S. cliency relationship with Israel did not reach its current high level until the early 1970s. Israel should therefore probably be regarded as only a moderately important U.S. client between 1954 and 1977. Jordan and Tunisia also received substantial U.S. aid, making them moderately important U.S. clients. Similarly, Egypt and Syria received substantial amounts of Soviet aid and should be considered moderately important Soviet clients. Although South Yemen has become a major Soviet client in recent years, it was at best only a weak Soviet client between 1954 and 1977.[50]

Asia contained the largest number of important U.S. and Soviet clients. Cambodia, Indonesia, Laos, South Korea, and South Vietnam each received very large amounts of U.S. economic and military aid. With the exception of Indonesia, the United States also had a treaty of some kind with each of these countries and intervened extensively in their domestic politics.[51] Although the relative levels of U.S. aid to the Philippines and Taiwan for the entire period were somewhat lower, the United States also had treaties with these two countries and intervened extensively in their domestic politics. These seven countries can therefore be considered

[47]The United States signed an executive agreement covering defense-related matters with Liberia in 1959.

[48]Since the mid-1970s, Ethiopia, Angola, and Mozambique have become important Soviet clients, and Somalia has become a moderately important U.S. client.

[49]Iran also signed a treaty with the Soviet Union in 1921, which is still technically in force.

[50]Since the mid-1970s Egypt has become an important U.S. client, and Libya has become an important Soviet client. Iraq was also an important Soviet client in the 1970s. Saudi Arabia is widely regarded as a U.S. client; because the U.S.-Saudi relationship is much less asymmetric than the others discussed here, I prefer to regard this relationship as an informal alliance rather than a cliency relationship.

[51]South Korea was a member of SEATO. Laos, Cambodia, and South Vietnam did not actually sign the SEATO treaty but were included under its defensive provisions in a separate protocol.

Table 2. United States and Soviet clients, 1954–1977

Type of client	United States	USSR
Strong	Guatemala, Nicaragua, Panama, Cambodia, Iran, Indonesia, Laos, Philippines, South Korea, South Vietnam, Taiwan	Bulgaria, Czechoslovakia, East Germany, Hungary, Poland, Rumania, Cuba, Mongolia, North Vietnam
Moderately important	Greece, Turkey, Bolivia, Brazil, Colombia, Costa Rica, Dominican Republic, Ecuador, El Salvador, Haiti, Honduras, Paraguay, Liberia, Zaire, Israel, Jordan, Tunisia, Pakistan, Thailand	Guinea, Somalia, Egypt, Syria, Afghanistan, North Korea
Weak	Argentina, Chile, Peru, Ethiopia, Japan	Mali, South Yemen

strong U.S. clients in the 1954–77 period. The United States also gave moderate amounts of aid to Pakistan and Thailand and had treaties with each, making these two countries moderately important U.S. clients. Japan had undoubtedly been an important U.S. client in the immediate post–World War II period, but Table 1 indicates it was, at best, only a weak U.S. client after 1953. Missing data on Soviet military trainees and government expenditures make it more difficult to classify the Soviet clients in Asia. Nevertheless, it is probably safe to conclude that Mongolia and North Vietnam were strong Soviet clients and that Afghanistan and North Korea were at least moderately important Soviet clients.[52]

Two important conclusions can be drawn from Table 2. First, the global distribution of U.S. and Soviet clients clearly confirms the idea that patrons tend to establish cliency relationships with countries located in strategically important areas. The strongest U.S. cliency relationships in this period were with countries located in Central America, the northern tier of the Middle East (bordering on the Soviet Union), and east and Southeast Asia (bordering on the Soviet Union and China). Most of the moderately important U.S. clients were located in these regions as well. Similarly, all of the strong Soviet clients and most of the moderately important Soviet clients were located on or near the borders of the Soviet Union, the United States, and China. Second, Iran is just one of twenty countries that have had strong cliency relationships with one of the superpowers. The ideas developed in this chapter should therefore be broadly applicable to all twenty, and perhaps to some of the moderate and weak clients as well.

[52]South Vietnam and Taiwan both ceased to be U.S. clients in the mid-1970s Cambodia (Kampuchea) and Laos have become Soviet/Vietnamese clients since the mid-1970s. On U.S. and Soviet cliency relationships in Asia see Mark J. Gasiorowski and Seung-hyun Baek, "International Cliency Relationships and Client States in East Asia," *Pacific Focus* 2 (Fall 1987), 113–43.

2

Domestic Politics and Foreign Penetration in Iran, 1800–1951

To understand how the U.S.-Iran cliency relationship affected Iran's domestic politics, we must first examine the structural determinants of state-society relations in Iran in the era before this cliency relationship began. The origins of the modern Iranian state lie in the late nineteenth century, when foreign penetration began to transform Iran's economy and social structure and alter the basic focus of its domestic politics. In the first few decades of the twentieth century these changes brought about the collapse of the ruling Qajar dynasty and the establishment of a highly autonomous, Bonapartist state by the father of the late shah. They also created new societal groups, however, which became increasingly powerful in the first half of the twentieth century and were on the verge of establishing hegemony over the Iranian state in the early 1950s, when the U.S.-Iran cliency relationship began. The U.S.-Iran cliency relationship interrupted this process by helping to reestablish a highly autonomous state, thereby disrupting the forces that had shaped Iranian politics since the late nineteenth century.

Iranian Politics in the Nineteenth Century

The Iranian economy in the early nineteenth century was based essentially on agriculture. Unlike patterns of landholding in comparable preindustrial societies in Europe, however, most of the land in Iran at this time was owned by the state and was merely rented or assigned to private landlords. Moreover, the Iranian state, at least in theory, enjoyed extensive powers that it exercised arbitrarily, unconstrained by contractual obligations. The mode of production in Iran at this time is therefore best described as oriental despotism rather than feudalism.[1] One important consequence is that a hereditary landed aristocracy did not exist. Rather, Iranian society at this time contained several different power centers, and the state enjoyed a moderate degree of independence from each.

Iranian society in the early nineteenth century had four main, "traditional" social strata: an upper class of wealthy landlords, tribal leaders, and top clergymen; a middle class of bazaar merchants, artisans, bureaucrats, army officers, petty landlords, and low-level clergymen; an urban lower class of bazaar workers, peddlers, and the lumpenproletariat; and a rural lower class of poor peasants and nomadic tribespeople. Because the Iranian economy was based on agriculture, the landlords were the most powerful group and formed the core of the upper class. This class was closely interlinked through kinship and patronage bonds, and many of its members were linked to the state through membership in the extended royal family or through positions in the state bureaucracy. The middle class was socially mobile, both upward and downward, and was therefore not always clearly distinguishable from the upper and lower classes. The urban and rural lower classes encompassed most of the population: roughly one-seventh of the total population lived in six major cities, and one-half were nomadic tribespeople. Most members of the urban and rural lower classes lived at or near the subsistence level. This class stratification was embedded in a complex mosaic of regional, ethnic, tribal, and religious distinctions.[2]

The Iranian state in the early nineteenth century was quintessentially authoritarian: curbed by neither a constitution nor participatory institutions, the state maintained its authority through repression and mechanisms of co-optation deeply rooted in Iran's traditions and social customs. The shah (or king) controlled the state with the assistance of numerous retainers and advisers. He exercised power through ministries and provincial bodies headed by court appointees drawn mainly from the upper class and staffed with middle-class bureaucrats. The most important component of the state apparatus was the army, composed mainly of irregular tribal contingents. The shah used the army to maintain his dominance and

[1]Ervand Abrahamian, "Oriental Despotism: The Case of Qajar Iran," *International Journal of Middle East Studies* 5 (January 1974), 3–31; Homa Katouzian, *The Political Economy of Modern Iran: Despotism and Pseudo-Modernism, 1926–1979* (New York: New York University Press, 1981), chap. 2.

[2]This discussion draws on Ahmad Ashraf, "Iran: Imperialism, Class, and Modernization from Above" (Ph.D. diss., New School for Social Research, 1971), chap. 5; see also James Alban Bill, *The Politics of Iran: Groups, Classes, and Modernization* (Columbus, Ohio: Charles E. Merrill, 1972), chap. 1. Population figures are from Charles Issawi, ed., *The Economic History of Iran, 1800–1914* (Chicago: University of Chicago Press, 1971), 20, 26.

prerogatives, defend Iran from foreign invaders, suppress tribal uprisings, and generally enforce the state's authority. Other branches of the state apparatus were responsible for collecting taxes. With the state apparatus and state revenues, the shah maintained an extensive patronage network that helped him co-opt the most powerful societal groups. Both secular and clerical courts administered justice in a haphazard and arbitrary manner. The few schools that existed were run by the clergy.[3]

By outward appearances the state was quite powerful: the shah owned most of the land; he appointed all major secular and clerical officials; he could raise an army and condemn his subjects to death at will; and he could confiscate land, fix prices, and grant concessions, privileges, and monopolies. The power of the state was limited in practice, however, by the existence of many competing power centers among the upper class, which in turn reflected the heterogeniety of Iranian society. Far from being omnipotent, the state therefore enjoyed only a moderate degree of autonomy.[4]

The most powerful group in Iran was the landlord class. Iran's large landlords were quite wealthy, often had close personal connections to the shah and his top advisers, occasionally held powerful positions in the state bureaucracy, and served as the state's main source of tax revenue, giving them a considerable amount of power vis-à-vis the state. Most tribal leaders and many top clergymen were also landlords, giving them considerable influence over the state in this capacity. In addition, certain other factors affected the political power of these two groups. Most of the tribes were armed and posed serious threats to the state's authority, giving their leaders further influence over the state. Although the Shi'i clergy ostensibly regarded the state's secular authority as illegitimate, top clerical leaders tolerated and often explicitly approved it in practice, providing legitimation for the state and giving the clergy some influence over it. The clergy also wielded great influence over other societal groups through their positions as spiritual leaders, their judicial functions, and their control over religious taxes. By mobilizing these groups against the state's authority, the clergy could exercise further influence over the state.[5]

[3]See Nikki R. Keddie, *Roots of Revolution: An Interpretive History of Modern Iran* (New Haven, Conn.: Yale University Press, 1981), chaps. 2–3. For a study of the Iranian state apparatus as a patronage network somewhat later see A. Reza Sheikholeslami, "The Patrimonial Structure of Iranian Bureaucracy in the Late Nineteenth Century," *Iranian Studies* 11 (1978), 199–258.

[4]This argument is based partly on Abrahamian, "Oriental Despotism."

[5]On the landlord class in this period see Ann K. S. Lambton, *Landlord and Peasant in Persia* (London: Oxford University Press, 1953), chap. 6. For an excellent study of relations between the state and one of the most powerful tribal groups see Gene R. Garthwaite, *Khans and Shahs: A Documentary Analysis of the Bakhtiyari in Iran* (Cambridge: Cambridge

Iran's middle and lower classes had no independent means of influencing the state at this time. Poverty, ignorance, cultural traditions, and fractionalization along regional, ethnic, tribal, and religious lines prevented any real political awareness from emerging among them. Most members of these classes were associated with communal groups such as tribes, guilds, and religious communities which tied them to the upper class through patronage bonds associated with employment, tribal affiliation, religious practice, and other social relationships. The upper class leaders of these communal groups often tried to influence the state on behalf of their middle- and lower-class clientele, who reciprocated with loyalty, labor, and participation in group activities. These patronage bonds therefore served both as limited, indirect channels of influence over the state and as mechanisms for co-opting middle and lower class members of these communal groups. Consequently, to the extent that Iran's middle and lower classes could exert any influence at all over the state, it was usually through alliances with members of the upper class.[6]

Since middle- and lower-class groups had no independent means of influencing the state, politics was almost exclusively the domain of the upper class. Political activity at this time consisted mainly of tribal conflict and intrigue among members of the upper class and was usually directed at acquiring or retaining wealth, power, and prestige. The shah was both a participant and a mediator in this process, using the state apparatus to amass as much wealth as possible but also trying to promote order and stability to maintain his dominant position in society.

In the course of the nineteenth century, Iran was gradually drawn into the imperial competition of the major European powers. The political and economic incursions of these powers into Iran increasingly affected Iran's social structure and its domestic politics, eventually causing fundamental changes in state-society relations.

Since the beginning of the nineteenth century, Iran had been trapped between the advances of two great imperial powers. Russia was expanding southward into the Caucasus and central Asia, seeking a transporta-

---

University Press, 1983). On clergy-state relations in this period see Said Amir Arjomand, *The Shadow of God and the Hidden Imam* (Chicago: University of Chicago Press, 1984), chaps. 10–11; and Hamid Algar, *Religion and State in Iran, 1785–1906* (Berkeley and Los Angeles: University of California Press, 1969).

[6]On the intragroup dynamics of such communal groups see, e.g., Garthwaite, *Khans and Shahs*, chap. 3; Algar, *Religion and State in Iran*, chap. 1; and Mohammad Reza Afshari, "The *Pishivaran* and Merchants in Precapitalist Iranian Society: An Essay on the Background and Causes of the Constitutional Revolution," *International Journal of Middle East Studies* 15 (May 1983), 133–55.

tion link to the Persian Gulf and covetously eyeing India. Britain was expanding its domination over India and seeking control over the Persian Gulf and Red Sea trade routes. Iran concluded several treaties with Britain and France between 1801 and 1814 aimed mainly at blocking Russian expansionism. After defeats by the czar's armies in 1804–13 and 1826–28, Iran signed treaties with Russia in 1828 and 1881 which ceded large amounts of Iranian territory to Russia and established the modern Russo-Iranian border. Iran also fought a war with Britain in 1856–57 over Afghanistan, after which the two countries signed a treaty recognizing Afghanistan's independence. In 1892, George Curzon, the quintessential British diplomat of the era, aptly described Iran and the territories surrounding it as "pieces on a chessboard upon which is being played out a game for the dominion of the world."[7]

Once the European powers had established themselves in the region, and after the Suez Canal opened in 1869, the foreign economic penetration of Iran grew rapidly. Iran's foreign trade increased fourfold between 1850 and 1914. Most of Iran's imports in the late nineteenth century were manufactured goods, and Iran increasingly became an exporter of agricultural products. The country's trade balance was consistently negative, leading Nasir al-Din Shah (who ruled Iran from 1848 until 1896) to obtain large loans from Russian and other European sources and to grant commercial concessions to European entrepreneurs. The first such concession was granted in 1863, for the construction of a telegraph line to India. Concessions for various transportation and mining projects, for the production and distribution of tobacco, and for banking and customs services followed over succeeding decades. The most important of these went in 1901 to an Englishman named William D'Arcy for the exploitation of oil and gas in all but the northernmost parts of Iran.[8]

This foreign economic penetration had the effect of commercializing the Iranian economy and changing its structural composition. This began a process, which continued well into the twentieth century, in which Iran's mode of production gradually evolved from oriental despotism into dependent capitalism. These exogenous and endogenous structural factors thoroughly transformed Iran's social structure and eventually brought about tremendous changes in the nature of state-society relations.

[7]George N. Curzon, *Persia and the Persian Question*, vol. 1 (London: Cass, 1966), 3–4. On Iran's foreign relations in this period see Firuz Kazemzadeh, *Russia and Britain in Persia, 1864–1914* (New Haven, Conn.: Yale University Press, 1968), and Rouhollah K. Ramazani, *The Foreign Policy of Iran: A Developing Nation in World Affairs, 1500–1941* (Charlottesville: University of Virginia Press, 1966), chaps. 2–3.

[8]Issawi, *Economic History of Iran*, 132–37; Ramazani, *Foreign Policy of Iran*, 65–72; Kazemzadeh, *Russia and Britain in Persia*, chaps. 2–5.

Handicraft industries, which had been firmly established in Iran in the early nineteenth century, were seriously weakened by the growing imports of manufactured goods and increasing competition in the export market. Although a limited amount of industrialization did occur during the late nineteenth century, almost all of it was undertaken by foreign entrepreneurs. Consequently, while a small industrial working class had emerged in Iran by 1900, foreign economic penetration had prevented the emergence of more than a handful of industrial capitalists, who would eventually constitute a "modern" upper class. By contrast, the rapid growth of Iran's exports invigorated and commercialized the agricultural sector and greatly strengthened the landlord class. Moreover, Nasir al-Din Shah sold off large amounts of state-owned land to raise cash, further strengthening the landlord class. The expansion of the agricultural sector provided new rural employment opportunities, which led many tribal groups to settle on the land. Iran's nomadic tribal population therefore declined from 50 percent of the total in the early nineteenth century to only 25 percent by the end of the century, and the power of Iran's tribal leaders declined accordingly. The rapid growth of trade also benefited certain bazaar merchants, who constituted a small but growing commercial bourgeoisie.[9]

The general growth of commerce and the corresponding expansion of the state bureaucracy also created a new, "modern" middle class of teachers, journalists, bureaucrats, and other professionals, which emerged mainly out of the existing "traditional" middle class. The distinctiveness of this class lay both in its occupational character and in its Western intellectual orientation, which resulted from its growing contact with Europeans and its access to Western education, both in Iran and abroad. The modern middle class was strongly attracted to Western political concepts like democracy and nationalism and it advocated sweeping political and economic reforms and reduced foreign interference. By contrast, the traditional middle class continued to associate mainly with its communal groups and saw no such urgent need for reform. The modern middle class was not particularly wealthy and did not generally have close personal connections with the shah and his advisers. Rather, its main sources of power lay in the key positions it occupied in the economy and the state bureaucracy and in its high level of social mobilization. The general growth of commerce also created new employment opportunities for the

[9]Issawi, *Economic History of Iran*, 258–61; A. Ashraf and H. Hekmat, "Merchants and Artisans and the Developmental Processes of Nineteenth-Century Iran," in A. L. Udovitch, ed., *The Islamic Middle East, 700–1900: Studies in Economic and Social History* (Princeton, N.J.: Darwin, 1981), 725–50; V. F. Nowshirvani, "The Beginnings of Commercialized Agriculture in Iran," in ibid., 547–91; Lambton, *Landlord and Peasant in Persia*, chap. 7.

urban lower class, bringing about a steady increase in the size of the urban population.[10]

These changes in Iran's social structure, as well as other, more direct consequences of foreign penetration, had fundamentally changed Iranian politics by the last decade of the nineteenth century. Two major changes had occurred. First, the autonomy of the Iranian state had declined considerably. The landlord class had become powerful enough to exercise virtual hegemony over the state. Moreover, the state's autonomy was increasingly restricted by foreign actors as well, as it became increasingly dependent on foreign loans and commercial concessions for revenue, and as Britain and Russia began to impose restrictions on Iran's foreign and domestic policy and intrigue in its domestic affairs.

Second, the main actors in Iranian politics had grown increasingly polarized over the issue of foreign influence in Iran. The main protagonists in this conflict were the state, backed by the landlord class and Britain and Russia, and an incipient coalition of the modern middle class, the traditional middle class, and the Shi'i clergy. The state had become dependent on foreign loans and concessions and therefore was unwilling to restrict foreign influence. The landlord class, having benefited from the growing export market for agricultural products, supported the state on this issue. The modern middle class, though still fairly small, had grown increasingly nationalistic and resentful of Nasir al-Din Shah's despotism. The bazaar merchants and artisans, who formed the core of the traditional middle class, had been adversely affected by growing inflation and by the foreign concessions and increasing imports of manufactured goods, which prevented them from expanding into transportation and finance and from exploiting the growing domestic market for manufactured goods. The clergy had always maintained close ties with the bazaar and had become increasingly concerned about the growth of Western and secular influence, which it blamed on Nasir al-Din Shah. The traditional middle class and most of the clergy therefore sided with the modern middle class in its opposition to the growth of foreign influence.[11]

Because the immediate focus of this conflict was on foreign influence, its

[10]On the modern middle class see Ashraf, *Iran: Imperialism, Class, and Modernization,* 294–331; and Bill, *Politics of Iran,* chap. 2. On the expansion of the state bureaucracy and Western education in Iran see Shaul Bakhash, *Iran: Monarchy, Bureaucracy, and Reform under the Qajars, 1858–1896* (London: Ithaca Press, 1979).

[11]See Nikki R. Keddie, "The Origins of the Religious-Radical Alliance in Iran," in idem, ed., *Iran: Religion, Politics, and Society* (London: Cass, 1980), 54–55; and Richard W. Cottam, *Nationalism in Iran* (Pittsburgh: University of Pittsburgh Press, 1979), chaps. 3, 11. On the rapid growth of inflation in Iran in this period see Gad G. Gilbar, "Trends in the Development of Prices in Late Qajar Iran, 1870–1906," *Iranian Studies* 16 (Summer–Autumn 1983), 177–98.

primary theme soon became anti-imperialism, expressed in the metaphors of nationalism and Islam. In a more fundamental sense, however, this conflict was a dispute over political power and the state's policies: it pitted a coalition drawn from the modern and traditional middle classes and the clergy against the state and its domestic and foreign allies in a dispute over fundamental aspects of state policy making. Democracy, which had gained many adherents among the modern middle class by this time, therefore became a prominent theme in this conflict as well. Democracy and nationalism thus became closely linked as guiding principles for the main political conflict of the time.

The simmering dispute over the growth of foreign influence came into focus in 1891 when Nasir al-Din Shah granted a British citizen a concession for the production and sale of tobacco, which was widely used in Iran and had been an important source of livelihood for many Iranian merchants. These merchants were greatly angered and sought to have the concession annulled. The Shi'i clergy were also incensed because an item of intimate personal use would now be handled by non-Muslims. Activists such as Sayyid Jamal al-Din al-Afghani, a widely traveled clergyman who had been strongly influenced by contemporary anti-imperialist movements in India and the Arab world, quickly seized upon the granting of the tobacco concession. Secular nationalists, bazaar leaders, and members of the clergy organized massive nationwide protests that spring. At times bordering on insurrection, these protests continued for almost a year, ending only in early 1892 when Nasir al-Din Shah withdrew the concession. Although the tobacco protests did not fundamentally change state-society relations, they did signal the emergence for the first time of a mass-based opposition movement.[12]

Most leaders of the tobacco protest remained active in the following years, publishing opposition newspapers and pamphlets, organizing secret societies to discuss and plan political activity, and staging rallies and demonstrations against foreign influence and the state's policies. The opposition's increasing pressure for the establishment of a democratic regime reflected the modern middle class's growing prominence in the movement. After a series of unpopular actions by Mozaffar al-Din Shah (who had replaced Nasir al-Din Shah in 1896), Tehran merchants staged a general strike in May 1905. In another general strike in December 1905, groups of protesters took *bast* (a form of sanctuary) in the Masjid-e Shah Mosque and the shrine of Abdul Azim in Tehran to dramatize their demands for reform. Large demonstrations in Tehran in the summer of

[12]On the tobacco protest see Nikki R. Keddie, *Religion and Rebellion in Iran: The Tobacco Protest of 1891–1892* (London: Cass, 1966).

1906 culminated in the occupation of the British Legation by a crowd of some fourteen thousand people. The demonstrators demanded that a constitution be enacted and a *majles* (or parliament) be established. After rumors began to circulate that army units were about to defect, and amid fears of an armed uprising, Mozaffar al-Din Shah agreed to the demonstrators' demands.[13]

The Creation of the Modern Iranian State, 1906–1941

The establishment of democratic institutions after the Constitutional Revolution was the first step in the creation of a modern Iranian state. It also signaled the end of the hegemony of the landlord class and raised the possibility that one or more of the groups that had participated in the constitutional movement might soon gain control over the state. The modern middle class had become the driving force behind the constitutional movement, but the transition to dependent capitalism was still far from complete, leaving that class still too weak to gain control over the state by itself. Major differences within the opposition coalition so weakened this coalition that it, too, was incapable of establishing hegemony. With the absence of class hegemony, the basic precondition for the emergence of a Bonapartist state existed. However, two factors prevented such a state from emerging until the mid-1920s. First, Britain and Russia remained heavily involved in Iran's domestic affairs after the Constitutional Revolution and were determined to prevent an independent government from coming to power; in effect, *they* exercised hegemony over the Iranian state. Second, it was not until the mid-1920s that a ruler emerged with the strength and leadership ability needed to establish a Bonapartist state.

An efflorescence of popular political activity followed the victory of the constitutional movement in the summer of 1906. A constituent assembly was quickly convened to draw up an electoral law for the new majles, and an election was held in October 1906. The new Majles quickly drafted a constitution based on the Belgian model, which was ratified by Mozaffar al-Din Shah in December 1906. The Majles also began to implement a program of reforms which largely reflected the agenda of the modern middle class: royal expenditures were restricted; the salaries and pensions of many top officials and members of the royal family were reduced or

[13]On the Constitutional Revolution see esp. Edward G. Browne, *The Persian Revolution of 1905–1909* (London: Cass, 1966), chap. 5.

eliminated; and the system of land tenure was modified to undermine the power of the large landlords. A wide variety of journals, newspapers, and political organizations also appeared in this period.[14]

The initial euphoria sparked by the Constitutional Revolution was, however, short lived. Mohammad Ali Shah, who succeeded Mozaffar al-Din Shah soon after the constitution was ratified, quickly began a protracted effort to undermine the constitutional regime. Britain and Russia joined in this effort by signing a treaty in August 1907 which, in effect, turned Iran into a joint protectorate. Debates in the Majles between factions representing the modern middle class and those representing the traditional middle class and the clergy became increasingly bitter and spilled over into the streets of Tehran. In June 1908 the Russian-officered Cossack Brigade attacked and closed the Majles building, killing hundreds of constitutionalists and torturing or murdering many of their leaders. Proconstitutional revolts then broke out in Tabriz and several other cities, plunging the country into civil war. Russian troops entered Iran in 1909 to put down the uprising in Tabriz. A force of constitutionalists from Rasht and a column of Bakhtiari tribesmen then marched on Tehran, deposed Mohammad Ali Shah, and installed his young son Ahmad on the throne. A government was quickly formed, and the Second Majles was convened in November 1909. Tehran was soon engulfed in a series of strikes and demonstrations, however, and much of the country was plunged into tribal warfare. Seeking to restore order, British and Russian troops entered Iran in late 1911 and presented the government with a series of humiliating demands. Bowing to these demands, the government closed the Majles in November 1911, ending Iran's brief experiment in constitutional rule.[15]

Iran remained in a state of near-anarchy for the next decade. British and Russian troops maintained a semblance of authority in the major cities, but tribal unrest continued in many outlying areas. The government was controlled for several years by Bakhtiari tribal leaders, who had gained some popular support for their role in restoring the constitutional regime in 1909. With the outbreak of World War I, Ottoman troops occupied parts of western Iran, and German agents intrigued among the tribes and among remnants of the constitutional movement. Czarist forces in northern Iran and in the Caucasus collapsed after the 1917 Russian Revolution. British troops then advanced northward through Iran into the Caucasus to counter a German-Turkish drive toward Baku. Soviet agents soon

[14]Ervand Abrahamian, *Iran between Two Revolutions* (Princeton, N.J.: Princeton University Press, 1982), 86–93; Lambton, *Landlord and Peasant in Persia*, 178–80, 260.

[15]Abrahamian, *Iran between Two Revolutions*, 86–109. For an eyewitness account of this period see W. Morgan Shuster, *The Strangling of Persia* (London: T. Fisher Unwin, 1912).

began to intrigue in the northern provinces, where several separatist movements had emerged. After the British left the Caucasus in 1920, Soviet troops entered northern Iran in pursuit of White Russian forces. An Iranian Communist party was established in Enzeli in June 1920. A Soviet republic was briefly created in Gilan in September 1920, and separatist revolts occurred in Azerbaijan and Khorasan. Soviet and British troops remained on Iranian territory until 1921.[16]

After the collapse of czarist Russia and the end of World War I, Britain tried to impose on Iran a treaty designed to bring the country more firmly under British control. By late 1920 there had emerged in Iran widespread opposition to this treaty and to the failure of the Iranian government to stop the revolts in the northern provinces. Several groups of army officers apparently began plotting to overthrow the government. In early 1921 a coalition of officers led by Colonel Reza Khan and constitutionalists led by a journalist named Sayyid Zia al-Din Tabatabai seized power, apparently with British support, and installed Sayyid Zia as prime minister and Reza Khan as commander of the armed forces. Reza Khan soon forced Sayyid Zia out of office, had himself appointed prime minister in 1923, and acceded to the throne as Reza Shah in 1925.[17]

During his rapid ascent to power, Reza Shah had solicited support from the traditional upper class by releasing many members of this class who had been jailed by Sayyid Zia, restoring the positions of many officials who had been purged from the state bureaucracy, closing leftist newspapers, and briefly supporting the premiership of Ahmad Qavam, a member of the Qajar royal family who had gained a reputation as a moderate. He had also sought support from the modern middle class by entering into an alliance with two progressive political parties and instituting compulsory military conscription, a measure that promised to undermine the traditional bases of support of the landlord class and the clergy. Thus Reza Shah had enjoyed broad support in his effort to become shah. He had been opposed only by the left and by a small group of Majles deputies led by a lawyer and wealthy landowner named Mohammad Mosaddeq.[18]

Reza Shah's ability to gain support from both the traditional upper class and the modern middle class indicates that neither of these classes was then capable of exercising hegemony over the state. Moreover, as tensions

[16]Ramazani, *Foreign Policy of Iran*, chaps. 6–7; George Lenczowski, *Russia and the West in Iran, 1918–1948: A Study in Big-Power Rivalry* (Ithaca, N.Y.: Cornell University Press, 1949), chaps. 2–3.

[17]See Donald N. Wilber, *Riza Shah Pahlavi: The Resurrection and Reconstruction of Iran* (Hicksville, N.Y.: Exposition, 1975), chap. 3.

[18]Ibid., chaps. 5–7.

in the region declined in the early 1920s, Britain and the Soviet Union had rapidly reduced their presence in Iran. The absence of class hegemony and the sharp decline in foreign influence enabled Reza Shah to establish a highly autonomous, Bonapartist state during the 1920s.

Reza Shah's efforts to establish a highly autonomous state were bolstered by his strong leadership and his extensive use of repression and co-optation, tactics that were to remain important features of the Iranian state after his fall from power. He became adept at playing groups and individuals against one another, as in his maneuvering between the traditional upper class and the modern middle class during his rise to power. He expanded the state bureaucracy and used it as an instrument of co-optation by giving top positions to powerful political figures, raising pay scales for public employees, and providing public services to important groups and individuals. During his tenure as commander of the armed forces, he had made extensive efforts to reorganize the army and consolidate his control over it. He was then able to use the army to crush the separatist movements in the north and tribal uprisings in other parts of the country, at once eliminating the main threats to his rule and gaining the respect and support of other elements of society. The army and the police thereafter became pillars of Reza Shah's regime, enabling him to rig elections, close down newspapers, break up political gatherings, and intimidate, arrest, torture, and murder his opponents. Repression became so severe in Iran that a U.S. embassy official in 1934 described the country as "strongly reminiscent of Soviet Russia in the period of militant communism, 1917–1921."[19]

Once he had established a highly autonomous, Bonapartist state, Reza Shah was able to use the state apparatus to carry out virtually any policies he desired. This enabled him to amass a great fortune, including, by one account, as much as 15 percent of the arable land in Iran.[20] But the state's high degree of autonomy also enabled him to undertake an extensive program of reforms aimed at modernizing and secularizing Iran and reducing foreign influence. Reza Shah's reforms gradually transformed Iranian society, unleashing forces that were to revolutionize Iranian politics in the period after he was ousted from power in 1941.

Reza Shah directed his first modernization efforts at the military and the civil service. As commander of the armed forces, he had eliminated foreign officers from Iran's diverse military units and united them into a single command. He also purged the officer corps, instituted compulsory con-

[19]Ibid., chaps. 8–12; Hornibrook to Secretary of State, April 19, 1934, 119.254/2119, National Archives.

[20]Ashraf, *Iran: Imperialism, Class, and Modernization*, 156.

scription, and established a small navy and air force. He reorganized the civil service in 1922, establishing uniform regulations for the hiring, promotion, and professional conduct of state employees. The civil code and judicial system also underwent extensive reforms. The number of civilian government employees increased from twenty-five thousand to one hundred thousand between 1923 and 1943, and the armed forces grew to nearly four hundred thousand men.[21]

Reza Shah made comparable efforts to establish a modern, secular educational system. The number of students enrolled in secular primary and secondary schools increased by an astonishing 1,300 percent between 1925 and 1939. The University of Tehran was established in 1934, and some thirty-six teachers' colleges and thirty-two vocational schools had been opened by 1941. Reza Shah started a program that awarded one hundred state scholarships each year for study overseas; over fifteen hundred Iranians had returned from studying abroad by 1938. Schools for the military and the civil service and a large adult education program were established, as were an academy for the study of Persian language and literature and many libraries, museums, and athletic facilities.[22]

Reza Shah also used the state extensively to promote industrialization and expand Iran's economic infrastructure. A state-owned national bank and state-owned domestic and foreign trade monopolies were established. Tariffs were restructured to promote industrialization. Some sixty-four state-owned factories had been built by 1941, accounting for roughly 50 percent of Iran's nonoil industrial production and employment. The Trans-Iranian Railroad, built under Reza Shah, connected the major northern cities of Iran to the Persian Gulf. Thousands of miles of roads were built. Reza Shah also levied various direct and indirect taxes to finance these efforts.[23]

In addition to these social and economic reforms, Reza Shah made great efforts to reduce foreign influence. Soon after the coup of 1921, Sayyid Zia's government had repudiated the 1919 treaty advanced by Britain and signed a treaty with the Soviet Union in which all czarist claims on Iran were renounced. Arthur Millspaugh, an American financial analyst, was hired in 1922 to reorganize the Iranian economy. Trade with the Soviet Union, Germany, Japan, and the United States was increased in order to reduce Iran's economic dependence on Britain. The Trans-Iranian Rail-

[21]Amin Banani, *The Modernization of Iran, 1921–1941* (Stanford, Calif.: Stanford University Press, 1961), chap. 4; Ashraf, *Iran: Imperialism, Class, and Modernization*, 300.

[22]Banani, *Modernization of Iran*, chap. 6; Julian Bharier, *Economic Development in Iran, 1900–1970* (London: Oxford University Press, 1971), 38.

[23]Bharier, *Economic Development in Iran*, 73–78, 84–88, 176–80; Banani, *Modernization of Iran*, chap. 7.

road was financed with domestic capital and built with advisers and equipment drawn from several foreign countries. Foreign exchange controls and import-substitution measures were implemented to broaden and protect the economy. A widely despised system of capitulations was rescinded. These measures substantially increased Iran's independence from foreign powers, although Britain continued to wield considerable influence through its control over the oil industry and its ties to prominent Iranian political figures, businessmen, tribal leaders, and members of the clergy.[24]

Reza Shah's reforms had a tremendous impact on the Iranian economy, completing the transformation of the mode of production from oriental despotism to a relatively primitive form of dependent capitalism. The agricultural sector, though still the backbone of the economy, had declined from 80–90 percent of GNP in 1900 to about 50 percent by the 1930s and had become heavily commercialized. In its place, the oil industry and the manufacturing and service sectors had grown substantially. Oil production grew by almost 600 percent between 1926 and 1937. Manufacturing grew from almost nil to about 5 percent of GNP between 1926 and 1947. Factories for producing textiles, cement, matches, and processed foods were built in this period. These factories mainly used domestically produced inputs and therefore constituted an initial stage of import substitution. Service industries such as construction, transportation, and communications also grew substantially. Although Iran was still economically dependent at the end of Reza Shah's reign, the nature of this dependence had changed considerably because of these reforms: oil had joined agricultural goods as a major export product; Britain was no longer Iran's dominant trading partner; a modest level of import substitution had been achieved; Iran's foreign debt had been eliminated; and foreign investment had grown very little, except in the oil industry.[25]

These changes in the mode of production, as well as the social reforms undertaken by Reza Shah, had important long-term consequences for Iranian domestic politics. The landlord class was considerably weakened by the decline of agriculture, by land confiscations, and by measures that undermined its authority in rural areas, such as military conscription and the promotion of literacy. Reza Shah's harassment and forced settlement of tribes reduced Iran's nomadic population from roughly 25 percent of the total in 1900 to under 10 percent by the early 1930s and thus undermined the power of tribal leaders. Similarly, policies such as the promotion of a secular educational system, military conscription, and legal

[24]Ramazani, *Foreign Policy of Iran*, chaps. 8–12.
[25]Bharier, *Economic Development in Iran*, 59, 157–58, 172–81.

reform, as well as more direct forms of harassment, undermined the power of the Shi'i clergy. Because of the prevalence of state-owned industries and trade monopolies, very few industrial capitalists emerged in this period, but Iran's bazaar merchants benefited considerably from the expansion of the economy and remained politically important.[26]

Reza Shah's economic and social reforms also increased the size and latent political power of the modern middle class and the industrial working class. The modern middle class grew considerably as a result of the educational reforms and the expansion of the economy and state bureaucracy. Moreover, as the state became increasingly involved in economic and social affairs, it became more dependent on the expertise of the modern middle class. The strong support of the modern middle class for Reza Shah's reforms continued to alienate it from the clergy and made it increasingly difficult for these two groups to work together. The industrial working class grew from roughly thirteen thousand in 1900 to about ninety thousand in 1941, of whom thirty thousand worked in the oil industry. Moreover, despite intense harassment by Reza Shah, Iran's Communist party had become more militant and better prepared to mobilize the working class in the post–Reza Shah era. Only the peasantry remained socially unmobilized and political inactive.[27]

Reza Shah's reforms therefore sharply accelerated changes that had already begun to affect Iranian domestic politics: the conflict between the landlord-dominated traditional upper class and the modern middle class continued; the political power of the traditional upper class continued to decline, and that of the modern middle class increased; and the industrial working class grew and became large enough to play an important role in politics. After Reza Shah's overthrow, these changes were to produce a period of considerable turmoil which greatly affected the autonomy of the Iranian state.

Iranian Politics during and after World War II

Reza Shah was abruptly ousted from power in September 1941 when British and Soviet forces invaded Iran and crushed the hapless Iranian

[26]Ibid., 26, 31; Lambton, *Landlord and Peasant in Persia*, 260, 285–86; Ahmad Ashraf, "Historical Obstacles to the Development of a Bourgeoisie in Iran," in M. A. Cook, ed., *Studies in the Economic History of the Middle East* (London: Oxford University Press, 1970), 328–31; Shahrough Akhavi, *Religion and Politics in Contemporary Iran: Clergy-State Relations in the Pahlavi Period* (Albany: State University of New York Press, 1980), chap. 2.

[27]Ashraf, "Historical Obstacles," 329; Bharier, *Economic Development in Iran*, 162; Sepehr Zabih, *The Communist Movement in Iran* (Berkeley and Los Angeles : University of California Press, 1966), chap. 2; Farhad Kazemi and Ervand Abrahamian, "The Nonrevolutionary Peasantry of Modern Iran," *Iranian Studies* 11 (1978), 259–304.

army. The primary motive for the invasion was to secure the Trans-Iranian Railroad as a supply route for the Soviet war effort. British and Soviet officials were also concerned, however, about the rapid growth of German influence in Iran. Germany had become Iran's largest trading partner, and some three thousand Germans were living in Iran in 1941. German agents had set up clandestine cells throughout the country, and Reza Shah, who had been attracted to Hitler's Pan-Aryan nationalism, had rejected Allied demands that German agents and sympathizers in Iran be arrested. Reza Shah was exiled to Mauritius and later to South Africa, where he died in 1944. Crown Prince Mohammad Reza Pahlavi, aged twenty-one, succeeded his father on September 17, 1941.[28]

After Reza Shah was overthrown, Iranian politics returned in some ways to the pattern that had prevailed at the beginning of the century: the state's autonomy declined considerably, and conflict reemerged among the most powerful societal groups over fundamental aspects of the state's foreign and domestic policy. The decline in the state's autonomy was due initially to extensive British and Soviet intervention in Iran's domestic affairs and to the absence of strong state leadership. But the modern middle class and industrial working class, which had both grown considerably under Reza Shah, became increasingly active in Iranian politics and clashed with the traditional upper class, trying, in effect, to establish hegemony over the state. The growing power of the modern middle class and the weak leadership of the young shah enabled state power to pass largely into the hands of the prime minister and the Majles, which had authority under the constitution to nominate and approve candidates for the premiership. Control over the Majles therefore became a key goal of the various groups contending for power, and domestic politics became much more pluralistic. The growing prominence of the modern middle class brought the reemergence of anti-imperialism and democracy as the most prominent themes in Iran's political discourse.

With the demise of Reza Shah's repressive regime, the vigorous political activity of the preceding era quickly reemerged. A general amnesty for political prisoners was declared. Political figures who had gone into exile under Reza Shah returned and immersed themselves once again in politics. Censorship was lifted and a broad spectrum of newspapers and periodicals quickly reappeared. Political parties and trade unions were permitted to operate, and dozens were soon formed. Strikes and demonstrations,

[28]Rouhollah K. Ramazani, *Iran's Foreign Policy, 1941–1973: A Study of Foreign Policy in Modernizing Nations* (Charlottesville: University of Virginia Press, 1975), chap. 1; T. Vail Motter, *United States Army in World War II: The Middle East Theater, the Persian Corridor, and Aid to Russia* (Washington: Department of the Army, Office of the Chief of Military History, 1952), 481–83; Office of Strategic Services, Research and Analysis Branch, "Iran: Ripe for the Nazis," R & A Report 509, November 27, 1941, National Archives.

which had become rare under Reza Shah, occurred with growing frequency. Soviet, British, and German agents intrigued among the emerging political forces, adding to the rich political ferment of the time.

Most of the political parties that emerged in this period were merely instruments of particular members of the upper class; lacking popular support, many quickly disappeared. The two most important were the National Will party, led by Sayyid Zia and known for its pro-British orientation, and the Democrat Party, led by Ahmad Qavam. Some of the parties established in this period were, however, based on the support of specific societal groups and were therefore much more durable. Although political parties had existed in Iran since the turn of the century, these were the first representative parties with popular bases of support.

The largest and most active party established in this period was the Tudeh (Masses) party, formed in October 1941 by the survivors of a group of fifty-three Iranian Marxists who had been jailed by Reza Shah and amnestied after the Anglo-Soviet invasion. Its base of support lay among the modern middle class and the industrial working class. The Tudeh initially adopted a democratic, antifascist, and leftist but noncommunist program: it supported the constitution, participated in Majles elections, and strongly opposed nazism and the remaining vestiges of Reza Shah's regime. One of the Tudeh's top priorities was to organize trade unions; in 1946 its Central Council of Federated Trade Unions claimed a total membership of 335,000 workers. The Tudeh party had become so popular by 1946 that a *New York Times* reporter estimated it would have received 40 percent of the votes in a free nationwide election. Since its inception, the Tudeh had contained both communist and democratic factions. A major rift developed between these factions during the August 1944 party congress, and the communist faction soon became dominant. By late 1944 the Tudeh party had therefore begun to identify openly with the Soviet Union.[29]

Several smaller leftist parties also appeared, some of which soon merged with the Tudeh. Mass-based leftist parties advocating regional autonomy were established in the provinces of Azerbaijan, Gilan, and Kurdistan. The social democratic Iran party was established by a small group of Western-oriented intellectuals. The centrist Justice party was established by a group of intellectuals supported by bazaar merchants. Finally, an enigmatic, ultranationalist organization known as the Pan-Iranist party was formed by a small core of intellectuals and a large group of urban lower-class toughs. Although each of these parties was to become influen-

[29]Zabih, *Communist Movement in Iran*, chap. 3; *New York Times*, June 15, 1946, 2:2; U.S. Department of State, Office of Intelligence and Research, *The Tudeh and Associated Parties in Iran*, OIR No. 3523.5, April 1, 1946.

tial in the years after World War II, none could match the Tudeh party in size or organizational ability.

Another important political organization to appear at this time was the Fedayan-e Islam (Devotees of Islam), a small but highly active group of Muslim extremists supported by certain Shi'i clergymen and bazaar merchants. Much like the contemporary Muslim Brotherhood in Egypt, the Fedayan sought to promote Islamic fundamentalism through agitation and terrorist attacks against targets it regarded as anti-Islamic. The Fedayan was anathema to the mainstream Shi'i clergy, which tended to side with the traditional upper class but had largely abandoned its earlier political activism. One prominent clergyman who did maintain ties with the Fedayan-e Islam was Ayatollah Abul Qassem Kashani, a rabble-rousing clerical activist who was also associated with a notorious Nazi spy named Franz Meyer.[30]

Since elections for the Thirteenth Majles, which sat from November 1941 until November 1943, had been nearly completed before the Anglo-Soviet invasion, these emergent parties played no role in determining the composition of this Majles. They did, however, become active in the elections for the Fourteenth Majles (March 1944–March 1946), giving it a fairly diverse character. During the Fourteenth Majles elections, tensions had emerged between pro- and antishah elements over attempts by the shah to rig the elections in his favor. These tensions continued to exist after the elections, splitting the Fourteenth Majles into a fairly small royalist faction and a large, heterogeneous antishah faction that included a group of pro-British deputies, a group of tribal leaders, a group of upper-class deputies from Iran's northern provinces (which were occupied by the Soviet army), and groups based on the Justice party, the Iran party, and the Tudeh party. The antishah coalition quickly gained control over the most important Majles committees and began to form a cabinet. It then tried to gain control over the armed forces, which had been Reza Shah's main power base, by imposing restrictions on its budget and forcing it to adopt certain reforms. This effort quickly came to an end, however, when a series of violent strikes in Isfahan, led by the Tudeh party, brought about the collapse of the antishah coalition.[31]

[30]For good descriptions of the political organizations that emerged in this period see L. P. Elwell-Sutton, "Political Parties in Iran, 1941–1948," *Middle East Journal* 3 (January 1949), 45–62; and Katouzian, *Political Economy of Modern Iran*, chap. 8. On the Fedayan-e Islam see Farhad Kazemi, "The Feda'iyan-e Islam: Fanaticism, Politics, and Terror," in Said Amir Arjomand, ed., *From Nationalism to Revolutionary Islam* (Albany: State University of New York Press, 1984), 158–76; and Amir H. Ferdows, "Khomaini and Fadayan's Society and Politics," *International Journal of Middle East Studsies* 15 (May 1983), 241–57.

[31]"Iranian Political Parties and the Forthcoming Elections for the XIVth Parliament," July 22, 1943, Record Group 59, Box 5192; Abrahamian, *Iran between Two Revolutions*, 199–224.

The Iranian government had begun secret negotiations in 1943 with several British and American oil companies to grant new oil concessions in the northern and southeastern parts of Iran. The Soviet Union soon learned about these negotiations and began to pressure the Iranian government in the summer of 1944 to grant it the oil concession for northern Iran.[32] This dispute began a period of growing tension between pro- and anti-Soviet elements in Iran that was to dominate Iranian politics for several years. The Tudeh party quickly backed the Soviet demands, openly identifying itself with the Soviet Union for the first time. The antishah Majles deputies from Iran's northern provinces also backed the Soviet demands, further weakening the antishah forces. Most of the remaining Majles deputies then passed a bill in December 1944 authored by Mohammad Mosaddeq which outlawed all further oil concessions. The Soviet Union nevertheless continued to press for an oil concession, creating growing tension between pro- and anti-Soviet elements. By August 1945 Tudeh-led uprisings had begun to occur in the Soviet-occupied provinces of Azerbaijan, Mazandaran, and Gorgan; Soviet troops prevented the Iranian army from suppressing these uprisings. The Soviet Union helped establish the Democratic party of Azerbaijan and Democratic party of Kurdistan, which advocated autonomy for the ethnically distinct provinces of Iranian Azerbaijan and Kurdistan. Tension increased throughout the fall of 1945, culminating in the establishment, by these two parties, of the Autonomous Republic of Azerbaijan in December 1945 and the Kurdish People's Republic in January 1946. Soviet support for the rebel governments was blatant and led most observers to conclude that the Soviet Union was trying to establish client states on its Iranian border similar to those being created at this time in Eastern Europe and Korea. Moreover, Soviet troops still occupied much of northern Iran, including the areas claimed by the rebel governments. Iran therefore quickly became a major battlefield in the emerging Cold War.

Backed by the United States and Britain, the Iranian government asked the United Nations Security Council to address the issue of continued Soviet military occupation of northern Iran. Ahmad Qavam, who had been named prime minister in January 1946, traveled to Moscow in March 1946 for direct negotiations over the dispute. He eventually obtained an agreement from the Soviet Union that it would withdraw its troops from Iran in exchange for an oil concession, subject to Majles approval. Although Soviet troops did leave in May 1946, rebel forces backed by Soviet civilian advisers remained in control of the two autono-

[32]On the origins of this dispute see L. P. Elwell-Sutton, *Persian Oil: A Study in Power Politics* (London: Lawrence and Wishart, 1955), chap. 9.

mous republics, and the Tudeh party continued to create chaos throughout the country. Encouraged by Qavam and by U.S. and British officials, the Qashqai tribe revolted and laid siege to Shiraz in September 1946. Under the pretext of restoring order for the Fifteenth Majles elections, which had already been delayed for several months, Qavam sent troops into Azerbaijan in December 1946. Spontaneous popular uprisings overthrew the government of the Autonomous Republic of Azerbaijan before the Iranian army had even reached Tabriz; the Kurdish Republic also soon fell. Hundreds of rebels were killed or imprisoned, and over ten thousand fled to the Soviet Union. A bill to approve the Soviet oil concession was later presented in the Majles and soundly defeated.[33]

With the departure of Soviet troops and the collapse of the two autonomous republics, external actors again assumed the secondary role in Iranian domestic politics that they had come to play under Reza Shah. In the open political environment that prevailed, the withdrawal of foreign actors left Iran turbulent and in a state of flux. The immediate consequences of the Soviet withdrawal were a collapse of the Tudeh's large base of support and a surge in the popularity of Qavam's Democrat party. Qavam had begun an extensive crackdown on the Tudeh party and its affiliates in October 1946. During the reoccupation of Azerbaijan and Kurdistan, this crackdown continued, greatly weakening the Tudeh. As a result, the Tudeh party underwent a period of reorganization and ideological purification: it boycotted the Fifteenth Majles elections, purged much of its top leadership, and identifyed more closely with Marxist-Leninist principles and the policies of the Soviet Union.[34]

In the Fifteenth Majles elections, held after the collapse of the two autonomous republics, Qavam's Democrat party obtained a strong majority. But like the antishah coalition in the Fourteenth Majles, the Democrat party contained very diverse elements ranging from wealthy landlords and tribal leaders to members of the modern middle class and working class. Friction soon emerged, leading to defections and ultimately to Qavam's ouster from the premiership in late 1947. A coalition of royalist and pro-British Majles deputies then elected Ibrahim Hakimi prime minister by one vote over Mohammad Mosaddeq, who was supported by remnants of the Democrat party and various independents.

[33]Robert Rossow, Jr., "The Battle of Azerbaijan," *Middle East Journal* 10 (Winter 1956), 17–32; Archie Roosevelt, Jr., "The Kurdish Republic of Mahabad," *Middle East Journal* 1 (July 1947), 247–69; Lois Beck, *The Qashqa'i of Iran* (New Haven, Conn.: Yale University Press, 1986), 148–52. For an excellent study of the role this crisis played in the Cold War see Bruce Robellet Kuniholm, *The Origins of the Cold War in the Near East* (Princeton, N.J.: Princeton University Press, 1980).

[34]Zabih, *Communist Movement in Iran*, chap. 4.

Hakimi made proposals designed to enhance the shah's power, including an increase in military spending and the establishment of an upper house of parliament, called the Senate, half of whose members would be appointed by the shah.[35]

With an ally in the prime minister's office and his opponents in the Majles still fairly disorganized, the shah in late 1947 began a protracted effort to increase his control over the state. Toward this end he began to play a more active role in politics, especially in the activities of the Majles, and began to solicit military and economic aid from the United States. This latter step angered the pro-British faction in the Majles, and they withdrew their support for the Hakimi government. The royalist faction then managed to secure the election of Abdul Hussein Hazhir as prime minister. Hazhir quickly set about strengthening the armed forces and began secret negotiations with the British-owned Anglo-Iranian Oil Company (AIOC) to increase the state's oil revenue. These actions led to further conflict with the pro-British Majles faction and to conflict with Ayatollah Kashani, who organized large demonstrations and a general strike. Hazhir resigned in late 1948, after only four months in office. The contending Majles factions then tried unsuccessfully to elect a new prime minister, leaving the position vacant for several weeks.

In the midst of this impasse an attempt was made in February 1949 to assassinate the shah. Although the political affiliations of the assailant were never conclusively established, the shah's allies claimed he had been associated with both the Tudeh party and the Fedayan-e Islam. The shah used the assassination attempt as a pretext to increase his control over the state: he declared martial law, outlawed the Tudeh party, deported Kashani to Lebanon, had other opposition figures arrested, and convened a constituent assembly, which established the court-controlled Senate proposed earlier and gave the shah authority to dissolve the Majles. Taking advantage of the crisis atmosphere, the shah also secured the election of a royalist named Mohammad Said as prime minister. Said then took steps to strengthen the armed forces, gave the shah authority to shut down newspapers, and returned to the shah the vast landholdings accumulated by Reza Shah, which had been placed under government control after the Anglo-Soviet invasion.

The shah tried to follow up on these victories by rigging the Sixteenth Majles elections, which were begun in July 1949. In October 1949 Mosaddeq led a large crowd of students, bazaar figures, and politicians onto

[35]The discussion in this and the following paragraphs draws mainly on Abrahamian, *Iran between Two Revolutions*, 242–67.

the royal palace grounds to protest the rigged elections. The demonstrators elected a committee of twenty prominent activists led by Mosaddeq to negotiate their demands with the shah's court minister. After receiving a promise that the elections would proceed freely, this committee retired to Mosaddeq's home, where it agreed to form an organization that would continue to press for political reforms. This organization, which became known as the National Front, initially engaged in efforts to democratize the political system by pressing for free elections and other political reforms, but it quickly became engrossed in the task of trying to regain control over Iran's oil resources, which were still controlled by the AIOC.

The National Front managed to elect eight of its members to the Sixteenth Majles, which convened in February 1950, including Mosaddeq and several other members of the original committee of twenty. Although the new Majles had a royalist majority, the National Front deputies quickly began to agitate for reforms aimed at reducing the power of the shah and improving the welfare of the middle and lower classes. In June 1950 the royalist government of Ali Mansur submitted a proposal to the Majles embodying the agreement that had been reached with the AIOC in the secret negotiations begun by Hazhir. The National Front and the Tudeh party immediately denounced this proposal as a sell-out. Large public demonstrations were held to protest the proposal, and a pro-British politician was assassinated. Mansur then resigned the premiership, leading the shah to nominate General Ali Razmara, a moderate nationalist who supported the oil proposal but had often criticized the shah. Razmara quickly won Majles approval and then sponsored a bill embodying the oil proposal, along with reform measures such as a tax increase for the wealthy, the creation of an anticorruption commission, a relaxation of anti-Tudeh measures, and a land reform bill.

The submission of the oil bill to the Majles provoked widespread popular unrest. The National Front began to call for outright nationalization of the oil industry; but Razmara continued to press for approval of the bill. In March 1951 he was assassinated by a member of the Fedayan-e Islam, apparently because of his support for the oil agreement. Extensive rioting throughout the country followed the assassination. A series of strikes took place at the oil port of Abadan. The Fedayan assassinated a former cabinet minister and threatened to kill the shah and other officials. The Majles, still dominated by a royalist majority, elected Hussein Ala, a moderate with close ties to the shah, to replace Razmara. Ala tried to appease the nationalist forces by bringing a National Front leader into his cabinet and backing a package of reforms. Opposition continued, and Ala soon resigned. In late April the Majles nominated Mosaddeq for the premiership and then voted to nationalize the oil industry. Bowing to the demands of the nationalist forces, the shah accepted Mosaddeq's nomination on April 29 and signed the nationalization bill into law on May 2.[36]

United States Policy toward Iran, 1941–1951

Before World War II, relations between the United States and Iran had been cordial but distant: U.S. foreign policy was guided largely by the principle of isolationism, and Iran was not located where the United States had important strategic or economic interests. The two countries had established diplomatic relations in 1856, but the United States did not assign a diplomat of ambassadorial rank to Iran until 1944. Contact between the United States and Iran in the nineteenth century had consisted mainly of missionary activity and archaeological expeditions. In the first few decades of the twentieth century, Iran's various rulers had tried to increase the U.S. presence in Iran in order to counterbalance British and Russian influence. This effort had produced two important U.S. economic advisory missions to Iran and a modest amount of trade, but the United States continued to have little tangible interest in Iran. Diplomatic relations between the two countries were evidently of so little importance in the late 1930s that they were suspended for several years because of derogatory statements about Reza Shah that appeared in the American press.[37]

With the opening of a supply route to the Soviet Union through Iran during World War II, however, U.S. involvement in Iran increased considerably. The United States first sent troops to Iran in December 1942 to assist in the supply effort; by early 1944 some thirty thousand U.S. soldiers were stationed there. During the war the United States made extensive improvements to Iran's transportation system and to the AIOC facilities and built plants for assembling aircraft, trucks, and oil drums. Arthur Millspaugh was brought back to Iran as an economic adviser in 1942 and given broad authority to set prices, raise taxes, and manage the state's budget. The United States sent missions to Iran under the command of General Clarence Ridley and Colonel Norman Schwartzkopf to train the Iranian army and Gendarmerie. Lend-lease aid was made available in 1942, and Iran received some eight and a half million dollars in U.S.

[36]For a good account of these events see Elwell-Sutton, *Persian Oil*, chap. 16.

[37]Abraham Yeselson, *United States–Persian Diplomatic Relations, 1883–1921* (New Brunswick, N.J.: Rutgers University Press, 1956); John A. Denovo, *American Interests and Policies in the Middle East, 1900–1939* (Minneapolis: University of Minnesota Press, 1963), chap. 9.

military and economic aid under this program. Moreover, U.S. oil companies, acting with the encouragement and assistance of the U.S. embassy in Tehran, tried to obtain oil concessions in Iran in 1943 and 1944.[38]

But despite this growing presence, the United States did not become actively involved in Iran's domestic affairs during World War II. Although State Department officials had expressed concern about postwar Soviet and British designs on Iran as early as January 1943, and while the U.S. Office of Strategic Services monitored German, Soviet, and British activities in Iran during the war, the need to maintain harmony among the wartime allies ruled out extensive U.S. involvement. The United States made no attempt to block Soviet efforts to obtain an oil concession and gain greater influence in Azerbaijan in 1944 and early 1945. President Roosevelt had, in fact, tried to appease the Soviet Union at Iran's expense during the 1943 conference of Allied leaders in Tehran by suggesting that Iran's railroad and a Persian Gulf port be placed under international control to serve as a warm-water outlet for Soviet exports.[39]

The U.S. policy of noninvolvement in Iran's domestic affairs slowly began to change after World War II, as events in Azerbaijan and Kurdistan grew increasingly ominous and as U.S.-Soviet tensions mounted over such issues as the future of Central Europe and the incipient civil war in Greece. President Truman began to press the Soviet Union to withdraw its troops from Iran in the late summer and fall of 1945. In January 1946 the United States strongly supported Iran's appeal to the United Nations for a Soviet withdrawal. After a deadline for the withdrawal of Soviet troops passed in March 1946, the U.S. embassy in Moscow issued notes of protest to the Soviet government, and the U.S. government dispatched the battleship *Missouri* to Istanbul to return the body of the Turkish ambassador to the United States, who had recently died in Washington. Heated exchanges over the situation in Iran subsequently occurred in the United Nations between U.S. secretary of state James Byrnes and Soviet ambassador Andrei Gromyko.[40]

The removal of Soviet troops from Iran in May 1946 did not imme-

[38]Motter, *United States Army in World War II*, chaps. 9, 20, 21; U.S. Department of Commerce, Office of Business Economics, *Foreign Aid by the United States Government, 1940–1951* (Washington: GPO, 1952), 88; Mark Hamilton Lytle, *The Origins of the Iranian-American Alliance, 1941–1953* (New York: Holmes and Meier, 1987), chaps. 2, 4.

[39]Yonah Alexander and Allan Nanes, eds., *The United States and Iran: A Documentary History* (Washington: University Publications of America, 1980), 93–99; Lenczowski, *Russia and the West in Iran*, 279–83; U.S. Department of State, *Foreign Relations of the United States, 1944*, vol. 5 (Washington: GPO, 1969), 483 (this series is hereafter cited as *FRUS*). State Department officials were horrified at Roosevelt's suggestion; see *FRUS, 1945* 8:523–26.

[40]On the U.S. role in the Azerbaijan crisis see Kuniholm, *Origins of the Cold War*, chaps. 5–6; and Lytle, *Origins of the Iranian-American Alliance*, chaps. 8–11.

diately end the crisis. The Iranian government made repeated requests to the United States in the summer and fall of 1946 for diplomatic support and a large aid package. In September and October the State Department, in consultation with the Joint Chiefs of Staff and other government agencies, conducted a thorough review of U.S. policy toward Iran. Although the Joint Chiefs considered Iran "of vital strategic interest" because its oil reserves would be critical in the event of global war,[41] no fundamental policy changes resulted. The United States continued to support Iran diplomatically by backing its appeal to the United Nations and encouraging it to remain firm, but tangible measures such as a large aid package were not forthcoming. While U.S. diplomatic support had undoubtedly helped to achieve the withdrawal of Soviet troops from Iran, it was the bold actions of Prime Minister Qavam, rather than a major U.S. initiative, that brought about the collapse of the two autonomous republics in December 1946.[42]

With the collapse of the autonomous republics, Iran quickly receded in importance for U.S. policy makers. In 1947 the United States unveiled the Truman Doctrine and the Marshall Plan, signaling a historic shift in U.S. foreign policy away from a posture of isolationism. The United States provided over ten billion dollars to countries in Western Europe and the eastern Mediterranean under these programs and began similar aid programs for major allies in east Asia (see Table 3). Despite continued unrest and its strategic location, Iran received less U.S. aid in this period than Ireland, Portugal, and Sweden, which had not participated in World War II and were not experiencing domestic unrest. United States officials believed a large aid package would not appreciably enhance Iran's security but would be seen as provocative by the Soviet Union. Although loans of $3.3 million and $22.5 million were approved for Iran in 1946 and 1947, U.S. officials brushed aside Iranian requests that payments on these loans be waived. When the Iranian ambassador to the United States submitted a request for a $100 million aid package, he was told merely that Iran "should keep the best possible relations with the Soviet Union."[43]

This reluctance to expand U.S. involvement in Iran continued in 1948 and 1949. United States officials expressed strong support for Iran's independence and maintained close contact with Iranian officials, but aside

[41]U.S. Joint Chiefs of Staff, *United States Strategic Interests in Iran*, JCS 1714/1, 4 October 1946, 6.

[42]*FRUS, 1946* 7:519, 529–36, 542; see also the account of these events by the U.S. ambassador to Iran at this time, in George V. Allen, "Mission to Iran," Allen Papers, Manuscript Department, Duke University Library.

[43]*FRUS, 1947* 5:905, 916, 925–26.

Table 3. United States aid to major recipients, 1946–1952 (in millions of current U.S. dollars)

Country	1946	1947	1948	1949	1950	1951	1952
Europe:							
Austria	65.8	100.4	161.7	374.2	224.0	118.6	118.4
Belgium	.6	30.6	.2	261.0	318.3	394.2	299.9
Britain	79.9	3,757.0	0	1,613.7	1,008.9	551.4	634.5
Denmark	0	1.0	0	126.1	126.6	153.4	92.3
France	302.6	42.8	363.7	1,313.3	1,162.3	1,726.9	1,698.5
West Germany	195.8	293.3	850.3	1,257.6	733.4	652.8	319.3
Ireland	0	0	0	85.6	45.3	16.6	0
Italy	423.3	416.7	331.0	684.1	445.7	665.9	567.1
Netherlands	24.5	1.3	10.2	504.8	331.8	519.4	449.3
Portugal	0	0	0	0	31.5	112.3	85.2
Sweden	.6	0	0	46.8	51.6	21.7	11.3
East Asia:							
China/Taiwan	128.7	464.1	50.9	344.6	51.1	193.8	275.8
Japan	106.7	389.3	483.7	501.5	365.3	290.3	63.6
Philippines	31.4	161.5	136.4	237.7	154.8	158.3	161.2
South Korea	5.6	75.5	100.1	141.8	102.6	93.9	159.8
Mediterranean/ Middle East:							
Greece	195.2	180.9	332.8	362.0	256.6	317.3	351.2
Iran	3.3	22.5	0	0	11.8	27.8	44.1
Turkey	6.1	2.6	72.1	117.3	182.2	219.8	259.0

Source: U.S. Agency for International Development, *U.S. Overseas Loans and Grants: Series of Yearly Data,* vols. 1–5 (Washington, 1984).
Note: Aid here includes both loans and grants of military and economic assistance.

from a "token" $10 million military aid grant in 1950,[44] substantial assistance was not forthcoming. The shah, the Iranian ambassador, and the various Iranian prime ministers of this period made frequent requests for aid and tried unsuccessfully to obtain formal and informal security agreements with the United States (and with Britain). The issues of aid and a security agreement were raised again during the shah's visit to Washington in November 1949. Although this trip ended amicably, the shah's failure to obtain a stronger U.S. commitment left him deeply disappointed and fueled growing anti-American sentiment among the Iranian elite.[45]

Although the United States did not offer Iran a large aid package or a security agreement in the late 1940s, it did slowly increase its involvement

[44]Kenneth W. Condit, *The History of the Joint Chiefs of Staff: The Joint Chiefs of Staff and National Policy*, vol. 2, *1947–1949*, Joint Chiefs of Staff, Joint Secretariat, Historical Division, February 1979, 80.

[45]*FRUS, 1948* 5:170–71, 175–77, 182–84; *FRUS, 1949* 6:528–29, 540–42, 572–82; *FRUS, 1950* 5:511.

in other ways. The agreements signed in 1943 for U.S. training and advisory missions to the Iranian army and Gendarmerie were renegotiated and extended in 1947 and 1948. The U.S. embassy staff in Tehran grew considerably, enhancing diplomatic, commercial, and cultural interactions. Moreover, the United States established a CIA station in its embassy in Tehran in early 1947 to take over covert operations previously carried out by U.S. military attachés and the embassy staff.[46]

The CIA conducted five types of covert operations in Iran in the late 1940s. First, it organized "stay-behind" networks among the Qashqai and other tribes of southern Iran which could be activated after a Soviet invasion to initiate guerrilla warfare behind Soviet lines.[47] Second, CIA officers mapped out escape and evasion routes for use by U.S. and Iranian personnel in the event of a Soviet invasion. Third, the CIA launched cross-border espionage and subversion operations into the Soviet Union from Iran using Azerbaijanis, Armenians, and members of other ethnic groups found on both sides of the border. Fourth, the CIA monitored the activities of the Soviet Union and its allies in Iran with espionage and surveillance programs. Fifth, in 1948 the CIA began an operation code-named BEDAMN that was designed to undermine Soviet and Tudeh influence in Iran.[48] Although BEDAMN was mainly a propaganda operation, it had begun to encompass covert political action by the early 1950s. These CIA operations, aimed ultimately at the Soviet Union, inevitably affected Iranian domestic politics by strengthening or weakening proxy groups such as the Qashqai and the Tudeh. But because they were not very extensive, these operations had little real impact on Iranian politics.

The reluctance of the United States substantially to increase its presence in Iran in the late 1940s was dictated by the global strategy U.S. policy makers were then pursuing: a "strongpoint defense" focused mainly on the industrial centers of Western Europe and Japan. These areas were to be defended from a Soviet attack by concentrating Allied military forces on the western and eastern borders of the Soviet Union and by promoting economic reconstruction in these regions. Other areas, including the non-Mediterranean Middle East, were accorded a lower priority. Respon-

[46]Ramazani, *Iran's Foreign Policy, 1941–1973*, 159–62. The CIA was known as the Central Intelligence Group (CIG) until September 1947. The details on early CIG and CIA activities in Iran given in this and the following paragraphs are from confidential interviews with three participants and with several retired CIA officers who served in Iran subsequently.

[47]The initial planning and feasibility studies for these networks were apparently carried out by U.S. embassy personnel (i.e., *not* by the CIA), in collaboration with the Iranian army; see U.S. Embassy, Tehran, "United States Attitude toward Formation of 'Free Government' in Iran," Record Group 59, Box 6980a, October 14, 1948; and idem, "Political Situation and Military Potentialities . . . ," in ibid., November 19, 1948.

[48]CIA code names and cryptonyms always begin with a two-letter prefix that identifies the country involved; it is omitted in all such references here.

sibility for defending the Middle East, including Iran, was left mainly to Britain, which had eighty thousand troops stationed in the region and a naval base with eight ships in Bahrain. Because of its strategic location between the Soviet Union and the Middle East oilfields, which were vital to European recovery and to the West's ability to fight a major war, Iran was clearly very important to U.S. national security. Nevertheless, it was far from the "strongpoints" of Western Europe and Japan, and it was thought to be comparatively stable and safe from a Soviet invasion in the aftermath of the Azerbaijan crisis. Iran was therefore not included on a list of strategically important countries the Joint Chiefs of Staff targeted for aid in April 1947. Economic development and political reform were viewed as the best means of promoting political stability in Iran. As an alternative to U.S. aid, Iranian officials were encouraged to seek loans from the World Bank.[49]

In early 1950, U.S. global strategy began to change and unrest began to grow in Iran, producing a fundamental reevaluation of U.S. policy toward Iran and a steady increase in U.S. involvement there in the next few years. In late 1949, after the first Soviet test of a nuclear weapon and the establishment of a communist government in China, U.S. officials began to formulate a new, more aggressive strategy for containing Soviet expansionism. Codified in the National Security Council study NSC-68, this new strategy was implemented in April 1950. NSC-68 called for "a renewed initiative in the cold war," beginning with a substantial U.S. military buildup and large increases in U.S. military and economic aid programs.[50] Much of this aid was to be given to countries located, like Iran, on the perimeter of the Soviet sphere of influence, which now included China. The extension of U.S. aid under NSC-68 to countries far from the industrial centers of Western Europe and Japan implied a fundamental shift away from strongpoint defense toward a new concept, "perimeter defense": rather than concentrate simply on countries near the western

[49]John Lewis Gaddis, *Strategies of Containment* (New York: Oxford University Press, 1982), chaps. 2–3; U.S. Joint Chiefs of Staff, *Review of Policy Regarding Persia*, JCS 1714/12, 31 October 1950, 84–85; U.S. Department of State, Office of Intelligence and Research, *The British Position in the Middle East*, OIR No. 5980, October 2, 1952; *FRUS, 1947* 5:924–27; U.S. Joint Chiefs of Staff, *United States Assistance to Other Countries from the Standpoint of National Security*, JCS 1769/1, April 29, 1947, 83, in Thomas H. Etzold and John Lewis Gaddis, eds., *Containment: Documents on American Policy and Strategy, 1945–1950* (New York: Columbia University Press, 1950); *FRUS, 1948*, 5:90; *FRUS, 1950* 5:451–57, 504; State-War-Navy Coordinating Committee, Special Ad Hoc Committee, *Appreciation of the Situation Regarding U.S. Aid to Iran*, SWN-5231, April 7, 1947, 9–10. The basic statement of U.S. policy toward Iran in this period is contained in U.S. National Security Council, *The Position of the United States with Respect to Iran*, NSC-54, July 21, 1949.

[50]U.S. National Security Council, *United States Objectives and Programs for National Security*, NSC-68, April 14, 1950, 434, in Etzold and Gaddis, *Containment*.

and eastern borders of the Soviet Union, the United States would now seek to defend countries along the entire Sino-Soviet periphery.[51]

In the first months of 1950, U.S. policy makers were also becoming increasingly concerned about political instability in Iran. Unrest had been building for several years; the National Front had emerged as a major actor; and the Tudeh party, though outlawed since the February 1949 attempt to assassinate the shah, had regained some of its earlier strength. Moreover, a serious economic depression had begun in early 1950, after a bad harvest. A top State Department official visited Iran in late March of 1950 and described the situation there as "dangerous and explosive." After a similar visit in early April, the U.S Army chief of staff warned that Iran might become a "second China." Policy makers in the State Department privately criticized the shah as an ineffective leader and recommended pressuring him to install a more capable government. At the London Foreign Ministers' Conference in May 1950, U.S. officials asked the British to make major concessions in the ongoing oil negotiations in order to avert further unrest in Iran.[52]

In response to these changes, the State Department in April 1950 carried out a thorough review of U.S. policy toward Iran. As a result, the United States took a number of steps to enhance U.S. influence in Iran and strengthen the Iranian state. A Mutual Defense Assistance Agreement was signed in May 1950 which provided for an average of twenty-three million dollars a year in military aid through 1956. A special economic survey mission went to Iran in July to assess the country's economic needs. A twenty-five-million-dollar Export-Import Bank loan was approved in October (although never actually provided), and a modest Point Four aid program was begun. The United States also supported Iran's request for a ten-million-dollar loan from the World Bank. Henry Grady, a highly regarded diplomat who had served as U.S. ambassador to Greece during the post–civil war reconstruction effort there, was appointed ambassador to Iran. The U.S. embassy staff in Tehran was expanded considerably, and several more CIA officers were added.[53] By the eve of Mosaddeq's appointment as prime minister in late April 1951, the United States had positioned itself to play a major role in Iranian domestic politics.

[51]Gaddis, *Strategies of Containment*, chap. 4, esp. 91–92; see also Paul Y. Hammond, "NSC-68: Prologue to Rearmament," in Warner R. Schilling, Paul Y. Hammond, and Glen H. Snyder, eds., *Strategy, Politics, and Defense Budgets* (New York: Columbia University Press, 1962), 267–378.

[52]*FRUS, 1950*, 5:492, 510, 517–18, 523; *FRUS, 1950*, 3:487.

[53]*FRUS, 1950* 5:509–29, 551, 604; U.S. Department of State, *Bulletin*, June 5, 1950, 922, and July 10, 1950, 59; William E. Warne, *Mission for Peace: Point 4 in Iran* (Indianapolis: Bobbs-Merrill, 1956), 18; U.S. Department of State, *Foreign Service List, January 1, 1951* (Washington: GPO, 1951), 66–67.

3

The Mosaddeq Regime and Its Demise, 1951–1953

Mosaddeq's appointment as prime minister brought the Iranian state temporarily under the control of a coalition led by the modern middle class, as had the inauguration of the constitutional regime in 1906. That previous attempt by the modern middle class to achieve hegemony over the state had been thwarted by the instability of its coalition with the clergy and the traditional middle class and by British and Russian intervention. A weak coalition was no longer a major obstacle to modern middle class hegemony in 1951. Reza Shah's reforms had greatly strengthened the modern middle class, making it less dependent on the support of other groups. Although members of the clergy and the traditional middle class had joined with the modern middle class under the banner of the National Front, they were much less central to this coalition than they had been in 1906. Moreover, the industrial working class had also grown considerably under Reza Shah, and much of it joined the modern middle class in support of Mosaddeq. The likelihood that the modern middle class would succeed in establishing hegemony over the state was therefore much higher in 1951 than it had been in 1906, at least in this regard.

But Iran's rich oil resources and strategic location had made it a prime target for great power intrigue by the early 1950s, as it had been at the time of the Constitutional Revolution. The nationalization of the British-controlled oil industry led the British government to try repeatedly to overthrow Mosaddeq in 1951 and 1952. Although unsuccessful, these efforts did undermine Mosaddeq's base of support. By 1953 the U.S. government had become increasingly concerned about the possibility of a communist takeover. After the inauguration of the stridently anticommunist Eisenhower administration in January 1953, the United States fomented a successful coup d'état against Mosaddeq that also severely weakened both the National Front and the Tudeh party. United States involvement in the 1953 coup also marked the beginning of a cliency relationship between the United States and Iran. Although these foreign interventions were motivated by economic and strategic concerns rather then a desire to influence Iranian politics per se, they greatly weakened the most popular Iranian opposition organizations of this era and began a process by which a highly autonomous state was reestablished in Iran, blocking once again the attempt by the modern middle class to establish hegemony.

Mosaddeq and the National Front

By 1951, Mohammad Mosaddeq and the National Front had become the most prominent actors in Iranian politics. Born in 1882, Mosaddeq was a wealthly landowner who had spent much of his life in public service, gaining a reputation as an ardent nationalist, a staunch defender of the constitution, and one of Iran's few honest politicians. He had participated in the constitutional movement and was exiled to Europe in 1906, where he studied law. Returning to Iran in 1914, he held a variety of positions in the state bureaucracy and was elected to the Majles in 1924. He gained notoriety in 1925 by opposing the coronation of Reza Shah, who later retaliated by forcing him into internal exile. Back in public life in 1944 as a deputy in the Fourteenth Majles, he became a prominent critic of the corruption and intrigue that dominated Iranian politics at the time and authored the 1944 bill that outlawed further foreign oil concessions. Mosaddeq was the most prominent figure in the oil nationalization movement of the late 1940s and sponsored the nationalization bill that was signed into law in May 1951. He had led the October 1949 demonstration against the shah's attempt to rig the Sixteenth Majles elections and emerged as the leader of the newly established National Front after this demonstration.[1]

By the time Mosaddeq was appointed prime minister in late April 1951, the National Front had evolved into a coalition containing most of the groups that favored nationalization of the AIOC. The National Front's leadership was drawn primarily from the Iran party, which was led by Karim Sanjabi and Allahyar Saleh. The Iran party embodied the views of

[1]Fakhreddin Azimi, "The Reconciliation of Politics and Ethics, Nationalism and Democracy: An Overview of the Political Career of Dr. Muhammad Musaddiq," in James A. Bill and William Roger Louis, eds., *Musaddiq, Iranian Nationalism, and Oil* (Austin: University of Texas Press, 1988), 47–68; Farhad Diba, *Mohammad Mossadegh: A Political Biography* (London: Croom Helm, 1986), chaps. 1–6.

the modern middle class; its prominent role in the National Front therefore gave this organization a distinctly modern-middle-class character. The large popular base of the National Front was drawn, in part, from three mass-based organizations: the Toilers' party, an anticommunist leftist group with a large working-class base, recently established by Mozaffar Baqai and Khalil Maleki; the Pan-Iranist party, led by Dariush Foruhar and Mohsen Pezeshkpour; and the Mojahedin-e Islam (Islamic Warriors), a loosely organized Islamic group based in the Tehran bazaar and closely associated with Ayatollah Kashani. The National Front also attracted many followers with no organizational affiliation, especially among the modern middle class and the industrial working class and in the bazaar. The broad appeal of its program and the charisma of Mosaddeq gave the National Front a great deal of popular support, a fact that even British officials acknowledged. The main groups favoring nationalization of the AIOC at this time that were *not* affiliated with the National Front were the Tudeh party and the Fedayan-e Islam.[2]

The diverse elements of the National Front had joined together mainly to bring about the nationalization of the AIOC, which was almost universally resented in Iran. The 1933 agreement under which it was operating was widely regarded as exploitative and an infringement on Iran's sovereignty. Moreover, the AIOC had consistently violated the terms of this agreement and had been reluctant to renegotiate it as the oil nationalization movement grew in the late 1940s. Although the AIOC was highly profitable, its Iranian workers were poorly paid and lived in squalid conditions. The AIOC, usually in collusion with the British embassy, had also become heavily involved in Iran's domestic politics, arming and bankrolling elements of the Bakhtiari tribe and intriguing among the politicians and notables of Tehran. As a result, it was widely blamed for most of Iran's economic, social, and political problems, and public support for nationalization was very strong.[3]

[2]T. Cuyler Young, "The Social Support of Current Iranian Policy," *Middle East Journal* 6 (Spring 1952), 125–43; Richard W. Cottam, *Nationalism in Iran* (Pittsburgh: University of Pittsburgh Press, 1979), 264–68; see also U.S. Embassy, Tehran, "The Workers Parties of Iran," June 5, 1953, Record Group 59, Box 5498; ibid., "Pan-Iranism: The Ultimate in Iranian Nationalism," February 6, 1952, Record Group 84, Box, 29; Yann Richard, "Ayatollah Kashani: Precursor of the Islamic Republic?" in Nikki R. Keddie, ed., *Religion and Politics in Iran: Shi'ism from Quietism to Revolution* (New Haven, Conn.: Yale University Press, 1983), 101–24; and U.S. Embassy, Tehran, "Political Significance of the Tehran Bazaar Organization," December 19, 1953, Record Group 59, Box 4110. On the popularity of the National Front see U.S. Department of State, Office of Intelligence and Research, *Mossadeq's Current Position in the Internal Iranian Situation*, OIR No. 5676, October 26, 1951; and "Assessment of the State of Public Opinion," September 4, 1951, FO/371/91463. For typical coverage of Mosaddeq in the Western press that emphasizes his popularity see *Times* (London), August 22, 1951, 7; and *New York Times*, November 25, 1951, IV, 6:6.

[3]For a good discussion of the AIOC's abuses in Iran see L. P. Elwell-Sutton, *Persian Oil: A Study in Power Politics* (London: Lawrence and Wishart, 1955), chaps. 7–8.

Although a desire to nationalize the AIOC was the main point of unity for the National Front's diverse supporters, most of them also wanted substantial changes in the political status quo. The need for political change had been the most prominent theme in Iranian politics since the ouster of Reza Shah in 1941, and it had taken on new urgency in 1949 and 1950, as the shah tried to increase his control over the state and as economic problems grew. By 1951 the pressure for political change had become inextricably linked to the drive for oil nationalization: the AIOC and the British embassy wielded considerable influence in Iran and used this influence to help their traditional upper-class allies and the shah, who reciprocated by supporting the British position in the oil dispute. This linkage both enhanced the popularity of the nationalization movement and increased the pressure for political change; it also placed the National Front squarely in the tradition of the constitutional movement, which had been organized around the themes of democracy and nationalism.

While most of the National Front's supporters favored extensive political change, they held diverse views about what form this change should take and what tactics should be used to achieve it. Most members of the Iran party and the Maleki wing of the Toilers' party were democratic socialists and advocated the full implementation of the 1906 constitution and measures such as restrictions on private capital and large-scale redistributions of land and wealth. While Baqai's wing of the Toilers' party publicly espoused similar goals, it generally supported any cause that would enhance its power and often engaged in intimidation and violence. The more moderate members of the Iran party and most unaffiliated National Front supporters were not committed socialists; they advocated instead simply the establishment of a genuinely democratic constitutional monarchy as spelled out in the 1906 constitution and mild economic reforms such as higher social spending and moderate land reform. The Pan-Iranist party was a quasi-fascist organization that opposed both traditional forms of authority, like the monarchy, the clergy, and the landlord class, and more modern political phenomena such as capitalism and communism. While the Mojahedin-e Islam advocated implementation of the Shari'a (Islamic law) and measures that would benefit the bazaar, it served in practice mainly as an instrument for advancing the political goals of Ayatollah Kashani. Neither the Pan-Iranists nor the Mojahedin-e Islam were committed to democratic ideals and practices.[4]

Despite the diversity of views within the National Front, Mosaddeq pursued reformist measures aimed at reducing inequality and democratiz-

[4]See the references cited in n. 2, above, and Ervand Abrahamian, *Iran between Two Revolutions* (Princeton, N.J.: Princeton University Press, 1982), 190–92, 256–58.

ing the political system: he enacted laws designed to improve the plight of peasants, workers, and tenants; he took steps to improve Iran's educational and public health systems; he restructured the state's revenue and judicial systems; and he made efforts to democratize local-level politics and reduce the powers of the shah.[5] The mildness of these measures reflected the moderate and democratic character of Mosaddeq and the other top leaders of the National Front and their ability to restrain the more radical members of this coalition.

Although democratizing the political system was fundamentally a moderate goal, it nevertheless meant reducing the power and privileges of the traditional upper class, which held many seats in the Majles and exercised a fair amount of influence over the shah. The National Front therefore came into confrontation with the traditional upper class, much as the constitutionalists had after the 1906 revolution. However, Reza Shah's social and economic reforms and the splits that had occurred in the traditional upper class during World War II had weakened this class, preventing it from blocking Mosaddeq's appointment as prime minister. The National Front therefore seemed likely to succeed in establishing modern middle class hegemony over the state. Indeed, it was to be U.S. intervention rather than the efforts of the traditional upper class that would prevent the National Front from establishing such hegemony.

Democratizing the political system also involved reducing the power of the shah. Although Reza Shah had exercised almost complete control over the state, his son was much less successful and had proven himself relatively weak in the face of a large popular movement. The National Front also had to reckon with the Tudeh party. Outlawed since the assassination attempt on the shah in February 1949, the Tudeh had nonetheless regained some of its popularity since the debacle of 1946. By early 1952 the Tudeh reportedly had some thirteen thousand hardcore members organized into well-disciplined cells and perhaps forty or fifty thousand additional supporters. The Tudeh operated various front organizations and published several newspapers; it had also infiltrated several state agencies and was in the process of installing an elaborate espionage network in the armed forces.[6] Although the Tudeh party competed with the National

[5]Habib Ladjevardi, "Constitutional Government and Reform under Musaddiq," in Bill and Louis, *Musaddiq, Iranian Nationalism, and Oil*, 69–90.

[6]CIA, *Probable Developments in Iran in 1952 in the Absence of an Oil Settlement*, NIE-46, February 4, 1952, 2–3; Sepehr Zabih, *The Communist Movement in Iran* (Berkeley and Los Angeles: University of California Press, 1966), chap. 5; Gurney to Henderson, August 30, 1952, Record Group 84, Box 32; Farhad Kazemi, "The Military and Politics in Iran: The Uneasy Symbiosis," in Elie Kedourie and Sylvia G. Haim, eds., *Toward a Modern Iran* (London: Cass, 1980), 217–40.

Front for the support of the modern middle class and the industrial working class, it was severely handicapped by its close association with the Soviet Union. The Tudeh's main adversaries and some of its goals overlapped with those of the National Front, so the two often worked in parallel, if not in tacit cooperation. Nevertheless, irreconciliable differences between the Tudeh and the National Front led to frequent clashes. The Tudeh was not a serious threat to the Mosaddeq government, but it was clearly a disruptive force with the potential for rapid expansion in the event of a protracted crisis.

The Anglo-Iranian Oil Crisis and British Policy, May 1951–November 1952

The nationalization of the AIOC brought Mosaddeq and the National Front into direct confrontation with the British government, which owned 50 percent of the AIOC's stock. Nationalization posed an obvious threat to the AIOC's investments in Iran and threatened to eliminate a major source of Britain's foreign exchange earnings: the AIOC had earned $93 million in profits in 1950, mainly from its operations in Iran, and the British government had collected $142 million in tax revenues from the AIOC in that year.[7] Britain was running an annual trade deficit of roughly $1 billion at this time and struggling to recover from the effects of World War II, so the AIOC's operations in Iran were quite important to it. Moreover, because Britain was in the process of liquidating its vast colonial empire, the nationalization of the AIOC was a major blow to its dwindling prestige, a fact not lost on the embattled government of Prime Minister Clement Attlee.[8] In the months after the nationalization bill was signed into law, Britain therefore adopted a three-track strategy designed to reestablish its control over Iran's oil industry by either pressuring Mosaddeq into a favorable settlement or removing him from office.

The first component of this strategy was a series of legal and diplomatic measures, starting with an appeal to the International Court of Justice to arbitrate the oil dispute. A British negotiating team went to Tehran with a proposal that recognized the principle of nationalization but called for the

[7]These figures are from Julian Bharier, *Economic Development in Iran, 1900–1970* (London: Oxford University Press, 1971), 163; and Fereidun Fesharaki, *Development of the Iranian Oil Industry: International and Domestic Aspects* (New York: Praeger, 1976), 17. Britain reaped other benefits, too, such as foreign exchange earnings from salary remittances and price discounts on fuel for the British navy. For a good discussion of British interests in Iran at this time, see "Persian Oil: Paper on UK Objectives," June 9, 1951, FO/371/91543.

[8]For a good study of the British perspective on the oil crisis see William Roger Louis, *The British Empire in the Middle East, 1945–1951* (Oxford: Clarenden, 1984), 632–90.

AIOC to market Iran's oil on a fifty-fifty profit-sharing basis. Mosaddeq rejected this proposal in June 1951. Negotiations began again in August when Sir Richard Stokes led another mission to Tehran. Stokes's proposal differed little from the previous British offer and was also rejected. The British thereafter refused to negotiate directly with Mosaddeq, relying instead on appeals to the International Court and the United Nations and on mediation by the United States.[9]

The second component of the British strategy was to undermine Mosaddeq's domestic base of support by imposing stiff economic sanctions on Iran and carrying out hostile military maneuvers in the region. The AIOC began a production slowdown in May and prevented tankers from loading oil at the port of Abadan. By the end of July these steps had evolved into a full-fledged oil blockade, which was joined by the other major international oil companies, who feared that nationalization might spread to other oil-producing countries. Britain positioned a paratroop brigade on Cyprus in mid-May for possible use in Iran and sent the cruiser *Mauritius* to Abadan. Private discussions with U.S. officials about the possibility of using force to protect AIOC facilities elicited strong U.S. opposition. These actions led Mosaddeq to announce that the first shot fired would "signal the start of World War III."[10]

With the collapse of the Stokes negotiations, the AIOC announced it would take legal action against anyone who tried to buy Iranian oil. Britain asked its European allies to discourage their citizens from seeking employment with the newly formed National Iranian Oil Company (NIOC). Early September brought an embargo on British exports to Iran of iron, steel, sugar, oil-processing equipment, and any goods that could be resold for dollars. Twenty thousand Iranian oil workers were laid off by the AIOC, forcing Mosaddeq to put them on the government payroll. Sterling conversion privileges were canceled and other financial restrictions were imposed, violating a memorandum of understanding between the two governments. Four British destroyers joined the *Mauritius* in September and held firing practice in the waters off Abadan. British land and air forces in the region were also strengthened.[11]

The third component of the British strategy was to try to remove

[9]For a complete account of the oil negotiations in this period see Elwell-Sutton, *Persian Oil*, chaps. 16–18.

[10]U.S. National Security Council, "The Position of the United States with Respect to Iran, NSC Action No. 473," May 17, 1951, Record Group 59, Box 4107; Dean Acheson, *Present at the Creation* (New York: Norton, 1969), 507.

[11]"Reports Persians Trying to Recruit Oil Technicians," August 20, 1951, FO/371/91579; "Exports to Persia," December 17, 1951, FO/371/98634; U.S. Embassy, Tehran, "Monthly Economic Report," September 25, 1951, Record Group 59, Box 5490; "Financial Restrictions on Persia," September 12, 1951, FO/371/91491; Elwell-Sutton, *Persian Oil*, 257.

Mosaddeq from office and replace him with a more compliant prime minister. This was to be achieved mainly through covert action, which was to be carried out with the help of a network of pro-British politicians, businessmen, military officers, and clerical leaders. The principal figures in this network were the Rashidian brothers, who had been the main British agents in Iran since the early 1940s. Also important were the politicians Sayyid Zia, whom the British were trying to install as prime minister, and Jamal Emami, who then headed the pro-British faction in the Majles.[12]

The British had begun to pressure the shah to appoint Sayyid Zia even before Mosaddeq was nominated by the Majles. This pressure increased after Mosaddeq assumed office, and planning began to oust Mosaddeq and install Sayyid Zia. The shah was sympathetic to the British demands but remained paralyzed with indecision throughout the summer of 1951. After the collapse of the Stokes negotiations in late August, the British used all available means in their effort to oust Mosaddeq. Stokes met with the shah shortly after the negotiations broke down and implored him to dismiss Mosaddeq. The pro-British Majles faction was called upon to foment disruptions and prevent a quorum from forming. The Foreign Office developed a set of guidelines for dealing with Mosaddeq's successor (whom it presumed would be Sayyid Zia), including a loan from the AIOC and a plan calling for the AIOC's return under a different name. More ominously, plans were made to invade Iran to oust Mosaddeq forcibly. But when President Truman was told about the invasion plan in September 1951, he responded that the United States would not support an invasion and encouraged the British to resume negotiations. Attlee was then forced to tell his cabinet that "in view of the attitude of the United States Government, [he did not] think it would be expedient to use force to maintain the British staff in Abadan."[13]

[12]Documentary evidence on the British network is fragmentary but gives some indication of its size; see, for example, "Les Follies Imperiales," March 18, 1952, FO/248/1541; and "Oriental Counsellor's Political and Economic Conversations," n.d., FO/248/1515. "Action in the Persian Situation Advocated by M. Kaivan," July 3, 1951, FO/371/91461, gives a list of pro-British political figures obtained from a British agent in the Iranian labor movement; for a description of this agent's network see "Trade Unions in Persia," January 6, 1952, FO/371/98731; and "Political Affairs: Isfahan and Bakhtiari," n.d., FO/248/1520. The Rashidians are referred to as "the brothers" in the account of these events given in Christopher Montague Woodhouse, *Something Ventured* (St. Albans, Hert.: Granada, 1982), chaps. 8–9.

[13]"Record of Interdepartmental Meeting," March 20, 1951, FO/371/91525; "Records Conversation with Miss Lambton," June 15, 1951, FO/371/91548; "American Assistance to the Persian Oil Dispute," July 2, 1951, FO/371/91559; "Reports on Conversation with the Shah," July 16, 1951, FO/371/91462; "Record of a Luncheon Party Given by the Shah," August 5, 1951, FO/371/91577; "Encloses Short Account of Talks," September 1, 1951, FO/371/91584; "View That HMG Should Refrain from Any Statement," August 26, 1951, FO/371/91582; "Approach to a New Persian Government," September 8, 1951, FO/371/

Having failed to reverse the nationalization law or to oust Mosaddeq, and with their main candidate for the premiership by now thoroughly discredited, the British began to search for other options. One soon materialized. Ahmad Qavam had approached the British several times since Mosaddeq's appointment seeking support for his bid to be named prime minister. Julian Amery, a Conservative member of Parliament, met with Qavam in Paris in March 1952. Qavam then returned to Tehran to build support for his candidacy. He produced a list of possible cabinet ministers and submitted it to the British for approval. The British supported Qavam by asking pro-British Majles members to help him and backing his plan to end the oil dispute. By early 1952 the British had also begun a covert effort through the Rashidians to create friction among the leaders of the National Front. In a telegram to his superiors, Robin Zaehner, a professor of Persian language and literature at Oxford who was working for MI-6 (the British intelligence service) in Iran at this time, claimed the Rashidians had been responsible for the tensions that emerged in early 1952 between Mosaddeq and National Front notables Kashani and Hussein Makki.[14]

Mosaddeq was evidently aware of these activities. He retaliated suddenly on July 16 by resigning from office, after trying unsuccessfully to wrest control over the armed forces from the shah. The shah appointed Qavam prime minister, although plans for his premiership had apparently not yet been completed. The National Front organized massive demonstrations calling for Mosaddeq's return to office. At least 69 people were killed and over 750 injured when army and police units attacked the demonstrators. Since Qavam had no popular following, Mosaddeq's supporters dominated the streets of Tehran and other cities during these demonstrations, and Mosaddeq was triumphantly swept back into office on July 21.[15]

The Qavam episode had serious repercussions. Morale in the armed forces dropped precipitously, particularly after Mosaddeq purged the officer corps upon his return to office. The Tudeh party became more

---

91590; "Text of Reply from President Truman," September 26, 1951, FO/371/91591; "Persian Oil Dispute," September 28, 1951, FO/371/91592; CAB 128/20, 231–34 (British cabinet records, Public Records Office, London). The invasion plan was described to me in a confidential interview with a retired MI-6 (British intelligence) officer involved in these events.

[14]"American Assistance to the Persian Oil Dispute," July 2, 1951, FO/371/91559; "Qavam's Proposals," January 7, 1952, FO/371/98683; "Intervention of Mr. Julian Amery," February 7, 1952, FO/371/98683; "Qavam's Proposals," March 25, 1952, FO/371/98683; interview with Sir George Middleton, London, January 16, 1985, "Internal Situation," n.d., FO/248/1531.

[15]Henderson to Acheson, August 3, 1952, Record Group 84, Box 29.

active. Mosaddeq quarreled bitterly with Kashani and other National Front leaders over cabinet appointments and over his request to the Majles to grant him emergency powers. The Pan-Iranist party turned against Mosaddeq, leading Foruhar and his wing of the party to establish a new pro-Mosaddeq organization known as the Party of the Iranian Nation. More ominously, a group of military officers led by Fazlollah Zahedi began to plot against Mosaddeq with the Rashidians. Zahedi was a retired general who had been arrested by the British during World War II for working with German agents. He was currently a member of the Senate and headed an organization known as the Retired Officers' Association. He had briefly held a cabinet post under Mosaddeq and had supported the National Front until the July 1952 uprisings, when the resurgence of Tudeh activity and the disintegration of the armed forces apparently drove him into the opposition.[16]

Zahedi and the Rashidians began to plot against Mosaddeq soon after he returned to office. A Kashani emissary and National Front leaders Makki, Baqai, and Abol Hassan Haerizadeh approached Zahedi and expressed their dissatisfaction with Mosaddeq. Zahedi apparently gained Kashani's support as a result of this meeting by giving him a role in the selection of his prospective cabinet members. From this point on, Kashani, Makki, Baqai, and Haerizadeh worked against Mosaddeq in loose collaboration with Zahedi and were among Mosaddeq's staunchest opponents. Zahedi also obtained the support of Abul Qasem Bakhtiari, a tribal leader who had worked with him for the Germans during World War II. Zahedi met with British embassy officials, who agreed to help him after consulting with London. The British apparently provided arms to certain Bakhtiari tribal groups. A British embassy official discussed Zahedi's prospects with U.S. ambassador Loy Henderson, who was noncommital. Either Zahedi or a close lieutenant also met with Henderson, who listened to their case but remained noncommital.[17]

As with the Qavam plot, Mosaddeq had evidently learned of Zahedi's plans and moved to stop him before they could be implemented. Arrest

[16]"Annual Report on Persian Army for 1952," September 12, 1952, FO/371/98638; "Internal Situation"; *New York Times*, August 15, 1952, 2:8, August 20, 1952, 1:1; Henderson to Acheson, August 3, 4, and 15, 1952, Record Group 84, Box 29; Muslim Students Following the Line of the Imam, *Documents from the U.S. Espionage Den*, vol. 22 (Tehran: n.p., n.d.), 38; Henderson to Acheson, July 7 and 21 and October 17, 1952, Record Group 84, Box 29; Fitzroy Maclean, *Eastern Approaches* (London: Cape, 1950), 266.

[17]"Internal Situation"; "Oriental Counsellor's Political and Economic Conversations"; "Tribal Affairs and Tribal Policy," n.d., FO/248/1521; Middleton interview; interview with retired MI-6 officer (n. 13); U.S. Embassy, Tehran, "Intrigues among the Bakhtiari Tribes," November 28, 1952, Record Group 84, Box 28; Henderson to Acheson, September 9, 1952, Record Group 84, Box 29.

warrants were issued on October 13 for the Rashidians and for General Abdul Hussein Hejazi, a Zahedi ally who had been dismissed in August from his position as head of the war college. General Bahram Aryana was dismissed from the army in connection with the plot, and Zahedi was saved from arrest only by his parliamentary immunity. Three days later, on October 16, Mosaddeq broke diplomatic relations with Britain.[18] Lacking a base for operations inside Iran, the British henceforth were forced to rely on the United States to break the impasse with Mosaddeq.

The Truman Administration and the Anglo-Iranian Oil Dispute

After the oil nationalization bill was approved by the Majles, the Truman administration pursued two main goals regarding the oil dispute. First, Iran was to be kept in the Western camp at all costs: its strategic location between the Soviet Union and the Persian Gulf oilfields dictated not only that it be kept from falling under Soviet control but also that it be prevented from adopting a "neutralist" posture. Second, because a protracted oil crisis might damage the U.S. economy and threaten U.S. and Western European security, stability was to be maintained in the world oil market. Neither goal necessitated undermining the Mosaddeq government at this time. Rather, the Truman administration publicly expressed its support for Mosaddeq; it strongly opposed British efforts to use military force against Iran; it provided the Mosaddeq government with moderate amounts of military and economic aid; and it made extensive diplomatic efforts to bring an early end to the oil dispute.[19]

Soon after the oil nationalization bill was enacted, U.S. officials began to implement a plan to ease the effect of the British oil blocade on the

[18]*New York Times*, October 13, 1952, 4:1, October 16, 1952, 6:4; "Annual Report on Persian Army for 1952," December 9, 1952, FO/371/98638.

[19]On the initial goals of U.S. policy toward the oil dispute see U.S. National Security Council, *The Position of the United States with Respect to Iran*, NSC 107/2, June 27, 1951. For public statements of the U.S. position at this time see U.S. Department of State, *Bulletin*, June 4, 1951, 891, and July 23, 1951, 131. United States policy makers of course were aware of British efforts to undermine Mosaddeq and occasionally discussed these activities with British policy makers; see U.S. Department of State, "Memorandum of Conversation, Subject: Iran," May 16, 1952, Record Group 84, Box 29; and "Anglo-U.S. Discussions about the Persian Internal Situation and the Oil Question," July 29, 1952, FO/371/98691. These discussions were confirmed to me in an interview with Henry Byroade, Patomac, Md., August 7, 1984. But U.S. officials repeatedly expressed opposition to British efforts to intervene in Iran; see "U.S. Views on Questions Raised during Discussions," April 19, 1951, FO/371/91471; and "Approach to the Shah to Remove Mussadiq," December 1, 1951, FO/371/91465.

world oil market. Under this plan, U.S. oil companies were asked to provide oil to U.S. allies that had been adversely affected by the blocade. Some forty-six million barrels of oil were delivered under this plan in the first year of the blocade, amounting to roughly 20 percent of Iran's 1950 production. Although undertaken to promote stability in the world oil market,[20] this plan had the effect of strengthening the British oil blocade and therefore inadvertently helped to undermine the Iranian economy and weaken domestic support for the Mosaddeq government.

At the same time, the United States made diplomatic efforts to resolve the oil dispute. United States officials publicly called for a negotiated settlement and pledged not to interfere in Iran's internal affairs. They privately advised Britain to "pay lip service" to the principle of nationalization, accept a fifty-fifty division of profits, and avoid using force against Iran. After the first round of oil negotiations broke down, Averell Harriman went to Tehran to press for new talks, leading to the second round of negotiations under Stokes. After the Stokes mission collapsed, U.S. officials repeatedly pressed the British to resume negotiations,[21] and President Truman sent a note imploring the British not to invade Iran.

Mosaddeq traveled to the United States in October 1951 to address the United Nations about the oil dispute. While there, he went to Washington and was warmly received by President Truman and other U.S. officials. Meanwhile, a new U.S. approach toward the oil dispute was being developed. This plan recognized Iran's desire for an end to British control over its oil industry and distanced the United States considerably from the British position. The new U.S. proposal called for Iran's oil to be produced by the NIOC and marketed by a consortium that would initially include Royal Dutch/Shell and several major U.S. oil companies. When antitrust concerns led the U.S. majors to back out of this plan, a similar package was arranged involving independent U.S. oil companies. When this plan fell apart in the fall of 1952, a third plan was worked out in which antitrust laws would be waived to permit the U.S. majors to participate. United States officials had come to believe that the participation of the U.S. majors was essential to provide adequate marketing capacity for Iran's large volume of oil exports and to secure an Export-Import Bank loan for Iran. They also debated purchasing one hundred million dollars

[20]See U.S. National Security Council, *National Security Problems concerning Free World Petroleum Demands and Potential Supplies*, NSC 138, December 8, 1952, 9–10.

[21]Yonah Alexander and Allen Nanes, eds., *The United States and Iran: A Documentary History* (Washington: University Publications of America, 1980), 215–17; *New York Times*, May 22, 1951, 24:4; "Washington Talks," April 10, 1951, FO/371/91470; "Message from S. of S.," September 10, 1951, FO/371/91463; "Text of State Department's Views," September 21, 1951, FO/371/91589; "Persian Oil Dispute," September 28, 1951, FO/371/91592.

worth of Iranian oil and acting with greater independence from Britain, even at the risk of damaging U.S.-British relations.[22] Mosaddeq rejected the consortium package in late 1952.

The United States also increased its covert political operations in Iran at this time. Working through two Iranians code-named Nerren and Cilley, CIA officers had been carrying out various anti-Soviet and anti-Tudeh propaganda activities since 1948 under operation BEDAMN: anticommunist articles and cartoons were planted in Iranian newspapers; books and leaflets critical of the Soviet Union and the Tudeh party were written and distributed;[23] rumors were started. As the Tudeh party began to reemerge in the early 1950s, the BEDAMN operation also began to encompass covert political action. Its political action arm engaged in both direct attacks on Soviet allies in Iran and so-called black operations designed to turn Iranians against the Tudeh. Attacks on Soviet allies typically involved hiring street gangs to disrupt Tudeh rallies and financing anticommunist groups, including the Pan-Iranist party and the Somka party (a small neonazi organization), which regularly fought with Tudeh mobs in the streets of Tehran. Black operations included infiltrating agents provocateurs into Tudeh demonstrations to provoke outrageous acts, paying clerical leaders to denounce the Tudeh as anti-Islamic, and organizing attacks on mosques and public figures in the name of the Tudeh.[24] These activities complemented more benign, overt activities with the same

[22]George McGhee, *Envoy to the Middle World* (New York: Harper and Row, 1983), chap. 31; Dean Acheson, *Present at the Creation* (New York: Norton, 1969), 509–11; "Record of Talks," October 4, 1951, FO/371/91595; "American Proposal That the Royal Dutch/Shell Group Should Take Over and Operate the Abadan Refinery Considered Impractical," November 6, 1951, FO/371/91610; interview with Paul Nitze, Washington, D.C., July 5, 1984; Alexander and Nanes, *United States and Iran*, 229; "Mr. Acheson's Suggestions for Settling the Oil Dispute," October 9, 1952, FO/371/98700; "Memorandum for the President," November 6, 1952, *Declass. Docs.* 6, no. 4 (1980), 408B; Walter S. Poole, *The History of the Joint Chiefs of Staff: The Joint Chiefs of Staff and National Policy*, vol. 3, 1950–1952 (Joint Chiefs of Staff, Joint Secretariat, Historical Division, December 1979), 365.

[23]A particularly effective project under BEDAMN was the production of a fictionalized autobiography of the well-known Iranian poet and Tudeh party member Abul Qasem Lahuti, who was then living in the Soviet Union. Although Lahuti later denounced the forgery over Radio Moscow, many Iranians still believe it to be accurate. An oblique reference to this project is contained in Donald N. Wilber, *Adventures in the Middle East: Excursions and Incursions* (Princeton, N.J.: Darwin, 1986), 191; see also chaps. 11, 12, and 14 for further references to BEDAMN operations. The material in this and the following paragraph was obtained in confidential interviews with seven retired CIA officers who participated in these activities. Except where noted, all details were confirmed by more than one source.

[24]One such operation was the organization of a "fake" Tudeh attack on the Harriman mission in the summer of 1951; see Kermit Roosevelt, *Countercoup* (New York: McGraw Hill, 1979), 95. Several people were killed in the ensuing riots, which were widely blamed on the Tudeh. Roosevelt, who then headed the CIA's Middle East operations, believes this

general goal which were being carried out by the U.S. embassy staff and the U.S. Information Agency. By the time of Mosaddeq's appointment as prime minister, the annual budget for the BEDAMN program had apparently grown to around one million dollars.[25]

Despite the Truman administration's policy of supporting Mosaddeq and opposing British efforts to overthrow him, the BEDAMN program was also used in ways that undermined the popular base of the National Front. CIA officers tried to detach Kashani and his followers from the National Front using propaganda, which was often quite vulgar, that depicted Mosaddeq as a corrupt and immoral person who was exploiting Kashani. They also gave money to a mullah named Mohammad Taqi Falsafi to try to build a clerical alternative to Kashani and encouraged other mullahs to adopt a more fundamentalist line to drive them away from Mosaddeq. Similar efforts to turn the Toilers and Pan-Iranists against Mosaddeq and provoke splits in these organizations were carried out through Iranians working in the BEDAMN network, who generally concealed their CIA connections. In a particularly noteworthy case, a CIA contract officer working under cover as an employee of the American Friends of the Middle East approached Mozaffar Baqai in September or October of 1952 and encouraged him to break with Mosaddeq; Baqai subsequently received money from the CIA. Kashani, Makki, and Ayatollah Sayyid Mohammad Behbehani may have received similar approaches.[26]

By the fall of 1952, not only had Kashani, Baqai, Makki, and several other National Front leaders turned against Mosaddeq, but Dariush Foruhar and his followers had left the Pan-Iranist party after it broke with Mosaddeq and Khalil Maleki and his followers had left the Toilers' for

---

operation may have been carried out by Nerren and Cilley *without* the approval of their CIA case officers (personal interview, Washington, D.C., June 5, 1985). Another black operation apparently involved setting off several small explosions in Tehran mosques and blaming them on the Tudeh. The British conducted similar black operations through the Lankarani brothers, who were their agents in the Tudeh party, according to one CIA officer (n. 23).

[25]This figure was given to me by one CIA officer (n. 23). I have been unable to determine exactly when political action began under the auspices of BEDAMN, but it appears to have started in 1950 or 1951. The U.S. embassy and U.S. Information Agency staff sought to undermine Soviet and Tudeh influence in Iran through routine conversations with Iranian political figures and by making pro-American and anti-Soviet books and other materials available to the Iranian public, for example.

[26]Kermit Roosevelt told me in my interview with him that these other figures were probably approached in this way by the CIA, but he was not absolutely certain of this. I have been unable to confirm or disprove his assertion in interviews with other participants in these events. Discussions were held with a prominent Iraqi Shi'i cleric named Sharestani about undermining Kashani; see Henderson to Acheson, September 29, 1952, Record Group 84, Box 42; and Berry to Acheson, October 4, 1952, Record Group 84, Box 42. Baqai also had close ties with the British at this time; see U.S. Embassy, Tehran, "Recent Activities of Iranian Toilers Party," August 23, 1952, Record Group 59, Box 4109.

similar reasons and established an organization known as the Third Force. Even the Iran party split, when Mohammad Nakhshab and his followers established the Iranian People's party (which, however, continued to support Mosaddeq).[27] It is, of course, impossible to determine the degree to which BEDAMN was responsible for these splits. Most Iranian political figures at the time were extremely opportunistic and ambitious and would have had many reasons for turning against Mosaddeq. This was especially true of Kashani, Baqai, and Makki. Furthermore, the Rashidians were carrying out similar activities on behalf of the British. The CIA officers who operated the BEDAMN program are themselves uncertain of its impact; one has described it as "important" in encouraging Kashani and Baqai to split with Mosaddeq, while another has described its effect as "limited."[28] While the CIA thus cannot be credited entirely with provoking these splits in the National Front, it probably played a significant role.

It is also unclear who in the U.S. government authorized these attacks against Mosaddeq and the National Front. The official policy of the Truman administration was to support Mosaddeq and *not* undermine his government, so these actions directly contradicted official U.S. policy. The State Department, headed at the time by Dean Acheson, undoubtedly upheld this policy. It therefore appears that the decision to undermine Mosaddeq through BEDAMN was taken within the CIA itself. Since the top CIA officials with responsibility for covert operations at the time either have passed away or are "unable to recall" who authorized these actions, it is impossible to determine where in the CIA chain of command this rogue-elephant component of the BEDAMN program originated.[29]

[27]On the split in the Pan-Iranist party see U.S. Embassy, Tehran, "Pan-Iranism," which refers to a "mysterious mastermind" directing the Pan-Iranists, who may have been the head of the BEDAMN program, according to one CIA officer (n. 23). Both the British and the Soviets were aware of U.S. support for Baqai at this time; see "Internal Situation," n.d., FO/248/1531; and "Visit of General Schwartzkopf to Persia," August 6, 1953, FO/371/104569. On the split in the Iran party see "Internal Affairs," April 24, 1953, FO/371/104567; and U.S. Embassy, Tehran, "A Survey of the Nationalist Movement in Iran since the Fall of Mosadeq," May 8, 1957, 4.

[28]Confidential interviews with two CIA officers (n. 23).

[29]Covert operations by the CIA were then authorized under National Security Council Directive NSC-10/2, which permitted activities "against hostile foreign states or groups or in support of friendly foreign states or groups"; see U.S. Senate, Select Committee to Study Governmental Operations, *Foreign and Military Intelligence*, Bk. 1, 94th Cong., 2d sess., April 26, 1976, 475–509. In the parlance of the time, this meant that covert action could be used against the Soviet Union and its allies. While the anti-Soviet and anti-Tudeh activities carried out under BEDAMN clearly fell within these guidelines, activities against the National Front certainly did not, since the National Front was not regarded as communist or pro-Soviet. It therefore seems unlikely that this component of BEDAMN would have been authorized by the CIA director or his top deputies. My assumption is that it originated either with the head of the BEDAMN program or with Kermit Roosevelt, who is "unable to recall" whether he authorized these activities (personal interview).

The Overthrow of Mosaddeq

After the break in diplomatic relations between Britain and Iran, the British embassy staff left Tehran on November 1, 1952, symbolically ending the long era of British domination in Iran. Although they left behind the Rashidian network and several deep-cover operatives, the British position in Iran had clearly become very weak. Accordingly, Christopher Montague Woodhouse, the chief MI-6 officer in Iran at the time, was sent to Washington to seek U.S. support for a tentative plan to overthrow Mosaddeq.[30] Woodhouse's plan called for the Rashidians and certain Bakhtiari tribal leaders to engineer a coordinated uprising against Mosaddeq, with or without the shah's support. Although the British had been conspiring with Zahedi since August, they put forward several other names in addition to his as possible leaders of the uprising. Woodhouse went first to the CIA, where his plan was enthusiastically received by Frank Wisner (head of the CIA's covert operations branch), Allen Dulles (Wisner's deputy, and soon to be named director of the CIA), and Kermit Roosevelt (Wisner's Middle East division chief). Several lower-level CIA specialists on Iran were opposed to the idea, however, as was the CIA station chief in Tehran, who is said to have viewed it as "putting U.S. support behind Anglo-French colonialism." Woodhouse also held discussions with State Department officials. Woodhouse was told that the Truman administration would not agree to the plan, but that President-elect Eisenhower probably would.[31]

Zahedi continued to intrigue, although the departure of the British had undoubtedly set his efforts back. Arms and money continued to flow into the Bakhtiari region, where Abul Qasem Bakhtiari was trying to enlist the support of other tribal leaders. Zahedi reportedly promised to establish a "Free South in Iran," where the Bakhtiari would be given autonomy under the leadership of Abul Qasem. In January 1953, Zahedi's Majles allies, led by Kashani, fomented a major dispute in an apparent attempt to create conditions that would lead to Mosaddeq's ouster. This effort came to an end on January 19, when Mosaddeq won a vote of confidence fifty-nine to one.[32]

[30]Woodhouse, *Something Ventured*, 116–19.

[31]Ibid.; Roosevelt interview; Byroade interview. The quotation of the station chief's view was related to me in a confidential interview with a retired CIA officer who claims to remember it from a telegram written by the station chief at the time.

[32]U.S. Embassy, Tehran, "Intrigues among the Bakhtiari Tribes;" Henderson to Acheson, January 18, 1953, Record Group 59, Box 4115; Henderson to Acheson, January 19, 1953, Record Group 59, Box 4117; see also articles in the *New York Times* for this period. The Majles vote was on a bill to extend Mosaddeq's emergency powers.

In mid-February, Zahedi asked several Iranian army generals to support him in a coup. His son Ardeshir told U.S. embassy officials that Zahedi was about to seize power and identified the prospective members of his postcoup cabinet. About the same time, a group of Bakhtiari tribesmen led by Abul Qasem and members of the Retired Officers' Association attacked an army column in Khuzestan province, causing many casualties. Mosaddeq retaliated by arresting Zahedi and several other conspirators and threatening to resign. The shah then announced that he was about to take a vacation abroad, provoking widespread unrest. A large crowd organized by Kashani, the Somka party, and pro-Zahedi military officers gathered at the Shah's palace and marched toward Mosaddeq's home, calling for Mosaddeq's dismissal. Violent clashes erupted between this crowd and a larger, pro-Mosaddeq crowd. The U.S. embassy reported that the "present probability is that the Mosaddeq Government will fall,"[33] but Mosaddeq managed to escape the hostile crowd, and loyal army units eventually restored order.

In late April, the chief of the National Police, General Afshartous, was kidnapped and murdered. MI-6 had apparently planned the kidnapping to provoke a coup, but the murder was not part of the plan. Zahedi, Baqai, and several of their associates (including Kashani's son) were implicated in the killing, and warrants were issued for their arrest. Kashani, as president of the Majles, helped Zahedi avoid arrest by giving him bast, or sanctuary, in the Majles; Baqai was protected by parliamentary immunity. Mosaddeq charged that the conspirators had also intended to kill the defense and foreign ministers and that their goal had been to install Baqai as prime minister. Afshartous had been widely regarded as courageous, uncorrupt, and staunchly loyal to Mosaddeq. His murder was a blow to the morale of the National Front, and it demonstrated clearly the ruthlessness of the anti-Mosaddeq conspirators.[34]

These events added considerably to the turmoil that had gripped Iran since the summer of 1952. After the February riots, rumors of a coup began to circulate in the army, and unrest simmered among the Bakhtiari. The pro-Mosaddeq Qashqai tribe made plans to attack the Bakhtiari and

[33]"Internal Affairs," February 18, 1953, FO/371/104562; "Internal Affairs," February 24, 1953, FO/371/104562; "Internal Affairs," February 28, 1953, FO/371/104563; "Internal Affairs," March 1, 1953, FO/371/104562; "Dr. Musaddiq's Quarrel with the Shah," February 23, 1953, FO/371/104563; "An Assessment of the Internal Situation in Persia," March 2, 1953, FO/371/104563; "Internal Affairs," March 10, 1953, FO/371/10463; "The Friendly Relationship . . . ," June 10, 1953, FO/371/104568.

[34]The role of MI-6 in the Afshartous murder is described in *Iran Times*, May 31, 1985, 1; see also "The Murder of the Persian Chief of Police Afshartus," April 24, 1953, FO/371/104565; "The Murder of Chief of Police Afshartus," May 8, 1953, FO/371/104566; "Summary for the Period April 30–May 13 1953," June 23, 1953, FO/371/104568.

march on Tehran in the event of a coup. The Tudeh party had been quite active in the February riots and remained so in the weeks that followed, leading Mosaddeq to order a wave of arrests of suspected Tudeh members.[35] More significantly, Mosaddeq's once-unchallenged position as leader of the nationalist movement grew increasingly precarious. Because Kashani, Baqai, and Makki held great sway over the urban lower classes, their defections into the opposition had weakened Mosaddeq's popular support and his support in the Majles. Majles debates over the causes of the February incident and Baqai's role in the murder of Afshartous served as forums for further attacks against Mosaddeq. By the summer of 1953, the battle lines had been drawn.[36]

While Zahedi and his associates were engaged in these activities, the Eisenhower administration was beginning to develop plans to overthrow Mosaddeq. Top CIA officials had already become convinced that a coup was necessary. Secretary of State John Foster Dulles had been discussing plans for a coup with his brother, CIA director Allen Dulles, since the November election. Top U.S. and British officials met on February 3, 1953, only two weeks after Eisenhower's inauguration, to review the situation. A decision was taken at this meeting to develop and implement a plan to overthrow Mosaddeq and install Zahedi as prime minister. The operation, code-named AJAX, was to be led by Roosevelt. United States officials had previously described Zahedi as "unscrupulous" and "an opportunist"; now they viewed him as a strong leader capable of the decisive steps needed to bring Iran firmly back into the Western camp.[37] Roosevelt traveled to Iran several times in the following months to prepare for the coup. He and another CIA officer met frequently with Zahedi and may have given him financial assistance. A well-known American specialist on Iran working under contract for the CIA went to Nicosia in mid-May to develop a detailed plan for the coup with an Iran specialist from MI-6 and then reviewed the plan with Roosevelt in Beirut. The two flew to London in mid-June to discuss the plan with British officials; final U.S. approval came at a June 25 State Department meeting.[38]

[35]"Internal Situation," n.d., FO/371/10463; "Internal Affairs," March 1, 1953; "*New York Times*, March 9, 1953, 12:2, and March 10, 1953, 4:5; "Change of Government Tribal Administration," April 10, 1953, FO/371/104565; "Internal Situation," August 13, 1953, FO/371/104569; U.S. Embassy, Tehran, "Iranian Political Trends. . . ," April 24, 1953, Record Group 59, Box 4110.

[36]U.S. Embassy, Tehran, "Iranian Political Trend"; idem, "Iranian Political Developments from the End of March to the Overthrow of the Mosadeq Regime . . . ," October 28, 1953, Record Group 59, Box 4110; Cottam, *Nationalism in Iran*, 277–82.

[37]Roosevelt interview. The February meeting is described in Roosevelt, *Countercoup*, 120–24. For U.S. views on Zahedi see U.S. Department of State, "Memorandum of Conversation, Subject: Iran."

[38]These events and the outline of the coup plan given in the next paragraph were recounted to me by the American Iran specialist in a confidential interview.

The coup plan had four components: (1) the propaganda and political-action capabilities of BEDAMN were to be turned immediately against Mosaddeq; (2) opposition figures were to be encouraged thereby to take bast in the Majles, creating a disturbance that would inflame the situation; (3) since the shah had not been consulted about the coup, his agreement to dismiss Mosaddeq and appoint Zahedi was to be obtained; and (4) the support of key active-duty military officers was to be sought. The idea of a Bakhtiari tribal uprising was dropped, presumably because Abul Qasem Bakhtiari had recently been arrested. Diplomatic means were to complement these covert activities: Iran was dropped from the itinerary of Secretary of State Dulles's trip to the Middle East in May 1953, and President Eisenhower sent a much-publicized letter to Mosaddeq in late June stating that the United States would not provide Iran with further economic aid until the oil dispute had been settled.[39] The Rashidian and BEDAMN networks and several officers in the Tehran CIA station were also expected to help with the coup. The Rashidians had been turned over to the CIA by MI-6 when the British left Tehran in November 1952. The CIA station was augmented for AJAX. The station chief (who apparently opposed the coup) was replaced with a former journalist who had covered the Azerbaijan crisis and knew many prominent Iranians, and a CIA paramilitary expert with recent experience in Korea went to Iran to take responsibility for liaison with the Iranian military officers involved in the plot.[40]

Mosaddeq's position grew more precarious in June and July, with almost daily demonstrations by pro- and anti-Mosaddeq crowds and the Tudeh party. The Majles was the scene of continual disputes between pro- and anti-Mosaddeq deputies over issues such as the February riots, Baqai's role in the Afshartous killing, control over the armed forces, and elections for a new speaker. Fistfights broke out in the Majles in early June. On July 1 Mosaddeq achieved a major victory when Abdullah Moazemi, a Mosaddeq supporter, was elected by a vote of forty-one to thirty-one to replace Kashani as speaker. After further opposition attacks, a group of Mosaddeq supporters resigned en masse from the Majles. In late July a group of deputies loyal to Haerizadeh and Baqai took bast in the Majles. With the Majles paralyzed by these actions, Mosaddeq decided to adjourn it and hold new elections. But because of the opposition's threat to prevent a quorum, he was forced to hold a public referendum on the issue in early August. The referendum was blatantly rigged by government forces, causing a great public outcry against Mosaddeq.[41]

[39]"Iranian Political Developments ," 15; Alexander and Nanes, *United States and Iran*, 234–35.

[40]These details were obtained in confidential interviews with several of the participants.

[41]The events of this period are fairly well covered in the *New York Times*; see also "Dr. Musaddiq's Move to Dissolve the Majles," July 21, 1953, FO/371/104569; "Dissolution of

The CIA had already begun to undermine Mosaddeq through the BEDAMN network by this time. CIA participants in these activities have described them as "an orchestrated program of destabilization" and "an all-out effort."[42] BEDAMN was at least partially responsible for both the demonstrations and the Majles unrest that plagued Mosaddeq in this period.[43] Here again, it is impossible to determine the effectiveness of these actions, but they probably played a significant role in undermining Mosaddeq's popular support.

Several efforts were made to persuade the shah to back Zahedi. First, Ambassador Henderson met with the shah on May 30 and was told that Zahedi would be acceptable if he had broad public support, came to power through parliamentary means, and was backed by a large aid package from the United States or Britain. The United States was clearly in no position to satisfy the first two of these conditions. In a second attempt in late July, a U.S. Army colonel and an MI-6 officer traveled to France to locate Princess Ashraf, the shah's twin sister, who was gambling at the casinos in Deauville. Princess Ashraf agreed to speak to her brother after apparently receiving an unauthorized promise from the colonel that the United States would support the shah in the style to which he was accustomed, should the coup fail. Princess Ashraf arrived in Tehran on July 25, but Mosaddeq prevented her from seeing her brother. In a third attempt a week later, General Norman Schwartzkopf, who had commanded the Iranian Gendarmerie from 1942 until 1948, managed to see the shah, who refused to commit himself to the CIA plan. Schwartzkopf then advised Roosevelt to visit the shah personally. Arrangements were made through the Rashidians. The shah agreed to support the plan, once official U.S. and British involvement had been confirmed to him in special radio broadcasts.[44]

Having obtained the shah's concurrence, Roosevelt's team was able to proceed with the coup. *Firmans* (royal decrees) dismissing Mosaddeq and

---

the 17th Majles," August 4, 1953, FO/371/104569; USARMA Tehran to DEPTAR, WASH DC, March 3, 1953, Record Group 59, Box 4113; U.S. Embassy, Tehran, "Political Events July 25–31, 1953," July 31, 1953, Record Group 59, Box 4110.

[42]Confidential interviews. One BEDAMN activity was a propaganda campaign to portray Mosaddeq as having Jewish ancestry.

[43]Mosaddeq later charged that this Majles unrest had been the work of foreign agents; see U.S. Embassy, Tehran, "Prime Minister's Radio Address of July 27, 1953," July 28, 1953, Record Group 59, Box 4116. Six new anti-Mosaddeq newspapers suddenly appeared in Tehran at this time, and U.S. embassy officials, unaware of the CIA's activities, were suspicious about the source of funding; see USARMA Tehran to DEPTAR.

[44]"Ambassador Henderson's Report," June 2, 1953, FO/371/104659; confidential interview with the colonel; Roosevelt, *Countercoup*, 147–49, 156–57. For Princess Ashraf's account of her trip see Princess Ashraf Pahlavi, *Faces in a Mirror* (Englewood Cliffs, N.J.: Prentice Hall, 1980), 134–40.

appointing Zahedi as prime minister were drawn up and signed by the shah. On the night of Saturday, August 15, Colonel Nematollah Nassiri, the commander of the Imperial Guard, delivered to Mosaddeq the firman dismissing him. Mosaddeq, who had been warned of the plot, probably by the Tudeh party, denounced the firman as a forgery and had Nassiri arrested. Troops loyal to Mosaddeq set up roadblocks throughout the city. Opposition deputies, military officers suspected of plotting with Zahedi, and the shah's minister of court were arrested. A massive search was begun for Zahedi, and a reward of one hundred thousand rials was offered for his arrest. Armored units assigned to move into Tehran in conjunction with the delivery of the firmans failed to arrive. Without informing Roosevelt's team, the shah fled the country in panic, traveling first to Baghdad, then to Rome.[45]

Nassiri's arrest completely disrupted the coup plan, forcing Roosevelt and his team to improvise a new strategy. Contingency plans were made for Roosevelt, Zahedi, and a few other key participants to be evacuated from Iran in a U.S. military attaché's airplane. Zahedi was brought to a CIA safehouse, where he remained in hiding until the final hours before Mosaddeq was overthrown. Roosevelt's team then made several diverse and uncoordinated efforts to trigger a coup. The first of these was an attempt to publicize the shah's decision to dismiss Mosaddeq and replace him with Zahedi, which Mosaddeq had not publicly announced. On Sunday, August 16, CIA officers made copies of the firmans announcing these decisions and had Nerren, Cilley, and two American newspaper reporters distribute them throughout Tehran. The two reporters were also taken to meet Ardeshir Zahedi at the home of one of the CIA officers. He told them about the firmans and characterized Mosaddeq's attempt to arrest his father as a coup, inasmuch as his father had legally been appointed prime minister. This information was quickly published in the *New York Times* and elsewhere.[46]

After the firmans had been distributed, the CIA team tried to generate support for Zahedi in the armed forces. A declaration calling for the military to support the shah was drawn up and circulated. The U.S.

[45]The details of the coup presented in this and the following paragraphs are based on my confidential interviews with four of the five key CIA participants and on *New York Times* articles written by correspondent Kennett Love, who covered the coup in Tehran. The Tudeh party had evidently infiltrated the network of officers recruited for AJAX; details of the coup plan had been reported by Tass on July 15 and in Tudeh newspapers as early as August 13. See "Dr. Musaddiq's Move to Dissolve the Majles"; and "Persian Army Officers Attempt to Overthrow Dr. Musaddiq," August 16, 1953, FO/371/104569.

[46]The role of the two reporters is described in Kennett Love, "The American Role in the Pahlavi Restoration on 19 August 1953," Allen Dulles Papers, Princeton University Library, 1960.

military advisory mission distributed military supplies to pro-Zahedi forces. Efforts were also made to gain the support of garrisons in other cities: messengers were sent to Kermanshah and Isfahan, using forged travel documents previously obtained from CIA headquarters. Colonel Teimur Bakhtiar, the garrison commander at Kermanshah, led a column of tanks and armored cars toward Tehran, but the Isfahan commander refused to cooperate.[47]

As these events were unfolding, Nerren and Cilley hired a large crowd to march into central Tehran on Monday, August 17, shouting Tudeh slogans and carrying signs denouncing the shah. This "fake" Tudeh crowd, paid for with fifty thousand dollars a CIA officer had given to Nerren and Cilley the previous evening, was designed to provoke fears of a Tudeh takeover and thus to rally support for Zahedi. The crowd was soon joined by real Tudeh members, who were unaware that the demonstration was a CIA provocation. The combined crowd attacked the Reza Shah mausoleum and several mosques and tore down statues of the shah and his father. These demonstrations continued the next day, leading Ambassador Henderson to demand that they be broken up by the police, who were still in their barracks. In what was to be a fateful decision, Mosaddeq acquiesced. The Tudeh retaliated by ordering its cadres off the street. On Wednesday, August 19, most of the Tehran police were to turn against Mosaddeq, while Tudeh crowds remained off the streets and did not attack the pro-Zahedi crowds that appeared on that day.[48]

Once copies of the firmans had been circulated and steps had been taken to rally the armed forces behind Zahedi, Roosevelt's team began to look for ways to trigger an uprising against Mosaddeq. The most obvious way to do this was through the clergy, preferably through a popular figure like Kashani. The CIA team, having no direct ties with Kashani, asked the Rashidians to make such an arrangement through their allies among the

[47]*New York Times*, August 19, 1953, 1:3–4; U.S. Congress, House, Committee on Foreign Affairs, *The Mutual Security Act of 1954: Hearings*, 83d Cong., 2d sess., April 3, 1954, 503–4, 509.

[48]The CIA role in organizing this fake Tudeh crowd, which played a critical role in the coup, was confirmed to me in confidential interviews with at least five retired CIA officers. One told me the CIA station later learned from its Tudeh informants that the Tudeh's decision to pull its crowds off the streets came after it had realized that the original crowd had been a provocation. Several of these sources suggested that Nerren and Cilley may have used their contacts with leaders of the Pan-Iranist party to mobilize part of this crowd. This is consistent with the observation by U.S. Embassy personnel that this crowd contained "an unusual mixture of Pan-Iranists and Tudeh" members; see Mattison to Dulles, August 17, 1953, Record Group 59, Box 4110. Henderson's conversation with Mosaddeq is described in his 1972 interview with the Columbia University Oral History Research Office (15–18). The Tudeh later reevaluated its role in these events and concluded that it should have been more supportive of Mosaddeq; see Zabih, *Communist Movement in Iran*, 219–21.

clergy. The Rashidians reported back that such an uprising could not be arranged until Friday, when weekly prayers would be held. Fearing that Mosaddeq's net would soon close in around them, Roosevelt asked the Rashidians how he could contact Kashani. He was directed to a Rashidian ally named Ahmad Aramesh. Two CIA officers met with Aramesh on the morning of Wednesday, August 19, and gave him ten thousand dollars to pass on to Kashani. Kashani then apparently arranged to have an anti-Mosaddeq crowd march from the bazaar into central Tehran. Similar crowds were probably organized independently by the Rashidians and by Nerren and Cilley, possibly through Ayatollah Behbehani and a mob organizer named Shahban "the brainless" Jafari.[49]

The combined crowd, joined by army and police units and by onlookers opposed to Mosaddeq, attacked government office buildings and the offices of pro-Mosaddeq newspapers and political parties. Mosaddeq refused to use the security forces to break up the crowd. An army unit seized the radio station and began to broadcast pro-Zahedi bulletins. Air force general Guilanshah led a column of tanks to the CIA safehouse where Zahedi was hiding. Together with a group of proshah demonstrators, these forces then seized the army headquarters and marched on Mosaddeq's home. There, a nine-hour battle ensued in which some three hundred people were killed. The walls around the home were destroyed with tank and artillery fire, the house was stormed, and Mosaddeq escaped over the roof. He surrendered to Zahedi's forces the next day.[50]

The Significance of the 1953 Coup

The overthrow of Mosaddeq was a seminal event in modern Iranian history. Our understanding of the subsequent cliency relationship between the United States and Iran requires the answers to three important questions about this coup: (1) how important was the U.S. role; (2) what

[49]A report of the plan to organize demonstrations on Friday appeared several weeks later in the *Times of India*; see "Transmits a Further Series of Articles," June 16, 1953, FO/371/104568. Neither of the CIA officers who delivered the money to Aramesh could confirm that it went to Kashani, though both believe that it did (confidential interviews). The pro-Zahedi demonstrators included members of the Somka and Pan-Iranist parties; see Henderson to Acheson, August 19, 1953, Record Group 59, Box 4110. All the people involved either directly or indirectly in the coup with whom I spoke believe that the Aramesh-Kashani connection was *not* the only source of funding for the crowds that appeared on August 19. Most of these sources assume the other figures mentioned here were also involved, although none could confirm this positively.

[50]Roosevelt, *Countercoup*, 176–97; *New York Times*, August 20, 1953, 1:6.

motives led the United States to become involved; (3) what were the consequences for Iranian domestic politics?

Although Britain and various Iranian actors obviously made important contributions to Mosaddeq's overthrow, the evidence suggests that the Mosaddeq regime probably would have survived had it not been for U.S. intervention. During the twenty-eight months of his premiership, British and Iranians efforts had clearly reduced Mosaddeq's popularity but failed to remove him from office. Indeed, while Mosaddeq remained in power in the summer of 1953, each of his major challengers had been severely weakened or eliminated: Sayyid Zia and Qavam had disappeared from the scene; the British had been expelled; Kashani had lost much of his support in the Majles; and Zahedi had failed twice to oust Mosaddeq and had gone into hiding to evade an arrest warrant. Indeed, aside from the Tudeh party, which was still relatively weak at this time,[51] *no* Iranian political group or figure appears to have been capable of ousting Mosaddeq in the summer of 1953 without substantial foreign assistance.

This conclusion is reinforced by an examination of each participant's contributions to the coup. United States officials had planned the coup (with help from a British intelligence officer) and financed and directed it. When the original plan failed, the CIA officers leading the operation improvised the new strategy. Although various Iranians played important roles in the coup, each was acting under instructions from the CIA team. Fazlollah Zahedi, the nominal coup leader, was hiding in a CIA safehouse during most of the operation. The shah was not consulted about the decision to undertake the coup, about the coup plans, or even about the candidate chosen to replace Mosaddeq. He supported the coup only reluctantly and fled to Baghdad at the first sign of failure. Although some Iranian army units supported the coup, others remained loyal to Mosaddeq. It therefore seems highly unlikely that Zahedi and his small group of collaborators could have carried out the coup without U.S. support. Moreover, extensive U.S. assistance in the months after the coup was vital in enabling the Zahedi government to consolidate power.

Not only was a coup very unlikely in the summer of 1953 without U.S. help, but Mosaddeq's domestic position was less precarious than commonly believed. Although Iran's economy had initially been badly hurt by the British oil embargo and other economic sanctions, stimulative fiscal policies undertaken in 1952 had brought unemployment down below its 1951 level and produced a modest recovery by the end of the year. The

[51] The CIA had concluded in November 1952 that a Tudeh takeover was not likely before the end of 1953; see CIA, *Probable Developments in Iran through 1953*, NIE-75, November 13, 1952.

Mosaddeq government had tried to sell oil to Japan and Italy in early 1953, and although these efforts eventually failed, the oil blocade probably would have been broken soon. The U.S. economic attaché described business in Iran as "brisk" in May 1953, and Iran's nonoil exports were reportedly doing well.[52] Moreover, Mosaddeq still retained considerable support in organizations such as the Iran party and the Third Force, in the bazaar,[53] among the urban lower and middle classes in general, and in the military. In the absence of a strong opponent, then, Mosaddeq would probably have either remained in power for some time to come or relinquished power to another National Front figure.

What motives led the United States to become involved in the coup? It is often argued that the primary U.S. motive was the desire of U.S. policy makers to advance the interests of U.S. oil companies by helping them gain a share in Iran's oil industry.[54] The Eisenhower administration was decidedly supportive of U.S. business interests, and the Dulles brothers had been prominent Wall Street lawyers specializing in international business. Moreover, the final agreement worked out in 1954 with the Zahedi government gave U.S. oil companies a 40 percent share of Iran's oil production, which had been controlled entirely by the British-owned AIOC before nationalization.

Although this argument has a superficial appeal, it ignores the contemporary realities of the international oil market. Since a glut existed in the early 1950s, U.S. oil companies had no compelling reason to seek new sources. The U.S. majors had increased production in Saudi Arabia and Kuwait in 1951 to make up for the loss of Iran's oil, so operating in Iran would have forced them to reduce production in these other countries, creating tension with Saudi and Kuwaiti leaders. Furthermore, the intensity of nationalist sentiments in Iran made operations there very risky.

[52]U.S. Embassy, Tehran, "Monthly Economic Report," November 2, 1951, Record Group 59, Box 5490; "Labor Attaché's Report for January–June 1952," July 21, 1952, FO/371/98732; U.S. Embassy, Tehran, "Quarterly Economic and Financial Review, Iran, Fourth Quarter 1952," January 17, 1953, "Quarterly Economic and Financial Review, Iran, First Quarter, 1953," April 17, 1953, "Quarterly Economic and Financial Review, Iran, Second Quarter, 1953," July 18, 1953, "Monthly Economic Survey, Iran, April 1953," May 12, 1953, and "Monthly Economic Survey, Iran, July 1953," August 14, 1953, all in Record Group 59, Box 5490; see also U.S. Department of State, Office of Intelligence and Research, *Iran's Political and Economic Prospects through 1953*, January 9, 1953, 13–17; Homa Katouzian, "Oil Boycott and the Political Economy: Musaddiq and the Strategy of Non-Oil Economics," in Bill and Louis, *Musaddiq, Iranian Nationalism, and Oil*, 203–27; and Patrick Clawson and Cyrus Sassanpour, "Adjustment to a Foreign Exchange Shock: Iran, 1951–1953," *International Journal of Middle East Studies* 19 (May 1987) 1–22.

[53]See "Comments on the Political Significance of the Tehran Bazaar Organization," December 19, 1953, FO/371/109986.

[54]See, e.g., Bahman Nirumand, *Iran: The New Imperialism in Action* (New York: Monthly Review Press, 1969), 5.

Because of these considerations, U.S. oil company executives had repeatedly told U.S. officials that they were not interested in buying Iranian oil at this time.[55] Indeed, the Truman administration had even tried to persuade U.S. oil companies to participate in a consortium by offering to scale back a major antitrust suit brought against them by the Justice Department, and this arrangement was later incorporated into the settlement of the oil dispute arranged by the United States in 1954. Thus not only did the U.S. majors not want to buy Iranian oil at this time, but U.S. policy makers were forced to take drastic steps to persuade them to do so.

The timing of the initial U.S. decision to overthrow Mosaddeq (two weeks after Eisenhower's inauguration) suggests that this decision was due primarily to the more activist foreign policy views of the new administration rather than to the evolving situation in Iran at the time. Indeed, the coup actually served as something of a test of the Eisenhower administration's new strategy for combating Soviet expansionism.

Since early 1950 the Truman administration had expanded the U.S. presence in Iran under its perimeter defense strategy. Iran's strategic location on the southern border of the Soviet Union and its large oil reserves made it "of critical importance" to U.S. national security, according to a November 1952 National Security Council study.[56] United States intelligence analysts did not regard Mosaddeq as a communist and did not believe that a Tudeh takeover was likely at this time. Rather, they believed that the Tudeh was following a "popular front" strategy by infiltrating the armed forces and government bureaucracy and trying to gain favor with Mosaddeq and other National Front leaders. Although the Truman administration was deeply concerned about Tudeh influence, it did not believe that a Tudeh takeover was imminent and therefore did not try to overthrow Mosaddeq.[57]

During the 1952 election campaign the Republicans had accused the Truman administration of dealing inadequately with Soviet expansionism, arguing that it had "lost" China and Eastern Europe and become bogged down in a seemingly endless war in Korea. Once in power, the new administration began to formulate a new global strategy, which became known as the "New Look." This strategy retained Truman's perimeter

[55]See U.S. Senate, Committee on Foreign Relations, *The International Petroleum Cartel: The Iranian Consortium and U.S. National Security*, 93d Cong., 2d sess., February 21, 1974, esp. 27–28; and "Anglo-U.S. Discussions," December 13, 1952, FO/371/98704.

[56]U.S. National Security Council, *United States Policy regarding the Present Situation in Iran*, NSC 136/1, November 20, 1952, 1.

[57]CIA, *Probable Developments in Iran*; U.S. Department of State, Office of Intelligence and Research, *Iran's Political and Economic Prospects through 1953*, OIR No. 6126, January 9, 1953. The Tudeh's "popular front" strategy was described to me in a confidential interview with a retired CIA officer who worked on Iran at this time.

defense approach but sought to regain the initiative against the Soviet Union by acting more aggressively and using a broader variety of policy instruments, including covert action. Iran, which John Foster Dulles had described as a potential "second China" during the 1952 campaign,[58] quickly became a test case. Although no major changes had occurred in Iran since the election and a Tudeh takeover was still not viewed as imminent, the administration decided almost immediately after the inauguration to overthrow Mosaddeq. Most middle-level U.S. officials involved in Iranian affairs did not favor a coup,[59] which indicates that the decision was made by top officials without extensive consultation. After the coup, which had marked the first peacetime use of covert action by the United States to overthrow a foreign government, similar efforts followed in Guatemala, Egypt, Syria, Indonesia, and Cuba. Moreover, the U.S. press was informed about the U.S. role in the coup to demonstrate the Eisenhower administration's determination to combat Soviet expansionism.[60] These actions support the idea that the coup was an important test case for the Eisenhower administration.

Finally, what were the consequences of the coup for Iran's domestic politics? The immediate consequence was that the shah and Zahedi were able to carry out an extensive series of arrests and install a rigid authoritarian regime under which all forms of opposition political activity were prohibited. These measures severely weakened not only the National Front and its affiliates but also organizations that had opposed the National Front, such as the Tudeh and Toilers' parties and Kashani's network, which never regained the prominence they had enjoyed during the Mosaddeq era. The National Front and these other organizations were the primary means through which the modern middle class, the industrial

[58]"The United States' Ideas of a Settlement of the Oil Dispute," October 20, 1952, FO/371/98702. On the "New Look" see John Lewis Gaddis, *Strategies of Containment* (New York: Oxford University Press, 1982), chap. 5.

[59]A coup was opposed by Assistant Secretary of State Henry Byroade, Ambassador Henderson, the Tehran CIA station chief, and several lower level Iran specialists in the State Department and CIA; Byroade interview; interviews with Gordon Mattison, Bethesda, Md., June 30, 1984, and Roy Melbourne, Chapel Hill, N.C., February 1, 1984; confidential interviews with several retired CIA officers. Byroade and Henderson both went along reluctantly, according to these sources; the main proponents seem to have been the Dulles brothers, Wisner, and Roosevelt. For evidence that a Tudeh takeover was not viewed as imminent, see CIA, "Comment on Tudeh Position in Current Iranian Situation," March 3, 1953.

[60]The account of the coup given in Richard Harkness and Gladys Harkness, "The Mysterious Doings of CIA," *Saturday Evening Post*, November 6, 1954, 66–68, was made available to the Harknesses by the CIA, according to several confidential sources. The importance of the 1953 coup in Iran as a precedent for similar activities elsewhere was emphasized to me in a telephone interview with Richard Helms, CIA director from 1965 until 1973, Washington, D.C., July 26, 1984.

working class, and the traditional middle and lower classes had been able to exert influence over the state. The coup and the subsequent consolidation of an authoritarian regime therefore greatly increased the state's autonomy vis-à-vis these classes. Moreover, the movement led by the National Front had, in effect, been an attempt by the modern middle class to establish hegemony over the state. These actions therefore also ended, at least temporarily, the prospects for such hegemony. Inasmuch as the United States had played a key role in fomenting the coup, it was largely responsible for these consequences.

4

The Establishment of a U.S. Client State in Iran

The United States had organized the coup d'état that overthrew Prime Minister Mosaddeq in August 1953 with the aim of restoring political stability in Iran and thus preventing an eventual communist takeover. Yet while Mosaddeq had been successfully removed from office, he and the National Front remained quite popular. If the newly installed Zahedi government failed to consolidate power quickly, political instability might soon reemerge and the National Front or some other organization might pose a serious challenge to it. Indeed, this began to happen in the first months after the coup. In order to strengthen the Zahedi government, the United States took a variety of actions which helped to create a new, more stable, authoritarian regime by the end of 1954. The United States then began to implement measures designed to enhance Iran's long-term political stability and integrate Iran into the U.S. global strategy for containing the Soviet Union. By the early 1960s, these measures had turned Iran into one of the major U.S. clients in the region. They had also had a considerable impact on Iran's domestic politics, enhancing the state's repressive and co-optative capabilities and therefore greatly increasing its autonomy.

The Postcoup Consolidation of Power

The 1953 coup had removed Mosaddeq and his government from office, but the National Front's base of support in the modern middle class, the traditional middle class, and the industrial working class remained largely intact. Similarly, the Tudeh party's base of support in the modern middle class and the industrial working class remained fairly strong, and the Tudeh had thoroughly infiltrated the armed forces and certain government agencies. Since the new Zahedi government had little popular support and could not even count on the full support of the shah or the armed forces,[1] strong measures were clearly needed. Accordingly, Zahedi immediately began a massive crackdown on all sources of opposition. A curfew was declared in Tehran, and tanks were deployed in the bazaar. Mosaddeq and his close associates were arrested or forced into hiding. Suspected Tudeh hideouts were raided. Newspapers were harassed or forced to close. Army and police units broke up sporadic demonstrations in Tehran and other cities. More than fourteen hundred people had been arrested by the end of September, and at least seven hundred more by the end of the year. Some three thousand government employees who allegedly belonged to the Tudeh party were dismissed from their jobs. The armed forces were purged of disloyal members, and some eighteen hundred loyal officers were promoted.[2]

Despite these harsh measures, a considerable amount of opposition political activity occurred in the first months after the coup. This activity was carried out by three distinct groups: loyal National Front supporters, the Tudeh party, and defectors from the National Front who had begun to oppose the Zahedi government.

Although most top National Front leaders had been arrested soon after the coup, many lower level figures and unaffiliated supporters remained at large and quickly began to engage in opposition activity. The most serious threat of this kind came from the Qashqai tribe, which, despite its close ties to the United States, had strongly supported Mosaddeq. The Qashqai khans returned to their tribal lands in the south and began to mobilize their forces. They then seized an army barracks and, in late September, laid siege to the city of Shiraz. Fearing that an armed confrontation would play into the hands of the Tudeh, National Front leaders in Tehran sent a message to the Qashqai khans asking them to withdraw. The CIA station chief in Tehran also visited the Qashqai khans and threatened to "crush" them if they continued their activities. The siege of Shiraz was soon lifted. The Iranian army began a campaign to disarm the Qashqai in November, and the khans were later forced into exile.[3]

[1]On the strength of the National Front and the Tudeh party at this time see "Persian Government Wish to Hold Elections Soon," December 31, 1953, FO/371/109986; and "Estimate of Tudeh Party Numerical Strength," September 23, 1953, FO/371/104573. On Zahedi's lack of support see "Internal Situation in Persia," August 25, 1953, FO/371/104570; and Henderson to Acheson, October 9, 1953, Record Group 59, Box 4110.

[2]*New York Times*, August 20, 1953, 1:8, August 21, 1953, 1:8, August 25, 1953, 1:5, August 28, 1953, 4:2, September 2, 1953, 13:1, September 13, 1953, 24:1; "Tehran Situation Reports," n.d., FO/371/104570; "The Newspaper Situation," August 28, 1953, FO/371/104570; *Journal de Tehran*, September 24, 1953. These arrest figures are based on those cited in *Journal de Tehran*, September 23, 1953, and in subsequent issues.

[3]"Tehran Situation Reports"; *New York Times*, September 28, 1953, 8:1–2; "Fortnightly

Another major source of opposition was the National Resistance Movement, an organization formed by National Front supporters soon after the coup. The National Resistance Movement attracted most of the prominent National Front loyalists still at large and served for a time as the de facto successor to the National Front. It published two newspapers and organized antigovernment demonstrations, including a large one by students and bazaar merchants in early October; a general strike by bazaar merchants in early November, led by restaurant owner, Hassan Shamshiri; and a series of demonstrations by Tehran University students in early December. Each was put down with severe force: several demonstrators were killed; hundreds were arrested; and the roof of the Tehran bazaar was torn off by the security forces after the Shamshiri demonstration. Although the National Resistance Movement remained in existence for several years, the severity of the government's repression forced it to stop organizing public demonstrations after December 1953.[4]

The Tudeh party was also very active, although it had been forced underground by the government's repression. It approached the National Resistance Movement and a pro-Mosaddeq organization that had been formed in the Tehran bazaar about collaborating against the Zahedi government, and apparently participated in the demonstrations mentioned above. In late September a Tudeh sabotage squad attacked an airbase and destroyed all but two of the Iranian air force's operational aircraft. Since these aircraft were being readied for use against the Qashqai siege of Shiraz, speculation arose that the Tudeh and the Qashqai were collaborating. The Tudeh also tried to sabotage several naval vessels at the port of Khorramshahr in October and led a large antigovernment uprising in Isfahan in November. Because it posed a major threat to the government, the Tudeh party was the main focus of repression; as a result, its active membership was cut in half by December 1953.[5]

Political Summary, Period November 16–November 29," December 1, 1954, FO/371/109985; "Fortnightly Political Summary, Period March 27–April 13," April 14, 1954, FO/371/109985. These National Front and CIA approaches to the Qashqai were described to me in an interview with Mohammad Hossein Qashqai (London, December 22, 1984) and the CIA approach was confirmed in a confidential interview with the CIA station chief. This confrontation apparently ended the close relationship between the Qashqai and the CIA.

[4]Houchang Esfandiar Chehabi, "*Modernist Shi'ism and Politics: The Liberation Movement of Iran*" (Ph.D. diss., Yale University, 1986), chap. 5; *New York Times*, October 9, 1953, 5:7; "Internal Affairs," November 9, 1953, FO/371/104571; "Kashani's Press Conference on Dec. 5," December 9, 1953, FO/371/104572.

[5]"Internal Situation Reports," n.d., FO/371/104571; U.S. Embassy, Tehran, "Political Significance of Tehran Bazaar Organizations," December 19, 1953, Record Group 59, Box 4110; *New York Times*, September 26, 1953, 2:1, October 10, 1953, 2:5; CIA, *Current Intelligence Bulletin* 29 (September 1953); "Political and Economic Developments in Iran," November 19, 1953, FO/371/104572; U.S. Embassy, Tehran, "Roundup of Tudeh Activities, Late November 1953," December 11, 1953, Record Group 59, Box 4110.

Oddly enough, a third source of opposition was the National Front defectors who had collaborated with Zahedi to overthrow Mosaddeq. Kashani and Baqai began to intrigue against Zahedi almost immediately after the coup, making inflammatory statements to the press and trying to build a new nationalist organization. Zahedi at first tolerated these activities but soon began to threaten Kashani and Baqai and restrict their access to the press. Kashani and Makki gradually dropped out of sight as Zahedi consolidated power, but Baqai remained very active: he was arrested and forced into internal exile in 1954, and he became one of the most visible critics of the shah's regime in the decade after the 1953 coup.[6]

Despite opposition efforts, the Zahedi government gradually managed to consolidate power. Although its main instrument in this process of consolidation was repression, two other tactics proved useful as well. One was a highly publicized trial of Mosaddeq in November and December of 1953. This trial helped weaken the National Front at this critical juncture by focusing its attention on Mosaddeq's fate rather than on the prevailing political situation. Moreover, because the trial focused on narrow legal issues rather than on the nature of Mosaddeq's regime, it enabled the Zahedi government to counter Mosaddeq's progressive image with charges that he had flagrantly violated the law. In the end, Mosaddeq received a three-year jail term and then remained under house arrest until he died in 1967; he was thus prevented from serving either as a martyr or as a leader of the nationalist movement. Highly publicized trials were also held at this time for Hussein Fatemi, who was eventually executed; for Ali Shayegan and Ahmad Razavi, who were given life sentences (later commuted); and for a group of army officers who had supported Mosaddeq during the coup.[7]

The other tactic was to rig the Eighteenth Majles elections, which were held in the first three months of 1954. The notorious mob organizer Shahban "the brainless" Jafari played a prominent role in rigging these elections by organizing gangs that assaulted and intimidated voters. The U.S. embassy reported that most of the candidates elected to the Eighteenth Majles were either pro-British or "old faces with bad reputations";[8]

[6]"Political and Economic Developments in Iran"; "Memorandum on the Present Political Situation," January 4, 1954, FO/371/109986; "Persia Quarterly Political Report," February 26, 1954, FO/371/109990; "Fortnightly Political Summary, Period May 29–June 12," June 12, 1954, FO/371/109985; "Preliminary Report on the Internal Situation in Persia," January 7, 1954, FO/371/109985.

[7]*Journal de Tehran*, October 12, 1954, and November 2, 1954; U.S. Embassy, Tehran, "Imprisonment of Pro-Mosadeq Political Figures," June 1, 1955. On the consequences of Mosaddeq's imprisonment and subsequent house arrest for the nationalist movement see Richard W. Cottam, *Nationalism in Iran* (Pittsburgh: University of Pittsburgh Press, 1979), 294–95.

[8]"Not Painless Is 'Brainless,'" *Life*, March 22, 1954, 38–40; "Elections," February 2, 1954, FO/371/109986.

no legitimate opposition figures were elected. By gaining control over the Majles in this way, the Zahedi government prevented it from serving as a forum for opposition activity, as it had since the early 1940s, and made it impossible for members of the opposition to avoid arrest through parliamentary immunity.

By the time the Eighteenth Majles elections had been completed in March 1954, the Zahedi government had severely weakened the National Front, the Tudeh party, and all other sources of opposition. It continued to use repression liberally during and after the elections, intimidating voters and arresting opposition leaders such as Shahpour Bakhtiar, Mozaffar Baqai, Daryush Foruhar, Mostafa Kashani, Ahmad Razavi, and Ali Shayegan. The overall rate of arrests declined considerably after the Eighteenth Majles elections, however.[9]

Two key events in the late summer and fall of 1954 essentially completed the consolidation of the post-Mosaddeq regime. The first was the September 1954 discovery by Zahedi's security forces of a large Tudeh network in the armed forces. This network consisted of at least 458 military officers organized independently of the main Tudeh network who reported directly to an intelligence officer in the Soviet embassy. Although this network had apparently been established primarily to gather intelligence rather than to conduct subversive activities, it had carried out the sabotage of the air force planes mentioned above and was a clear threat to the government.[10] The destruction of this network, together with the wave of arrests immediately after the coup and the arrest of 380 Tudeh members in Tehran in July 1954, eliminated the Tudeh party as a major political force thereafter. It also indicated that the government's security forces had attained a fair level of sophistication, a reality that undoubtedly pleased the government and its supporters and troubled the opposition.

The final step in the consolidation of the new regime was the signing of an agreement in October 1954 between the NIOC and a consortium of

[9]The *Journal de Tehran* reported a monthly average of some 243 arrests from September 1953 through February 1954 but only 24 per month from March through June of 1954, by my calculations.

[10]This description is based on confidential interviews with two CIA officers closely involved in the roll-up of this network; on "Government Anti-Tudeh Campaign," November 26, 1954, *Declass. Docs.* 1, no. 4 (1974), 309D; and on Farhad Kazemi, "The Military and Politics in Iran: The Uneasy Symbiosis," in Elie Kedourie and Sylvia G. Haim, eds., *Towards a Modern Iran: Studies in Thought, Politics, and Society* (London: Cass, 1980), 217–40. United States officials believed at this time that a second, independent Tudeh network had been established among noncommissioned officers in the Iranian armed forces, but none was ever uncovered. Just before it was detected by the security forces, the Tudeh military network had apparently sent many of its members to Tehran to carry out acts of sabotage while the Majles was debating the new oil agreement. Among these saboteurs was an assassination squad assigned to kill certain government officials; see Iran White Paper, sec. II.A-(2).

Western oil companies which enabled Iran to resume its oil exports. This agreement was negotiated by Ali Amini, Zahedi's minister of finance, with considerable U.S. help. It closely resembled contemporary agreements between oil-producing countries and the major international oil companies: profits were to be shared fifty-fifty between the NIOC and the consortium members; Iran was to receive royalty fees amounting to 12.5 percent of total sales; and British Petroleum (formerly the AIOC) was to receive adequate compensation for the nationalization of its assets. British Petroleum received a 40-percent share in the consortium; a group of U.S. companies together received a 40-percent share; Royal Dutch Shell received a 14-percent share; and Compagnies Française des Pétroles received the remaining 6-percent share. Although Iran's oil income nearly tripled as a result of this agreement, tax credits awarded by the home governments of the consortium members largely offset members' losses.[11] Iran's oil exports had resumed by the end of the year, giving a boost to the economy, providing the government with a much-needed source of revenue, and ending a turbulent chapter in Iran's history.

Anxious to promote political stability and prevent a Soviet takeover, U.S. officials began a major effort immediately after the coup to strengthen the Zahedi government, using diplomacy, financial aid, and covert political action. Soon after the coup, President Eisenhower sent a message of congratulations to the shah, and U.S. officials announced that an aid request from Iran would receive prompt and favorable consideration. There followed frequent public expressions of support in the fall of 1953, culminating in Vice-president Richard Nixon's December visit to Iran. On August 26 the Zahedi government formally requested an emergency U.S. economic aid package; within ten days the existing U.S. aid program in Iran had been augmented with $23.4 million and an additional $45 million in emergency aid had been given. More emergency aid followed in early 1954. In addition, roughly $1 million in cash left over from the AJAX operation was given to the Zahedi government by the Tehran CIA station shortly after the coup. Diplomatic and financial support of this kind helped consolidate the postcoup regime by enhancing the stature and self-confidence of the Zahedi government and giving it the financial resources it needed to restore order.[12]

[11]Fereidun Fesharaki, *Development of the Iranian Oil Industry: International and Domestic Aspects* (New York: Praeger, 1976), 47–55.

[12]*New York Times*, August 25, 1953, 11:6, August 28, 1953, 4:2, December 10, 1953, 3:1; Yonah Alexander and Allan Nanes, eds., *The United States and Iran: A Documentary History* (Washington: University Publications of America, 1980), 250–54; interview with Kermit Roosevelt, Washington, D.C., June 5, 1985. On the importance of U.S. emergency assistance to the Iranian government see U.S. House of Representatives, Committee on

The Tehran CIA station also began a variety of covert efforts to assist the new government. As mentioned above, the CIA station chief traveled to the Qashqai region shortly after the coup to dissuade the khans from using force against the new government. This initiative was particularly effective because the CIA had been giving financial and matériel assistance to the Qashqai for several years and had developed a good rapport with the khans. The CIA gave the government intelligence on the Tudeh party, provided a small amount of money to certain favorable candidates in the Eighteenth Majles elections, and may have helped suppress the Shamshiri demonstrations in November 1953. It also used the BEDAMN propaganda network to distribute books, pamphlets, and newspaper articles criticizing the Tudeh party and praising the government and began to help Esfandiar Bozorgmehr, Zahedi's minister of information, carry out similar propaganda activities. CIA officers in the United States planted articles favorable to the Zahedi government in the American press as well.[13]

The CIA also began to train Iran's intelligence forces. In September 1953 a U.S. Army colonel who had been working for the CIA in the Middle East for several years and had an extensive background in police and detective work was sent to Iran under cover as a military attaché. His mission was to organize and command a new intelligence unit then being established under the auspices of the Tehran military governorship, which was placed under the command of General Teimur Bakhtiar in December 1953. The colonel worked closely with Bakhtiar and his subordinates, commanding this unit and training its members in basic intelligence techniques such as surveillance and interrogation methods, the operation of intelligence networks, and organizational security. Bakhtiar's intelligence

---

Foreign Affairs, *The Mutual Security Act of 1954: Hearings*, 83d Cong., 2d sess., March 4, 1954–June 8, 1954, 498–505.

[13]These activities were described to me in confidential interviews with five of the participants. The CIA had been giving arms and money to the Qashqai in connection with the stay-behind networks set up in the late 1940s (see Chap. 2). In one anti-Tudeh operation, two CIA officers conducting surveillance of a Tudeh hideout learned of plans for a large Tudeh demonstration in the fall of 1953. This information was apparently passed along to the Zahedi government, which then broke up the demonstration. Although only a few Majles candidates received CIA support, this support was directly responsible for getting at least one of them elected, according to one of my sources. One major BEDAMN propaganda effort was its attempt to generate public support for the oil negotiations. On possible CIA involvement in suppressing the Shamshiri demonstrations see Kennett Love, "The American Role in the Pahlavi Restoration on 19 August 1953," 1960, Allen Dulles Papers, Princeton University Library; I have been unable to confirm the CIA involvement independently. On U.S. propaganda activities in Iran in this period see U.S. National Security Council, Operations Coordinating Board, *Progress Report on United States Policy toward Iran*, October 13, 1954, 3, DDE Library. One article the CIA planted in the American press was Richard Harkness and Gladys Harkness, "The Mysterious Doings of CIA," *Saturday Evening Post*, November 6, 1954, 66–68.

unit was the first modern, efficient intelligence organization to operate in Iran.[14]

The primary mission of this intelligence unit was to seek out and neutralize all threats to the shah and the Iranian government. These threats were anticipated mainly from the Tudeh party, but challenges from remnants of the National Front and from within the armed forces were also considered possible. The main achievement of this unit, which began to operate in early 1954, was the detection and destruction of the Tudeh military network discovered in September 1954. Although the U.S. Army colonel was in command of this unit at the time, it was his Iranian subordinates who discovered the Tudeh network.[15] This event played a key role in consoliding the postcoup regime and was a primary reason for the shah's subsequent decision to establish a modern, unified intelligence organization.

Perhaps the most significant U.S. activity on behalf of the new government was a major effort to resolve the oil dispute. In October 1953 the State Department hired Herbert Hoover, Jr., a prominent oil industry analyst, to negotiate a new oil agreement. The Eisenhower administration followed the approach adopted by its predecessor in agreeing to scale back an important antitrust case then pending against the major U.S. oil companies in exchange for their participation in a consortium to purchase and market Iranian oil. With the participation of the U.S. majors thus assured, Hoover traveled to Tehran and London in November 1953 and worked out the basic terms of an agreement, which was eventually signed and ratified by the Majles in October 1954.[16]

[14]The material here and in the next paragraph was related to me in a confidential interview with the U.S. Army colonel and confirmed in confidential interviews with two retired CIA officers then involved in Iranian affairs. This colonel is the officer who had contacted Princess Ashraf in France in connection with the 1953 coup (see Chap. 3). His police background included participation in the suppression of the coal mine strikes in "bloody Harlan County" in Kentucky in the early 1930s. United States and Iranian officials had briefly discussed in 1950 the possibility of hiring a retired FBI agent to train an intelligence unit in Iran's National Police force, but these discussions ended when Iranian officials lost interest; see Acheson to Wiley, June 30, 1950, Record Group 59, Box 4106; and Acheson to Grady, December 12, 1950, Record Group 59, Box 4106.

[15]This network was uncovered when, after a routine traffic accident, a Tudeh courier was arrested carrying coded documents with the names of all members of the network and other information. The main achievements of Bakhtiar's intelligence unit were the decoding of these documents and the arrest of almost all network members simultaneously. Although the U.S. Army colonel had made arrangements for CIA code breakers to examine the documents, his Iranian subordinates had already broken the secret codes before they could be sent to Washington.

[16]See Burton I. Kaufman, *The Oil Cartel Case: A Documentary Study of Antitrust Activity in the Cold War Era* (Westport, Conn.: Greenwood, 1978).

Iran and U.S. Global Strategy

United States policy makers had fomented the 1953 coup to restore political stability in a country they regarded as vital to the U.S. global strategy for containing the Soviet Union. Iran continued to play a vital role in U.S. global strategy for the next decade and remained extremely important to the United States thereafter, providing the basis for a strong cliency relationship between the two countries.

The U.S.-Iran cliency relationship was initially dictated by the Eisenhower administration's New Look strategy. Set forth in the October 1953 National Security Council study NSC-162/2, the New Look was an effort to regain the initiative in the global confrontation with the Soviet Union while reducing U.S. defense expenditures. Although it was based on the Truman administration's idea of containing the Soviet Union through perimeter defense, the main goal of the New Look was to do this more effectively and at a lower cost by changing the basic orientation of the U.S. armed forces: conventional ground forces, which were very costly and had become hopelessly bogged down in Korea, were to be scaled back, and the U.S. strategic bomber fleet was to be given the capacity to carry out both limited nuclear strikes and "massive retaliation."[17]

The New Look also called for a major effort to strengthen pro-Western countries along the entire periphery of the Soviet sphere of influence, a project begun by the Truman administration in 1950 but stalled by the reconstruction of Europe and the Korean War. Accordingly, the Eisenhower administration began to establish cliency relationships all along the Sino-Soviet periphery, making extensive use of security assistance, economic aid, alliances, and covert action, which the previous administration had not used very extensively in the Third World. The result was a fundamental shift in U.S. military and economic aid programs away from Europe and toward countries in the Middle East and east Asia (Table 4); Iran, Pakistan, Thailand, South Vietnam, Taiwan, and South Korea all became important U.S. clients in this period. By enhancing the U.S. ability to contain Soviet expansionism, these cliency relationships accorded well with the administration's desire to regain the initiative against the Soviet Union while reducing U.S. defense expenditures.[18]

Iran was to play a key role in the Eisenhower administration's more

[17]See Glen H. Snyder, "The 'New Look' of 1953," in Warner R. Schilling, Paul Y. Hammond, and Glen H. Snyder, eds., *Strategy, Politics, and Defense Budgets* (New York: Columbia University Press, 1962), 379–524; and John Lewis Gaddis, *Strategies of Containment* (New York: Oxford University Press, 1982), chap. 5.

[18]See ibid.

Table 4. Average yearly U.S. foreign aid to selected countries (in millions of current U.S. dollars)

	1949–1953		1954–1961		1962–1969	
Country	Military	Economic	Military	Economic	Military	Economic
Europe:	1,867.5	2,982.6	613.5	402.7	113.6	105.3
Austria	0	146.0	12.2	9.3	2.3	.5
Belgium/Luxembourg	64.1	112.2	107.7	0	9.9	0
Denmark	37.5	56.1	40.2	0	14.7	0
France	244.4	662.7	378.2	0	13.5	0
Ireland	0	29.6	0	0	0	0
Italy	121.6	324.4	180.0	54.4	42.9	7.3
Netherlands	38.0	197.0	121.0	.9	12.1	0
Norway	33.1	55.4	62.6	.1	31.0	0
Portugal	14.8	10.3	27.6	3.4	5.0	6.6
Spain	0	12.5	54.4	113.1	27.7	8.3
United Kingdom	29.3	720.1	109.1	29.4	5.0	0
West Germany	36.5	515.4	94.2	15.2	.3	.1
Yugoslavia	46.3	61.9	58.9	114.5	.2	65.7
Near East/south Asia:	303.1	352.3	384.8	896.2	471.4	1,382.7
Egypt	0	2.8	0	36.1	0	72.6
Greece	22.9	16.5	0	27.7	88.7	19.3
India	0	58.8	0	292.8	16.2	654.6
Iran	17.6	9.7	60.0	64.5	103.3	28.5
Israel	0	32.0	.1	54.2	110.8	22.1
Jordan	0	1.6	2.0	34.0	30.8	43.9
Pakistan	0	24.2	62.1	163.6	8.8	39.5
Turkey	144.0	56.7	162.1	129.3	165.9	153.4
East Asia:	278.1	690.9	773.6	897.6	1,221.5	857.2
Cambodia	0	0	8.5	27.5	3.0	7.2
China/Taiwan	56.6	114.7	209.0	109.2	113.5	36.5
Indonesia	.9	24.1	3.1	25.9	6.0	62.4
Japan	18.4	244.1	98.2	23.7	30.7	.4
Laos	0	0	12.3	33.4	51.8	49.2
Philippines	19.3	116.4	25.2	33.5	29.8	31.9
South Korea	3.2	133.1	183.4	299.9	338.9	207.3
Thailand	8.3	4.5	34.4	31.3	67.4	37.8
South Vietnam	n.a.	n.a.	65.8	193.1	737.9	388.3
Latin America:	28.0	27.0	54.7	189.4	99.4	784.7
Brazil	12.8	4.7	13.3	37.0	26.1	229.2
Chile	1.6	.7	4.9	21.2	12.9	92.9
Africa:	0	6.6	11.1	37.8	32.0	365.2
Morocco	n.a.	n.a.	.9	48.3	8.5	47.1
Tunisia	n.a.	n.a.	1.6	40.1	3.3	46.9
World	2,476.7	4,059.4	1,837.7	2,520.7	1,937.9	3,495.1

Source: U.S. Agency for International Development, *U.S. Overseas Loans and Grants: Series of Yearly Data,* vols. 1–5 (Washington, 1984).

Notes: Period averages are calculated from the year of independence, where applicable. "N.a." indicates a country was not yet independent during the period. Only countries that received an average of more than $25 million per year in 1949–1953 or 1954–1961 are included.

active perimeter defense strategy. In the view of U.S. policy makers, Iran's location on the northern tier of the Middle East made it vital for the defense of that region, for the forward defense of the Mediterranean region, and as a base for staging air or ground attacks into the Soviet Union. Iran's oil resources and those of the other Persian Gulf countries were crucial to the reconstruction of Western Europe and to the ability of the West to sustain a protracted war. Short of general war, Iran was also valuable as a base for staging intelligence-gathering operations against the Soviet Union, both cross-border espionage and, beginning in 1957, electronic surveillance directed at the Soviet missile-testing facilities in central Asia. For these various reasons, the Eisenhower administration labeled Iran "of critical importance" to U.S. national security.[19]

Initially, the Eisenhower administration's policy toward Iran under its version of the perimeter defense strategy focused simply on reducing political instability and eliminating the threat posed by the Tudeh party. These goals had largely been accomplished with the overthrow of Mosaddeq and the consolidation of power by Zahedi. U.S. policy makers therefore began to develop a new approach in early 1955 which sought to transform Iran "from a weak nation traditionally seeking a 'neutralist' position in world affairs into an anti-Communist asset."[20] This approach, which guided U.S. policy toward Iran for the remainder of Eisenhower's term, involved building a strong client state under the leadership of the shah and integrating Iran into an alliance with other U.S. allies in the region. An Iranian client state was expected to contribute to perimeter defense by maintaining political stability in Iran, helping to deter a Soviet invasion of the Middle East, and if necessary, joining in the defense of the Middle East by temporarily holding a front against Soviet forces in the Zagros Mountains of southwestern Iran. The decision to build a client state in Iran meant, in effect, that U.S. efforts to influence Iranian domestic politics would henceforth be primarily indirect, consisting of measures designed to enhance the Iranian state's ability to contain domestic unrest,

[19]U.S. National Security Council, *United States Policy toward Iran, NSC-175*, December 21, 1953, 1, and Annex, 13–16; idem, *A National Petroleum Program*, NSC-97/6, November 16, 1953. On U.S. intelligence-gathering activities based in Iran see Chap. 2, above, and James Bamford, *The Puzzle Palace* (Boston: Houghton Mifflin, 1982), 198–201. The electronic listening posts in Iran were of great importance in evaluating the "missile gap" scare that followed the launching of Sputnik in 1957 and became even more critical after the May 1960 U-2 incident, after which U-2 flights over the Soviet Union were suspended. The importance of these listening posts was stressed to me in confidential interviews with several former top U.S. officials and is briefly discussed by former CIA director Richard Helms in Martin F. Herz, ed., *Contacts with the Opposition* (Washington: Georgetown University, Institute for the Study of Diplomacy, 1979), 23.

[20]U.S. National Security Council, *U.S. Policy toward Iran*, NSC 5504, January 15, 1955, 1.

rather than direct measures aimed at strengthening or weakening specific societal actors. Thus the CIA discontinued almost entirely its covert political action programs in Iran in the mid-1950s and worked instead on intelligence gathering and on its training and liaison relationship with Iran's intelligence services.[21]

Despite the successful consolidation of a new regime in Iran, U.S. policy makers remained concerned that political unrest might soon reemerge. These concerns grew rapidly in 1956 and 1957, as the winds of nationalism swept through the Middle East. Several National Security Council policy guidance papers on Iran noted growing political unrest and recommended that the Iranian government be pressured to undertake political and economic reforms. In 1958, U.S. policy makers grew even more alarmed about Iran's domestic political situation after several reported coup plots and the July 1958 overthrow of the Iraqi monarchy. A November 1958 CIA study stated that the shah was likely to be overthrown "within a year or so" unless he were to begin a program of reforms. In response, the National Security Council adopted a new policy guidance paper on Iran in mid-November, designated NSC-5821/1, which called for major changes in U.S. policy. It stated that the shah's main base of support came from the "large landholders and their conservative business associates, the top ranks of the government bureaucracy, and senior military officers," and that the growing unrest was due to "awakening popular expectations for reform of Iran's archaic social, economic, and political structure." Arguing that the shah was not likely to carry out reforms on his own, NSC 5821/1 directed that pressure be brought to bear on him and that contact be established with any noncommunist

[21]In the mid- and late 1950s and early 1960s, the CIA maintained roughly half a dozen paid agents in the Tudeh party and somewhat fewer in the National Front, among them several well-known leaders of the two organizations. The CIA also had a long-standing agent with good contacts among the Shi'i clergy, a few agents in the Iranian student groups in Europe, and a few in key government agencies, such as the oil ministry. All were used to gather intelligence rather than to conduct covert political operations. Nevertheless, the CIA did carry out a few inconsequential covert political operations in Iran after the early 1950s. For example, it gave some financial assistance in the early 1960s to one of its Iranian agents who was running for a Majles seat. This was done as a favor to the agent, not as an attempt to increase U.S. influence in the Majles, which was by then no longer an important policy-making body. There were also some informational and cultural programs that were quite benign and were, in any case, designed mainly to improve the U.S. image and generate support for the shah's regime rather than to strengthen or weaken specific societal actors. The CIA also operated the electronic listening posts aimed at the Soviet Union and, oddly enough, even established a listening post in the U.S. embassy compound in Tehran in the mid-1960s to monitor radio transmissions by Iranian intelligence. All the material in this note comes from my interview with a retired CIA officer who was directly involved, and it was confirmed in broad outline by several other retired CIA officers and a former Iranian intelligence officer. The FBI also apparently monitored Iranian student groups in the United States; see *Washington Post*, August 9, 1979, A-12.

opposition group that might emerge. If the shah failed to undertake the necessary reforms, NSC 5821/1 recommended that the United States be prepared to reduce its identification with the shah and support a successor government.[22]

This policy guidance not withstanding, little was done about the growing crisis in Iran for the remainder of Eisenhower's term. The U.S. military and economic aid programs were expanded. The U.S. ambassador and the CIA station chief in Tehran were instructed to press the shah on reforms, and at least one high-level emissary went to Iran (in April 1959) with a similar message. Although the CIA station chief held frequent discussions with the shah on the issue of reform, the ambassador was apparently reluctant to do so. Moreover, Eisenhower himself met with the shah in December 1959 but apparently did not raise the issue of reform. The failure of U.S. officials to press more forcefully for reforms was due in part to the growing threat posed by Iraq and to the shah's flirtation with the Soviet Union, which reduced the ability of U.S. officials to exert influence over him. Furthermore, the shah was able to deflect U.S. pressures for reform temporarily by launching a token anticorruption drive and announcing a new seven-year development program.[23]

The Kennedy administration adopted the same basic view of U.S. strategic interests in Iran as its predecessor. However, the new administration, having come to office in the aftermath of a series of major crises in the Third World, adopted a new general strategy for U.S. foreign policy toward the Third World which differed considerably from that of the Eisenhower administration. This new strategy, together with growing domestic problems in Iran, produced major changes in U.S. policy toward Iran in the early 1960s.

The new strategy, which became known as "flexible response," advocated the use of a broader variety of foreign policy instruments to contain Soviet expansionism. In the view of Kennedy administration officials, the previous administration's reliance on nuclear rather than conventional military forces and its emphasis on security assistance and covert action to create client states in the Third World, together with its rigid ideological outlook, had left it incapable of dealing with Third World crises such as

[22]U.S. National Security Council, *Progress Report on United States Policy toward Iran*, NSC 5504, July 25, 1956; idem, *U.S. Policy toward Iran*, NSC 5703/1, February 8, 1957; idem, *Operational Guidance with Respect to Iran in Implementation of NSC 5703/1*, May 22, 1957; Wailes to Dulles, August 14, 1958, DDE Library; CIA, Office of National Estimates, "Prospects in Iran," November 10, 1958; U.S. National Security Council, *U.S. Policy toward Iran*, NSC 5821/1, November 15, 1958, 1–2, 15, 17.

[23]Interviews with the CIA station chief and with Fraser Wilkins, Washington, D.C., July 9, 1985; Donald N. Wilber, *Adventures in the Middle East: Excursions and Incursions* (Princeton, N.J.: Darwin, 1986), 190; Herter to Wailes, December 20, 1959, DDE Library; *New York Times*, October 22, 1958, 14:4, and November 5, 1958, 14:4.

the spread of Nasserism, the conflicts in Southeast Asia, and the emergence of Castro. Under flexible response, the Kennedy administration began to rebuild U.S. conventional forces, especially counterinsurgency units that could be used in the Third World. It also placed a greater emphasis on economic aid (see Table 4), on cultural programs like the Peace Corps, and on diplomatic efforts to foster peaceful political and socioeconomic change in the Third World. With political unrest widespread in Iran by early 1961, the Kennedy administration used these latter policy instruments extensively there. It also began to expand U.S. involvement in Third World countries not located along the Sino-Soviet periphery, reducing the salience of perimeter defense in U.S. global strategy.[24]

Soon after it entered office, the Kennedy administration established a special task force on Iran headed by Assistant Secretary of State Phillips Talbot. In May 1961 this task force issued a report that echoed many of the concerns and recommendations of NSC-5821/1. Its main recommendation was to give strong support to the newly installed reformist government of Ali Amini, including an immediate increase in U.S. economic aid and measures to forestall any military coup against him. Over the long term, the task force report recommended that U.S. officials encourage Iranian leaders to carry out social, economic, and political reforms and strengthen the armed forces; that the United States increase its contact with the nationalist opposition; and that moderate opposition figures be encouraged to resist pressures from more extreme opposition groups.[25]

These recommendations shaped U.S. policy toward Iran for the next two years. United States ambassador Edward Wailes and his successor, Julius Holmes, expressed strong support, both publicly and privately, for Amini and his reform program. Although U.S. officials did not threaten to reduce U.S. aid, they did pressure the shah gently but firmly to broaden his base of support and make overtures to the moderate opposition. Embassy and CIA personnel in Tehran increased their contact with the opposition, meeting with prominent opposition leaders and encouraging them to moderate their demands. Amini's tenure as prime minister did prove to be the start of a wide-ranging program of reform. Although it is impossible to determine the extent to which U.S. pressure was responsible for these reforms, top U.S. officials involved in these events believe it did play an important role.[26]

[24]Gaddis, *Strategies of Containment*, chap. 7; see also Robert A. Packenham, *Liberal America and the Third World* (Princeton, N.J.: Princeton University Press, 1973), 59–85.

[25]U.S. Department of State, Office of Director S/P, *A Review of Problems in Iran and Recommendations for the National Security Council*, May 15, 1961, Iran White Paper, doc. I.B-69.

[26]Interviews with Stuart Rockwell, Washington, D.C., July 16, 1985, and Phillips Talbot, New York, August 5, 1985; *Washington Post*, October 23, 1977, A-27. On U.S. contacts

By 1963, U.S. officials had become much more confident about the durability of the shah's regime. An April 1963 CIA study stated that while the shah remained "dependent on the continuing support of the armed forces and the security apparatus," his chances of remaining in power in the next few years were "relatively good." Shortly thereafter, the National Security Council issued a new policy guidance paper that advocated continued support for the shah's social and economic reforms but did not call for further pressure for political reform. The massive clergy-led demonstrations that erupted in June 1963 at first alarmed U.S. officials, but they quickly dismissed them as "a flash in the pan."[27]

The Johnson administration's global strategy differed little from that of its predecessor. It became increasingly preoccupied with the Vietnam War and later with the Arab-Israeli conflict, however, distracting its attention from Iran and further reducing the salience of perimeter defense. These preoccupations, together with U.S. policy makers' growing confidence in the shah's ability to contain domestic unrest, led the United States to reduce the scope of the cliency relationship considerably in the mid-1960s. Sharply declining U.S. military and economic aid reduced the ability of U.S. policy makers to pressure the shah for further reforms. The State Department and the CIA also drastically reduced their intelligence-gathering capabilities in Iran in the mid- and late 1960s. The size of the Tehran embassy's political section fell from twenty-one in 1963 to ten in 1969 and only six in 1972. The CIA dropped many of its Iranian agents, including all of its agents in the Tudeh party. Increasingly, it focused its intelligence-gathering capabilities on such matters as regional relations, Iran's oil and nuclear power industries, and the ability of the armed forces to absorb advanced military equipment, and it relied on Iran's intelligence services for information on domestic politics.[28]

The Nixon administration's global strategy reflected the U.S. experi-

---

with the opposition see Muslim Students Following the Line of the Imam, *Documents from the U.S. Espionage Den*, vols. 20–22 (Tehran: n.p., n.d.).

[27]CIA, *The Iranian Situation*, SNIE 34–63, April 10, 1963; U.S. National Security Council, *Report on United States Strategy for Iran: Reply to NSAM 228*, April 20, 1963; quotation is from Rockwell interview. For a prescient dissenting view on this NSC study see Executive Office of the President, Bureau of the Budget, "Memorandum for Mr. Komer," May 7, 1963, *Declass. Docs.*, vol. 5, no. 2 (1979), 226A.

[28]Iran White Paper, sec. III.D-(1); U.S. Department of State, *Foreign Service List* (Washington, various years); interview with a retired CIA officer. The figures on the size of the embassy's political section include some CIA officers, who were usually given positions in the embassy to provide them with cover and diplomatic immunity. The lists of U.S. embassy contacts published in Muslim Students, *Documents from the U.S. Espionage Dens*, vol. 17, 1–24, indicate that U.S. embassy officials had very little contact then with the Iranian opposition: of the seventy-five Iranian contacts named, I could identify only seven as possible members of the opposition.

ence in Vietnam. Under the guidance of Henry Kissinger, the administration developed several strategies for containing the Soviet Union which avoided entanglements like the Vietnam quagmire. One such strategy was the Nixon Doctrine, under which the United States sought to avoid direct involvement in proxy wars with the Soviet Union by heavily arming some of its Third World clients and encouraging them to combat Soviet proxy forces. Because of its strategic location and its neutrality in the Arab-Israeli conflict, Iran became an important focus of the Nixon Doctrine. The United States sold large amounts of sophisticated weaponry to Iran under the Nixon Doctrine and encouraged the shah to act as a policeman in regional conflicts between U.S. and Soviet allies. Outside of the Persian Gulf region, Iran became increasingly active in Africa and in the Arab-Israeli conflict. Moreover, with the emergence of this more equal relationship between the United States and Iran, U.S. policy makers were much less able to influence the shah and were forced to acquiesce to his desire for a reduction of U.S. intelligence-gathering activities inside Iran. By the early 1970s, the volume of CIA political reporting on Iran had apparently dropped below that of the late 1940s, and the U.S. embassy staff in Tehran included few officers who could speak Farsi or had served previous tours in Iran. The United States was thus entirely unprepared for the revolution that was to occur in Iran in 1978 and 1979.[29]

Unlike its predecessors, the Carter administration did not develop a coherent set of foreign policy principles that could be described as a global strategy. Although it placed considerable emphasis on promoting human rights in the Third World, this emphasis, by itself, did not constitute a strategy. The Carter administration initially pursued the same basic approach toward Iran as the Nixon and Ford administrations: it agreed to sell Iran large quantities of sophisticated weapons, and it consistently blocked the efforts of human rights advocates in the State Department and Congress to pressure the shah to undertake political liberalization.[30] Before the Carter administration could formulate a new global strategy, or even a new approach toward Iran, the first manifestations of the Iranian revolution began to appear. Moreover, President Carter and many of his top foreign policy advisers were preoccupied during most of 1978 with

[29]Gaddis, *Strategies of Containment*, chap. 9; interviews with Ambassador Douglas MacArthur (telephone, October 9, 1987) and the retired CIA officer mentioned in n. 28; William H. Sullivan, *Mission to Iran* (New York: Norton, 1981), 40; U.S. House of Representatives, Permanent Select Committee on Intelligence, *Iran: Evaluation of U.S. Intelligence Performance Prior to November 1978: Staff Report* (Washington, 1979). For a candid discussion of the inadequacies of CIA intelligence on Iran see CIA, "Research Study: Elites and the Distribution of Power in Iran," February 1976, reprinted in Muslim Students, *Documents from the U.S. Espionage Den*, vol. 7, 82–83.

[30]Sullivan, *Mission to Iran*, 19–22.

the negotiations that culminated in the Camp David agreement between Egypt and Israel. The Carter administration thus never managed to integrate Iran into a general plan for U.S. foreign policy.

Economic Assistance

After the 1953 coup, the United States sharply increased its economic aid to Iran. The roughly $68 million in U.S. economic aid given to Iran immediately after the coup was used mainly to supplement the Iranian government's budget, accounting for more than one-third of the estimated $200 million in oil revenue Iran had lost since May 1951 as a result of the British oil blockade. An additional $15 million in budgetary assistance provided in May 1954 brought total U.S. economic aid to Iran in fiscal year (FY) 1954 to $84.5 million. Together with $25.6 million in military aid, total U.S. aid to Iran in FY 1954 accounted for 60 percent of Iranian government expenditures in that year (see Table 5).[31] Since Iran's oil revenue was negligible, the remainder of the Iranian government's expenditures in FY 1954 had to be financed mainly through domestic and foreign borrowing. Iran's oil revenue grew rapidly after the October 1954 oil agreement, but U.S. policy makers believed it would need U.S. economic aid for several more years to carry out the economic improvements needed to achieve long-term political stability. Accordingly, the emergency economic aid program begun after the coup was replaced in November 1954 with a more permanent program, under which U.S. economic aid grants and loans averaged $75 million per year in FYs 1955 and 1956.[32]

Iran's economy had largely recovered from the effects of the oil blockade by the end of 1955, so U.S. policy makers concluded that budgetary assistance was no longer needed. Moreover, both the shah and U.S. military planners wanted to build up Iran's armed forces. In 1956, U.S. policy makers therefore undertook a comprehensive review of the U.S. economic

[31] *New York Times*, September 30, 1953, 8:3; Iran White Paper, sec. IV.D, 3. Since the aid figures in Table 5 refer to the fiscal year *ending* in the year shown and the remaining figures refer to the Iranian calendar year *beginning* in the year shown, the FY 1954 aid figures are not strictly comparable to the Iranian government expenditure figure for 1954; they are more appropriately compared with the 1953 government expenditure figure. Although the percentage figure given here and similar figures given below slightly understate the relative magnitude of U.S. aid to Iran because of this problem of comparability, I have decided to make these comparisons in this manner for the sake of simplicity.

[32] Iran White Paper, sec. IV.D, 3–6; U.S. Agency for International Development, *U.S. Overseas Loans and Grants: Series of Yearly Data*, vol. 1, Near East and South Asia (Washington, 1984).

Table 5. Iran's domestic and external finances (in millions of current U.S. dollars)

	U.S. aid to Iran								Iranian domestic finances			
Year	Total aid (1)	Aid grants (2)	Aid loans (3)	Other loans (4)	Economic grants (5)	Military grants (6)	U.S. direct investment (7)	World bank loans (8)	Oil revenue (9)	Government spending (10)	Plan spending (11)	GDFCF[a] (12)
1950	11.8	11.8	0	0	0	11.8	1.0	0	25.0	297.2	10.2	366.7
1951	27.8	27.8	0	0	1.5	26.3	1.0	0	n.a.	208.7	4.2	281.0
1952	44.1	44.1	0	0	15.0	29.1	1.0	0	n.a.	n.a.	2.2	285.1
1953	52.5	52.5	0	0	31.9	20.6	1.0	0	n.a.	n.a.	2.1	292.3
1954	110.1	110.1	0	0	84.5	25.6	25.0	0	36.7	183.3	15.9	373.9
1955	90.7	58.7	32.0	48.7	43.2	15.5	57.0	0	33.0	293.1	21.7	450.2
1956	97.7	85.3	12.4	0	62.3	23.0	76.0	0	85.8	308.9	129.4	534.7
1957	138.5	115.5	23.0	0	33.0	82.5	125.0	75.0	138.6	406.6	129.9	609.9
1958	157.0	117.0	40.0	0	12.1	104.9	178.0	0	216.5	524.1	188.6	786.8
1959	132.6	94.3	37.7	0	9.7	84.6	176.0	72.0	239.6	632.3	189.5	657.4
1960	123.4	123.4	0	0	38.1	85.3	179.0	47.2	262.7	694.4	241.3	763.0
1961	146.8	94.9	51.9	21.3	36.3	58.6	205.0	0	282.5	723.4	252.9	698.3
1962	113.4	88.6	24.8	0	43.9	44.7	209.0	0	299.7	722.1	213.6	629.7
1963	103.5	81.3	22.2	0	20.6	60.7	221.0	0	338.0	735.3	245.5	679.9
1964	54.7	49.4	5.3	8.5	12.5	36.9	217.0	18.5	372.3	847.5	352.5	823.8
1965	101.6	39.7	61.9	21.7	5.6	34.1	325.0	40.5	491.1	986.1	488.4	1,128.7
1966	175.1	71.0	103.2	1.8	7.4	64.5	314.0	10.0	625.7	1,411.2	500.3	1,188.1
1967	202.4	39.8	162.6	102.3	3.2	36.6	317.0	25.0	727.3	1,771.9	714.0	1,577.5
1968	124.1	24.3	100.0	39.7	2.3	22.0	382.0	47.0	837.5	2,167.7	926.7	1,817.5

1969	128.4	24.1	104.3	6.5	1.4	22.7	402.0	70.0	620.6	3,553.8	1,098.0	2,073.9
1970	4.0	4.0	0	44.7	1.4	2.6	319.0	48.5	790.8	5,580.0	1,264.7	2,190.4
1971	3.3	3.3	0	203.6	1.2	2.1	309.0	165.0	885.0	5,197.7	1,518.7	2,837.1
1972	16.0	16.0	0	143.2	2.4	13.6	313.0	125.0	1,590.7	5,925.6	1,725.6	3,762.8
1973	1.6	1.6	0	281.9	1.3	.3	129.0	149.5	2,593.1	8,412.4	2,345.8	5,286.7
1974	1.4	1.4	0	290.6	1.4	0	−561.0	265.0	4,603.3	11,608.7	5,156.4	8,310.5
1975	1.7	1.7	0	5.3	1.7	0	−98.0	52.5	17,818.1	28,134.7	7,788.4	15,754.2
1976	1.1	1.1	0	40.0	1.1	0	−360.0	0	17,755.1	32,898.5	8,424.7	21,046.1
1977	0	0	0	0	0	0	−144.0	0	19,952.7	44,657.8	13,124.3	25,941.3
1978	0	0	0	17.9	0	0	392.0	0	20,376.0	50,090.1	8,119.2	n.a.

Sources: Cols. 1–6: U.S. Agency for International Development, *U.S. Overseas Loans and Grants: Series of Yearly Data,* vol. 1, *Near East and South Asia* (Washington, 1984); Col. 7: (1950–76) U.S. Department of Commerce, Bureau of Economic Analysis, *Selected Data on U.S. Direct Investment Abroad, 1950–1976* (Washington, 1982), 1–27; (1977–78) worksheets provided by the Department of Commerce; Col. 8: International Bank for Reconstruction and Development (World Bank), *Annual Report* (Washington, various years); Cols. 9–10: United Nations, *Statistical Yearbook* (New York, various years); Col. 11: (1950–62) Julian Bharier, *Economic Development in Iran, 1900–1970* (London: Oxford University Press, 1971), 68; (1963–78) Bank Markazi Iran, *Annual Report and Balance Sheet* (Tehran, various years); Col. 12: (1950–58) Bharier, *Economic Development in Iran,* 50–51; (1959–78) United Nations, *Yearbook of National Account Statistics* (New York, various years).

Notes: U.S. aid data for the 1976–77 transitional quarter (when the U.S. fiscal year was changed) are included in the 1976 figures. Other loans (Col. 3) are mainly Export-Import Bank loans. The data in Col. 7 refer to the *stock* of *net* U.S. direct investment in Iran; negative values indicate that Iranian investment in the United States exceeded U.S. investment in Iran. Data in Cols. 1–6 and 8 refer to the fiscal years ending in June (or September, after 1976) of the year shown; data in Col. 7 refer to the Gregorian calendar year; and data in Cols. 9–12 refer to the Iranian calendar year beginning in March of the year shown. In Cols. 9–12, rials are converted to dollars using exchange rates given in (1950–54) International Monetary Fund, *International Financial Statistics: 1971 Supplement* (Washington, 1971), 122–23; and (1955–78) idem, *International Financial Statistics: 1983 Yearbook* (Washington, 1983), 280–91. The average of the buying and selling rates for the rial is used for 1950–54 exchange rates; the period average market rate is used for 1955–78. In Col. 9, values for 1956 and 1959 were not given in the source used to construct this series; the values shown in the table are the averages of the values given for the preceding and subsequent year.

[a]GDFCF is "gross domestic fixed capital formation."

and military aid programs in Iran under the auspices of a committee headed by Deputy Undersecretary of State Herbert Prochnow. The Prochnow committee concluded that a moderate level of economic development and a substantial military buildup would require a major shift of U.S. aid away from budgetary assistance and toward increased technical and military assistance in FYs 1957–60.[33] Budgetary assistance was therefore largely discontinued after FY 1956, and economic aid was reduced in favor of a large increase in military aid (see Table 5).

Political unrest began to grow in Iran in the late 1950s, especially after the July 1958 coup in Iraq. Moreover, widespread corruption and the shah's failure to undertake much-needed economic reforms had produced economic stagnation by the end of the decade. United States policy makers responded to these emerging problems by increasing economic aid grants by roughly $30 million per year beginning in FY 1960, reducing military aid by a similar amount the next year, and providing Iran with a $21.3 million Export-Import Bank loan (see Table 5). By 1961, a major crisis was brewing. In May, the Kennedy administration's special task force recommended that economic aid be increased immediately and military aid be continued at the current (reduced) level. Both military and economic aid remained at roughly these levels for several more years, with loans gradually replacing grants. The U.S. aid program in Iran was officially discontinued in November 1967, although small amounts of previously allocated aid continued to flow for several more years.[34]

To understand how this economic aid affected the Iranian state's autonomy, we need to take a closer look at how it was used and what effect it had on the Iranian economy. After accounting for 60 percent of the Iranian government's expenditures in FY 1954, U.S. military and economic aid grants together averaged 22 percent of government expenditures in the 1955–59 period and 14 percent in the 1960–63 period; U.S. loans (including Export-Import Bank loans) accounted for another 9 percent and 4 percent respectively. United States aid was thus a major source of revenue for the Iranian state in the decade after the 1953 coup, helping it finance social services, economic development projects, and domestic security forces and therefore enhancing its ability to co-opt and repress domestic societal groups. Table 5 shows that U.S. loans and grants to Iran equaled 80 percent of spending by the Plan Organization (the main state agency charged with promoting economic development) and 21

[33]U.S. National Security Council, *Report by the Interdepartmental Committee on Certain U.S. Aid Programs*, NSC-5610, Iran Annex, August 3, 1956.
[34]U.S. Department of State, *Review of Problems in Iran*, 44.

percent of gross domestic fixed capital formation (GDFCF) in the decade. These figures suggest that Iran's economic growth was significantly enhanced by the U.S. aid program.[35]

Table 5 also contains data on Iran's oil revenue (see Col. 9). A comparison of these figures with those for total U.S. aid to Iran indicates that Iran's oil revenue only began to exceed its U.S. aid receipts by a significant amount in 1958. Oil revenue and income from U.S. aid programs accounted for similar amounts of Iran's total spending in the 1954–59 period (33 and 31 percent, respectively) but diverged sharply in the 1960s as oil exports grew. Oil revenue amounted to 119 percent of Plan Organization spending and 31 percent of GDFCF in the 1954–63 period, roughly 50 percent higher than the proportions contributed by U.S. loans and grants. Oil income was the main engine of growth in the 1960s and 1970s, easily exceeding total Plan Organization spending in these two decades and amounting to 49 percent of GDFCF in the 1964–77 period.

Aggregate figures such as these give only a rough indication of how U.S. economic aid affected the Iranian economy. A more detailed picture emerges from an examination of how this aid was used. The $709.7 million in U.S. economic aid provided between 1950 and 1965 fell into three broad categories: 67.4 percent was capital assistance, another 15.9 percent was Food for Peace aid, and the remaining 16.7 percent was financing for technical assistance.[36]

Capital assistance was used for two main purposes. First, something less than half of the total amount given was used as budgetary support for the Iranian government, especially in FYs 1954–56, when approximately $150 million was used for this purpose. Second, the remainder was used to finance development projects, which were then carried out with U.S. technical assistance. In 1955, 1961, and after 1963, U.S. development financing was supplemented with large Export-Import Bank loans (see Table 5). The U.S. government also encouraged private American capital and the World Bank to invest in Iran in this period, and each played a role in financing Iran's development efforts (see Cols. 7 and 8 of Table 5).[37]

The way Iran spent its $60 million in U.S. budgetary assistance in the first year after the coup reflects Iran's general use of U.S. budgetary

[35]Although relatively little of this aid contributed directly to Plan Organization spending or to GDFCF, it did offset state spending. To ensure comparability across time, the percentages based on Table 5 given in this paragraph and below were calculated from an inflation-adjusted version of the figures in the table. The inflation index used for this purpose was the GDP deflator given in International Monetary Fund, *International Financial Statistics Yearbook, 1983* (Washington, 1983), 280–81.

[36]U.S. AID Mission to Iran, *Summary Highlights of A.I.D. Economic Assistance Activities in Iran* (n.p., 1966), AID Library.

[37]Ibid., 43–46.

support. Of this $60 million, $27 million went to pay the salaries of government employees, who had been paid irregularly under Mosaddeq because of the fiscal problems associated with the oil blockade. In November 1953, $3 million of this $27 million went into pay raises for government employees, which averaged 4.4 percent. A further $12.2 million paid the expenses of the NIOC, which consisted mainly of the salaries of some fifty thousand disgruntled oil workers, and $1.4 million provided bonuses to the army, police, and Gendarmerie. United States budgetary assistance also financed imports of consumer goods such as sugar, tea, medical supplies, cotton and wool fabrics, auto and truck parts, and high-visibility social service projects such as street paving, a malaria eradication program, and the construction of schools, low-cost housing, hospitals, a nationwide telecommunications system, and a water system for Tehran. United States aid provided over two million worker-days of direct employment and several million more indirectly. The increased availability of dollars in Iran caused by the U.S. aid program also brought inflation down to reasonable levels by the end of 1954.[38] There can be little doubt that these measures were important in preventing popular unrest in this critical period and thus in helping to consolidate the post-Mosaddeq regime.

As U.S. capital assistance went increasingly into development projects in the late 1950s and early 1960s, U.S. Food for Peace aid subsidized the commodity imports that had been financed with capital assistance in the mid-1950s. Food for Peace aid increased from virtually nothing before FY 1956 to an average of $3.1 million per year in FYs 1956–60 and $15.3 million per year in FYs 1961–66. Under this program, surplus U.S. agricultural products such as wheat, rice, dry milk, butter, vegetable oil, cotton, and feed grains were provided through grants and loans payable in Iranian currency. About one-third of the Food for Peace aid was disaster relief assistance for victims of earthquakes, droughts, floods, and cold weather.[39]

Budgetary support and Food for Peace aid brought about fairly rapid improvements in the welfare of the Iranian people and therefore helped promote political stability in the short term. By contrast, the development projects financed with U.S. capital assistance and Export-Import Bank loans and implemented with U.S. technical assistance were aimed at achieving more sustained improvements in living conditions and therefore at promoting political stability in the long term. These projects were

[38] Ibid., 37–41; U.S. House of Representatives, Committee on Government Operations, *United States Aid Operations in Iran*, House Report No. 10, 85th Cong., 1st sess., January 28, 1957, 45–48.

[39] U.S. AID Mission, *Summary Highlights*, 47–54; U.S. Agency for International Development, *U.S. Overseas Loans and Grants*, vol. 1.

mainly of three kinds:[40] economic development projects, both in agriculture and industry; social welfare projects, particularly in public health and education; and administrative reforms, including a public administration program and community and labor development projects.

Because agriculture was still important to the Iranian economy at this time, agricultural development was a major focus of the U.S. technical assistance program. Probably the most effective aspect of U.S. agricultural assistance was its focus on education. Many Iranian farmers and technicians received training in modern agricultural techniques, both in the United States and in Iran. U.S. advisers helped establish a variety of agricultural training facilities in Iran, including the Karaj Agriculture College, a series of vocational agricultural schools, an agricultural extension service, and many demonstration farms and livestock stations. Several major projects were carried out under the U.S. aid program to improve agricultural productivity, including pest control programs, groundwater and river control projects, and the establishment of rural cooperatives and the Agriculture Credit and Rural Development Bank. Technicians associated with the U.S. aid program also provided advice on such matters as irrigation, livestock breeding, soil classification, and the use of new crop varieties, fertilizers, and cultivation techniques.[41]

Industrial development assistance consisted mainly of projects designed to promote further industrialization by improving the country's economic infrastructure. Major projects improved Iran's highways, ports, airports, railroad system, telecommunications network, and public water facilities. Plans were drawn up to coordinate and develop Iran's national electric power system. Power generating facilities were upgraded in Tehran and other major cities. Intensive geologic surveys promoted the exploitation of Iran's plentiful nonoil mineral resources. The U.S. Agency for International Development made large loans to the Industrial Mining and Development Bank of Iran, which served as a primary source of financing for private industrialization efforts. More specific projects developed the textile, cement, bottle-making, and sugar-refining industries.[42]

Technical assistance also encompassed social welfare projects. Many Iranian doctors and public health officials were trained in the United States and in Iran under the U.S. aid program. Public health programs

[40]A fourth kind of project, public safety, is, because of its security implications, discussed below with security assistance programs.

[41]U.S. AID Mission, *Summary Highlights*, 14–20; USOM-Iran, *Review of U.S. Technical Assistance and Economic Aid to Iran, 1951–1957*, 4 vols. (n.p., n.d.), chaps. 9–10, AID Library.

[42]U.S. AID Mission, *Summary Highlights*, 28–31; USOM-Iran, *Review of U.S. Technical Assistance*, chap. 5.

were established in several of Iran's medical schools, as was a public health research and training institute at the University of Tehran. Very successful programs were begun to combat diseases such as malaria and smallpox. United States advisers also helped establish a network of rural public health centers and a program for teaching basic hygiene in public schools. The U.S. aid program also established teacher training programs and helped construct and equip many schools and training centers. Perhaps the most noteworthy effort in education was a major project carried out through the University of Pennsylvania to expand Pahlavi University in Shiraz.[43]

Of the many steps the U.S. aid program took to increase the efficiency of Iran's antiquated administrative infrastructure, the most notable was a large public administration training and assistance program carried out in part through the University of Southern California's School of Public Administration. Under this program, organizational and procedural studies were made of each cabinet ministry to improve their operational efficiency. Other programs began upgrading the government's financial management practices, especially accounting, auditing, budgeting, and tax and customs administration. A modern civil service code was drawn up and implemented. A statistical information system was established to collect reliable demographic and economic data. Other efforts focused on promoting administrative decentralization and improving municipal-level taxation, budgeting, accounting, and personnel administration procedures. Training programs were begun in tax administration, budgeting, accounting, auditing, records management, and personnel administration. Tehran University's Institute for Administrative Affairs was established with U.S. assistance, and most of its faculty were educated in the United States. The U.S. aid program also provided managerial assistance to the Plan Organization through the Washington-based Governmental Affairs Institute.[44]

United States efforts to improve Iran's administrative infrastructure also included community and labor development programs. The basic goals of the community development program were to strengthen potential democratic institutions, promote local self-government, and foster self-reliance among the rural population. Village councils were set up in some rural areas to administer agricultural development projects and

[43]U.S. AID Mission, *Summary Highlights*, 23–28; USOM-Iran, *Review of U.S. Technical Assistance*, chaps. 11–12.

[44]USOM-Iran, *Review of U.S. Technical Assistance*, chaps. 3–4; University of Southern California, School of Public Administration, *Seven Years in Iran: The Final Report of a Technical Assistance Project in Public Administration* (Los Angeles, 1962); Jahangir Amuzegar, *Technical Assistance in Theory and Practice: The Case of Iran* (New York: Praeger, 1966), 16.

implement the government's land reform program. United States advisers provided these councils with administrative training and with financing for agricultural loans and construction projects. Advisers were also attached to the Ministry of Labor to train its employees in the fundamentals of labor demand analysis, occupational analysis, and placement. Apprenticeship programs were begun for foundry workers, boilermakers, blacksmiths, machinists, plumbers, pipefitters, patternmakers, textile workers, carpenters, and automobile and locomotive repairmen. Training manuals were compiled and translated into Farsi for vehicle and equipment maintenance, electrical work, textile plant operation, and other skills.[45]

For our purposes the most important consequence of the U.S. economic aid program in Iran was that it helped the Iranian state co-opt many groups that were potential sources of unrest and therefore enhanced its autonomy. Budgetary assistance and Food for Peace aid helped reduce unrest by financing the state's expenditures on salary increases, consumer goods, and social services and by providing food products and disaster relief directly to the Iranian people. Assistance of this kind was especially important immediately after the coup. Technical assistance and development financing helped reduce unrest in the long term by improving the country's economic and administrative infrastructure, thereby enhancing economic growth and the effectiveness of the state bureaucracy.

Security Assistance

Under the Truman administration, the main purpose of the U.S. military aid program in Iran had been to enhance the armed forces' ability to maintain domestic security, primarily by curbing urban unrest and tribal disturbances. Toward this end, the U.S. military mission had been reorganized in 1947 and again in 1950, when it became known as the U.S. Military Assistance Advisory Group (MAAG). The main purpose of MAAG was to train and assist the Iranian army in using the military equipment provided under the U.S. military aid program. Although \$67.4 million in U.S. military aid to Iran had been budgeted for the 1950–52 period, only \$17.4 million in aid had actually been delivered. The Eisenhower administration in its first year in office followed the same basic approach, providing a further \$27.8 million in U.S. military aid.[46]

[45]U.S. AID Mission, *Summary Highlights*, 21–23, 31; USOM-Iran, *Review of U.S. Technical Assistance*, chaps. 8, 13.

[46]U.S. National Security Council, *United States Policy regarding the Present Situation in Iran*, NSC-136/1, November 20, 1952, 3; Thomas M. Ricks, "U.S. Military Missions to Iran, 1943–1978: The Political Economy of Military Assistance," *Iranian Studies* 12 (Summer–Autumn 1979), 168–77; U.S. Department of Defense, Defense Security Assistance Agency, *Fiscal Year Series, 1980* (Washington, 1980), 82–83.

After the Zahedi government had established an adequate degree of political stability, U.S. policy makers began to consider expanding the capabilities of the Iranian armed forces. Toward this end, they began a wide-ranging review in early 1954 to determine what role the Iranian armed forces could play in U.S. global defense strategy. This review and subsequent discussions with the shah resulted in early 1955 in a decision to strengthen the Iranian armed forces sufficiently to enable them to conduct defensive delaying actions in the Zagros Mountains in the event of a Soviet invasion. This decision would change the basic mission of the Iranian armed forces: the task of maintaining domestic security would gradually be turned over to the Gendarmerie and the National Police, and the armed forces would concentrate mainly on national defense. Moreover, it was understood that Iran would soon join a U.S.-sponsored regional defense organization then being planned, which came to be known as the Baghdad Pact.[47]

The type and volume of U.S. military aid provided to Iran in the mid-1950s reflected these changing priorities. Despite strong pressure from the shah for a rapid military buildup, U.S. policy makers decided in early 1955 that a major U.S. effort to strengthen the Iranian armed forces should be put off until Iran had officially joined the Baghdad Pact (which occurred in November 1955) and its military needs had been fully assessed. Moreover, military aid was to be conditional on the health of the economy and the ability of the armed forces to absorb new equipment. In the meantime, moderate amounts of military aid would suffice. Five U.S. military training teams, consisting of a total of 65 officers and 125 enlisted men, were attached to the Iranian army at the division and brigade levels, and plans were made to train Iranian army units to defend strategic passes in the Zagros Mountains. The United States also agreed at this time to provide Iran with F-84G jet fighters and other modern equipment.[48]

As it turned out, the final decision to expand Iran's military capabilities was not made until early 1957. In 1956 the Prochnow committee report on the U.S. aid programs in Iran concluded that the capability of the Iranian armed forces to defend a front in the Zagros Mountains for up to thirty days could be developed by roughly doubling U.S. military aid for four years. Also, 1956 saw the rapid spread of militant nationalism and an

[47]U.S. Embassy, Tehran, "Shah's Proposals regarding Expansion of United States Aid to Iranian Armed Forces," April 7, 1954, Record Group 59, Box 4117; U.S. National Security Council, *U.S. Policy toward Iran*, NSC-5504, 7; idem, Operations Coordinating Board, *Progress Report on NSC 5402 (Iran)*, October 15, 1954, 6 DDE Library.

[48]Operations Coordinating Board, *Progress Report on NSC 5402*, 11–12; Iran White Paper, sec. I.B, 26; U.S. National Security Council, *U.S. Policy toward Iran*, NSC-5504, 27–28.

increase in Soviet influence in the Middle East, especially after Egyptian president Gamal Abdel Nasser nationalized the Suez Canal. In response, the Eisenhower administration began to formulate a new strategy for containing Soviet influence in the Middle East which became known as the Eisenhower Doctrine. This strategy, which was formally articulated in a March 1957 congressional resolution, called for increased U.S. aid to countries in the Middle East that were threatened by the Soviet Union or its proxies. Plans to expand the U.S. military aid program in Iran were necessarily delayed until the full implications of the Eisenhower Doctrine for Iran could be assessed.[49]

A firm decision to expand U.S. military aid to Iran came in February 1957, while Congress was debating the Eisenhower Doctrine, and details of the new aid package were worked out in the following months. As shown in Table 6, U.S. military aid to Iran increased sharply between FY 1956 and FY 1957 (which ended on June 30, 1957), enabling Iran's military expenditures to increase by 69 percent. This sharp increase in military aid was offset by a reduction in economic aid. The number of U.S. military advisers in Iran also grew rapidly after FY 1956, as did the number of Iranian military personnel being trained in the United States (see Table 6). Of the $240 million in U.S. military aid earmarked for Iran in early 1957 for FYs 1958–60, 47 percent was to be spent on military equipment and supplies, including more F-84G fighters and other aircraft, naval vessels, tanks, armored cars, trucks, artillery, communications equipment, small arms, and a thirty-day supply of ammunition. A further 39 percent was to be spent on military construction projects, including access roads, barracks, and airbases in Tehran, Dezful, and Qom. The remainder was earmarked for training and shipping costs. After the July 1958 coup in Iraq, $28.6 million in U.S. budgetary assistance to Iran was diverted to the armed forces, deliveries of previously committed equipment were speeded up, and the United States authorized an expansion of the Iranian armed forces by thrity-seven thousand troops.[50]

In the wake of the Iraqi coup, the shah intensified his efforts to obtain more U.S. military aid, ultimately submitting a request for $600 million in additional aid in January 1960. But U.S. policy makers were becoming increasingly concerned that Iran's military buildup was placing serious

[49]U.S. National Security Council, *Report by the Interdepartmental Committee, Iran Annex*, 7–8. On the Eisenhower Doctrine see John C. Campbell, *Defense of the Middle East: Problems of American Policy*, rev. ed. (New York: Praeger, 1960), chaps. 8–9.

[50]U.S. National Security Council, *U.S. Policy toward Iran*, NSC-5703/1, 7, and Financial Appendix, 16–17; U.S. Joint Chiefs of Staff, "Briefing Paper for Presidential Use in Discussions with the Shah of Iran," June 9, 1958, 6–7, DDE Library; U.S. National Security Council, *U.S. Policy toward Iran*, NSC-5821/1, 12; Wailes to Herter, August 19, 1958, DDE Library.

Table 6. United States military assistance to Iran

Year	U.S. military aid (1)	U.S. military sales (2)	Iranian military expenditures (3)	Iranian military trainees (4)	U.S. military advisers (5)	Iranian military personnel (6)
1950	11.8	0	68.8	0	n.a.	n.a.
1951	26.3	0	51.2	0	11	135,000
1952	29.1	0	42.7	103	29	n.a.
1953	20.6	0	41.5	149	53	n.a.
1954	25.6	0	50.3	196	n.a.	n.a.
1955	15.5	0	64.7	98	n.a.	n.a.
1956	23.0	0	81.9	227	403	n.a.
1957	82.5	0	138.1	363	408	n.a.
1958	104.9	0	168.6	660	439	143,000
1959	84.6	0	207.2	190	794	n.a.
1960	85.3	.1	181.6	947	704	n.a.
1961	58.6	.2	187.2	1,346	573	185,000
1962	44.7	.7	186.9	1,095	561	200,000
1963	60.7	.1	191.2	1,077	496	208,000
1964	36.9	.2	219.2	950	509	208,000
1965	34.1	12.9	301.3	609	473	206,000
1966	64.5	33.2	414.1	480	467	225,000
1967	36.6	38.9	528.4	408	467	225,000
1968	22.0	56.7	603.7	318	447	225,000
1969	22.7	94.9	556.6	765	471	230,000
1970	2.6	127.7	714.5	504	389	238,000
1971	2.1	106.9	733.7	354	315	255,000
1972	13.6	257.2	1,098.3	186	315	265,000
1973	.3	264.8	1,820.5	0	760	285,000
1974	1.4	682.8	4,730.5	0	871	310,000
1975	1.7	1,035.2	6,697.3	0	872	385,000
1976	1.1	1,998.9	7,789.6	0	1,077	420,000
1977	0	2,550.0	7,958.4	0	1,034	350,000
1978	0	1,801.8	9,506.9	0	n.a.	350,000

Sources: Col. 1: U.S. Agency for International Development, *U.S. Overseas Loans and Grants: Series of Yearly Data,* vol. 1, *Near East and Southeast Asia* (Washington, 1984); Cols. 2, 4: U.S. Department of Defense, Defense Security Assistance Agency, *Fiscal Year Series, 1980* (Washington, 1980), 82–83; Col. 3: (1950–55) Stockholm International Peace Research Institute, *Yearbook of World Armaments and Disarmament 1968/69* (London: Duckworth, 1969), 206; (1956–78) idem, *World Armaments and Disarmament SIPRI Yearbook 1980* (London: Taylor and Francis, 1980), 26; Col. 5: (1951) U.S. Embassy, Tehran to Dept. of State, March 11, 1951, Record Group 59, Box 4118; (1952–53) "Fiscal Year 1954 Mutual Defense Assistance Program Budget Estimate, MAAG, Iran," February 20, 1953, Record Group 334, Box 2; (1956–77) U.S. Senate, Committee on Foreign Relations, *U.S. Military Sales to Iran,* 94th Cong., 2d sess., July 1976, 34–36; Col. 6: (1951) "Strength of the Iranian Armed Forces," September 11, 1951, Record Group 59, Box 4118; (1958) National Security Council, *U.S. Policy toward Iran, NSC-5821/1,* November 15, 1958, 12; (1961–70) U.S. Arms Control and Disarmament Agency, *World Military Expenditures, 1971* (Washington, 1972), 36; (1971–78) idem, *World Military Expenditures and Arms Transfers, 1969–1978* (Washington, 1980), 94.

Notes: Figures in Cols. 1–3 are in millions of current U.S. dollars. Iranian military trainees (Col. 4) are those trained in the United States. U.S. military advisers (Col. 5) include members of the MAAG unit and technical assistance field teams (which began to operate in Iran in 1969) but not advisers assigned to the Iranian Gendarmerie or employees of private U.S. defense contractors.

strains on its fragile economy and fueling domestic unrest. Moreover, congressional hearings in the late 1950s had uncovered evidence of widespread corruption and mismanagement in the U.S. aid programs in Iran. These concerns produced a decision in 1959 to reduce military aid for FY 1960 and increase economic aid in the following years (see Table 5).[51]

By the time the Kennedy administration entered office in early 1961, domestic political problems in Iran had become acute. The administration's special task force on Iran recommended in May 1961 that military aid be kept at the current reduced levels and that the Iranian armed forces be encouraged to undertake reforms such as assigning army units to carry out civic action projects and providing vocational and literacy training to draftees. As Table 6 shows, the concerns expressed by U.S. policy makers slowed the military buildup that had begun in 1957. The United States also authorized the Iranian armed forces to adopt a "forward defense" strategy under which army and air force units were redeployed into the northern regions to defend Iran's borders, rather than simply a front in the Zagros Mountains, against a Soviet or Iraqi invasion.[52]

Fueled by growing oil exports, the Iranian economy expanded rapidly in the mid-1960s. An increasingly confident shah continued to press for a military buildup and took steps to distance his regime from the United States, threatening to sign a nonaggression treaty with the Soviet Union and making a large arms purchase from the Soviets in 1967. As a result, the United States discontinued military and economic aid programs in November 1967, reducing the intensity of the cliency relationship. United States military aid to Iran was gradually replaced with a military sales program in the mid-1960s, and U.S. training of Iranian military personnel declined as well (Table 6).[53]

No longer dependent on U.S. aid, the shah began a massive military buildup in the late 1960s, purchasing advanced U.S. military equipment such as F-4 fighters and M-47 tanks. In May 1972, President Nixon agreed to permit the shah to purchase virtually any type of conventional weaponry in the U.S. arsenal, including advanced F-14 and AWACS aircraft, Phoenix and Maverick missiles, Spruance-class destroyers, and a

[51]Iran White Paper, sec. I.B, 31; U.S. National Security Council, *U.S. Policy toward Iran*, NSC-6010, June 8, 1960, 12; idem, Operations Coordinating Board, *Report on Iran*, December 9, 1959, 4–6; U.S. House, *United States Aid Operations*.

[52]U.S. Department of State, *Review of Problems in Iran*; interview with Talbot; Holmes to Rusk, September 22, 1962, JFK Library. The task force recommendations for military reform were echoed by Defense Department specialists on Iran at this time; see "Observations on the Situation in Iran," n.d. *Declass. Docs.*, vol. 7, no. 2 (1981) p. 145A.

[53]Iran White Paper, sec. I.B, 39–49; Rouhollah K. Ramazani, *Iran's Foreign Policy, 1941–1973 A Study of Foreign Policy in Modernizing Nations* (Charlottesville: University Press of Virginia, 1975), chap. 13.

five hundred million dollar IBEX electronic surveillance system. This decision, together with the quadrupling of world oil prices in late 1973 and early 1974, resulted in a 600-percent increase in Iranian military expenditures between 1972 and 1977 and a tenfold increase in U.S. military sales to Iran in this period (Table 6). By the late 1970s, massive U.S. arms sales to Iran had created serious management and supply problems in the Iranian armed forces and fueled growing unrest in Iran. But despite President Carter's emphasis on human rights and his desire to reduce U.S. foreign military sales, the policy of unlimited Iranian access to U.S. conventional weaponry continued under the Carter administration.[54]

As part of its strategy of strengthening anti-Soviet forces in the Third World, the Eisenhower administration began a major effort in the mid-1950s to train and equip paramilitary, police, and intelligence services in friendly Third World countries. This initiative was intended both to enhance internal security in the affected countries and to enable the regular armed forces in these countries to concentrate on external threats.[55] Although the United States had been giving limited assistance of this kind to some Third World countries before this initiative, such assistance had not been an important instrument of U.S. foreign policy. In Iran, three internal security services received training of this kind from the United States: the Gendarmerie, a paramilitary force whose main task was to maintain order in rural areas; the National Police; and the intelligence unit established under General Teimur Bakhtiar in 1953. These three organizations served as the shah's main instruments of repression, leaving the armed forces free to deter external threats.

United States assistance to the Gendarmerie had begun in 1942, when the U.S. Army Mission to the Imperial Iranian Gendarmerie (GENMISH) was established under the command of Colonel Norman Schwartzkopf. GENMISH served primarily in an advisory capacity until 1950, when large amounts of U.S. equipment and training were given to the Gendarmerie. Although GENMISH was formally independent, it cooperated closely with the MAAG unit in Iran, particularly in supplying equipment to the Gendarmerie. The personnel strength of GENMISH varied from

[54]U.S. Senate, Committee on Foreign Relations, Subcommittee on Foreign Assistance, *U.S. Military Sales to Iran*, 94th Cong., 2d Sess., July 1976, viii–xiii, 13–32; *Washington Post*, January 2, 1977, 1. On Nixon's decision to sell large amounts of military equipment to Iran see Gary Sick, *All Fall Down: America's Tragic Encounter with Iran* (New York: Random House, 1985), 13–18; and Sullivan, *Mission to Iran*, 20–21.

[55]For the study that initiated this program see U.S. National Security Council, *Report to the National Security Council Pursuant to NSC Action 1290-d*, November 23, 1955, DDE Library.

twenty-seven to forty between 1954 and 1976 (when it was finally deactivated), generally including eight U.S. Army officers and a few civilian advisers.[56]

GENMISH's main task after 1950 was to improve the Gendarmerie's mobility, firepower, and communications capabilities. Toward this end, it provided the Gendarmerie in the early- and mid-1950s with a large number of trucks and bicycles, several dozen armored cars, two light airplanes, and a variety of small arms. GENMISH installed a sophisticated radio system in the mid-1950s to link Gendarmerie headquarters in Tehran with each of the provincial Gendarmerie headquarters and, through them, with the 142 regional field stations and 32 mobile units. This equipment was later upgraded and supplemented with helicopters and small patrol boats. GENMISH trained Gendarmerie personnel in the use of this equipment, in basic tactics, and in specialized tactics such as counterinsurgency, border patrol, and narcotics interdiction. Some Gendarmerie personnel also received literacy training. Lastly, GENMISH provided operational and organizational advice, overseeing the expansion of the Gendarmerie from twenty-four thousand men in 1957 to some seventy thousand men in the mid-1970s and encouraging it to adopt new capabilities and tactics, such as an intelligence branch and special mobile strike units.[57]

United States assistance to the National Police began in the summer of 1954, when the State Department's International Cooperation Administration (ICA) sent a three-man advisory team to conduct a review of police operations in Iran. This team developed a detailed reorganization plan for the National Police which covered virtually all aspects of its operations and was gradually implemented with U.S. assistance over the next few years.[58]

The plan's most important feature was a major effort to revise the training facilities of the National Police. An ICA public safety adviser went to Iran in October 1957 to begin a reorganization along the lines of U.S. police academies. One of his first changes was to hire a full-time faculty, which consisted initially of five Iranian police officers recently trained in the United States and four others trained by U.S. advisers in Iran. The ICA adviser then worked with these instructors to develop new

[56]U.S. Senate, *U.S. Military Sales to Iran*, 34; Victor J. Croziat, "Imperial Iranian Gendarmerie," *Marine Corps Gazette*, October 1975, 28–31; U.S. President's Citizen Advisors on the Mutual Security Program (Fairless Committee), *U.S. Army Military Msn. with the Imperial Iranian Gendarmerie, GENMISH*, January 1957, DDE Library.

[57]U.S. President's Citizen Advisors, *U.S. Army Military Msn.*; Croziat, "Imperial Iranian Gendarmerie." The existence of a Gendarmerie intelligence branch was revealed to me by a retired CIA officer who had helped train Iran's main intelligence unit.

[58]USOM-Iran, *Review of U.S. Technical Assistance*, 483.

training material and specialist courses on narcotics law enforcement, criminal investigation, traffic control, police station and prison management, and the use of communications equipment. The ICA adviser also established a program to train provincial police forces, an in-service training program, an audiovisual training program, a central library, and a facility for translating manuals and documents into Farsi. Further organizational changes in the following years included the development of a specialist course on civil disturbance control in the early 1960s. In addition, by 1974, some 218 Iranian police officers had been sent to the United States for training at the International Police Academy, the FBI Academy, the U.S. Border Patrol Academy, and other facilities.[59]

The United States also helped the National Police in other ways. In 1957, U.S. advisers began a major expansion and upgrading of National Police communications capabilities. Together with advisers from the U.S. economic aid program attached to the Ministry of Post, Telephone, and Telegraph, U.S. police advisers helped design and install a nationwide telecommunications system with links to the Central Treaty Organization regional system then being installed in Iran. This system provided the National Police with a nationwide telephone and teletype communications network. Advisers also installed a separate radio network linking National Police headquarters in Tehran with all regional police stations and with Interpol headquarters in Paris. Mobile two-way radio systems were installed in National Police patrol and riot-control vehicles. Advisors also set up a modern crime and photographic laboratory and an efficient records management system, and they helped implement a thorough reorganization of police operations at the precinct level, both in Tehran and in other cities.[60]

The U.S. Army colonel who had been sent to Iran shortly after the 1953 coup to train and command General Bakhtiar's new intelligence unit remained in Iran until March 1955, when he was replaced with a more permanent team of five career CIA officers. In 1956, after consulting with U.S. officials, the shah decided to reorganize and expand this intelligence

[59]International Cooperation Administration, "Completion of Tour Report, Mr. Michael G. McCann," September 29, 1959, AID Library; U.S. Department of State, "End of Tour Report, Public Safety Advisor, Training," 13 August 1963, ibid.; Michael Klare and Nancy Stein, "Police Terrorism in Latin America," *NACLA Latin America and Empire Report* 8 (January 1974), 20, 22. For a general description of U.S. foreign police training programs see Michael T. Klare, *Supplying Repression* (New York: Field Foundation, 1977).

[60]International Cooperation Administration, "Completion of Tour Report, Mr. Norman Snyder," July 10, 1959; idem, "End of Tour Report, Public Safety Advisor," June 12, 1961; and idem, "End of Tour Report, Telecommunications Advisor," December 27, 1961, all in AID Library; U.S. Department of State, "End of Tour Report, Public Safety Advisor," April 10, 1963, and "End of Tour Report of Public Safety Advisor for Patrol," June 8, 1964, ibid.; U.S. AID Mission, *Summary Highlights*, 35.

unit. The new agency, known as SAVAK,[61] was placed under the command of Bakhtiar, who was made a deputy prime minister and given direct access to the shah. The shah's primary intention in establishing SAVAK was to create a modern, efficient intelligence agency that would be capable of monitoring and combating both domestic and foreign threats to his rule and would be free from the petty rivalries and bureaucratic inertia that plagued the existing intelligence agencies (i.e., units of the army, Gendarmerie, and National Police). Bakhtiar had demonstrated his loyalty during the 1953 coup and had shown considerable skill in commanding SAVAK's predecessor, most notably in directing the breakup of the Tudeh military network in 1954; he was therefore the logical choice to head SAVAK. Bakhtiar traveled to the United States in 1956 to consult with U.S. officials and study the workings of the CIA and the FBI. Although U.S. advice and training were vital to SAVAK's development into an effective intelligence agency, the shah rejected a U.S. recommendation that he establish separate domestic and foreign intelligence agencies.[62]

The five-man CIA training team remained in Iran until 1960 or 1961, with occasional changes in personnel. This team consisted of a chief of base, a deputy chief of base, and specialists in covert operations, intelligence analysis, and counterintelligence. Although formally under the command of the CIA station chief in Tehran, this team was based in SAVAK headquarters and had very little interaction with CIA station personnel. Its basic mission was to provide SAVAK with the training necessary to turn it into a modern, effective intelligence agency.

This training consisted of courses in the fundamentals of intelligence work, similar to those taught at CIA training facilities like the one at Fort Peary, Virginia. SAVAK officers learned the basic tools of spycraft, such as agent recruitment, the use of message drops and safehouses, surveillance and interrogation methods, and personal security. SAVAK intelligence analysts learned modern analytic techniques, such as how to set up biographical files, how to judge the reliability of intelligence sources, how to integrate material from different sources into an intelligence report, and how to write and disseminate reports effectively. SAVAK counterintelligence specialists learned the basic skills of this arcane field as well as the

[61]SAVAK is an acronym for Sazman-e Ettela'at va Amniyat-e Keshvar (National Intelligence and Security Organization).

[62]The description of SAVAK and its relations with the CIA in this and the following paragraphs was obtained mainly in confidential interviews with four retired CIA officers who worked closely with SAVAK in this period and with a top SAVAK official who was directly involved in SAVAK's training programs. All important details obtained from one of these sources were corroborated independently by at least one other source. Additional sources for specific details are cited in the following notes.

organization and operational techniques of the Soviet-bloc intelligence agencies. Many SAVAK officers received specialized training in the United States in fields such as forgery detection, the Russian language, and the use of computers and special equipment for surveillance, interrogation, and communications. SAVAK officers also went to Britain, France, and West Germany in the late 1950s for specialized training. By the time the CIA training program ended in the early 1960s, virtually all first-generation SAVAK personnel had been trained by this CIA team.[63]

The CIA training team was removed in 1960 or 1961, in conjunction with the shah's efforts in this period to reduce his dependence on the United States. It was replaced with a team of instructors from Mossad, the Israeli foreign intelligence service. This Mossad team, which generally had between two and eight members, remained in Iran until 1965 and provided training similar to that given by the CIA. While the Mossad training team was in Iran, SAVAK began to develop its own training program. Under the direction of General Hussein Fardust, a top SAVAK official and close friend of the shah, SAVAK acquired training manuals and other relevant material from the intelligence agencies of the United States, Israel, Britain, France, West Germany, India, Pakistan, and Taiwan. SAVAK officers studied this material carefully and used it to develop their own full-scale training curriculum. All SAVAK training had been carried out by foreign intelligence agencies in the 1950s and early 1960s, but by 1966 SAVAK was capable of training its own personnel in the fundamentals of intelligence work. Although SAVAK officers often went to the United States, Israel, Britain, France, and West Germany for specialized training, and instructors from these countries occasionally came to Iran to provide such training, most of SAVAK's training was done by its own instructors after 1965.[64]

The CIA and SAVAK also cooperated in other ways, though on a selective and rather limited basis. The two agencies maintained a close liaison relationship, especially in the 1950s and early 1960s. The CIA

[63]It is often alleged that the CIA trained SAVAK to use torture. This allegation was vehemently denied by all my CIA sources, who generally maintained that torture training was explicitly prohibited for both CIA and "friendly" trainees and that SAVAK, in any case, was already well skilled in the use of torture.

[64]Most of the material in this paragraph is from my interview with the SAVAK official in n. 62. Although it was impossible to confirm many of the details he provided, his general scenario of SAVAK training was consistent with that of the other sources in n. 62 and was specifically corroborated by one of them. The Israeli training mission began in 1964, according to Avner Yaniv, *Deterrence without the Bomb: The Politics of Israeli Strategy* (Lexington, Mass.: Lexington Books, 1987), 95. After the Iranian revolution, several top SAVAK officials testified at revolutionary tribunals that they had received training in Israel and had worked closely with Mossad; see, e.g., *Iran Voice* (Washington), August 8, 1979, 1, 12, and January 21, 1980, 1.

station chief in Tehran maintained regular contact with the shah and the SAVAK director, and the main SAVAK representative in the United States, who worked under cover at the United Nations, met frequently with CIA officials in the United States and actually worked as an agent for the CIA. The five-man CIA training team, and subsequently a small CIA liaison unit that occupied an office in SAVAK headquarters after the training team had left, also maintained a close working relationship with SAVAK. Through these channels, the CIA and SAVAK exchanged intelligence information. The CIA provided SAVAK with considerable intelligence on other countries in the region, including the Arab states, Afghanistan, and the Soviet Union. The CIA passed along intelligence on Soviet missile tests and other Soviet military activities near Iran's northern border, which it obtained from its electronic listening posts. It also provided SAVAK with material on the Tudeh party in the 1950s and early 1960s, but did not give SAVAK intelligence on other Iranian political organizations, such as the National Front, clerical activists, or the guerrilla groups that emerged in the late 1960s. SAVAK in turn provided the CIA with considerable intelligence on regional matters and on the Tudeh party, the guerrilla groups, and other Iranian political organizations, much of it unreliable or even deliberately deceptive.[65]

The CIA also ran some joint covert operations with SAVAK and with units of the Iranian armed forces. The two intelligence agencies occasionally launched joint cross-border intelligence-gathering operations into the Soviet Union. SAVAK typically provided logistical support in exchange for some of the intelligence obtained. These operations were much less frequent after 1957, when the electronic listening posts were installed. The CIA also occasionally helped SAVAK interrogate Soviet agents captured in Iran. Although the CIA offered to conduct joint operations with SAVAK against the Tudeh party in the early 1960s, SAVAK refused; conversely,

[65]On the SAVAK representative in the United States see Mansur Rafizadeh, *Witness: From the Shah to the Secret Arms Deal* (New York: Morrow, 1987), chap. 12 and elsewhere; while much in this book is unreliable, a former CIA officer who knew Rafizadeh confirmed to me that he had been a U.S. agent. The listening posts, described in Bamford, *Puzzle Palace*, 198–201, were operated by CIA technicians on bases provided (and guarded) by the Iranian air force and under the operational command of the CIA station chief in Tehran. Information obtained by these listening posts which was useful to Iran was given directly to the shah by the CIA station chief, bypassing SAVAK and the Iranian armed forces. Intelligence on domestic matters in Iran was not given to SAVAK because U.S. intelligence sources in Iran might thereby have been compromised, because the shah might have become alarmed at the extent of U.S. intelligence-gathering activities in Iran, and because it was generally believed that SAVAK had better intelligence than the CIA on these matters anyway. The former SAVAK officer (n. 62) described the material SAVAK gave the CIA as "trash" and told me the shah himself had ordered that the CIA be given such material. The liaison between the CIA and SAVAK often involved very mundane matters, such as requests by Iranian officials to help relatives living in the United States.

the CIA turned down SAVAK requests to conduct joint cross-border operations into Iraq in this period. The CIA did, however, provide arms and financial assistance for the Iranian effort to back the Barzani Kurds in their guerrilla war against the Iraqi government between the early 1960s and 1975 (an effort in which Israel was also deeply involved). All these joint CIA-SAVAK operations were directed against foreign targets; the CIA did not assist SAVAK in its domestic operations. SAVAK was, however, given permission to operate in the United States, where many Iranian students and dissidents were living, after it agreed to respect U.S. laws.[66]

CIA-SAVAK relations became much more distant in the early 1960s, as the overall intensity of the U.S.-Iran cliency relationship declined. The CIA training team was removed, and fewer SAVAK officers were trained in the United States. Liaison and joint operations occurred less often, and contact between CIA and SAVAK personnel was increasingly restricted. CIA-SAVAK relations deteriorated mainly because the primary U.S. goal of strengthening Iran's intelligence capabilities had been accomplished and because security considerations inevitably prevent intelligence agencies from cooperating too closely.[67] At the same time, SAVAK began to diversify its contacts with Western intelligence services, maintaining limited training and liaison relationships with the British, French, and West German services. Most significant, SAVAK established a very close relationship with Mossad in the early 1960s.

United States security assistance programs greatly improved the effectiveness of Iran's security forces and therefore substantially increased the

[66]SAVAK personnel were included in cross-border operations into the Soviet Union primarily for training purposes, according to one of my sources (n. 62). On the Barzani Kurds' guerrilla war against Iraq see Edmund Ghareeb, *The Kurdish Question in Iraq* (Syracuse, N.Y.: Syracuse University Press, 1981). This operation was carried out by both SAVAK and the Iranian army. The CIA refused to run joint operations into Iraq because it already had adequate capabilities inside Iraq for its operations there. The United States did, however, help arrange a series of joint SAVAK-Mossad cross-border operations into Iraq which began in the early 1960s, according to the former SAVAK officer (n. 62); these operations are described in some detail below. Joint operations against Iranian targets were not carried out because SAVAK was unwilling and because U.S. officials believed SAVAK was capable of undertaking such operations by itself; indeed, the primary reason for building up SAVAK in the 1950s and early 1960s had been to give it that capability. On SAVAK operations in the United States see Iran White Paper, sec. III.B.

[67]It is often said in intelligence circles that "there are no 'friendly' intelligence services." The shah was striving to reduce both his dependence on the United States and the magnitude of U.S. intelligence activities in Iran, and the weakening of CIA-SAVAK relations was merely one aspect of this effort. The CIA strove to maintain close ties with SAVAK in this period in order to monitor SAVAK's activities and effectiveness; toward this end, there were occasional efforts to recruit SAVAK personnel as CIA agents (see n. 65). One reason for the CIA's desire to monitor SAVAK was basic counterintelligence: SAVAK was trying to "bug" the U.S. embassy and monitor U.S. intelligence-gathering activities in Iran.

Iranian state's ability to use repression as an autonomy-enhancing capability. The most important of these programs was the CIA's training and liaison relationship with SAVAK, which enabled it to play a pervasive role in Iranian politics under the shah. Although most of the U.S. assistance to the Iranian armed forces was intended to improve its war-fighting capability, the better training and equipment and higher morale that ensued improved the armed forces' effectiveness in domestic security matters. United States aid to the Gendarmerie and National Police transformed these organizations into modern, relatively efficient security services. Inasmuch as repression was the Iranian state's most important autonomy-enhancing capability in the 1960s and 1970s, U.S. security assistance significantly increased the Iranian state's autonomy.

Regional Security Cooperation

The third major element of U.S. policy toward Iran under the Eisenhower administration's perimeter defense strategy was to engage Iran in a regional security organization similar to those being created in Western Europe and Southeast Asia. United States policy makers had considered establishing such an organization in the final years of the Truman administration, and the idea had quickly became a high priority for the Eisenhower administration in 1953. Secretary of State Dulles traveled to the Middle East that spring to discuss the idea with regional leaders. In April 1954, Turkey and Pakistan signed a treaty of friendship and cooperation, with strong U.S. encouragement. Though anxious to have Iran join the emerging alliance, U.S. policy makers preferred to wait until an oil agreement had been reached and the post-Mosaddeq regime had been fully consolidated. The new alliance was formalized in February 1955, when Iraq and Turkey signed what came to be known as the Baghdad Pact. Britain entered several weeks later, and Pakistan and Iran joined in September and October. Although the United States had been the major architect of the Baghdad Pact and remained the driving force behind it, its deepening involvement in the Arab-Israeli conflict prevented the United States from formally joining.[68]

The Baghdad Pact was primarily a defense alliance for deterring a Soviet invasion. It called for security cooperation among the member states, including joint military planning and exercises and mutual pledges of

[68]Campbell, *Defense of the Middle East*, chaps. 4, 5; U.S. Department of State, *History of CENTO*, January 1964, 1–23, Iran White Paper, doc. I.B-45; U.S. National Security Council, *United States Policy toward Iran*, NSC–5402, January 2, 1954, 4.

nonintervention. Its formal structure consisted of a council of ministers, located in Baghdad, and special committees for military planning, economic cooperation, communications, and countersubversion. Although not an official member, the United States joined the economics and countersubversion committees, established a permanent liaison with the military planning committee, and indirectly supported the pact by giving its regional members considerable military aid and training. The dubious benefits of security cooperation with the other pact members were largely offset for Iran by the increased hostility its membership provoked from the Soviet Union and other regional actors; the main advantage for Iran was probably the higher levels of U.S. aid associated with membership.[69]

From its very inception, the Baghdad Pact was beset with problems. Incensed at Iraq's decision to join the pro-Western alliance, Egyptian president Nasser began to foment unrest in Iraq and took steps to isolate the Iraqi government in the Arab world. Regional tensions increased further when Nasser concluded a major arms deal with Czechoslovakia in September 1955 and nationalized the Suez Canal in the summer of 1956, giving Britain, France, and Israel a pretext for invading Egypt. The Soviet Union also reacted to the pact with great hostility, strengthening its ties with Egypt and bitterly denouncing Iran and the other pact members. The U.S. response was the Eisenhower Doctrine, which authorized the use of U.S. military force on behalf of any Middle Eastern country threatened by the Soviet Union or its regional allies. Privately, a special U.S. envoy assured the shah that "if Iran were attacked, the U.S. would be at its side."[70]

The July 1958 overthrow of the Iraqi monarchy dealt the Baghdad Pact a fatal blow. The new Iraqi government boycotted subsequent pact meetings and officially withdrew from the organization in March 1959, leading the remaining members to move its headquarters to Ankara and rename it the Central Treaty Organization (CENTO). To bolster the alliance, the United States began in late 1958 to negotiate bilateral treaties with the three remaining regional members. The Soviet Union strongly denounced this effort and briefly tried to negotiate a nonaggression treaty with Iran. The three bilateral treaties, signed in March 1959, reaffirmed U.S. willingness to intervene militarily in defense of these countries but stopped short of providing them with formal guarantees of U.S. support. United States policy makers also quietly developed contingency plans to use tactical nuclear weapons in the region in the event of general war.[71]

[69]Campbell, *Defense of the Middle East*, 60–61, 233.
[70]Ibid., chap. 6; Ramazani, *Iran's Foreign Policy*, 292–94; Iran White Paper, sec. I.B, 29.
[71]John Donovan, ed., *U.S. and Soviet Policy in the Middle East, 1957–1966* (New York:

Although CENTO survived the crises of the late 1950s, its development as a security alliance was limited in comparison with the anti-Soviet alliances the United States was establishing at this time in Western Europe and Southeast Asia. The members of CENTO could not agree in the 1950s and early 1960s on such basic matters as a joint military command structure and contingency plans for limited war. Although joint military planning and exercises did occur under CENTO, the alliance's contribution to the military capabilities of the member countries was "marginal," according to a 1964 State Department study.[72] Similarly, while the countersubversion committee of CENTO provided an institutional basis for cooperation among member intelligence agencies, most of the cooperation that actually occurred among these agencies was bilateral and outside of CENTO. The main functions of the CENTO countersubversion committee were coordination and dissemination of intelligence on Soviet activities in the region and planning for guerrilla warfare in response to a Soviet invasion. Although Iran cooperated with other CENTO members on military and intelligence activities against rebellious tribes (such as the Kurds and Baluchis) and occasionally on other matters, it did so *outside* the CENTO framework.[73]

As the Cold War receded in the mid-1960s and regional economic issues became more salient, CENTO gradually evolved into an instrument for limited economic cooperation. Under the auspices of the CENTO communications committee, and with financing from the United States and Britain, regional railroad, highway, air, post, and telecommunications links were expanded. The CENTO economics committee organized conferences and symposia and oversaw technical assistance projects in fields such as agriculture, public works, and nuclear power development. The regional members also established a regional planning committee to foster economic cooperation among themselves. Although this committee made extensive plans to promote increased trade and joint economic planning, little was actually accomplished. CENTO continued to function in this limited fashion until Iran and Pakistan withdrew from the organization in March 1979, bringing about its demise.[74]

Facts on File, 1974), 128–42; Iran White Paper, sec. I.B, 31–32; U.S. Joint Chiefs of Staff, "Briefing Paper for Presidential Use in Discussions with the Shah of Iran," June 9, 1958, 3, DDE Library.

[72]U.S. Department of State, *History of CENTO*, 60.

[73]Confidential interviews with a retired CIA officer, a retired U.S. Army officer who headed the U.S. MAAG mission in Iran for several years, and a former SAVAK official who served on the CENTO countersubversion committee in the 1960s.

[74]U.S. Department of State, *History of CENTO*, 78–90; W. M. Hale and Julian Bharier, "CENTO, R.C.D. and the Northern Tier: A Political and Economic Appraisal," *Middle*

Iran also maintained cooperative bilateral security relationships with several Middle Eastern countries and participated in two informal regional security organizations in the 1960s and 1970s. Although the United States was not directly involved in any of these relationships, it generally approved of them and apparently encouraged the shah to enter into them. Taken together, these various informal regional security relationships probably made a larger net contribution to the security of the shah's regime than did CENTO.

Of these relationships the most important, after that with the United States, was Iran's relationship with Israel. The primary basis for this relationship was the antipathy Iran and Israel both felt toward the Arab countries, particularly toward radical Arab states such as Egypt (under Nasser), Iraq, and Syria. This shared antipathy provided a natural basis for cooperation in intelligence activities directed against the Arab countries. Moreover, Israel's intelligence services were highly skilled, had excellent operational capabilities throughout the Middle East, and were willing to provide Iran with services the United States and other countries would not or could not offer, making cooperation with Israel particularly attractive to the shah.[75]

The security relationship between Iran and Israel began for all practical purposes in 1960 or 1961, when a team of Israeli intelligence officers replaced the CIA team training SAVAK personnel. The Israeli team remained in Iran until 1965, apparently with U.S. encouragement.[76] At the same time, Iran and Israel began to run joint covert operations against radical Arab states and organizations throughout the Middle East. Mossad and SAVAK set up a joint intelligence-gathering operation in the city of Abadan (in southwestern Iran) that developed an extensive network of informants inside Iraq. This network, which apparently had access to virtually the entire spectrum of Iraqi political life, was later complemented by a series of electronic listening posts set up and jointly operated by the Iranian and Israeli armed forces along the Iran-Iraq

Eastern Studies 8 (May 1972), 217–26; Shirin Tahir-Kheli, "Proxies and Allies: The Case of Iran and Pakistan," *Orbis* 24 (Summer 1980), 344.

[75]On Iran's ties with Israel see Shahram Chubin and Sepehr Zabih, *The Foreign Relations of Iran* (Berkeley and Los Angeles: University of California Press, 1974), 156–62; and Yaniv, *Deterrence without the Bomb*, 93–95. It is widely believed that Israeli intelligence officers trained SAVAK personnel in torture techniques and helped them interrogate political prisoners. Although I have seen no reliable evidence of this, several retired CIA officers knowledgable about the Iran-Israeli intelligence relationship in this period have described it to me generally as a no-holds-barred relationship, indicating that they believe such activities may well have occurred.

[76]This is the view of the former SAVAK official in n. 62.

border. In the mid-1960s Iran, Israel, and the United States began jointly to provide arms, training, financial support, and intelligence and medical assistance to the Barzani Kurds in their protracted uprising against the Iraqi government. This operation continued until 1975, when Iran and Iraq signed a treaty that ended Iranian support for the Barzani forces and thus permitted the Iraqi government to crush the uprising. In the mid-1960s, Israel provided Iran with captured Soviet-made arms for use by the forces of Imam al-Badr of Yemen, who was receiving extensive Iranian assistance in his effort to put down an Egyptian-backed uprising in that country. Israel and Iran also exchanged considerable intelligence on the Arab world, including information obtained by SAVAK informants located in various Arab governments and in the Palestine Liberation Organization. Close economic ties also emerged between the two countries. Israel sent agricultural advisory missions to Iran and sold the shah large quantities of arms. In return, Iran sold large amounts of oil to Israel and helped finance construction of the Eilat-Ashkelon oil pipeline.[77]

The Iranian and Israeli intelligence services also maintained an informal liaison organization with the Turkish intelligence service in the 1960s and 1970s. This organization, known as Trident, served as a forum for exchanging information on Soviet and radical Arab activities in the Middle East, which were of great interest to the three member countries. Although Trident partially duplicated the role of the CENTO countersubversion committee, it had the obvious advantage for its members of providing a forum that excluded the United States, Britain, and Pakistan. Similarly, much of the cooperation between the Iranian and Israeli intelligence services was conducted outside of Trident to exclude Turkey.[78]

Iran maintained cooperative security relationships with several other pro-Western countries in the region as well. Iran's security forces cooperated with those of Saudi Arabia, which shared Iran's antipathy toward the Soviet Union and Arab radicalism. The most notable instance of Saudi-Iranian security cooperation was their joint support for the forces of Imam al-Badr in Yemen in the 1960s. Iran and Saudi Arabia also helped organize a secret, informal intelligence organization known as the Safari Club. This organization, which also included France, Egypt, and Morocco, was established in the early 1970s to combat communist influence

[77]Most of the material in this paragraph was obtained from the former SAVAK official in n. 62 and corroborated by one of the retired CIA officers mentioned there. On U.S. and Israeli support for the Barzani uprising see also Ghareeb, *Kurdish Question in Iraq*, esp. chap. 7. On economic ties between Iran and Israel see Muslim Students, *Documents from the U.S. Espionage Den*, vol. 36.

[78]The material in this paragraph was obtained from the two sources cited in n. 77.

in Africa by providing arms, intelligence, and financial support to friendly African countries under attack by Soviet-backed forces. The Safari Club helped President Mobutu of Zaire crush an uprising in Katanga in the mid-1970s and gave arms to President Siad Barre of Somalia to support his conflict with the Soviet-backed government of Ethiopia. Although the United States was deliberately excluded from the Safari Club, it strongly approved of its activities (which paralleled similar U.S. operations in Africa) and was apparently kept fully informed. In the mid-1970s Iran provided extensive military assistance to the government of Oman in its effort to crush the Dhofar rebellion and provided Egypt's intelligence agency with training and assistance. Iran also occasionally cooperated with Turkey and Pakistan in operations against rebellious Kurdish and Baluchi tribal groups.[79]

Although these cooperative regional security measures enhanced and supplemented the Iranian state's repressive apparatus and therefore presumably strengthened its autonomy-enhancing capabilities, it is difficult to determine, without more detailed information, exactly how much effect they had. The Baghdad Pact and CENTO seem to have had very little effect on Iran's domestic security, but the cooperation with Israel, Turkey, Pakistan, and the moderate Arab states, which was facilitated by the United States, may well have been very useful in monitoring Iranian dissidents living abroad and in combating tribal unrest and the guerrilla groups at home.

Informational and Cultural Measures

Although the U.S.-Iran cliency relationship primarily involved economic and security matters, the United States also conducted overt and covert informational and cultural programs in Iran through the United States Information Agency (USIA), the State Department, and the CIA. These programs were intended to generate support for the shah's regime, to enhance the image of the United States in Iran, and to undermine the image of the Soviet Union.

The USIA was formally established in August 1953 by combining into

[79]The material in this paragraph was obtained mainly from the two sources in n. 77. On Iranian involvement in the Yemen war see Chubin and Zabih, *Foreign Relations of Iran*, 153. On the Safari Club see Mohamed Heikel, *Iran: The Untold Story* (New York: Pantheon, 1981), 112–16; although this book contains many inaccuracies, its description of the Safari Club was corroborated by the two sources mentioned above (n. 77). On Iranian involvement in the Dhofar uprising see Fred Halliday, *Arabia without Sultans* (New York: Random House, Vintage, 1975), 364–66.

one agency certain foreign informational and cultural activities previously carried out by the State Department and other U.S. government agencies. The most important activities the USIA took over at this time were the Fulbright Exchange Program and the Voice of America. The Fulbright Program, which had begun to operate in Iran under a cultural exchange treaty signed in 1949, ultimately enabled 1,368 Iranians to study and teach in the United States and 293 Americans to do the same in Iran. The Voice of America had broadcast programs to Iran in Farsi during World War II. It reestablished this service in 1949, generally providing two or three hours of programming each day until 1960, when the service was discontinued. Under its Book Translation Program, the USIA translated and distributed at least ninety books in Iran in the 1950s and early 1960s, including *The Anatomy of Communism*, *Seven Years in Soviet Prison Camps*, *USA: The Permanent Revolution*, *A Pocket History of the United States*, and *The Story of My Life* (by Helen Keller). The USIA also operated several public libraries in Iran, provided informational materials to Iranian newspapers, published a Farsi-language magazine, and helped run the Iran-America Society, which sponsored English-language courses and a variety of cultural events.[80]

Although the State Department turned over most of its informational and cultural affairs programs to the USIA in 1953, it did subsequently undertake some important activities of this kind in Iran. The Peace Corps, which is administered by the State Department, sent more than two thousand volunteers to Iran between 1962 and 1976, when its operations there were discontinued. These volunteers engaged in such activities as English-language and vocational instruction, agricultural development, engineering, and architecture. The economics officers in the U.S. embassy in Tehran helped promote commercial ties between the United States and Iran by providing economic data and other information to U.S. and Iranian businessmen. The U.S. embassy also sponsored frequent parties and celebrations and sought to generate support for the shah and project a positive image of the United States through its public statements and activities.[81]

The CIA covertly carried out similar informational and cultural ac-

[80]U.S. Information Agency, *USIA: Its Work and Structure* (Washington, n.d.), 8–9; Ali Pasha Saleh, *Cultural Ties between Iran and the United States* (Tehran: n.p., 1976), 130–35; U.S. Information Agency, *Forty Years: The Fulbright Program, 1946–1986* (Washington, n.d.), 39; U.S. Information Agency, Voice of America, *Voice of America Languages* (Washington, 1986), 4; U.S. Information Agency, Book Translation Program, *Books Published Abroad* (Washington, various years). Additional details here were generously provided by Martin Manning of the USIA Historical Collection.

[81]Saleh, *Cultural Ties*, 383–92.

tivities in the 1950s and early and mid-1960s. The BEDAMN propaganda operation continued until 1954 or 1955, when its principal agents, Nerren and Cilley, emigrated to the United States. BEDAMN was then replaced with one or more new covert propaganda operations, which also used Iranian agents and continued to function at least until the early 1960s. These propaganda operations planted CIA-authored articles in the Iranian press and occasionally distributed books, pamphlets, and posters. These covert CIA activities were similar in many respects to the USIA's overt informational activities. The main difference was that operating covertly allowed the CIA to conceal or deliberate misrepresent the true source of the information it disseminated in order to increase its effectiveness.[82]

The CIA also operated in Iran through the American Friends of the Middle East (AFME), a philanthropic organization founded in 1951 to improve relations between the United States and the people of the Middle East. Several active or retired CIA officers occupied prominent leadership positions in AFME, and the CIA covertly provided AFME with financial assistance through its International Organizations Division, which had been established in the late 1940s to counter Soviet efforts to gain control over international organizations such as labor unions and student groups. The most important AFME program helped students from the Middle East gain entrance to colleges and universities in the United States and then facilitated their studies through financial support, counseling, and other means. AFME also promoted American tourism in the Middle East, sponsored speaking tours in the United States by prominent figures from the Middle East, disseminated information in the Middle East that was favorable to the United States or critical of the Soviet Union, and even sought to promote a Muslim-Christian dialogue in the Middle East. AFME continued to operate until 1967, when its CIA affiliation was publicly exposed in *Ramparts* magazine.[83]

[82]For example, a typical black operation might involve publishing a fraudulent issue of a Tudeh party newspaper containing statements that criticized or defamed Islam. The information in this paragraph was obtained in interviews with four retired CIA officers directly involved in these propaganda activities.

[83]Editors, "How the CIA Turns Foreign Students into Traitors," *Ramparts*, April 1967, 38–40. AFME's affiliation with the CIA was confirmed to me in numerous interviews with retired CIA officers, one of whom told me the *Ramparts* article was based on information provided to the authors by a Soviet intelligence agent. Although I have been unable to discover how much of AFME's funding came from the CIA, I have determined that in the 1950s at least two of its executive directors, two of its vice-presidents, and several members of its board of directors were active or former CIA employees. On AFME operations see American Friends of the Middle East, *Annual Report of the Executive Vice President* (various editions), and its magazine, *Viewpoints: Middle East, North Africa*, which was later renamed *Mid East: A Middle East–North African Review*. On the activities of the CIA's

Ironically, AFME set up its Tehran office in August 1953, just as the CIA was fomenting the coup that overthrew Prime Minister Mosaddeq. Its main function was to help Iranian students seek admission to American colleges and universities. In its first full year of operation (FY 1955), 6,795 Iranians visited this office seeking information about studying in the United States; of these, 375 ultimately applied for admission and 315 were accepted. AFME's student placement service grew substantially in the following years: 1,262 Iranians applied to study in the United States in FY 1959 (more than half of AFME's total for the Middle East), and 694 were accepted. AFME played a major role in establishing the Iranian Student Association (ISA) in the United States: it sponsored the December 1952 conference at which the ISA was founded and several subsequent conferences before ties between the two organizations were broken in 1959, when the ISA turned against the shah's regime. AFME also set up a program to help U.S.-educated Iranians find employment in Iran and supported Iranian organizations such as the Iran-America Society, the Tehran Boy Scout troop, the International Businessmen's Luncheon Club, and the Rotary Club. At least three of AFME's first five representatives in Iran were active or retired CIA officers. Although the CIA's main purpose in supporting AFME's activities was simply to generate a more favorable image of the United States, it did use the organization on at least one occasion to carry out a covert political operation in Iran.[84]

These informational and cultural measures generated some domestic support for the shah's regime and in this sense helped enhance the autonomy of the Iranian state. The most significant of these measures were probably the programs that enabled Iranians to study in the United States, for they helped foster a technocratic, modern-middle-class fraction that staffed the state bureaucracy and was fairly supportive of the shah's regime. To the extent that the informational programs helped create a positive public image of the shah, they made it more difficult for opposition organizations to mobilize against his regime.

International Organization Division see U.S. Senate, Select Committee to Study Governmental Operations with Respect to Intelligence Activities, *Supplementary Detailed Staff Reports on Foreign and Military Intelligence*, bk. 1, 94th Cong., 2d sess., 181–91; and Cord Meyer, *Facing Reality: From World Federalism to the CIA* (New York: Harper and Row, 1980), chap. 5.

[84]A CIA contract officer used his AFME affiliation as cover for a covert meeting with Mozafar Baqai in the fall of 1952 (see Chap. 3). This is the only specific instance of the CIA's use of AFME for a covert operation that I have been able to identify. The CIA officers mentioned in n. 83 generally believe, however, that AFME may have been used occasionally for routine activities such as low-level intelligence gathering and agent recruitment. The material in this paragraph is drawn from the sources in n. 83.

5

The State and Society in Iran under the Shah

The empirical analysis in this book thus far has focused on two distinct topics: the dynamics of Iranian politics, and the nature of the U.S.-Iran cliency relationship. This chapter begins to bring these two topics together by examining the changing character of the state and society in Iran after 1953 and the structural determinants that brought about these changes. Cliency was one such structural determinant: it helped weaken the main Iranian opposition groups during and after the 1953 coup, and it subsequently strengthened the state's repressive apparatus and its co-optative mechanisms. But profound changes in the stage and form of Iran's mode of production, caused mainly by its growing oil exports, also affected the character of the state and society in the post-1953 era. This chapter examines the effects of both cliency and changes in the mode of production on the state and society in Iran. The next two chapters then examine how these structural determinants affected Iran's "visible national politics" and state policymaking in the post-1953 period.

Changes in the Mode of Production, 1954–1977

Reza Shah had carried out wide-ranging reforms in the late 1920s and 1930s which completed the transformation of Iran's mode of production from oriental despotism to a relatively primitive, agriculturally based form of capitalism. However, the Anglo-Soviet invasion and World War II completely disrupted these development efforts. After the war, a state agency known as the Plan Organization was established to promote economic development, and the First Development Plan (1949–55) was launched under its auspices. As Table 7 shows, the First Plan emphasized agriculture, which received 40.4 percent of total First Plan expenditures.

Table 7. Expenditure under the five development plans (in billions of current rials)

Sector	First Plan (1949–55)	Second Plan (1956–62)	Third Plan (1963–67)	Fourth Plan (1968–72)	Fifth Plan (1973–75)
Agriculture/ irrigation	5.7 (40.4)	17.4 (24.9)	47.3 (23.1)	83.2 (16.4)	144.8 (14.0)
Transportation/ communication	3.5 (24.8)	27.3 (39.0)	53.8 (26.3)	110.1 (21.7)	153.0 (14.8)
Industry/mines	4.1 (29.1)	7.0 (10.0)	17.1 (8.4)	113.1 (22.3)	207.7 (20.0)
Fuel power	n.a.	n.a.	32.0 (15.6)	95.0 (18.7)	135.6 (13.1)
Other	.8 (5.7)	18.3 (26.1)	54.4 (26.6)	105.4 (20.8)	395.3 (38.1)
Total	14.1	70.0	204.6	506.8	1,036.4

Sources: Hossein Razavi and Firouz Vakil, *The Political Economy of Economic Planning in Iran, 1971–1983* (Boulder, Colo.: Westview, 1984), 21, 23, 27, 33; Jahangir Amuzegar, *Iran: An Economic Profile* (Washington: Middle East Institute, 1977), 168.

Notes: Figures in parentheses express sectoral expenditures as a percentage of total expenditures. Expenditures on fuel/power for the First and Second Plans are contained in the figures given for industry/mines and agriculture/irrigation. Expenditures on the Fifth Plan cover only the first three years of this plan. The "other" sector is primarily social services.

Unfortunately, the British oil embargo again disrupted Iran's development efforts, forcing the Mosaddeq government essentially to abandon the First Plan. After the oil nationalization dispute was resolved in October 1954, rapid increases in the state's oil revenue and extensive U.S. military and economic aid enabled the Iranian economy to recover rapidly. The state then began to use its growing revenue to promote rapid economic development through a series of development plans that were formulated and implemented by the Plan Organization.

Important steps toward developing the economy were taken under the Second Development Plan (1956–62), which was financed both with oil revenue and with loans from the United States and the World Bank. Considerable public investment was again channeled into the agricultural sector under this plan (Table 7), but its main objectives were to expand Iran's economic infrastructure, especially its transportation and communications systems, and to begin a process of import-substitution industrialization. Import substitution was to be achieved in part by making large amounts of public and foreign capital available to the private sector through a series of specialized development banks that were established or expanded in this period, including the Industrial Credit Bank, the Industrial and Mining Development Bank, and the Agricultural Bank of Iran.[1]

[1]Hossein Razavi and Firouz Vakil, *The Political Environment of Economic Planning in Iran, 1971–1983* (Boulder, Colo.: Westview, 1984), 23–25; Richard Elliot Benedick, *Industrial Finance in Iran* (Boston: Harvard University, Graduate School of Business Administration, 1964), 83–86, 102, 119–22.

The Third Development Plan (1963–67) adopted a comprehensive approach to development planning which was to guide Iran's development efforts until the mid-1970s. Formulated with the help of U.S. advisers and financed with oil revenue, the Third Plan was comprehensive in that the projects it financed were chosen according to a coordinated development strategy that contained guidelines not only for Plan Organization spending but also for development-related spending by other state agencies and by the private sector. The plan's main goal was to promote rapid import-substitution industrialization. Public investment grew tremendously under this plan and was directed mainly into infrastructure and heavy industry, including steel and other metals, petrochemicals, and machine tools. This approach was continued under the Fourth Plan (1968–72), which greatly expanded public investment in these areas (see Table 7). The private sector was encouraged to invest in medium and light industries under the Third and Fourth Plans. Lending to the private sector by the specialized development banks was expanded considerably. The Fourth Plan also increased public spending on social services and made an effort to address Iran's growing manpower and employment problems.[2]

The Iranian state also began an extensive land reform program in the early 1960s aimed ostensibly at alleviating the severe poverty that existed in rural areas and at reinvigorating the agricultural sector. The land reform program was the centerpiece of a wide-ranging reform program begun in this period which became known as the White Revolution. Carried out in several steps, the land reform program ultimately provided land to just over half of Iran's peasants and eliminated virtually all of its large landowners. Yet despite its scope, the land reform program did little to alleviate rural poverty: at least 75 percent of the peasants who owned land when the program was officially ended in 1971 owned less than the minimum needed for subsistence, and 32 percent of the peasants still owned no land at all. The large amounts of public investment channeled into agriculture under the Third and Fourth Plans in conjunction with the land reform program mainly financed large irrigation projects. Despite the magnitude of these efforts, however, agricultural production stagnated in the 1960s and 1970s.[3]

The Fifth Development Plan (1973–77) was initially designed to pursue the same general development strategy as its predecessors, though with

[2]Razavi and Vakil, *Political Environment of Economic Planning*, 25–35; George B. Baldwin, *Planning and Development in Iran* (Baltimore: Johns Hopkins Press, 1967), 40–42, 120–28; Plan Organization, *3rd Development Plan, 1341–1346: Final Report* (Tehran, 1970), chap. 3; idem, *Fourth National Development Plan, 1968–1972* (Tehran, 1968), chaps. 3–5, 8.

[3]Eric Hooglund, *Land and Revolution in Iran, 1960–1980* (Austin: University of Texas Press, 1982), chap. 5.

much higher investment targets. After world oil prices quadrupled in late 1973 and early 1974, however, the shah ordered the Plan Organization greatly to expand the scope of the Fifth Plan. As a result, development expenditures in the first three years of the Fifth Plan exceeded those in the entire five years of the Fourth Plan by considerable amounts in all categories (see Table 7). In an effort to address the fears of Plan Organization officials that this tremendous increase in investment would create infrastructural bottlenecks and therefore higher inflation, the shah agreed to raise public investment in infrastructure and manpower development. Investment in heavy industry and social services was increased as well. Although public investment in agriculture also increased under the Fifth Plan, its share of total public investment remained quite low.[4]

These development efforts transformed the mode of production in Iran from the relatively primitive, agriculturally based capitalism of the early 1950s into an increasingly industrialized, oil-based, rentier form of capitalism in the 1970s. Although accurate economic data are not available before the late 1950s, real economic growth apparently averaged around 7–8 percent annually in the mid- and late 1950s.[5] The share of agriculture in Iran's Gross Domestic Product (GDP) declined from approximately 50 percent in 1941 to 29.9 percent in 1959. In its place, the service sector emerged as the largest sector of the economy, accounting for 37.7 percent of GDP in 1959. Industry had also grown considerably by 1959, especially the oil industry and manufacturing and mining, which accounted, respectively, for 16.5 and 10.8 percent of GDP. Real economic growth averaged 9.8 percent annually between 1959 and 1972. Reflecting the emphasis on industrialization in the Third and Fourth Plans, the manufacturing and mining sector grew fastest in this period, accounting for 14.5 percent of GDP in 1972. The oil and service sectors also grew very rapidly in the 1960s and early 1970s, accounting, respectively, for 20.0 and 42.0 percent of GDP in 1972. Agriculture continued to decline, accounting for only 17.1 percent of GDP in 1972. Inflation and unemployment both remained quite low throughout this period, although a certain amount of underemployment existed in rural areas.[6]

[4]Razavi and Vakil, *Political Environment of Economic Planning*, 35–36, 68–77; Jahangir Amuzegar, *Iran: An Economic Profile* (Washington: Middle East Institute, 1977), 166–75.

[5]Julian Bharier, *Economic Development in Iran, 1900–1970* (London: Oxford University Press, 1971), 45.

[6]The figures in this and the next paragraph are based on Imperial Government of Iran, Plan and Budget Organization, Statistical Research Unit, *Economic Statistics and Trends of Iran*, 3d ed. (Tehran, 1976), 13–14, 39–40; Bank Markazi Iran, *Annual Report and Balance Sheet, 2535* (Tehran, 1977), 99, and idem, *Annual Report and Balance Sheet, 1358* (Tehran, 1980), 124–25. All figures are deflated with the GDP deflator in International Monetary Fund, *International Financial Statistics Yearbook, 1983* (Washington, 1983), 280–81. On employment and underemployment in Iran in this period see International Labor Office, *Employment and Income Policies for Iran* (Geneva, 1973), 26–27.

Iran's oil sector grew tremendously in the early 1970s. As the influx of oil revenue worked its way through the economy, and as the shah's grandiose development plans produced a variety of other economic distortions (see Chapter 7), inflation began to grow in the mid-1970s. Growing inflation, in turn, undermined real economic growth, which averaged 5.8 percent annually in the 1973–76 period and −3.5 percent annually between 1976 and 1978. Most of the growth that did occur in the mid-1970s was concentrated in the oil and construction sectors, which grew in real terms by 115 and 126 percent, respectively, between 1972 and 1977. By contrast, the service sector grew by only 27 percent in real terms, while the manufacturing and mining and agricultural sectors *declined* by 16 and 33 percent, respectively. By 1977 the oil and service sectors accounted for 32.5 and 40.3 percent of GDP, while the shares of agriculture and of manufacturing and mining had fallen to 8.5 and 9.1 percent.

The rapid economic growth of the post-1953 period was accompanied by a substantial increase in the availability of basic social services. The number of schools in Iran more than doubled between the late 1940s and 1960, raising the adult literacy rate from less than 10 percent of the population to 16 percent. Considerable improvements were also made during the 1950s in the number of doctors and health care facilities, in nutritional standards, and in the eradication of contagious diseases.[7] Nevertheless, as Table 8 shows, social conditions in 1960 were still quite primitive by Western standards and lagged well behind the average for all underdeveloped countries in infant mortality, educational enrollment, literacy, and newspaper circulation. Table 8 shows major improvements in each of these areas by 1975. The most dramatic improvements were in education: the adult literacy rate increased to 36.2 percent in 1975; enrollment in primary and secondary schools more than doubled between 1960 and 1975; and the number of Iranians enrolled in colleges and universities increased from 19,815 in 1960 to 195,826 in 1976, of whom 22 percent were studying abroad.[8] Nevertheless, Iran still remained below the average for all underdeveloped countries in 1970 in most of the categories shown in Table 8.

The Role of the State in the Iranian Economy

As the state's oil revenue and its autonomy grew in the 1960s and 1970s, it was able to play an increasingly dominant role in the economy,

[7]Bharier, *Economic Development in Iran*, 37–40.

[8]United Nations, *Statistical Yearbook, 1962* (New York, 1963), 630; Gail Cook Johnson, *High-Level Manpower in Iran: From Hidden Conflict to Crisis* (New York: Praeger, 1980), 19.

Table 8. Basic social indicators for Iran and other countries

	Iran			All under-developed countries		All developed countries	
	1960	1970	1975	1960	1970	1960	1970
Life expectancy at birth (years)	49.6	54.5	56.9	44.2	53.1	69.7	71.6
Population per physician	4,060	3,290	2,490[a]	13,774	8,160	816	705
Caloric supply per capita (% of daily requirement)	86.7	89.8	117.3	91.2	93.8	125.5	128.7
Protein supply per capita (grams per day)	55.4	58.5	74.4	54.5	54.9	92.7	94.9
Infant mortality rate (per thousand births)	163.0	136.2	122.1	153.0	112.2	29.7	19.6
Primary school enrollment ratio[b]	.410	.730	.950	.783	.854	1.139	1.089
Secondary school enrollment ratio[b]	.120	.270	.460	.166	.228	.639	.813
Adult literacy rate (% of adults)	16.0	36.9	36.2[c]	38.8	44.6	96.0	97.9
Newspapers per capita	.0034	.0078	.0138[c]	.0250	.0299	.3108	.3133

Source: World Bank, *World Tables,* 3d ed., vol. 2 (Baltimore: Johns Hopkins University Press, 1983), 44, 148–49.

[a]1978 data.

[b]Ratios are the total number of students enrolled at the given level (regardless of age) divided by the total population in the corresponding age category. Since younger and older students occasionally enroll at a given level, these ratios can be slightly higher than those in countries with nearly universal education.

[c]1976 data.

giving both itself and the economy a "rentier" character. The state used its dominance not only to promote rapid development but also to co-opt and control various societal groups, further increasing its autonomy. The state dominated the economy in three main ways. First, it channeled large amounts of its revenue directly into the economy in the form of public-sector investments. These investments were concentrated in the most critical and dynamic sectors of the economy, giving the state extensive control over it. Second, the state provided large amounts of capital to the specialized development banks, enabling it essentially to control these banks. Third, it maintained very high public consumption levels, enhancing its ability to use fiscal policy to control the economy. In addition, the extensive business activities of the royal family and various formal and informal regulatory mechanisms[9] served as further instruments of state control over the economy.

[9]See Robert Graham, *Iran: The Illusion of Power* (New York: St. Martin's, 1980), chap. 9.

The data in Table 9 on the sources of investment capital in Iran from 1959 through 1977 indicate how extensive the first two of these three mechanisms were. Columns 1 and 2 indicate that direct investment by the state accounted for a very large and growing share of total investment: state investment grew from 36.3 percent of GDFCF in the last four years of the Second Development Plan (1959–62) to 44.1 percent under the Third Plan (1963–67), 55.8 percent under the Fourth Plan (1968–72), and 58.5 percent under the Fifth Plan (1973–77). Similarly, Column 4 shows that direct foreign investment accounted for another 6.8 percent of Iran's GDFCF under the Third Plan and 4.7 percent under the Fourth Plan but fell to .5 percent under the Fifth Plan, after the NIOC renegotiated its relationship with the consortium that operated most of Iran's oilfields.[10] Domestic private investors therefore accounted for only 49.1 percent of gross direct investment in Iran under the Third Plan and only 39.5 and 41.0 percent, respectively, under the Fourth and Fifth Plans.

The specialized development banks were the main source of capital for private investors in Iran at this time.[11] Column 5, together with the calculations in the previous paragraph, show that 55.0 percent of Iran's domestic private investment capital was obtained from specialized development banks during the Third Plan. Columns 7 and 8 show that 81.0 and 2.6 percent of the attributable liabilities of these banks were provided by the state and by foreign sources, respectively, in this period, implying that 46.0 percent of domestic private investment capital was obtained from the state or from foreign sources during the Third Plan. The remaining 54.0 percent of this capital came from investors' savings and from loans made by commercial banks, bazaar moneylenders, and foreign banks. Since a small proportion of commercial bank liabilities also came from state agencies and from foreign sources (see Cols. 11 and 12), these figures imply that more than 66.0 percent of gross investment in Iran during the Third Plan actually originated with the state and less than 26.5 percent originated with domestic private investors. Similar calculations show that more than 74.6 and 74.2 percent of gross investment originated with the state during the Fourth and Fifth Plans and less than 18.0 and 20.6 percent originated with domestic private investors under these Plans.

In addition to direct state investment through the Plan Organization and state financing provided to the private sector through the specialized development banks, the private investments of the shah and other members of the royal family constituted an additional mechanism of state

[10]These negotiations occurred in 1972 and 1973 and essentially eliminated foreign investment in Iran's oil industry. I am indebted to Fereidun Fesharaki for this information.

[11]On Iran's specialized development banks see Amuzegar, *Iran*, 132–35 and esp. Table IX.2 on 133, which can be compared with Table 9 here.

Table 9. State involvement in the Iranian economy (in billions of 1975 rials)

	Fixed capital formation				Specialized development banks				Commercial banks			
					Private-sector loans	Attributable liabilities			Private-sector loans	Attributable liabilities		
Year	Total GDFCF (1)	State (2)	All private (3)	Foreign private (4)	(5)	Total (6)	State share (7)	Foreign share (8)	(9)	Total (10)	State share (11)	Foreign share (12)
1959	151.4	59.8	91.7	n.a.	n.a.	n.a.	n.a.	n.a.	n.a.	n.a.	n.a.	n.a.
1960	160.6	52.8	107.8	n.a.	n.a.	n.a.	n.a.	n.a.	n.a.	n.a.	n.a.	n.a.
1961	148.0	54.5	93.5	n.a.	n.a.	n.a.	n.a.	n.a.	n.a.	n.a.	n.a.	n.a.
1962	129.5	47.0	82.5	n.a.	32.5	43.2	38.9	.4	126.1	161.7	8.1	1.4
1963	139.6	55.3	84.3	11.7	38.1	49.3	42.5	.5	150.1	183.8	10.1	.9
1964	162.1	57.9	104.1	9.0	44.0	59.5	50.2	.7	172.1	207.2	13.9	1.0
1965	224.4	106.3	118.1	22.6	57.6	80.8	67.3	1.1	196.7	251.3	16.6	1.9
1966	238.1	104.5	133.6	15.9	71.1	83.0	65.8	2.5	234.1	295.1	17.5	1.5
1967	318.1	153.6	164.5	14.4	81.3	93.0	70.2	4.7	272.1	345.7	14.9	1.9
1968	387.8	216.2	171.6	19.9	101.7	113.4	86.2	7.3	352.8	445.7	13.3	1.9
1969	389.1	235.8	153.2	26.9	98.1	107.5	83.6	8.0	355.2	463.1	12.0	1.5
1970	467.3	281.0	186.3	19.0	131.4	142.7	111.3	11.6	487.3	632.0	14.1	2.4
1971	541.8	303.8	238.0	25.5	134.1	161.7	123.2	15.7	511.6	677.1	11.2	2.9
1972	673.1	335.8	338.6	23.4	159.9	213.2	142.4	36.5	622.8	828.7	11.1	3.4
1973	652.2	364.3	288.0	7.2	149.7	208.5	135.7	37.4	663.0	860.6	12.3	4.6
1974	622.2	401.8	220.4	5.0	148.6	194.4	134.6	28.6	530.8	767.8	9.2	6.2
1975	1,047.6	647.0	400.6	4.0	233.4	281.4	197.8	40.0	738.3	1,054.2	8.3	7.0
1976	1,222.4	674.0	548.4	5.4	297.9	329.7	205.5	69.6	861.0	1,240.4	9.6	6.7
1977	1,249.6	719.7	529.9	4.3	339.1	373.5	222.0	92.0	833.9	1,263.5	6.6	7.0

Sources: Cols. 1–3: (1959–75) Imperial Government of Iran, Plan and Budget Organization, *Economic Statistics and Trends of Iran,* 3d ed. (Tehran, 1976), 135–36; (1976–77) Bank Markazi Iran, *Annual Report and Balance Sheet, 1356* (Tehran, 1977), 96; Col. 4: Bank Markazi Iran, *Annual Report and Balance Sheet* (Tehran, various years); Cols. 5–12: International Monetary Fund, *International Financial Statistics Yearbook, 1983* (Washington, 1983), 280–81.

Notes: All rial figures are deflated using the GDP deflator given in International Monetary Fund, *International Financial Statistics Yearbook, 1983* (Washington, 1983), 280–81. Column 4 includes flows of foreign investment into the Iranian oil industry, which essentially ended in 1972 (I am indebted to Fereidun Fesharaki for the latter insight). *Attributable liabilities* are all liabilities except those reported under "Other Items (Net)." The government share of these liabilities are those reported under "Official Entities' Demand Deposits," "Credit from Central Bank," "Government Deposits," and "Government Capital." The *foreign share* of attributable liabilities are those reported under "Foreign Liabilities."

control over the economy. Much of the shah's personal wealth was held by the Pahlavi Foundation, an organization established in 1958 ostensibly to support humanitarian and philanthropic causes. In 1961 the shah claimed to have given 90 percent of his wealth, or $135 million, to the Pahlavi Foundation. The foundation reportedly had at least $2.8 billion in assets by the late 1970s, most of which was apparently invested inside Iran in large real estate holdings, agribusiness, banking, publishing, and automobile and tire manufacturing.[12] The shah presumably held other investments independently of the foundation, and other members of the royal family (especially Princess Ashraf) are widely known to have had considerable investments in Iran as well. Even if much of the royal family's wealth was invested abroad, it seems safe to assume that it invested at least $100–150 million annually in Iran in the mid-1970s. If so, then the royal family accounted for at least 5 percent of the proportion of GDFCF identified in the previous paragraph as originating with the domestic private sector during the Fifth Plan.

The Iranian state's very large share of gross domestic investment in this period enabled it to exercise a great deal of control over the economy. Tables 10 and 11 provide a more detailed understanding of how this control was manifested by breaking down the sources of investment capital in the main sectors of the economy and certain key industries into three categories: direct state investment through the Plan Organization, domestic private investment, and direct foreign investment. Although these data considerably understate the magnitude of total state investment by not taking into account state funds provided to the private sector through the specialized development banks or investments made by the royal family,[13] they nevertheless show clearly how the state used public investment to control the most important sectors of the economy.

The most important finding in Table 10 is that the state dominated the industry and mining sector, accounting for 66.5 percent of gross investment between 1965 and 1975. Domestic private investors accounted for only 24.1 percent of gross investment in this sector, and foreign investors accounted for the remaining 9.4 percent. Moreover, the industry and mining sector received 44.1 percent of total state investment and 96.3 percent of total foreign investment, the largest sectoral share in each case. Domestic private investment was concentrated in the service and construction sectors and accounted for more than half of gross domestic investment in each of these sectors. Surprisingly, the state was also the

[12]Graham, *Iran*, 157–60, 255–58.

[13]Complete data on the distribution of development bank loans and royal family investments by sector or industry are unavailable.

Table 10. Investment percentages in the Iranian economy by sector

	Agriculture	Industry/ mining[a]	Construction	Services	Total
1965–75 gross fixed investment (in billions of 1970 rials)	159.73	725.65	539.11	739.26	2,163.75
State share	54.5	66.5	31.1	48.2	50.6
Domestic private share	45.4	24.1	68.8	51.8	46.2
Foreign private share	.4	9.4	.1	0	3.3
Of national total:					
State	8.0	44.1	15.3	32.6	100.0
Domestic private	7.2	17.5	37.1	38.3	100.1
Foreign private	1.0	96.3	.8	.5	98.6[b]
1965–75 real growth in value added	9.9%	374.0%	364.6%	171.6%	202.7%
Sectoral contribution to 1970 GDP	19.4%	37.5%	5.0%	38.1%	100.0%

Sources: Gross investment and value added data are from Imperial Government of Iran, Plan and Budget Organization, *Economic Statistics and Trends of Iran,* 3d ed. (Tehran, 1976), 13–14, 143–44, 151–52. State and foreign investment data are from Bank Markazi Iran, *Annual Report and Balance Sheet* (Tehran, various years).

Notes: Data on foreign investment in the oil industry are converted to rials using exchange rates given in International Monetary Fund, *International Financial Statistics Yearbook, 1983* (Washington, 1983), 280–81, 516–17. Current rial figures are deflated with the GDP deflator in ibid. See also notes to Table 9 regarding foreign investment in the oil industry.

[a]Includes the oil and gas industry.

[b]The row does not add up to 100.0% because a small percentage of foreign investment was not attributed to a specific industry in the source used to construct this table.

largest investor in agriculture. The industry and mining sector was the leading sector of the economy in this period in the sense that it had the highest growth rate and the greatest potential for interindustry and intersectoral linkages. It is therefore not surprising that the state chose to dominate investment in this sector.

Because the industrial categories in Table 11 are more disaggregated than those in Table 10 and because the raw data used to construct it are drawn from a wider variety of sources, certain inconsistencies appear in Table 11. These inconsistencies are not severe enough, however, to prevent us from drawing a few broad conclusions from these data. Table 11 indicates that the state was the main investor in all parts of Iran's industry and mining sector except the food and tobacco industry and the "other" industries category, which consists mainly of textiles, footwear, glassware, china, and wood and paper products. These industries were dominated by the domestic private sector, which also controlled a small share

Table 11. Investment percentages in the industry and mining sector

	Food/ tobacco	Chemicals/ petrochemicals	Oil/gas	Metals/ mines	Mechanical/ transport/ electrical	Water/ power	Other	Total
1968–74 gross fixed investment (in billions of 1970 rials)	27.82	28.92	124.66	135.12	19.62	82.03	62.66	480.78
State share	23.1	99.6	56.3	62.2	77.2	128.0	7.3	65.3
Domestic private share	76.9	n.a.	16.7	36.1	9.2	n.a.	92.4	25.1
Foreign private share	0	23.9	27.0	1.7	13.6	0	.3	9.6
Of national total:								
State	.9	3.9	9.4	11.3	2.0	14.1	.6	42.2
Domestic private	3.3	n.a.	3.3	7.7	.3	n.a.	9.1	n.a.
Foreign private	.6	14.3	70.0	4.9	5.5	0	.4	95.7
1968–74 real growth in value added	−49.3%	54.8%	350.7%	271.7%	54.4%	18.2%	−24.9%	219.6%
Industry's contribution to 1970 GDP	3.3%	1.2%	22.2%	2.9%	1.5%	1.6%	4.9%	37.5%

Sources: Gross investment and value added data are from United Nations, *Growth of World Industry, 1973,* vol. 1 (New York, 1973), 229–30; idem, *Yearbook of Industrial Statistics, 1977,* vol. 1 (New York, 1977), 240–41. State and foreign investment data are from Bank Markazi Iran, *Annual Report and Balance Sheet* (Tehran, various years).

Notes: See notes to Table 10. This table contains inconsistencies in the percentage breakdowns of investment in the chemical and petrochemical industry and in the water and power industry. In the former case, the sum of public and foreign investment reported in the sources used to construct the table exceeded the amount reported for gross investment; in the latter case, the amount reported for public investment exceeded that reported for gross investment. These inconsistencies may have several causes: differences in where these sources obtained their information, how they identified the data on which an investment was actually made, how they classified certain industries, what kinds of expenditures they classified as investments, etc. These kinds of discrepancies seem largely to have canceled each other out in Table 10, where a much higher level of aggregation is used in classifying industries. They have created errors of roughly 20–30 percent in this table—not too large. Moreover, the data for the remaining industries appear to be fairly consistent. Incomplete data in some of the sources made it impossible to include earlier or later years.

of the oil and gas industry and the metals and mining industry. Foreign investors played a significant role in the chemical and petrochemical industry, the oil and gas industry, and the machinery, transportation, and electrical product industries. Most foreign companies working in Iran's oil and gas industry operated, however, under contract to the state-owned NIOC and therefore enjoyed little actual control over this industry. Similarly, because Iranian law prohibited foreign investors from owning more than a 25-percent share of companies in the chemical and petrochemical industry and in mechanical, transportation, and electrical industries,[14] the foreign sector exercised little real control in these industries as well. Table 11 indicates that the food and tobacco and "other" industries experienced negative real growth between 1968 and 1974. Moreover, these industries together accounted for a fairly small share of the industry and mining sector and were clearly much less critical to Iran's development efforts that the other industries shown in this table.

The main conclusions to be drawn from Tables 10 and 11 are that the Iranian state used its extensive revenue to control the most critical and dynamic parts of the industry and mining sector of the economy through public investment and that it relegated domestic private investment mainly to the construction and service sectors and to the least dynamic parts of the industry and mining sector. By directly controlling the most vital sector, and by indirectly controlling much of the remainder of the economy through the specialized development banks, royal family investments, and various regulatory mechanisms, the state was able to carry out its economic policies with almost complete independence from the Iranian bourgeoisie, thus severely limiting the ability of the bourgeoisie to exercise influence over it. The state's control over Iran's leading industries, over much of its economic infrastructure, and over the specialized development banks also left the bourgeoisie highly dependent on the state and thus further weakened it. Consequently, although Iran's bourgeoisie grew considerably in size during this period, it remained weak and highly dependent on the state. Tables 10 and 11 also indicate that foreign investment played a very minor role in the economy, especially after the NIOC renegotiated its relationship with the foreign oil companies in 1972 and 1973. Iran's economy therefore became less dependent on the world economy, at least in this respect.

The third way the state dominated the Iranian economy was through its high consumption levels. Table 12 contains data on Iran's public and private consumption levels and certain other aspects of the state's fiscal activity. Columns 1 and 2 show that public consumption grew much

[14]Citibank, *Investment Guide to Iran* (New York, n.d.), 20.

faster than private consumption in this period, rising from a modest 12.3 percent of total consumption in the last few years of the Second Development Plan (1959–62) to 16.6 percent under the Third Plan, 23.0 percent under the Fourth Plan, and 28.9 percent under the Fifth Plan. Column 3 indicates that defense spending accounted for only part of the increase in public consumption, falling from 43.9 percent of public consumption in the 1959–62 period to 32.8 percent under the Third Plan, 32.9 percent under the Fourth Plan, and 40.2 percent under the Fifth Plan. State spending in nondefense areas such as economic development and social services therefore accounted for a slightly *larger* share of the increase in public consumption than did defense spending. The state's high level of nondefense spending enhanced its ability to use fiscal policy to control the economy and made many Iranians from all social strata dependent on the state for their livelihoods, further increasing the state's autonomy. Table 12 also shows that the state relied increasingly on oil revenue rather than taxes to finance its expenditures, especially after the sharp increase in world oil prices in the early 1970s. This reduced the state's dependence on the upper and middle classes for revenue, increasing its independence from these classes.

Table 13 provides a comparative perspective on much of the forgoing discussion by presenting data for Iran and for certain comparable countries on several of the measures introduced above. In the first two columns, the values for Iran are higher than those for any other country and much higher than the average values for all countries, all developed countries, and all underdeveloped countries. This indicates that the Iranian state's investment and consumption levels were very high by world standards. The values for Iran in Columns 3 and 4 are smaller than those for any other country or group of countries, indicating that, by world standards, the Iranian state depended very little on domestic societal groups for tax revenue. The Iranian state's very high investment and consumption levels and its very low rate of taxation suggest that its oil revenue enabled it to play an extensive role in the economy and achieve a high degree of autonomy in the 1970s.

The Changing Structure of Iranian Society

The transformation of the mode of production in Iran from the relatively primitive, agriculturally based capitalism of the early 1950s to an increasingly industrialized, oil-based, rentier form of capitalism in the 1970s produced tremendous changes in the class structure of Iranian

Table 12. Expenditures and state revenue (in billions of 1975 rials)

Year	Consumption expenditures Private (1)	Consumption expenditures Public (2)	Defense expenditures (3)	State revenues (4)	State oil revenues (%) (5)	State tax revenues (%) (6)
1959	596.8	86.5	40.2	n.a.	n.a.	n.a.
1960	642.5	90.0	45.0	n.a.	n.a.	n.a.
1961	661.6	92.6	35.7	n.a.	n.a.	n.a.
1962	703.6	96.4	39.6	n.a.	n.a.	n.a.
1963	730.1	108.9	38.2	164.5	45.6	35.1
1964	770.5	127.4	37.4	177.2	52.7	34.0
1965	820.7	172.4	45.1	215.5	48.1	37.1
1966	872.5	197.4	64.6	257.1	48.8	35.6
1967	990.9	229.1	88.8	287.5	50.1	39.1
1968	1,202.0	287.5	119.0	361.6	48.5	41.3
1969	1,153.5	301.5	116.4	370.9	51.2	40.2
1970	1,459.8	395.5	114.2	481.3	49.2	41.6
1971	1,430.0	472.5	144.5	645.8	60.1	31.2
1972	1,608.0	591.6	128.8	707.5	59.0	32.9
1973	1,579.4	584.2	163.6	834.5	67.0	28.2
1974	1,246.2	694.3	149.1	1,540.8	86.4	11.3
1975	1,316.0	807.4	372.6	1,582.1	78.8	17.1
1976	1,267.6	830.1	393.7	1,518.9	77.4	18.7
1977	1,473.9	732.5	386.6	1,387.7	73.6	21.8

Sources: Cols. 1–2: (1959–75) Imperial Government of Iran, Plan and Budget Organization, *Economic Statistics and Trends of Iran,* 3d ed. (Tehran, 1976), 101–2; (1976–77) Bank Markazi Iran, *Annual Report and Balance Sheet, 1356* (Tehran, 1977), 97; Cols. 3–6: United Nations, *Statistical Yearbook* (New York, various years).

Note: All rial figures are deflated using the GDP deflator given in International Monetary Fund, *International Financial Statistics Yearbook, 1983* (Washington, 1983), 280–81.

society. These changes, in turn, had important implications for state-society relations and for the degree of state autonomy.

Although accurate demographic data for Iran before 1956 are unavailable, it is estimated that in 1946 approximately 75 percent of Iran's working male population of 5.104 million was engaged in agriculture and that roughly 2 percent of its work force, or some 94,000 workers, was employed in large manufacturing industries (i.e., those with ten or more employees), including the oil industry. These figures changed dramatically in the next few decades, as the mode of production changed. Employment in agriculture fell to 56 percent of total employment in 1956, to 46 percent in 1966, and to 34 percent in 1976. Meanwhile, industrial employment grew rapidly: the number of employees of large manufacturing industries grew to 114,000 in 1956, and total manufacturing employment grew from 13.8 percent of the work force in 1956 to 17.1 percent in 1966 and

Table 13. Degree of state involvement in the economy in Iran and selected other countries

Country/country group	State investment as % of total investment (1)	State consumption as % of total consumption (2)	Tax revenue as % of total revenue (3)	Tax revenue as % of GDP (4)
All countries	11.9[a]	20.7	89.8[a]	22.2[a]
Developed countries	8.6[a]	21.6	92.7[a]	24.2[a]
Underdeveloped countries:	22.3[a]	21.6	80.7[a]	16.4[a]
Argentina	13.8[b]	14.6	74.2[c]	10.2[c]
Brazil	7.9	13.9	91.3	17.9
Egypt	41.8[d]	27.3	72.1[d]	27.7[d]
India	7.4[d]	11.9	83.3[e]	10.3[e]
Iran	46.6	29.7	28.6	9.1
Mexico	16.2[a]	11.9	93.1[a]	11.0[a]
Pakistan	21.7[b]	12.0	83.3[b]	11.1[b]
Philippines	7.8[a]	11.9	89.8[a]	12.4[a]
South Korea	12.6	12.3	90.4	13.6
Turkey	32.6	15.4	86.5	16.9

Sources: International Monetary Fund, *International Financial Statistics: Supplement on Government Finance* (Washington, 1986), 26–27, 64–65, 70–71, 78–79; idem, *International Financial Statistics: Yearbook* (Washington, 1984), 50–61.

Notes: The data used to construct this table were unavailable for the years before 1970. Comparative data on the state's role in bank financing and in other matters discussed in the text either were not available or were not consistent enough to be included in the table. The countries included in the table were chosen because they are among the most widely studied underdeveloped countries and because their states are generally said to play very active roles in their economies. All figures are averages for 1970–78, except as noted:

[a]1972–78 data.
[b]1973–78 data.
[c]1971–78 data.
[d]1975–78 data.
[e]1974–78 data.

18.9 percent in 1976. This dramatic shift in occupational structure also produced a rapid increase in the size of the urban population, which grew from 26 percent of the total population in 1946 to 31 percent in 1956, 39 percent in 1966, and 47 percent in 1976.[15]

A clearer picture of how changes in the mode of production affected Iran's social structure in the post-1953 period is given in Table 14, which provides a breakdown of employment by occupational categories in 1966

[15]Bharier, *Economic Development in Iran*, 26, 34, 181; Djamchid Behnam and Mehdi Amani, *La population de L'Iran* (Paris: CICRED, 1974), 45; Statistical Centre of Iran, Plan and Budget Organization, *National Census of Population and Housing: Total Country* (Tehran, 1976), 73. Urban areas here and below are defined as cities and towns with 5,000 or more inhabitants.

Table 14. Occupational structure of Iran

Occupational group	1966			1976		
	Number of workers	% of total	% urban	Number of workers	% of total	% urban
Agriculture	3,137,876	45.7	6.3	2,969,848	33.8	7.9
Manufacturing and equipment operators	1,291,926	18.8	55.2	2,090,856	23.8	57.4
Construction:	739,655	10.8	58.2	1,207,798	13.7	47.0
Skilled construction workers	221,601	3.2	57.9	325,488	3.7	66.7
Laborers	518,054	7.6	58.3	882,310	10.0	39.7
Services:	1,431,688	20.9	75.1	2,054,260	23.4	83.6
Housekeepers, cooks, barbers, etc.	364,601	5.3	71.9	259,864	3.0	80.3
Police and firefighters	82,316	1.2	61.2	126,909	1.4	76.3
Working proprietors	335,718	4.9	70.9	407,304	4.6	78.1
Other sales workers	197,990	2.9	79.3	210,483	2.4	84.7
Clerical workers	201,148	2.9	92.6	449,328	5.1	90.7
Administrators and managers	11,937	.2	93.2	48,032	.5	89.5
Teachers	110,634	1.6	75.1	264,512	3.0	79.2
Clergymen and assistants	12,455	.2	61.1	23,863	.3	68.8
Other professionals	79,855	1.2	90.0	248,058	2.8	91.3
Other service workers	35,034	.5	21.8	15,874	.2	79.2
Subtotal	6,601,145	96.2	36.6	8,322,729	94.7	44.7
Occupation not specified	257,251	3.8	75.3	466,165	5.3	82.5
Total	6,858,396	100.0	38.1	8,788,894	100.0	46.7

Sources: (1966) Plan Organization, Iranian Statistical Centre, *National Census of Population and Housing,* vol. 168 (Tehran, 1968), 74–115; (1976) Plan and Budget Organization, Statistical Centre of Iran, *National Census of Population and Housing: Total Country* (Tehran, 1976), 94–109.

Notes: Forestry workers, fishermen, and hunters are included under the figures for agricultural workers. Equipment operators include transportation workers. Housekeepers, cooks, barbers, etc., also include waiters, building caretakers, charworkers, launderers, undertakers, and related workers. College and university professors are classified here as professionals rather than teachers.

and 1976.[16] The data in Table 14 are the basis for the profile of Iran's changing class structure developed in the next few paragraphs and summarized in Table 15.

Table 14 indicates that agricultural workers accounted for 45.7 percent of the work force in 1966 but only 33.8 percent in 1976. Of the roughly 68 percent of agricultural workers who owned some land after 1971, less than 25 percent owned more than the minimum needed for subsistence. If the lower class is defined as people who live at or near the subsistence level, and if landless peasants are assumed to live at the subsistence level, then these figures suggest that roughly 83 percent of all agricultural workers were members of the lower class. Almost all of the remainder can probably be classified as lower middle class.

The working class, including manufacturing workers, equipment operators, and construction workers, accounted for 29.6 percent of the work force in 1966 and 37.5 percent in 1976. This rapid increase and the corresponding decline in the size of the agricultural work force suggests that most of the peasants who left agricultural employment were subsequently employed in manufacturing, equipment operation, and construction. It is probably safe to assume that laborers lived at or near the subsistence level and therefore can be classified as lower class. The remainder of the working class was quite heterogeneous, however, ranging from poorly paid carpet weavers and food handlers to relatively well-paid oil workers, electrical workers, and mechanics. Lacking more detailed data on occupational and income structure, it is probably safe to assume that manufacturing workers, equipment operators, and skilled construction workers were evenly spread among the lower class, the lower middle class, and the "middle" middle class.[17]

Table 14 indicates that the service sector was quite diverse, both in income level and in the distinction between modern and traditional occupations. Housekeepers, cooks, barbers, and "other" sales workers (mainly shop assistants) generally lived at or near the subsistence level and therefore can be classified as members of the lower class. The traditional middle class consisted mainly of working proprietors (mostly bazaar

[16]Since workers are classified by occupation group rather than by type of industrial establishment in this table, these figures differ slightly from those given in the previous paragraph.

[17]Although the sources used to construct Table 14 give a much more detailed breakdown of manufacturing and construction occupations, these more detailed categories are not very useful for distinguishing lower-class from lower-middle-class occupations. For example, while the number of spinners, weavers, knitters, and other textile workers is given, it is impossible to determine what proportion was employed in small carpet-weaving shops, where salaries were very low, and what proportion was employed in large textile plants, where salaries were somewhat higher.

merchants) and clergymen and ranged from lower middle to upper middle class The modern middle class included most clerical workers, administrators and managers, teachers, and other professionals and generally ranged from "middle" middle to upper middle class. (The distinction between the traditional and modern middle classes was, of course, much less clear in practice than this discussion implies.) An important fraction of the modern middle class, which emerged in the post-1953 period but is not easily identified from the occupational categories shown in the table, is the "technocratic" modern middle class, which consisted of top administrators in the state bureaucracy and in the private sector who had generally received advanced education in certain "technocratic" fields in the West. Iran's police and firefighters and "other" service workers were mainly lower middle class and were not easily classified as either traditional or modern.

A small fraction of the administrators and managers and other professionals listed in the table were members of the upper class. The bourgeoisie formed the main core of a "modern" upper class, which also included some high-ranking state officials and professionals. This modern upper class had interests and political views very different from Iran's "traditional" upper class, which consisted of large landowners, tribal leaders, top clergymen, and bazaar merchants. Iran's traditional upper class was shrinking rapidly as a result of land reform and the shah's efforts to weaken the tribes and the clergy (see Chap. 6). This shrinkage, together with the bourgeoisie's increasing dependence on the state, indicates that the Iranian upper class was changing rapidly in character and becoming increasingly subservient to the state.

Because classes are defined by occupational category rather than by income level or type of political consciousness in Table 15, this breakdown does not necessarily provide an ideal characterization of class structure. Nevertheless, it does show very clearly how changes in Iran's mode of production affected its social structure. One important conclusion we can draw from this table is that a great deal of rural-urban migration occurred between the mid-1960s and the late 1970s. The urban work force grew by 54 percent between 1966 and 1976, while the rural work force grew by only 10 percent. Although some of the increase in urban population was caused by normal population growth and the emergence of new urban centers, one study suggests that roughly 35 percent of this increase was due to rural-urban migration.[18] Most rural-urban migrants in this period were poor peasants uprooted by the land reform program.

[18] Farhad Kazemi, *Poverty and Revolution in Iran* (New York: New York University Press, 1980), 14.

Table 15. Class structure of Iranian society

	1966 population			1976 population		
	% of urban	% of rural	% of total	% of urban	% of rural	% of total
Lower class	48.3	72.3	63.5	37.8	69.9	55.5
Middle class:	49.4	27.5	35.5	60.3	29.9	43.5
Lower	18.6	18.1	18.3	19.6	17.6	18.5
Middle	21.3	8.1	12.9	26.8	10.4	17.7
Upper	9.5	1.3	4.3	13.9	1.9	7.3
Traditional	10.2	2.5	5.3	9.0	2.1	5.2
Modern	12.2	1.0	5.1	21.9	2.5	11.1
Workers	23.2	10.7	15.3	25.4	14.5	19.4
Upper class	2.4	.2	1.0	2.0	.2	1.0
Total	100.1	100.0	100.0	100.1	100.0	100.0
Total number of employees	2,416,596	4,184,549	6,601,145	3,719,522	4,603,207	8,322,729

Notes: The percentages are calculated as follows from the data in Table 14: 83 percent of agricultural workers are classified as lower class, 15 percent as lower middle class, and 2 percent as "middle" middle class; one-third of manufacturing and equipment operators and skilled construction workers are classified as lower class, one-third as lower middle class, and one-third as "middle" middle class; all laborers, housekeepers, cooks, barbers, and "other" sales workers are classified as lower class; all police, firefighters, and "other" service workers are classified as lower middle class; all working proprietors and clergymen and assistants are classified as traditional middle class and distributed evenly among the lower middle, "middle" middle, and upper middle classes; the upper class is assumed to comprise one percent of the total population and to consist of administrators and managers and "other" professionals; all clerical workers, teachers, and remaining administrators and managers and "other" professionals are classified as modern middle class and distributed evenly among the "middle" middle and upper middle classes; and the nonspecified workers are excluded from this table. These classifications are used for both urban and rural workers in both 1966 and 1976.

Many of these urbanized peasants settled in large shantytowns on the fringes of major cities and obtained subsistence-level employment as unskilled workers.[19] Although the urban lower class declined from 48.3 percent of the urban population in 1966 to 37.8 percent in 1976, it grew in absolute size by 20 percent and continued to grow rapidly in the next few years. The large size of the urban lower class enabled it to engage extensively in collective political action and therefore made it potentially quite powerful. The urban lower class was to play a key role in the political upheaval of the late 1970s.

Table 15 also indicates that most of the growth in Iran's urban popula-

[19]For an excellent study of Iran's migrant poor see ibid.

tion occurred among the middle class, which grew from 49.4 percent of the total urban population in 1966 to 60.3 percent in 1976. Most of this growth was due to the tremendous expansion of the modern middle class, which grew from 12.2 percent of the urban population in 1966 to 21.9 percent in 1976. The working-class fraction of the urban middle class grew slightly, from 23.2 percent of the urban population in 1966 to 24.5 percent in 1976, and the traditional urban middle class *declined* from 10.2 percent of the urban population in 1966 to 9.0 percent in 1976. The rapid growth of the modern middle class and the slower growth of the industrial working class greatly increased both classes' ability to engage in collective political action and therefore made them much more powerful vis-à-vis the state. Iran's student population, whose political views generally resembled those of the modern middle class, nearly quadrupled between 1966 and 1976,[20] enabling students, too, to play a much more active role in politics.

The growth of the modern middle class and the industrial working class after 1953 continued trends that had begun in the late nineteenth century and accelerated rapidly in the 1930s, as the mode of production gradually evolved. It was this endogenous structural change that had helped create a Bonapartist regime under Reza Shah and incipient modern-middle-class hegemony in the 1940s and early 1950s. The continued rapid growth of these two classes after 1953 suggests that the modern middle class, together with the industrial working class as a junior partner, would probably have been able to establish hegemony over the state in this period, had other structural factors not intervened.[21]

Table 16 provides further insight into how Iran's social structure affected its domestic politics in this period. The first four columns show that Iran's industrial work force was proportionally much larger than the average for all underdeveloped countries in 1960 and 1970 and its agricultural work force was proportionally much smaller. The remainder of Iran's work force, which was employed in the service sector, was also proportionally larger than the average for all underdeveloped countries in

[20]The number of secondary school students in Iran grew from 658,467 to 2,356,878 between 1966 and 1976, and the number of college students grew from 36,742 to 154,215; see United Nations, *Statistical Yearbook, 1968* (New York, 1968), 751; and ibid., *Statistical Yearbook, 1978*, 914.

[21]For more extensive descriptions of the class structure of Iranian society in the postwar period see Ahmad Ashraf, "Iran: Imperialism, Class, and Modernization from Above" (Ph.D. diss., New School for Social Research, 1971), chap. 6; James Alban Bill, *The Politics of Iran: Groups, Classes, and Modernization* (Columbus, Ohio: Charles E. Merrill, 1972); and U.S. Department of State, Office of Intelligence and Research, *Analysis of Communist Propaganda in Iran*, Report No. 5714.15, June 1, 1954, 42–47.

Table 16. Occupational structure, urbanization, and income distribution in Iran and selected other countries, 1960–1975

	Occupational structure (%)						Urbanization (%)			Income distribution			
	1960		1970		1975								
Country/country group	Ag.	Ind.	Ag.	Ind.	Ag.	Ind.	1960	1970	1975	Lowest 40%	Middle 40%	Top 20%	Year
Argentina	20.0	35.9	16.4	32.1	14.7	30.1	73.6	78.4	80.5	445	974	2557	1970
Brazil	51.9	14.8	45.6	18.3	37.4	21.4	46.1	55.9	61.8	98	277	1199	1970
Egypt	58.0	12.0	54.0	19.0	52.4	24.1	37.9	42.3	43.5	n.a.	n.a.	n.a.	
India	74.0	11.0	74.0	11.0	71.7	12.1	18.0	19.8	20.9	40	79	257	1964
Iran	54.0	23.0	46.0	28.0	42.5	30.9	33.6	40.9	45.4	104	274	905	1968
Iraq	53.0	18.0	47.0	22.0	44.5	24.0	42.9	58.4	65.7	34	126	680	1956
South Korea	66.0	9.0	50.0	17.0	41.9	22.6	27.7	40.7	48.1	106	217	529	1970
Lebanon	38.0	23.0	20.0	25.0	15.0	26.2	44.4	61.8	69.8	165	330	1549	1960
Mexico	55.1	19.1	45.2	22.9	40.3	24.4	50.8	59.0	63.0	169	411	2064	1969
Pakistan	61.0	18.0	59.0	19.0	58.0	19.5	22.1	24.9	26.3	44	94	150	1964
Philippines	61.0	15.0	53.0	16.0	49.5	16.5	30.3	32.9	34.3	69	207	643	1971
Saudi Arabia	71.0	10.0	66.0	12.0	63.5	13.0	29.7	48.7	58.7	n.a.	n.a.	n.a.	
Turkey	78.5	10.5	67.7	12.1	61.0	12.6	29.7	38.4	42.3	66	211	857	1968
All underdeveloped countries	69.0	12.2	64.6	13.6	n.a.	n.a.	23.6	27.8	n.a.	n.a.	n.a.	n.a.	
All developed countries	17.6	38.2	10.6	38.5	n.a.	n.a.	68.1	73.5	n.a.	n.a.	n.a.	n.a.	n.a.

Sources: World Bank, *World Tables,* 3d ed., vol. 2 (Baltimore: Johns Hopkins University Press, 1983); Hollis Chenery et al., *Redistribution with Growth* (London: Oxford University Press, 1974), 8–9.

Notes: Industrial workers here include construction workers. Income distribution figures are the average yearly income of the given income group, expressed in 1971 U.S. dollars, calculated from percentage distribution figures for the year indicated. "N.a." indicates that data were not available for a particular country or group of countries.

1960 and 1970. Similarly, Iran's rate of urbanization was higher than the average for all underdeveloped countries in this period. Iran's relatively large industrial and service sector work forces and its high rate of urbanization indicate that its urban middle class (including its industrial working class) was relatively large for an underdeveloped country. The figures for specific countries suggest that Iran's urban middle class was probably somewhat smaller proportionally than those in Argentina and Lebanon; probably larger than those in Egypt, India, Iraq, South Korea, Pakistan, the Philippines, Saudi Arabia, and Turkey; and roughly comparable in size to those in Brazil and Mexico.

The data on the average yearly income levels of the middle 40 percent and top 20 percent of the population provide some idea of how wealthy the middle and upper classes in these countries were in 1971. The figures for Iran are somewhat lower than those for Argentina, Brazil, Lebanon, and Mexico but higher than those for India, Iraq, South Korea, Pakistan, the Philippines, and Turkey. Although the income figures for the poorest 40 percent of the population suggest that Iran's lower class was also comparatively well off in this period, Table 8 indicated that Iran was well behind the average for all underdeveloped countries in this period in the availability of certain basic social services bearing on health and education.

Table 16 indicates that Iran's urban middle class in the 1960s and 1970s was roughly comparable in size and level of wealth to those in Brazil, Mexico, and perhaps Turkey and was more advanced in this regard than those in Egypt, India, Iraq, South Korea, Pakistan, the Philippines, and Saudi Arabia. Iran's urban middle class should therefore have been similar to those in Brazil, Mexico, and Turkey in its level of social mobilization and therefore also in the amount of influence it could wield over the state, ceteris paribus. Although it is not possible to carry this comparative analysis any further here, there can be little doubt that Iran's urban middle class wielded much *less* influence over the state than those in Brazil, Mexico, and Turkey, and probably also less than the urban middle classes in several other countries identified above as having smaller and poorer urban middle classes. This suggests that changes in the mode of production were not the only important factor affecting state-society relations in Iran in this period.

The Repressive Apparatus

The rapid growth of Iran's modern middle class and, to a lesser extent, of its industrial working class and urban lower class greatly increased the ability of these groups to engage in collective political action and therefore made them potentially much more powerful vis-à-vis the state. Since group power limits state autonomy, these changes in social structure would have undermined the state's autonomy if other factors had not intervened. This book argues that two other factors did intervene: the U.S.-Iran cliency relationship, and the extensive revenue accruing to the state from Iran's growing oil exports. These exogenous structural factors greatly increased the state's autonomy by directly weakening the main opposition groups and by strengthening the repressive apparatus and co-optative institutions and mechanisms that were the state's primary autonomy-enhancing capabilities.

The repressive apparatus was the state's most effective autonomy-enhancing capability and consequently the main pillar supporting the shah's regime. The repressive apparatus had four main components: SAVAK, the National Police, the Gendarmerie, and the armed forces. In addition, the shah created a small, secretive organization, known as the Imperial Inspectorate, to monitor the security forces and other state agencies; and special interagency committees were occasionally established to carry out particular tasks. The repressive apparatus enhanced the state's autonomy by enabling it to weaken opposition political organizations and by creating a climate of fear that discouraged many Iranians from engaging in political activity. Since effective political organizations and high levels of mobilization are critically important determinants of the political power of middle- and lower-class groups, the repressive apparatus served especially to enhance the state's autonomy vis-à-vis these groups.

SAVAK was by far the most important and most effective component of the repressive apparatus. Although its personnel were initially drawn mainly from the armed forces and the National Police, it soon established rigorous recruitment procedures that enabled it to attract highly competent recruits from Iran's growing pool of college graduates. As its level of training and technical capabilities improved, its strength lay increasingly in its ability to use modern intelligence techniques, such as electronic surveillance, computerized biographical files, rigorous analytic methods, and sophisticated provocation and propaganda operations. Nevertheless, SAVAK retained (and even cultivated) a very brutal image by routinely torturing and executing opponents of the shah and creating a pervasive climate of fear and intimidation among the opposition.[22]

SAVAK's full-time personnel grew from roughly 2,000–2,400 in the early 1960s to 7,000–10,000 in the late 1970s. In addition, SAVAK

[22]Except where indicated, the material on SAVAK in this and subsequent paragraphs was obtained in interviews with the sources mentioned in Chap. 4, n. 62.

employed numerous part-time informers and thugs, totaling perhaps 20,000–30,000 in the late 1970s. SAVAK was initially organized into eight general departments: an administrative department, including the director of SAVAK and his immediate staff; a foreign operations department, which conducted SAVAK's overseas intelligence-gathering and covert operations; a domestic security department; an organizational security department, which was responsible for the security of SAVAK operations and personnel; a technical services department; a logistics and supplies department; a department to analyze and disseminate foreign intelligence; and a counterintelligence department. Two other general departments were subsequently added: a training department, which assumed the main responsibility for training SAVAK employees in the mid-1960s; and a central records department, which maintained biographical files on many Iranian citizens. SAVAK also maintained five operational branches in Tehran and an operational branch in each province. These branches carried out most of SAVAK's routine intelligence-gathering and repressive activities in their areas of jurisdiction.[23]

SAVAK's domestic security department (also known as the "third department") was the single most important component of the entire repressive apparatus. It employed roughly 10 percent of SAVAK's regular personnel and was divided into four sections. The first section carried out investigations of and operations against certain key opposition groups and organizations: the Tudeh party, the National Front and related parties, students and other Iranians living abroad, the Arab and Baluch minorities, the Kurds, and the clergy. This section was responsible for most of the repression in this period. The second section focused on public opinion and public institutions, including the press, the tribes, worker and peasant organizations, the state-sponsored political parties, schools and universities, and government agencies. Although this section undertook some operational activities, its primary function was to gather intelligence on these institutions and their members. The third section maintained the

[23]The SAVAK personnel figures are from CIA, *Political Prospects for Iran*, SNIE 34–62, September 7, 1962, 5; and John D. Stempel, *Inside the Iranian Revolution* (Bloomington: Indiana University Press, 1981), 25. Grossly exaggerated figures on the number of SAVAK employees and informers circulated widely in the 1970s; see, e.g., *Newsweek*, October 14, 1974, 61. Details on SAVAK's organizational structure are from National Front of Iran (operating abroad), "A Portion of the Secrets of the Security Organization (SAVAK)" May 1971; Earnest R. Oney, "The Eyes and Ears of the Shah," *Intelligence Quarterly* (February 1986), 1–3; and Thomas Plate and Andrea Darvi, *Secret Police: The Inside Story of a Network of Terror* (New York: Doubleday, 1981), 318–20. The first of these three sources, which contains a wealth of information on SAVAK, was apparently based on material provided by a SAVAK employee with access to the records of the administrative department, including extensive personnel records. The general accuracy of this document was confirmed to me by the SAVAK official and one of the CIA officers mentioned in Chap. 4, n. 62.

records of the domestic security department. The fourth section was responsible for specialized activities such as censorship, indoctrination, special training and operations, and judicial matters, including interrogation. The domestic security department also operated four prisons, including the notorious Bagh-e Mehran Prison, which reportedly contained torture chambers and an execution yard. (The equally notorious Evin Prison was run by SAVAK's counterintelligence department.)[24]

The domestic security department worked closely with the other SAVAK departments, with SAVAK's operational branches, and occasionally with the National Police, the Gendarmerie, and units from the armed forces. Its first and second sections relied heavily on cooperation with SAVAK's operational branches and their extensive networks of local informers to gather information about, and conduct operations against, the groups and institutions they focused on. This department also drew heavily on the foreign operations and intelligence departments for information on students and other Iranians living abroad in order both to monitor Iranian political organizations operating abroad and to obtain information on Iranians for use when they returned home. Similarly, the central records department was of considerable value as a source of information on opposition figures; and the counterintelligence department provided information on contacts between domestic opposition groups and foreign organizations. The technical services department had a surveillance team that monitored telephone conversations and carried out other forms of surveillance on behalf of the domestic security department; it also provided this department with advanced equipment of various kinds, including communications and surveillance equipment. SAVAK's domestic security department also exchanged information and conducted joint operations with the National Police, the Gendarmerie, and units of the armed forces. The most notable instance of such interservice cooperation was the Joint Police-SAVAK Counter-Dissidence Committee, which was set up in the 1970s to conduct joint operations against Iranian guerrilla groups.[25]

Although SAVAK was the state's main instrument of repression, the National Police, the Gendarmerie, the armed forces, and the Imperial Inspectorate each played a significant role as well. The National Police,

[24]National Front, "Portion of the Secrets."

[25]Most of the material in this paragraph is based on ibid. and on interviews with the sources mentioned in Chap. 4, n. 62. On SAVAK operations abroad see *Times* (London), May 12, 1974, 17; *Washington Post*, August 9, 1979, A-12; and Confederation of Iranian Students (National Union), *Documents on Iranian Secret Police, SAVAK* (n.p., 1976). On the Joint Police-SAVAK Counter-Dissidence Committee, see Muslim Students Following the Line of the Imam, *Documents from the U.S. Espionage Den*, vol. 7 (Tehran: n.p., n.d.), 100; and Plate and Darvi, *Secret Police*, 169–70.

which had a personnel strength of twenty-six thousand men in the mid-1970s, operated exclusively in urban areas and served mainly in a routine law enforcement capacity. It was, however, often called upon to arrest opposition figures or to break up opposition rallies and meetings, frequently in conjunction with SAVAK or with army units. The Gendarmerie, which had a strength of seventy thousand men in the mid-1970s, was the counterpart to the National Police in rural areas. In addition to routine law enforcement tasks, it policed Iran's borders, suppressed tribal uprisings, and carried out operations against the guerrilla groups that operated in rural areas.[26]

Although the primary focus of the armed forces had changed in the mid-1950s from maintaining domestic security to deterring and defending against foreign invasions, army units were occasionally used to break up public demonstrations in the 1960s and 1970s, most notably in June 1963 and in 1978. The army also developed counterinsurgency units in the 1960s and 1970s, although these units were intended mainly for use in the event of a Soviet or Iraqi invasion. Moreover, the armed forces had a competent intelligence staff; and the Gendarmerie had a small intelligence unit as well. Although the military intelligence staff was geared mainly toward the war-fighting mission of the armed forces rather than toward domestic unrest, one of its primary functions was to monitor unrest and subversion within the armed forces. The intelligence unit of the Gendarmerie monitored tribal unrest and occasionally worked with SAVAK against guerrilla groups operating in rural areas.[27]

The Imperial Inspectorate was an independent organization that monitored the other security services and state agencies in general. Initially established in 1958 and revitalized in the late 1960s, it had a small staff, and its director reported exclusively to the shah. Its main function was to prevent top officials in the other security services from plotting against the shah, which happened repeatedly in the late 1950s and early 1960s. In the mid-1970s the shah began to transform the Imperial Inspectorate into a kind of watchdog agency responsible for monitoring corruption and the performance of state officials.[28]

Much of the repression carried out by the security forces was very simple and very brutal. All opposition organizations were outlawed and

[26]Muslim Students, *Documents from the U.S. Espionage Den* 7:100; Victor J. Croizat, "Imperial Iranian Gendarmerie," *Marine Corps Gazette*, October 1975, 28–31; interview with one of the CIA sources mentioned in Chap. 4, n. 62.

[27]Interview with General Leo Soucek, commander of the army section of the U.S. MAAG group in Iran in the early 1970s, Rosslyn, Va., July 14, 1987.

[28]U.S. Embassy, Tehran, "New 'Critical' Role for Three Official Groups," September 19, 1977, 3–4; interview with the source mentioned in n. 26, above.

thus forced to operate clandestinely; their leaders were frequently arrested; and their occasional attempts to hold public meetings or rallies often ended in mass arrests and bloodshed. The security forces also rigged elections to prevent opposition organizations from obtaining seats in the Majles. Armed opposition groups—guerrillas and rebellious tribal groups—were treated particularly brutally. Mass organizations such as labor unions and student groups were heavily penetrated by SAVAK and their leaders were systematically harassed. Prominent intellectuals, artists, and clergymen who criticized the regime were harassed and often arrested. Censorship was quite severe: censors in the Ministry of Information and the Ministry of Arts and Culture scrutinized all books and articles before publication, and newspapers and publishing houses that printed controversial material were often harassed or forced to close.[29]

As guerrilla groups became more active in the early 1970s, repression became more severe. Estimates of the number of political prisoners being held in Iran in the mid-1970s range from a low of three thousand, according to the shah himself, to as many as one hundred thousand, as claimed by certain opposition groups. Although the actual number was probably close to the shah's figure, this is still a very large number for a country with a population of less than forty million. Many of these political prisoners were held under vague laws that permitted the state to make arrests for strictly political offenses, such as belonging to organizations that opposed the monarchy or espoused a "collectivist" ideology. Moreover, SAVAK was empowered to make arrests under these laws and to act as the sole investigator in the resulting trials, which were closed to the public. Defendants in these cases were held incommunicado before trial, given limited access to legal counsel, and prevented from calling defense witnesses and cross-examining prosecution witnesses. In an investigation of such trials, Amnesty International could not identify even a single case in which a defendant had been acquitted.[30]

[29]On the state's harassment of labor unions see Habib Ladjevardi, *Labor Unions and Autocracy in Iran* (Syracuse, N.Y.: Syracuse University Press, 1985), chaps. 9–10. For a good description of censorship in this period see Reza Baraheni, "The Perils of Publishing," *Index on Censorship* 7 (September/October 1978), 12–17. As a result of these measures, the number of books published in Iran reportedly fell from roughly 4,000 in 1970 to around 1,000 in 1975; and 37 of Iran's 60 newspapers and periodicals were reportedly closed down in 1974; see Ahmad Faroughy and Jean-Loup Reverier, *L'Iran contre le chah* (Paris: Simoen, 1979), 137–38. For an excellent study of the effects of this censorship see Gholam Hossein Razi, "The Press and Political Institutions in Iran: A Content Analysis of Ettela'at and Keyhan," *Middle East Journal* 22 (Autumn 1968), 463–74.

[30]Amnesty International, *Amnesty International Briefing: Iran* (London, 1976); see also William J. Butler and Georges Levasseur, *Human Rights and the Legal System in Iran* (Geneva: International Commission of Jurists, 1976). Many top SAVAK officers held commissions in the armed forces, enabling them to make arrests and participate in these political trials.

Numerous reports of torture appeared in the 1970s. The large number of these reports and the unassailable evidence that accompanied many of them suggests that torture was widely practiced. At least three hundred Iranians were executed between early 1972 and late 1976 after having been condemned by military tribunals, which were generally reserved for political prisoners. Many more Iranians were killed in shootouts with the security forces, "shot while trying to escape," tortured to death, or simply disappeared. Reports even surfaced in the 1970s that SAVAK assassination squads were pursuing Iranians living in exile in the United States and Europe. Much of this repression was directed at guerrilla groups, but moderate opposition figures such as Shahpour Bakhtiar, Hedayatollah Matin-Daftari, Abdul-Karim Lahiji, Mehdi Bazargan, and Ayatollah Sayyid Mahmoud Taleqani were also arrested, beaten, or tortured; prominent intellectuals and writers such as Jalal Ali Ahmad, Samad Behrangi, Behrouz Dehgani, Khosrow Golesorkhi, and Reza Baraheni were tortured or killed; and even Teimur Bakhtiar, the first head of SAVAK, was murdered by the security forces. Amnesty International declared in 1975 that "no country in the world has a worse record in human rights than Iran."[31]

Although Iran's security forces became notorious in the 1960s and 1970s for these brutal measures, they also employed much subtler methods that were often even more effective. The extensive biographical files in SAVAK's central records department were used routinely to screen applications for passports and for employment in government agencies and in many private firms. Members of the opposition were prevented from traveling or gaining meaningful employment in this way; and the fear of being denied a passport or employment discouraged many other disaffected Iranians from engaging in oppositional activity. The security forces also used sophisticated propaganda techniques. For example, it is rumored that Reza Baraheni's book *The Crowned Cannibals*, which gives an extensive account of SAVAK atrocities, was actually written under SAVAK's auspices in order to spread fear among the opposition. This may or may not be true; and SAVAK may well have instigated these rumors simply to discredit Baraheni. Either of these actions would indicate that SAVAK was quite sophisticated in the use of black propaganda. The

[31]*Libération* (Paris), May 29, 1976; *Washington Post*, August 9, 1979, A-12; Chapour Bakhtiar, *Ma fidélité* (Paris: Albin, 1982), 92; interviews with Matin-Daftari, Paris, November 2, 1983, and Lahiji, Paris, October 26, 1983; Baraheni, "Perils of Publishing"; Amnesty International, *Annual Report, 1974–1975* (London, 1975), 8. See also Confederation of Iranian Students, *Documents on the Pahlavi Reign of Terror, 3 vols.* (Frankfort, 1971); Committee against Repression in Iran, *Iran: The Shah's Empire of Repression* (London, 1976), 26–27; Reza Baraheni, *The Crowned Cannibals* (New York: Random House, Vintage, 1977); Iran Committee, *Torture and Resistance in Iran* (London, 1978); and Ali-Reza Nobari, *Iran Erupts* (Stanford, Calif.: Iran-America Documentation Group, 1978), 141–79.

rumors, if untrue, at least indicate that SAVAK had established for itself a very fearful reputation.[32]

SAVAK also carried out sophisticated provocation operations designed to spread fear and confusion among the opposition. The most elaborate of these involved the creation of "controlled" opposition groups, including student groups, political discussion groups, and even "fake" Tudeh party cells. SAVAK used these organizations to identify and control opposition elements and to provoke members of the opposition into carrying out activities for which they could then legally be arrested.[33] One such operation is worth describing in detail as an example of SAVAK's skill in carrying out covert operations. Teimur Bakhtiar was dismissed as head of SAVAK in 1961 and eventually settled in Iraq, where he began to build a political action network to overthrow the shah. According to one report, SAVAK managed to infiltrate over one hundred agents into this network, including many whom Bakhtiar placed in key positions. These agents pretended to develop an extensive network of cells; and SAVAK even set fires and staged a fake assassination in Tehran to convince Bakhtiar that his network was large and operational. In August 1970, just as Bakhtiar was preparing to launch an uprising against the shah, SAVAK had three other agents disguise themselves as students and hijack an airliner to Baghdad. Bakhtiar made contact with these "students" and took them on a hunting trip, where they assassinated him. SAVAK then arrested many legitimate members of the Bakhtiar network, which reportedly included top members of the Tudeh party and members of the Confederation of Iranian Students.[34]

The State Apparatus and Its Co-optative Institutions and Mechanisms

The overthrow of Prime Minister Mosaddeq in the 1953 coup and the subsequent suppression of the National Front, the Tudeh party, and all other popular political organizations left control over the Iranian state in the hands of the shah and a small group of top officials. The growing

[32]These accounts of SAVAK activities were related to me in an interview with one of the CIA sources mentioned in Chap. 4, n. 62.

[33]The retired SAVAK officer mentioned in Chap. 4, n. 62, told me SAVAK "ran the Tudeh party 100 percent," implying that it had so completely penetrated the Tudeh that it essentially controlled it. SAVAK also controlled the Iranian Society for Human Rights and an organization for Iranian intellectuals, according to Matin-Daftari (personal interview).

[34]Hubert Otis Johnson III, "Recent Opposition Movements in Iran" (M.A. thesis, University of Utah, 1975), 111–24. I have been unable to confirm or disconfirm this account independently.

effectiveness of the repressive apparatus and the era of prosperity created by the U.S. aid program and Iran's growing oil revenue kept opposition political activity to a minimum in the mid- and late 1950s, enabling the shah to consolidate his control over the state. Nominally democratic institutions and practices still existed, including elections, a legislature, legislative controls over the executive branch, and even political parties; but the absence of an effective opposition enabled the shah to subvert these institutions and practices, rendering them ineffective as mechanisms through which society could constrain the state. Moreover, the shah began to construct a variety of co-optative institutions and mechanisms that further undermined societal constraint. Although opposition political activity again flourished in the early 1960s, the shah managed to contain it and had established a highly autonomous state by about the end of 1963.

State policy making became increasingly centralized and personalized, leaving no institutional channels through which societal groups could effectively influence the state. The shah was intimately involved in all major aspects of state policy making, deciding such matters as what policies state agencies would pursue, who would be appointed to important positions in the bureaucracy, and which bills the Majles would pass. In making these decisions he relied on a small group of trusted advisers for information, and occasionally for advice, including Assadollah Alam, Manoucher Eqbal, Jafar Sharif-Emami, Amir-Abbas Hoveida, Jamshid Amuzegar, and generals Hussein Fardust, Nematollah Nassiri, Gholam Ali Oveissi, and Hassan Toufanian. These advisers came from fairly diverse backgrounds and were distinguished by their loyalty to the shah rather than to any societal group. Consequently, although they did serve to some extent as channels through which individuals could exert influence over the state, they did not represent the interests of particular societal groups per se. Moreover, the shah constantly played these advisers off against one another to test their loyalty to him and to prevent any of them from becoming too powerful, further undermining their ability to influence state policy on behalf of any group.[35]

Because of the shah's paramount role in decision making, state agencies possessed little or no independent authority. Prime ministers were selected exclusively by the shah after the early 1960s, with the Majles playing only a token role in this process, despite its constitutional prerogatives. The prime minister and his cabinet therefore became instruments for carrying out the shah's decisions rather than autonomous centers of power, as they

[35]U.S. Department of State, Bureau of Intelligence and Research, *Studies in Political Dynamics, no. 13, Iran*, December 1966, 12–14; U.S. Embassy, Tehran, "Decision-Making in Iran," July 22, 1976, reprinted in Muslim Students, *Documents from the U.S. Espionage Den* 7:102–27.

had been in the 1940s and early 1950s. The shah sought to promote loyalty among state officials by paying them well and tolerating corruption; and he used the security forces and a kind of "shadow cabinet" consisting of his closest advisers to monitor state officials' loyalty and effectiveness. These actions gave the shah extensive personal control over state officials and thus further undermined their ability to act independently. The state apparatus exhibited a growing degree of professionalism in this period and was vitally important in carrying out the shah's policies; but it exercised little or no independent authority. Similarly, the provincial offices of state agencies had very little independence from their headquarters in Tehran, where all important decisions were made.[36]

Iran's two legislative bodies also exercised no real authority after the early 1960s. Since Iranian law stipulated that the shah would appoint half the members of the Senate, this body had always been regarded as a tool of the shah and had not acquired any popular legitimacy or independent decision making authority. The Majles, however, had been the main source of attempts by almost all societal groups to influence the state since its establishment in 1906, and it had exercised considerable decision-making authority at certain times, most notably in the 1940s and early 1950s. Majles elections were routinely rigged by the security forces after the 1953 coup, however, so no more than a handful of popular candidates served in this body. As the shah consolidated his control over the state, he was able to control Majles elections more directly and thus ensure that this body would be personally loyal to him. After the heavily rigged election for the Twenty First Majles in September 1963, the Majles served as no more than a rubber stamp to approve the shah's decisions.[37]

Though political parties had been banned after the coup, the shah decided in 1957 to establish two official parties, the Melliyun (Nationalist) party and the Mardom (Peoples') party, in order to create the appearance of a competitive political system and to co-opt potential members of the opposition, especially among the modern middle class. The Melliyun party was headed by Prime Minister Manoucher Eqbal and served as the political vehicle for the incumbent government. The Mardom party was headed by Assadollah Alam and portrayed itself as a loyal opposition party, advocating land reform, political rights for women, and

[36]Muslim Students, *Documents from the U.S. Espionage Den* 7:102–27; Marvin Zonis, *The Political Elite of Iran* (Princeton, N.J.: Princeton University Press, 1971), chap. 4. For a good study of how the shah controlled the armed forces with such methods see U.S. Embassy, Tehran, "Impressions of the Iranian Military Officer Corps," May 6, 1976, reprinted in Muslim Students, *Documents from the U.S. Espionage Den* 7:205–18.

[37]CIA, *Research Study: Elites and the Distribution of Power in Iran*, February 1976, 42–47, reprinted in Muslim Students, *Documents from the U.S. Espionage Den* 7:22–24.

other reformist measures. Both parties tried to build large popular bases, opening offices throughout the country and advancing programs designed to generate popular support. Moreover, the security forces prevented opposition groups from establishing alternative parties, making the Melliyun and Mardom parties the only legal vehicles for political participation. Because they had been established by the state, however, neither party enjoyed much popular legitimacy, and neither managed to attract more than a few thousand members. The main attraction of these parties for most members was the prospect of benefiting from the patronage and opportunities for social and professional advancement they offered; these benefits, in turn, served as instruments of co-optation and therefore gave these parties a highly corporatist character.[38]

The Melliyun and Mardom parties were both severely discredited as a result of their complicity in the rigging of the Twentieth Majles elections of August 1960, and both thereafter became much less prominent. The Melliyun party was replaced as the progovernment party in late 1963 by the Iran Novin (New Iran) party, which was established by a small circle of young technocrats led by Hassan Ali Mansur, who became prime minister in early 1964. The Iran Novin party portrayed itself as a progressive party, embracing the shah's White Revolution reform program. It quickly became an appendage of the state apparatus, receiving financial assistance from SAVAK and from the prime minister's office and taking over many functions previously carried out by state agencies. By 1974, Iran Novin had evolved into an elaborate network of corporatist institutions, controlling roughly 90 percent of the labor unions and rural cooperative societies; maintaining affiliations with most of the bazaar guilds and with the health, literacy, and development corps established under the White Revolution; publishing sixty-seven newspapers and magazines; operating a nationwide network of youth centers; and even opening a college for political managers. Iran Novin claimed over two hundred thousand dues-paying members by 1974 and controlled 229 out of 268 Majles seats. Much like its predecessor, however, the Iran Novin party enjoyed no popular legitimacy as a representative institution. Most of its members were attracted mainly by the extensive patronage and opportunities for social mobility it offered.[39]

[38]For good descriptions of these parties and their successors see Leonard Binder, *Iran: Political Development in a Changing Society* (Berkeley and Los Angeles: University of California Press, 1962), 221–26; U.S. Embassy, Tehran, "The Mardom Party and the Coming Elections," June 6, 1960; and ibid., "The Recent Evolution of Power in Iran," April 11, 1975, reprinted in Muslim Students, *Documents from the U.S. Espionage Den* 7:198.

[39]U.S. Embassy, Tehran, "Political Parties: Recent Developments," October 11, 1960, ibid., "The New Iran Party's First Year," December 31, 1964; ibid., "Development of the Iran Novin Party," June 30, 1974.

Disappointed by the failure of the Iran Novin party and the nearly dormant Mardom party to mobilize adequate support for his policies, and unwilling to tolerate even the limited criticism the two-party system inevitably produced, the shah abruptly eliminated these two parties in early 1975 and replaced them with a single party, the Rastakhiz (Resurgence) party, which he hoped would serve as a vehicle for controlled mass mobilization. Toward this end, the Rastakhiz party took over most of the corporatist institutions the Iran Novin party had administered and assumed responsibility for many of the programs the shah had begun in the mid-1970s, such as the antiprofiteering campaign. Various enticements and coercive measures helped increase membership in the Rastakhiz party, until it reached 5.4 million by early 1977. Like its predecessors, the Rastakhiz party enjoyed little popular legitimacy, and its main attractions were patronage and opportunities for social mobility.[40]

In addition to the state-sponsored political parties, a variety of other corporatist institutions existed. The state controlled labor unions and guilds through the state-sponsored parties and through trade union federations and the High Council of Guilds, which were administered by the ministries of Labor and Interior. Associations for doctors, lawyers, engineers, and other professional groups were affiliated with the state-sponsored parties; and the state exercised further control over these associations by regulating entry into their professions and by directly employing many of their members. The Chamber of Commerce contained federations and special commissions for different types of businessmen and was closely regulated by the Ministry of Commerce, which appointed its top officers and controlled its budget. Social organizations for women, students, and graduates of foreign universities were affiliated with the state-sponsored parties. The state's Religious Endowments Organization exercised a fair amount of control over the clergy by regulating religious schools and the clergy's endowed properties. Even Iran's peasants were brought into corporatist institutions through the village councils, rural cooperative societies, and rural courts set up in conjunction with the land reform program. The security forces maintained close surveillance over these organizations and prevented the establishment of legitimate alternatives, which reinforced their corporatist character. Like the state-sponsored parties, these corporatist institutions co-opted their members by offering them patronage and opportunities for social mobility in exchange for loyalty and cooperation.[41]

[40]U.S. Embassy, Tehran "The Iranian One-Party State," July 10, 1975, reprinted in Muslim Students, *Documents from the U.S. Espionage Den* 7:185–94; ibid. "The Resurgence Party Begins Phase II," reprinted in ibid., 174–83; ibid. "Further Evolution of Iranian Politics," November 30, 1975.

[41]Binder, *Iran*, 177–201; Shahrough Akhavi, *Religion and Politics in Contemporary Iran*

Another important mechanism of co-optation was rapid economic growth, which enabled many Iranians to achieve substantial improvements in their material welfare. The state's dominant role in the economy and its high degree of autonomy enabled it to channel increases in income and other economic benefits to certain societal groups through its development programs and fiscal policies. The state used its influence over the distribution of these benefits to target the politically important urban middle and upper classes, including the modern middle class and the industrial working class, as the primary recipients; it made much less effort to improve the material welfare of the urban and rural lower classes.

The figures in columns 1 and 2 of Table 17 indicate that average per capita consumption was much higher in urban areas than in rural areas in the 1960s and 1970s and that it grew much faster than rural consumption. The bottom row of the table indicates that the average real income of industrial workers and laborers grew, respectively, by an average of 8.6 and 5.6 percent annually between 1968 and 1975. These figures are both substantially lower than the 10.1 percent average annual growth in urban consumption in this period. Assuming that the average incomes of industrial workers and laborers were fairly representative of the average incomes of the urban lower middle class and lower class, respectively, this finding suggests that these two classes benefited much less than the upper class and the remainder of the urban middle class from the tremendous growth in urban consumption in this period. In general, the data in Table 17 suggest that Iran's urban "middle" middle, upper middle, and upper classes benefited most from economic growth; its industrial working class benefited moderately; and its urban and rural lower classes benefited much less.[42] This income distribution pattern was a direct consequence of the state's economic development strategies, which emphasized capital-intensive industrialization at the expense of agriculture and traditional industries.

Iranians benefited from rapid economic growth not only through improvements in income but also through public consumption expenditures, which amounted to direct and indirect transfers from the state to particular societal groups. Lower- and middle-class groups benefited from the

---

(Albany: State University of New York Press, 1980), 56–59, 132–33; Hooglund, *Land and Revolution in Iran*, chap. 7.

[42]The data on urban household consumption expenditure in M. H. Pesaran, "Income Distribution in Iran," in Jane W. Jacqz, ed., *Iran: Past, Present, and Future* (New York: Aspen Institute, 1976), 278, are broadly consistent with this conclusion: the consumption expenditure of the poorest 50 percent of the urban population dropped from 20.07 percent of the total to 17.04 percent in 1959–73; that of the richest 30 percent increased from 63.64 percent of the total to 66.75 percent; and that of the remaining 20 percent declined slightly, from 16.29 percent of the total to 16.21 percent.

Table 17. Consumption and income of selected sectors of Iranian society

Year	Average real private consumption per capita (1975 rials)		Average income per capita (index)[a]	
	Rural (1)	Urban (2)	Industrial workers (3)	Laborers (4)
1959	14,735	31,361	n.a.	n.a.
1960	14,034	30,777	n.a.	n.a.
1961	13,637	29,197	n.a.	n.a.
1962	13,970	30,182	n.a.	n.a.
1963	13,915	30,290	n.a.	n.a.
1964	14,841	31,055	n.a.	n.a.
1965	15,312	30,613	n.a.	n.a.
1966	15,506	34,885	n.a.	64.3
1967	15,266	36,021	n.a.	62.6
1968	16,101	40,232	56.0	68.1
1969	16,053	41,673	57.9	74.0
1970	16,414	45,749	65.0	72.2
1971	15,140	46,284	68.9	66.8
1972	15,775	53,996	74.7	70.0
1973	17,899	61,878	80.2	70.9
1974	18,807	74,968	86.8	78.2
1975	20,382	78,870	100.0	100.0
1976	n.a.	n.a.	115.4	116.5
1977	n.a.	n.a.	113.5	117.7
1978	n.a.	n.a.	161.7	116.0
Average annual growth by period (%):				
1959–75	2.0	5.9	n.a.	n.a.
1968–75	3.4	10.1	8.6	5.6

Sources: Cols. 1–2: Imperial Government of Iran, Plan and Budget Organization, *Economic Statistics and Trends of Iran,* 3d ed. (Tehran, 1976), 109–10, 236–37; Col. 3: Bank Markazi Iran, *Annual Report and Balance Sheet* (Tehran, various years); Col. 4: ibid.; Plan Organization, Iranian Statistical Centre, *National Census of Population and Housing,* vol. 168 (Tehran, 1968), 138; Plan and Budget Organization, Statistical Centre of Iran, *National Census of Population and Housing: Total Country* (Tehran, n.d.), 101.

Note: All figures were deflated using the consumer price index given in International Monetary Fund, *International Financial Statistics Yearbook, 1983* (Washington, 1983), 280–81.

[a]This index was constructed by dividing the wage index data given in the Bank Markazi reference by an estimate of the number of employed laborers in each year, which was calculated on the basis of a linear extrapolation of the figures given in the latter two sources.

increased availability of social services, especially in health care and education. Table 8 indicates that considerable advances were made in nutritional standards and in the availability of physicians and educational opportunities, bringing about substantial increases in the life expectancy and literacy rates and a substantial decline in the infant mortality rate. Nevertheless, despite these improvements, Iran's literacy and infant mortality rates were still worse than the average for all underdeveloped countries in 1970, and its average life expectancy was only 54.5 years. Although the 1970s saw further improvements, these figures suggest that Iran's lower and lower middle classes did not benefit greatly. Since the availability of social services was inevitably much higher in urban areas, it is probably safe to conclude that the urban middle class benefited most from these advances and that the rural lower class benefited least.

Iran's upper middle class and upper class also received various direct and indirect transfers from the state. As the state bureaucracy grew in size, new employment opportunities in the upper levels of the bureaucracy became available to these classes. Employment in the state bureaucracy was often very attractive because it offered social mobility and the benefits of the corruption that was rampant in state agencies. Because the state controlled employment opportunities in universities and research institutes, many of the shah's staunchest intellectual opponents could be co-opted as well. The state made large direct transfers to members of the upper class in the form of lucrative business deals, subsidies, and other cash payments. It awarded highly inflated contracts to certain businessmen and influence peddlers for concessions of various kinds and made large payments to landowners in connection with the land reform program, enabling them to avoid the losses that land reform often entails. Many members of the clergy also received state subsidies. Although most of these transfers were entirely legal, many were not. As a result, corruption flourished, especially after the oil boom.[43] Weighing these transfers against the social services provided to the lower classes, one can see that the state's overall consumption expenditures probably benefited the urban middle and upper classes much more than the urban and rural lower classes.

Economic growth therefore greatly benefited Iran's upper middle class and upper class in the 1960s and 1970s; it provided substantial, though smaller, benefits to the remainder of the urban middle class and the industrial working class; and it produced only modest improvements in the living standards of the urban and rural lower classes. By helping to distribute the benefits of rapid economic growth in this way, the state's development and fiscal policies served to co-opt the urban middle and upper classes but produced growing frustration among the urban and rural lower classes, creating tensions that produced growing political unrest.

[43]On the growth and composition of the state bureaucracy see Bill, *Politics of Iran*, chap. 2. For good studies of the selective awarding of state contracts and of corruption see U.S. Embassy, Tehran, "The Iranian Aviation Mafia," April 27, 1971, reprinted in Muslim Students, *Documents from the U.S. Espionage Den* 17:45–47; and U.S. Embassy, Tehran, "Corruption in Iran: A Problem for American Companies," June 20, 1972, reprinted in ibid., 74–89. Much of this corruption was channeled through the Pahlavi Foundation; see Mark Hulbert, *Interlock* (New York: Richardson and Snyder, 1982), chap. 2. On state subsidies for the clergy see Akhavi, *Religion and Politics in Contemporary Iran*, 45, 141–42.

6

The Politics of the Iranian Client State

The last two chapters examined how Iran's cliency relationship with the United States and changes in the stage and form of its mode of production affected the characteristics and capabilities of the Iranian state and society in the post-1953 era. This chapter examines how these latter factors shaped and constrained Iran's "visible national politics" in this era and consequently how they affected the state's autonomy.

Iranian Politics in Transition, 1953–1959

Despite the suppression of the National Front and the Tudeh party after the 1953 coup, the Iranian state did not yet enjoy a high degree of autonomy in the mid-1950s. The modern middle class had been powerful enough in the early 1950s to make a bid for hegemony over the state, and both it and the industrial working class grew rapidly and played increasingly vital roles in the economy in the following years. Therefore, although their main political organizations had been temporarily neutralized, these two classes remained potentially quite powerful. The traditional upper class continued to play an important role in the economy and wielded considerable influence over the armed forces and over lower- and middle-class groups through patronage bonds. Consequently, although it had been in decline since the turn of the century, this class also remained fairly powerful. Moreover, the state's repressive and co-optative capabilities were still not sufficiently developed to enable it to act with a high degree of autonomy. Lacking adequate autonomy-enhancing capabilities, the state was forced to maintain a base of support in Iranian society in the mid-1950s.

The strong opposition expressed by remnants of the National Front and the Tudeh party toward the shah's regime and the continuing popularity of the National Front ruled out the modern middle class and the industrial working class as possible bases of support for the state, and the bourgeoisie, the traditional middle class, and the peasantry were too weak to serve as effective bases of support. The state therefore maintained an uneasy alliance with the traditional upper class after the 1953 coup while simultaneously trying to increase its autonomy vis-à-vis this class and all other societal groups. The modern middle class and the industrial working class were thus essentially excluded from political participation, and state policy largely reflected the interests of the traditional upper class.

The state's efforts to exclude the modern middle class and the industrial working class consisted mainly of further suppression of the remnants of the National Front and the Tudeh party. After the September 1954 discovery of the Tudeh military network, General Bakhtiar's intelligence unit, working closely with its CIA advisers, located and destroyed Tudeh targets such as the printing facilities of the newspaper Mardom, a large Tudeh arms dump, an extensive espionage network, an embezzlement ring, and the Tudeh's youth, women's, and railway workers' organizations. Further arrests and an extensive anti-Tudeh propaganda campaign were carried out in the mid- and late 1950s. SAVAK also penetrated the Tudeh party with spies and agents provocateurs, leading one SAVAK officer to claim that SAVAK "ran the Tudeh Party one hundred percent" by the 1960s.[1] These actions incapacitated the Tudeh, which ceased to be an effective political actor in Iran during the remainder of the shah's regime.

The remnants of the National Front were also harshly repressed, preventing this organization from exerting any real influence over the state. Following his arrest in August 1953, Mosaddeq served a three-year jail term and then remained under virtual house arrest in a remote provincial village until he died in 1967. National Front leaders were arrested repeatedly in the mid- and late 1950s and kept under surveillance by the security forces, forcing them sharply to curtail their political activities. Three leaders of the pro–National Front Qashqai tribe were forced into exile in 1955, and the state undertook a major effort in the next few years to disarm and settle the Qashqai.[2] Zahedi's efforts to rig the Eighteenth

[1]U.S. Embassy, Tehran, "Anti-Tudeh Campaign of the Iranian Government from November 20, 1954," April 30, 1955; idem, "Iran Political Summary: July 1955," August 9, 1955, 14; interview with a SAVAK officer (Chap. 4, n. 62). On the Tudeh party's decline after the 1953 coup see Sepehr Zabih, *The Communist Movement in Iran* (Berkeley and Los Angeles: University of California Press, 1966), chap. 6.

[2]Richard W. Cottam, *Nationalism in Iran* (Pittsburgh: University of Pittsburgh Press, 1979), 294–95; *Journal de Tehran*, October 12, 1954 and November 2, 1954; U.S. Embassy, Tehran, "Imprisonment of Pro-Mosadeq Political Figures," June 1, 1955; idem, "Political

Majles elections in early 1954 kept out all National Front figures, and martial law regulations, which remained in effect until April 1957, enabled the state to prevent opposition groups from using the press and organizing public demonstrations and rallies.

The state's repression and its co-optative activities also helped create several major cleavages in the nationalist movement after the 1953 coup, rendering this movement increasingly ineffective as the political voice of the modern middle class. One such cleavage was a split between the secular nationalists of the Iran party and the Islamic modernists[3] of the National Resistance Movement, which was formed shortly after the coup by Mehdi Bazargan, Ayatollah Sayyid Mahmoud Taleqani, and Yadollah Sahabi. Although the National Resistance Movement strongly supported Mosaddeq, it differed from the Iran party in emphasizing Islamic principles as well as anti-imperialism and democracy in its political program. The membership of the National Resistance Movement was drawn primarily from the bazaar and from academia and other professions; its social base therefore included elements of both the traditional middle class and the modern middle class. Despite the Islamic orientation of the National Resistance Movement, it worked very closely with the Iran party in the mid-1950s, and the two groups together constituted the dominant, Mosaddeqist wing of the nationalist movement. Differences between the two factions increased in the early 1960s, however, undermining their ability to work together in that critical period.

A second cleavage began to appear in the mid- and late 1950s with the emergence of political figures such as Ali Amini, Abol-Hassan Ebtehaj, Valliolah Qarani, and Hassan Arsanjani. These figures can be described as "independent nationalists" because they espoused nationalistic and fairly progressive ideas but were not aligned with the Mosaddeqists, who remained the most popular branch of the nationalist movement. Although some of these independent nationalists had previously been associated with the National Front and even with the Tudeh party, what distinguished them from the Mosaddeqists was their willingness to work within the constraints of the shah's regime, their nonideological character, and their limited popular support. Most of them were co-opted by the lure of important positions in the state bureaucracy, and they gradually became the de facto leaders of the emerging technocratic fraction of the modern

---

Potential of the Tribes of Iran," June 2, 1959; CIA, "The Outlook for Iran, NIE 34–59," March 3, 1959, 3.

[3]This term and most of the discussion in this paragraph are from Houchang Esfandiar Chehabi, "Modernist Shi'ism and Politics: The Liberation Movement of Iran" (Ph.D. diss., Yale University, 1986); see also U.S. Embassy, Tehran, "A Survey of the Nationalist Movement in Iran since the Fall of Mosadeq," May 8, 1957.

middle class. This technocratic fraction was fairly supportive of the shah's regime but too small and too apolitical to constitute an effective base of support for the state.[4] The emergence of this technocratic fraction did, however, undermine the Mosaddeqists by drawing away from them many bright and dynamic members of the modern middle class.

A third cleavage in the nationalist movement was created by an assortment of populist demogogues and political opportunists who espoused nationalistic ideas but were also not aligned with, and often worked against, the Mosaddeqists. This group included Mozaffar Baqai, Ayatollah Kashani, Ahmad Aramesh, Mohammad Derakhshesh, Mohsen Pezeshkpour, and perhaps also Khalil Maleki. Most of these figures had been associated with the National Front at the peak of its popularity in 1951 and early 1952 but had subsequently broken with Mosaddeq, and several had been involved in the 1953 coup. These figures appealed mainly to the traditional middle and lower classes and therefore complicated the efforts of the Mosaddeqists to establish alliances with these classes. Although the state generally suppressed these figures, it tolerated and even assisted some of them in order to undermine popular support for the Mosaddeqists.

Another potential source of opposition to the state in this period was the Shi'i clergy. The clergy had been deeply involved in the events leading up to the Constitutional Revolution of 1906 but thereafter had largely withdrawn from politics because of its differences with the main opposition groups and because of a gradual decline in its base of support due to social and economic development. By the early 1950s, the mainstream Shi'i clergy, led by Ayatollah Mohammad Hussein Borujerdi, took little interest in secular political matters. However, a small number of activist clerics, led by Ayatollah Kashani and the Fedayan-e Islam and based mainly on the traditional lower and middle classes, were highly active in politics at this time.[5]

After the coup, the shah tried to improve relations between the state and the mainstream Shi'i clergy and to isolate and suppress Kashani and the Fedayan-e Islam. His most important gesture toward the mainstream

[4]Although the technocratic fraction of the modern middle class staffed the state bureaucracy in the 1960s and 1970s, it never enthusiastically supported the shah's regime and never really opposed the more radical nationalist opposition. Although co-opted, it thus did not provide a base of support for the state. The clearest proof of this came in 1978–79, when the technocratic fraction made no effort to prevent the shah's downfall. For useful studies of some prominent independent nationalists in the 1950s see U.S. Embassy, Tehran, "Formation of 'New Iran Group,'" May 2, 1955; idem, "Formation of Pro-AMINI Political Party," July 24, 1957; idem, "The Qarani Affair: A Recapitulation," March 25, 1958; and idem, "Formation of the Freedom Society of Iran," September 3, 1957.

[5]Shahrough Akhavi, *Religion and Politics in Contemporary Iran* (Albany: State University of New York Press, 1980), chap. 3.

clergy was his tacit cooperation in the 1955 campaign against the Baha'is, who were viewed as apostates by the Shi'i. The shah also exchanged cordial notes with leading clergymen, received delegations from the clerical leadership, and carried out certain educational reforms favored by the clergy. Despite Kashani's key role in the overthrow of Mosaddeq, the shah viewed him as a threat. Therefore, when Kashani began to denounce the Zahedi government and resume his political activities, the security forces placed him under surveillance, arrested one of his sons, and eventually arrested him (twice) in 1956. After a November 1955 attempt on the life of Prime Minister Hussein Ala, the principal leaders of the Fedayan-e Islam were arrested and quickly tried; four were executed and the remainder were given long prison terms. These actions destroyed the Fedayan, although an organization bearing its name reappeared during the 1978–79 revolution.[6]

The shah's flirtation with the mainstream Shi'i clergy was one element in his broader strategy of establishing a base of support among the traditional upper class. That class shared the shah's desire to suppress the National Front and the Tudeh party and did not generally object to the establishment of a cliency relationship with the United States. Moreover, it was clearly in a position to frustrate many of the shah's plans, were he to ignore its interests. Since the state was still relatively weak and these shared goals were quite important to the shah, the traditional upper class was a natural base of support for the state. In exchange for this support, however, the shah was obliged to put off any plans he might have had to carry out extensive social and economic reforms, especially land reform. The main concession the shah made to the traditional upper class was to appoint prime ministers acceptable to this class, especially Fazlollah Zahedi. These prime ministers, in turn, filled the cabinet with ministers favorable to the traditional upper class, enabling this class to exert considerable influence over the state.

Although the shah quickly established a base of support among the traditional upper class, he evidently wanted to increase the state's independence from this class as rapidly as possible. Iranian politics in the mid- and late 1950s therefore consisted mainly of the shah's attempts to reduce the influence of the traditional upper class and corresponding attempts by this class to retain and even expand its influence. The shah's efforts took three main forms: he periodically purged representatives of the traditional upper class from top positions in the state apparatus, especially from the

[6]Ibid., chap. 3 and 177; *New York Times*, December 16, 1953, 11:1, February 1, 1954, 4:7, and January 19, 1956, 7:1; U.S. Embassy, Tehran, "Political Summary for the Month of January 1956," February 6, 1956, 3–5; idem, "Political Summary for the Month of November 1956," December 4, 1956, 6.

premiership; he took steps to strengthen the state's autonomy-enhancing capabilities; and he began to expand and co-opt the technocratic fraction of the modern middle class and fill the state bureaucracy with its members.

The first major confrontation between the shah and the traditional upper class was over Zahedi's tenure as prime minister, which lasted until April 1955. The shah was certainly happy with Zahedi's efforts to suppress the National Front and the Tudeh party and with the October 1954 oil agreement, but tension quickly emerged over flourishing corruption and Zahedi's heavy-handed efforts to rig the Eighteenth Majles elections, which brought many traditional upper-class conservatives into the Majles. The shah also undoubtedly saw Zahedi as a threat to his own ambitions for preeminence. Zahedi was abruptly dismissed and replaced with Hossein Ala, a career civil servant who was weak and devoted to the shah but also acceptable to most of the traditional upper class. Zahedi left Iran for his estate in Switzerland, where he died several years later, but a faction of his ardent supporters remained in the Majles and served as the primary spokesmen for the traditional upper class in its disputes with the shah and Ala during the remainder of the Eighteenth Majles.[7]

After the installation of the more compliant Ala government, the shah quickly acted to increase the state's independence from the traditional upper class. Supporters of the government soon clashed with the pro-Zahedi faction in the Majles over issues such as committee assignments, an inheritance tax bill, and a bill giving the state control over Iran's barren lands. The shah and his allies launched bitter attacks in the press against Iran's "fossilized feudal elements,"[8] who responded in kind. A major dispute erupted in June 1955, when the conservative opposition in the Majles tried unsuccessfully to assert control over the Plan Organization, which was headed by Abol-Hassan Ebtehaj, a moderately progressive technocrat who was trying to promote industrialization and certain economic reforms opposed by the traditional upper class. The government also succeeded in passing legislation that expanded its power to control the press and imprison its opponents, and it made extensive efforts to settle tribal groups. Some of the tension between the traditional upper class and the shah receded in August 1955, when the government made several minor personnel changes, and mutual attacks in the press began to subside.[9]

[7]Henderson to Dulles, March 9, 1954, Record Group 59, Box 4116; U.S. Embassy, Tehran, "Assessment of Likely Successors to General Zahedi as Iranian Prime Minister," December 20, 1954; idem, "Majles Opposition to the Ala Cabinet," May 16, 1955.

[8]U.S. Embassy, Tehran, "Iran Political Summary: April 6 to May 31, 1955," June 14, 1955, 2–5; idem, "Iran Political Summary: July 1955," August 9, 1955, 3.

[9]Idem, "Iran Political Summary: August 1955," September 4, 1955.

In another attempt to reduce the influence of the traditional upper class, the shah arranged the rigging of the Nineteenth Majles elections, held in April 1956. Just as Zahedi had used the Eighteenth Majles elections to pack the Majles with conservatives, the shah packed the Nineteenth Majles with moderate but essentially apolitical candidates who could be relied upon to support the government. This meant that many representatives of the traditional upper class (including the entire pro-Zahedi faction), as well as a few remaining nationalists and progressive independents, were forced out of the Majles. Predictably, the new Majles passed legislation, opposed by the traditional upper class, to approve a large World Bank loan, and it blocked renewed efforts by this class to restrict the activities of the Plan Organization. The Nineteenth Majles also approved a bill in March 1957 that formally created SAVAK, the new intelligence agency. Soon afterward, Prime Minister Ala was replaced with Manoucher Eqbal, a civil servant from a wealthy landowning family who had close ties to the traditional upper class but could also be counted upon to carry out the shah's policies.[10]

With the suppression of the National Front and the Tudeh party, the creation of a docile Majles, and the establishment of an increasingly effective intelligence agency, the shah was able in early 1957 to try to broaden the state's base of support by allowing a limited amount of political liberalization to occur. This liberalization was aimed primarily at the emerging independent nationalists and at a few populist demagogues, who could be counted upon both to oppose the traditional upper class and to draw support away from the Mosaddeqist opposition. The first step in this process was the lifting of martial law in Tehran, which occurred in April 1957. Although this was an important symbolic gesture, its practical effect was limited by the earlier enactment of a tough public security law and by the creation of SAVAK, which merely replaced and institutionalized the martial law administration. The second step was to establish the Melliyun and Mardom parties, which were intended to co-opt potential members of the opposition, especially among the modern middle class. These actions were accompanied by a limited but significant increase in freedom of the press. The shah also began to tolerate and even encourage overt political activity by certain independent nationalists and political opportunists. Hassan Arsanjani and a small group of Majles deputies and

[10]Idem, "1956 Majles Elections in Tehran," May 15, 1956; idem, "Political Summary for the Month of May 1956," June 6, 1956, 4; idem, "Political Summary for December 1956," January 5, 1957, 3–4; idem, "Political Summary for January 1957," February 6, 1957, 3–4; idem, "Political Summary for the Month of March, 1957," April 11, 1957, 3; idem, "An Analysis of the Eqbal Government as Seen after 22 Days in Office," April 27, 1957; Cottam, *Nationalism in Iran*, 236.

civil servants were permitted to form a political organization, known as the Freedom party, to support the political ambitions of Ali Amini, who was then Iran's ambassador to the United States. Mozaffar Baqai was permitted to hold a large rally of the Toilers' party in May 1957 and even given police protection for this purpose. Maleki, Aramesh, and Derakhshesh were widely rumored to be receiving assistance from SAVAK, and the Pan-Iranist party was revived and apparently assisted financially by SAVAK on direct orders from the shah.[11]

This limited political liberalization inevitably led the Mosaddeqist opposition, which was operating clandestinely, to increase its political activity. It soon became obvious, however, that these new political freedoms were not to apply to the Mosaddeqists. A group of progovernment Majles deputies introduced a bill in early 1957 to make the Iran party illegal. Although this bill never actually passed, it remained before the Majles for a long time and clearly had support from the government and from government-backed actors such as the Pan-Iranist party and Ahmad Aramesh. A further effort to intimidate the Mosaddeqist opposition occurred in September 1957, when some seventy members of the National Resistance Movement (including all of its top leaders) and several members of the Iran party were arrested. These arrests followed the publication of open letters by the National Resistance Movement criticizing the shah and a recently signed oil agreement. Although most of those arrested were soon released, several were reportedly tortured and four leaders of the National Resistance Movement remained in prison for eight months, effectively neutralizing this organization. These arrests inevitably produced increased dissatisfaction with the shah's regime among the Mosaddeqists and other disaffected elements and showed clearly the limits of the shah's political liberalization.[12]

Two events in early 1958 further demonstrated the growing unrest and the limits to political liberalization. The first occurred when Sam Pope Brewer, a reporter for the New York Times, traveled to Iran in late 1957 and met with several Mosaddeqists and other opposition figures. Brewer

[11]U.S. Embassy, Tehran, "Political Summary for the Month of April, 1957," May 1, 1957, 5; idem, "An Analysis of the New 'Press Freedom' of the Government," June 3, 1957; idem, "Formation of Pro-AMINI Political Party"; idem, "Meeting of the Toilers' Party," May 22, 1957; idem, "Iranian Government Critics and Opposition Leaders and the Status of the Latter," February 8, 1960, 10; confidential interviews with two retired CIA officers (regarding Aramesh and Derakhshesh); U.S. Embassy, Tehran, "Government-Sponsored Extreme Nationalist Political Grouping," March 26, 1958; idem, "Report on the Formation of a New Party in Iran," March 2, 1958.

[12]Idem, "Conversation with Vice-President of Majlis," February 7, 1957; idem, "Further Developments with Regard to the Iran Party Declaration," February 20, 1957; idem, "Arrests of Nationalists," September 24, 1957; idem, "Further Developments in Recent Arrests of Nationalists," October 24, 1957; Chehabi, "Modernist Shi'ism and Politics," 246–50.

then wrote an article, which appeared in early 1958, detailing unrest among the Iranian opposition. As a means of encouraging the shah to carry out reforms, CIA officers stationed in Tehran, acting with the approval of the U.S. ambassador, had invited Brewer to write the article and arranged his contacts with the opposition. The shah angrily denounced Brewer and opposition figures who "contact foreigners by night" and had at least eight members of the opposition arrested.[13]

The second incident, which was far more serious, was a plot to oust Prime Minister Eqbal and force the shah to "reign but not rule" as a constitutional monarch. This plot was led by General Valiollah Qarani, the commander of the army's intelligence branch, who was a progressive nationalist and something of a "young Turk" but was not directly associated with the Mosaddeqists or with any other political organization. Qarani had been voicing his displeasure with the shah's regime for some time, and it had become an open secret in Tehran that he was plotting a coup. What is not widely known, however, is that Qarani had told the shah that he was acting as an agent provocateur to draw prominent political figures into his plot to expose them as subversives; but that his plot was indeed genuine, and he had told the shah this so he could organize his plot openly without making the shah suspicious. Qarani was arrested two days before the coup was scheduled to occur and eventually given a three-year prison sentence. Qarani's collaborators were a diverse assortment of independent nationalists, traditional upper-class conservatives, and political opportunists. Ali Amini was implicated and removed (under a different pretext) from his post as ambassador to the United States.

The most striking aspect of the Qarani affair was the diversity of his collaborators. This indicated that the Mosaddeqists and many independent nationalists and members of the traditional upper class shared the goal of forcing the shah to reign as a figurehead and were capable of working together against the shah. United States embassy and CIA personnel had been following the plot for some time and had met repeatedly with Qarani. Although they apparently did not encourage him to carry out the coup, they also did not warn the shah about the seriousness of the plot. Perhaps for this reason, the shah suspected that the United States and Britain were behind the coup attempt. This suspicion increased his desire to become more independent from the West.[14]

[13]*New York Times*, January 2, 1958, 5:3, and February 25, 1958, 2:4 The CIA's role in this affair was described to me in a confidential interview with one of the officers involved.

[14]U.S. Embassy, Tehran, "Qarani Affair." Some details of this episode, including U.S. efforts to monitor the plot, were related to me in an interview (Washington, D.C., July 9, 1985) with the late Fraser Wilkins, minister-counselor in the U.S. embassy at the time, who

The shah's concerns about domestic unrest increased considerably after the July 1958 coup in Iraq, in which a conservative monarchy much like the shah's was suddenly and brutally overthrown by military officers led by General Abdel-Karim Qasim, a young nationalist who was similar in many ways to Qarani.[15] The Qarani affair and the Iraqi coup frightened the shah and led him to make policy changes in 1958 that were to become hallmarks of his regime in subsequent years: he became increasingly wary of the traditional upper class; he ended the trend toward political liberalization; he started a limited but highly visible program of social and economic reforms, including an anticorruption campaign and a limited land reform program; he pressured the United States for more military aid; and he began to improve Iran's ties with the Soviet Union in order to discourage Soviet subversion in Iran and improve his bargaining position with the United States. The shah did not, however, make any direct attempt to improve his relations with the Mosaddeqist opposition, relying instead on the two-party system to co-opt the Mosaddeqists' base of support.

The Qarani affair and the Iraqi coup were encouraging signs for the Iranian opposition. The Mosaddeqists were, however, in disarray as a result of the state's repression, especially the arrests of September 1957; and most of the remaining opposition organizations had been co-opted by the state or temporarily weakened as a result of their involvement in the Qarani plot. The main threat to the shah's regime at this time was, therefore, the prospect of another coup attempt by disaffected military officers, perhaps with support from the Mosaddeqists or other opposition elements.[16] The shah's security forces were well aware of this possibility, however, and no major threats of this kind emerged.

The Establishment of a Highly Autonomous State, 1960–1963

By 1960 the shah had constructed a regime in which the state was relatively autonomous. Relying mainly on his increasingly effective re-

---

had met with Qarani, and in confidential interviews with a U.S. military attaché and with two retired CIA officers who monitored the plot. One of these retired CIA officers maintains that the U.S. decision to meet with Qarani and not warn the shah constituted de facto U.S. support for the coup attempt.

[15]On Qasim and the Iraqi coup see Majid Khadduri, *Republican Iraq* (London: Oxford University Press, 1969).

[16]U.S. Embassy, Tehran, to Secretary of State, August 14, 1958; U.S. Embassy, Tehran, "Current Political Situation in Iran and Assessment of the Future," September 4, 1958.

pressive apparatus, he had thoroughly suppressed the National Front and the Tudeh party, the two main political organizations that represented the modern middle class and the industrial working class. He had also managed to reduce the influence of the traditional upper class by purging many of its representatives from the state apparatus and replacing them with relatively apolitical technocrats. The bourgeoisie and the emerging technocratic fraction of the modern middle class were still too small to exercise much influence and were, in any case, heavily co-opted by the state. The traditional middle class and the urban and rural lower classes remained poorly mobilized and bound to the traditional upper class through a variety of patronage bonds, leaving them still very weak.

Nonetheless, the modern middle class and certain other groups were still powerful enough to impose some limits on the state's autonomy, and the possibility existed that a large political movement might emerge and impose more extensive constraint on the state. Rapid economic growth in the mid- and late 1950s had increased the size and economic importance of the modern middle class, and this class was becoming increasingly restless because of the shah's failure to undertake much-needed social, economic, and political reforms. Several loosely organized political networks existed that were capable of providing the leadership for a new political movement based on the modern middle class: the Mosaddeqist wing of the nationalist movement remained essentially intact, though dormant, and independent nationalists such as Ali Amini and Hassan Arsanjani enjoyed some appeal. The Mosaddeqists could draw on the legacy of the National Front to mobilize support; and many young intellectuals and professionals had emerged who could infuse new energy into a political movement based on the modern middle class.

The industrial working class had also grown and become potentially more powerful, and the traditional middle class and urban lower class remained quite large, though politically inactive. The shah's failure to undertake extensive social and economic reforms left the urban lower class and much of the industrial working class still mired in poverty, creating unrest among these classes. Moreover, a harsh price stabilization program begun in September 1960 produced a mild recession that lasted until mid-1963, creating further unrest.[17] These classes therefore also constituted a potential source of opposition that could be mobilized into a popular movement by the Mosaddeqists, populist demagogues like Baqai, activist clerics in the tradition of Kashani, and perhaps even the independ-

[17] Idem, "Quarterly Economic Summary for the Fourth Quarter, 1960," February 14, 1961; idem, "Recent Actions. . . . to Get Iranian Economy Moving," July 30, 1963.

ent nationalists. Finally, the traditional upper class remained fairly powerful and was still capable of creating serious problems for the shah.

Iran's cliency relationship with the United States and its growing oil revenue were, however, rapidly strengthening the state's repressive and co-optative capabilities. Iranian politics was therefore very much in flux: conditions were ripe for the emergence of a large opposition movement, but the state's ability to contain such a movement was growing rapidly. These conflicting forces played themselves out between early 1960 and late 1963. By the end of this period the Iranian state had managed to defeat all of its challengers and defuse much of the unrest that had existed in 1960, leaving it highly autonomous.

The first sign that a popular opposition movement was beginning to reemerge came in January 1960, when roughly one thousand Tehran high school students staged the first public demonstration to be held in Iran since late 1953. Some two hundred of the demonstrators were arrested, including forty-one nonstudents. Although the immediate cause of the demonstration was a decision by the Ministry of Education to raise the minimum passing grade in Iran's high schools, the students also chanted slogans and carried signs denouncing the shah and his regime. This demonstration was not immediately followed by further overt oppositional activity, but the demonstrators' strong denunciations of the shah showed clearly that popular unrest was growing.[18]

In the months after the student demonstration, attention increasingly focused on the elections for the Twentieth Majles, scheduled for the summer of 1960. These elections were to be the first under the new two-party system and, because of changes in the election laws, were also to be the first in over four years. Initial preparations for the elections began in February. Confident that the two-party system could absorb popular unrest, and mindful of recent election-related unrest in Turkey and South Korea, the shah and Prime Minister Eqbal announced that the elections would be completely free and that independent candidates (i.e., those not affiliated with the two official political parties) would be permitted to participate. Privately, however, the shah told the U.S. ambassador in March that the elections would be rigged, and orders were soon given to SAVAK to secure the election of the shah's favored candidates.[19]

The shah's announcement that the elections would be free and the

[18]Idem, "The Students' Demonstration of January 11, 1960," March 12, 1960.

[19]Idem, "Political Parties Prepare for Coming Elections," March 5, 1960; idem, "Interim Report on Iran's 20th Majlis Elections," September 24, 1960, 2; idem, "Summary of Majlis Election Campaign, June 27–July 5," July 9, 1960.

obvious need to rig the elections to produce a compliant Majles set the stage for a major confrontation between the state and the opposition. Several independents quickly began to campaign, including Allahyar Saleh, Mozaffar Baqai, Hossein Makki, Ali Amini, and a group of Amini supporters that included Assadollah Rashidian and Sayyid Jafar Behbehani, a nephew of Ayatollah Behbehani. In a development with much greater long-term significance, a coalition known as the Second National Front was organized in July by the Iran party, the National Resistance Movement, the People of Iran party, Dariush Foruhar's Party of the Iranian Nation, and an anti-Maleki faction of the Third Force led by Mohammad Khonji. Concerned by this rapid increase in opposition activity, the state responded with a campaign of intimidation and repression: Eqbal privately threatened to reveal Amini's involvement in the Qarani affair; several SAVAK officers who had reputations for brutality were suddenly promoted as a warning to the opposition; and SAVAK, the National Police, and the army took steps to prevent Saleh and other members of the Second National Front from campaigning.[20]

The elections were held in August and were heavily rigged, producing considerable public resentment toward the government and the shah. The leaders of the Melliyun and Mardom parties had colluded with the shah to pick the winning candidates, usually by matching a strong candidate from one party against a weak candidate from the other. Shortly after voting had begun, the U.S. embassy was shown a list of the candidates slated for victory which indicated that the Melliyun party would win approximately 130 of the 200 Majles seats and that only four independents would win, including no members of the opposition. As word leaked out about which candidates had been chosen to win, several of the losing candidates and some election officials withdrew from the process. The elections themselves involved blatant irregularities, including the intimidation of candidates, restrictions on candidates' access to the press, fraudulent vote counting, and the use of preinscribed ballots and forged identity cards by voters hired by the government. The wide reporting of these irregularities in the press added to the growing public resentment. Violence at polling places resulted in several deaths. Voting was postponed or stopped al-

[20]Idem, "Summary of Majles Election Campaign"; Hassan Mohammadi-Nejad, "Elite-Counterelite Conflict and the Development of a Revolutionary Movement" (Ph.D. diss., Southern Illinois University, 1970), 134–35; U.S. Embassy, Tehran, "Election Developments," July 28, 1960; idem, "Iran on the Eve of Parliamentary Elections," July 13, 1960; idem, "Beginning of Voting in Majles Elections," August 4, 1960; idem, "Interim Report," 4–6.

together in several places as a result of popular unrest, and the elections were finally canceled on August 27.[21]

The election fiasco had two main consequences. First, both the shah and the Melliyun and Mardom parties were severely discredited. A campaign orchestrated partly by SAVAK tried to blame the election irregularities on Prime Minister Eqbal. Eqbal resigned from the premiership soon after the elections were nullified and was replaced by Jafar Sharif-Emami, a civil servant who had held several top positions in the state bureaucracy. Assadollah Alam, the founder and head of the Mardom party, was also widely criticized for his role in the elections, and he soon resigned from the party leadership. These resignations, however, did little to dampen public unrest. Second, opposition figures, such as Amini, Baqai, and Saleh, who had participated in the elections yet remained critical of the shah's regime gained considerable visibility and prestige.[22]

The shah took several steps immediately after the elections to prevent further damage to his regime. He tried to distance himself from the fiasco by blaming the elections on Eqbal and calling for new ones. To control the new elections, he announced that people who had been associated with Mosaddeq would not be allowed to participate, and he directed the security forces to draw up a new list of candidates. The shah also tried to weaken and divide the opposition through a combination of repression and co-optation. Amini was permitted to form a new political party, known as the Liberal party. Baqai was permitted to hold a large rally in early September but was then arrested two weeks later. Saleh and other National Front moderates were permitted to move about freely and were considered for appointment to cabinet posts and other top positions. A standing committee, consisting of the heads of all state security agencies, was created to deal with the growing unrest, and a ban was announced in early September on all unauthorized public gatherings.[23]

These actions temporarily halted overt opposition activity. Nevertheless, Amini soon began to prepare for the new elections by organizing a group of independent candidates which included Sayyid Jafar Behbehani and Mohammad Derakhshesh, who headed a prominent teachers' organi-

[21]Idem, "Interim Report," 4–7.

[22]Ibid., 5; idem, "Resignation of Mardom Party Head Assadollah Alam," September 24, 1960.

[23]Idem, "Interim Report," 9, 13; idem, "Preliminary Observations on Majles Elections," December 5, 1960; idem, "Political Parties: Recent Developments," October 11, 1960; idem, "Post-Eqbal Activities of Mozafer Baqai and 'Guardians of Freedom,'" September 1, 1960; idem, "Arrest of Mozafar Baqai," September 17, 1960; idem, "Alayar Saleh and the Coming Elections," December 21, 1960, 9.

zation. National Front leaders Saleh, Sanjabi, and Mohammad Ali Keshavarz-Sadr also began to prepare for the elections, as did Baqai and Maleki. Shortly after the new elections began in January 1961, the student wing of the National Front organized a series of large demonstrations (with crowds of up to twenty thousand) to protest election irregularities. Baqai organized several smaller protests. These demonstrations were broken up by the security forces or by groups of thugs hired by the Rashidians and their allies, and Baqai and many student leaders were arrested. On January 30 a group of National Front leaders took bast in the Senate for several weeks to protest election fraud and the harsh measures used by the security forces. Election violence also occurred in certain provinces, resulting in several deaths. The new Majles, convened in early February, was packed with allies of the shah and enjoyed no more popular legitimacy than its predecessors, though the shah did permit Saleh to win a seat in an effort to co-opt the moderate wing of the National Front.[24]

The fraudulent restaging of the Twentieth Majles elections further inflamed popular unrest. Student demonstrations continued, leading the shah to close Tehran University. Saleh used his position in the new Majles to launch public attacks on the regime. Eight demonstrators were killed and many more were hurt in rioting in Tehran in mid-March. In late April, Derakhshesh organized a teachers' strike to protest a government plan to improve teachers' working conditions. At a teachers' rally in front of the Majles on May 2, police killed one demonstrator.[25]

The intensity of popular unrest underscored the need for drastic new measures. United States officials began to pressure the shah gently but firmly to broaden his base of support and carry out social, economic, and political reforms. Embassy and CIA personnel in Tehran also began to meet with opposition figures such as Shahpour Bakhtiar, Abdorrahman Borumand, Dariush Foruhar, Mohammad Ali Keshevarz-Sadr, Hedayatollah Matin-Daftari, Allahyar Saleh, and Karim Sanjabi, soliciting their views and encouraging them to adopt more moderate positions.[26] Re-

[24]Idem, "Preliminary Observations on Majles Elections"; idem, "Recent Election Activities of the National Front and the Guardians of Freedom," January 26, 1961; idem, "Opposition Activities and Resulting Disturbances in Tehran," February 11, 1961; idem, "Election Violence in Borujen," March 20, 1961; U.S. Embassy, Tehran, to Secretary of State, May 4, 1961; U.S. Embassy, Tehran, "Majlis Elections: Part II, Analysis of New Majlis," April 25, 1961.

[25]*New York Times*, February 26, 1961, 14:2, and March 12, 1961, 9:4; U.S. Embassy, Tehran, to Secretary of State, May 17, 1961, and May 18, 1961.

[26]Interviews with Stuart Rockwell (Washington, July 16, 1985) and Phillips Talbot (New York, August 5, 1985), who were, respectively, the minister-counselor in the Tehran embassy and assistant secretary of state for Near Eastern and South Asian affairs; Muslim Students Following the Line of the Imam, *Documents from the U.S. Espionage Den*, vols. 20–22 (Tehran: n.p., n.d.).

sponding to the growing atmosphere of crisis and presumably also to this pressure from the United States, the shah finally began to undertake an extensive program of social and economic reforms.

It was clear, however, that extensive reforms would be opposed by the traditional upper class. The shah therefore took two important steps to undermine the political power of this class. First, he abruptly dismissed General Bakhtiar as chief of SAVAK in mid-March 1961 and replaced him with General Hassan Pakravan, who had been Bakhtiar's deputy. Several other top security officials were dismissed as well. Bakhtiar had been the main representative of the traditional upper class since the removal of Zahedi. As head of SAVAK he had become the second most powerful person in Iran, and he was widely believed to be plotting against the shah.[27] The dismissal of Bakhtiar and the other security officials ensured that the security forces would be more firmly under the shah's control in the coming confrontation with the traditional upper class. Second, the shah dismissed Sharif-Emami in May and appointed Amini to the premiership. Despite being from one of Iran's wealthiest families, Amini was relatively progressive and was therefore despised by the traditional upper class. United States officials had made it clear to the shah that they believed Amini was the best candidate for the premiership, although they apparently did not explicitly pressure him to appoint Amini.[28] Amini's appointment put the Iranian state for the first time in the hands of a government that was prepared to carry out reforms.

Amini quickly settled the teachers' strike by agreeing to all the teachers' demands and appointing Derakhshesh as his minister of education. He began a crackdown on corruption by arresting numerous military officers and officials from the previous government and preventing others from going abroad. On May 11 he announced a package of reforms that included measures aimed at resolving Iran's growing economic crisis and a land reform program, which he placed under the direction of Hassan Arsanjani, who had been named minister of agriculture. To facilitate Amini's efforts and silence lingering criticism about the recently held elections, the shah dissolved the Majles and announced new elections.[29]

Amini's reforms were staunchly opposed by the traditional upper class,

[27]Barry Rubin, *Paved with Good Intentions* (New York: Oxford University Press, 1980), 108. For an interesting fictionalized account of Bakhtiar's alleged plot see Gérard de Villiers, *S.A.S. contre C.I.A.* (Paris: Plon, 1965).

[28]Stuart Rockwell and Phillips Talbot (see n. 26, above) both strongly deny that the shah was explicitly pressured to appoint Amini but believe he was probably influenced by the obvious U.S. approval of Amini. The shah later stated that he *had* been pressured; see Mohammad Reza Pahlavi, *Answer to History* (New York: Stein and Day, 1980), 22.

[29]U.S. Embassy, Tehran, to Secretary of State, May 17, 1961; *Keesing's Contemporary Archives*, July 21–28, 1962, 18882.

which soon began to agitate against him. The traditional-upper-class opposition to Amini consisted of several interrelated groupings. The most active was the Rashidian network, which had been in existence for many years and had played an important role in the 1953 coup. Soon after Amini's appointment, the Rashidians formed an organization known as the Crusaders and Defenders of the Constitution, which publicly espoused a program of reforms but in fact sought a return to the status quo ante Amini. The members of this organization were mainly wealthy businessmen and bazaar leaders, many of whom maintained patronage bonds with members of the traditional middle class and urban lower class. The Rashidians also organized a small rightist group at Tehran University, which frequently clashed with National Front supporters. Through this network, the Rashidians regularly held rallies in the fall of 1961 which were attended by as many as five thousand people. Two smaller factions associated with the traditional upper class were Aramesh's Progressive Group and Sayyid Jafar Behbehani's Society of Friends, which were both loosely tied to the Rashidian network but served mainly as political vehicles for their respective leaders. Also loosely associated with the Rashidians was Teimur Bakhtiar, who increased his intrigues after being dismissed as head of SAVAK and was viewed by many members of the traditional upper class as the ideal candidate to replace Amini.[30]

A final source of traditional-upper-class opposition to Amini was the Shi'i clergy. The emergence of a women's rights movement in 1959 and the enactment of a land reform law in 1960 had angered much of the clergy and produced a gradual reemergence of clerical opposition to the state. After the death of the quietist Ayatollah Borujerdi in March 1961 and the appointment of Amini as prime minister, a prominent clerical faction led by Ayatollah Behbehani began to work closely with other members of the emerging traditional-upper-class opposition against Amini and his reform program. More ominously, a relatively junior ayatollah named Ruhollah al-Musavi Khomeini, who had developed a large coterie of students by the early 1960s, also began independently to agitate against Amini. Much like Kashani, who had become inactive by this time and was to die in 1962, Khomeini was able to mobilize large crowds from the traditional lower and middle classes, creating, in effect, a new coalition between these classes and the traditional upper class.[31]

[30]U.S. Embassy, Tehran, "Conservative Groups Opposing the Amini Government," February 8, 1962; idem, "Reflections on the Azmudeh and Aramesh Affairs," July 12, 1961; Marvin Zonis, *The Political Elite of Iran* (Princeton, N.J.: Princeton University Press, 1971), 51–52.

[31]Akhavi, *Religion and Politics in Contemporary Iran*, chap. 4; U.S. Embassy, Tehran, "Telegram of Ayatollah BEHBEHANI to Shah," February 14, 1962; idem, "Some Comments on Recent Religious Agitation in Iran," December 29, 1962.

The appointment of Amini to the premiership did not placate the Mosaddeqist opposition, which sought not only social and economic reforms but also a democratization of the political system. The Mosaddeqists therefore also opposed Amini. The first manifestation of Mosaddeqist opposition to Amini occurred on May 18, when the Second National Front held a rally to demand new elections which was attended by some eighty thousand people, the largest crowd assembled in Iran since the Mosaddeq era. Several weeks later, Amini met with National Front leaders and agreed to hold new elections in exchange for a promise that the National Front would refrain from further demonstrations. This agreement quickly broke down, however, as Amini failed to schedule new elections and began publicly to attack the National Front. In response, the National Front held another large rally on July 21. Amini had warned the National Front not to hold this rally and sent the security forces to break it up; 150 demonstrators were arrested, including all of the National Front's top leaders. Amini also began a crackdown on the growing group of student activists abroad. In August the leaders of the National Front again promised to refrain from holding large demonstrations, and although scattered protests occurred in the fall, this agreement held for several months. Then, in the absence of progress toward a new election, the National Front began in early December to organize a large rally. Amini refused to grant permission to hold this rally, and the National Front leadership ignominiously cancelled it. Frustrated by this lack of will, students at Tehran University held the rally anyway, creating serious strains within the Second National Front. A further embarrassment came in early January 1962, when Baqai was released from prison and immediately held a large rally.[32]

The Second National Front suffered another setback in late January, when a series of violent demonstrations rocked Tehran. The first occurred on January 21, when five thousand Tehran University students rallied to protest the arrest of three students for engaging in pro-National Front activities. Police units and paratroopers brutally attacked the protesters, in what one witness described as "a Mongol invasion."[33] Further unrest during the next few days left one demonstrator dead, hundreds injured,

[32]*New York Times*, May 19, 1961, 11:6, and July 22, 1961, 3:7; U.S. Embassy, Tehran, to Secretary of State, June 12, 1961, June 19, 1961, September 11, 1961, September 18, 1961, December 6, 1961, December 11, 1961, and January 6, 1962; U.S. Embassy, Tehran, "General Pakravan's Attitude Toward the Amini Government," July 31, 1961. Amini's ability to repress the National Front in this period was enhanced considerably by the shah's November 11 decision to grant him special powers; see *Keesing's Contemporary Archives*, July 21–28, 1962, 18882.

[33]U.S. Embassy, Tehran, "Political Disturbances in Tehran January 21–January 25," February 3, 1962, 3.

and hundreds more arrested, including most Second National Front leaders. Weakened by these arrests, the National Front was further discredited by its failure to control the demonstrators and organize a successful general strike. The Rashidians' student organization was also involved in the demonstrations; Assadollah Rashidian, Sayyid Jafar Behbehani, and several of their allies were arrested, and Teimur Bakhtiar was sent into exile.[34] Amini also increased press censorship after these demonstrations.[35]

Although most of its leaders were soon released from prison, the Second National Front had lost much of its momentum and never again posed a serious threat to the shah's regime. This occurred for two main reasons. First, Amini's reform program was fairly popular and co-opted many Iranians, especially members of the modern middle class, undermining the National Front's base of support. Second, the National Front was increasingly divided into a moderate faction associated with Saleh and the Iran party and a radical faction consisting mainly of students and members of the National Resistance Movement, which had been reconstituted as the Liberation Movement of Iran in May 1961. These two factions, which had existed within the Mosaddeqist wing of the nationalist movement since the mid-1950s, now clashed repeatedly over organizational matters and the issue of whether to adopt more confrontational tactics. The reluctance of the moderate faction to challenge Amini in the summer and fall of 1961 and its inept handling of events in December 1961 and January 1962 had greatly increased tension between the two factions and seriously undermined the Second National Front. Moreover, Amini and the shah worked subtly to aggravate these tensions by encouraging the moderates to work within the regime and by severely repressing the radicals; and SAVAK had thoroughly penetrated the National Front and also worked to aggravate tension between the two factions. This factionalism was eventually to split the Second National Front apart, when Bazargan and several of his allies abruptly walked out of its December 1962 congress, ending their association with the National Front.[36]

Amini's reforms and his success in weakening the Second National Front and the traditional-upper-class opposition had brought him consid-

[34]Bakhtiar continued to plot against the shah from exile, with support from the Iraqi government. In the late 1960s he assembled a diverse network that included the Tudeh party, leftists students abroad, disaffected members of the traditional upper class, and certain tribal elements. Bakhtiar was assassinated in Iraq in August 1970, apparently by SAVAK. See Chap. 5.

[35]Ibid.; idem, "Government Warns Tehran Press against Irresponsibility," February 6, 1962.

[36]Chehabi, "Modernist Shi'ism and Politics," chap. 5; Mohammadi-Nejad, "Elite-Counterelite Conflict," 129–32.

erable prestige in some circles by the summer of 1962. This raised the possibility that he might soon be in a position to challenge the shah, especially if he could control the Majles elections, which had still not been held. Moreover, other independent nationalists, such as Hassan Arsanjani, had also become prominent enough to pose a potential threat to the shah's preeminence. Accordingly, the shah dismissed Amini in July 1962 and replaced him with Assadollah Alam. Arsanjani was retained for a while as minister of agriculture but then dismissed in March 1963.

In the months after he dismissed Amini, the shah began to identify himself more clearly with the reform movement, publicly praising the land reform program and issuing decrees calling for other kinds of reforms. In January 1963 he unveiled a broad package of reforms, which he called the White Revolution, and announced a national referendum to approve the entire package. The White Revolution initially encompassed six major initiatives: an expansion of the land reform program, a workers' profit-sharing program, the nationalization of forests and pastures, the sale of state-owned factories, the enfranchisement of women, and the creation of a literacy corps. Other initiatives were subsequently added, including a health corps, a reconstruction and development corps, an antiprofiteering campaign, the nationalization of water resources, and the provision of free public education and public health services. Although frequently derided by critics of the shah, the White Revolution had a very positive effect on the living standards of many Iranians. Its most important aspect was the land reform program, which had provided land to roughly half of Iran's peasants by the time it officially ended in September 1971.[37]

The White Revolution had three very important long-term consequences for Iranian politics. First, it greatly expanded the state's cooptative capabilities and enabled the shah to portray himself as a progressive leader, thereby undermining popular support for the opposition. This was particularly true in the 1960s and early 1970s, while the land reform program was still being carried out and the other reforms still had some momentum. Second, by breaking up most large agricultural estates, the land reform program eliminated almost all of Iran's large landowners and therefore essentially destroyed the traditional upper class. Third, the land reform program, together with Iran's rapid economic growth, led many Iranian peasants to migrate to urban areas, swelling the ranks of the urban

[37]U.S. Embassy, Tehran, "Some Reflections on Current Political and Economic Developments in Iran," November 28, 1962; Rouhollah K. Ramazani, "Iran's 'White Revolution': A Study in Political Development," *International Journal of Middle East Studies* 5 (April 1974), 124–39; Eric Hooglund, *Land and Revolution in Iran, 1960–1980* (Austin: University of Texas Press, 1982), chap. 5.

lower class. These migrants were to become the focal point of revolutionary unrest in the late 1970s.

The shah's reform program produced considerable opposition activity, which was harshly suppressed. The Shi'i clergy, which had been agitating against the enfranchisement of women and against land reform, increased their opposition activity after the shah himself began to promote reforms. Clerical activists held a large public demonstration in Qom to protest these reforms in the early fall of 1962. A similar demonstration was organized in Tehran in late November but was canceled after Alam announced that a royal decree permitting women to vote was unenforceable. The promulgation of the White Revolution in January 1963 and the staging of a fraudulent referendum to legitimate it produced further oppositional activity. The Second National Front denounced the referendum, leading the shah to order the arrest of all of its leaders and many of their supporters. The leaders of the moderate faction were finally released from prison in September 1963, but Bazargan and other leaders of the radical faction were brought to trial in October 1963 and given two- to ten-year prison terms. Although scattered demonstrations occurred under the auspices of the Second National Front in September 1963, these arrests eliminated the National Front as an effective political force from this time on.[38]

The Shi'i clergy also reacted strongly to the promulgation of the White Revolution. Scattered demonstrations were held in January 1963, and the Tehran bazaar was closed for three days, resulting in the arrest of several clergymen, including Khomeini. Unlike the demonstrations organized by the Second National Front, which drew mainly from the modern middle class, these demonstrations drew mainly from the traditional middle and lower classes. The clergy organized further demonstrations in Mashad, Tabriz, and Qom in March and April. Violent tribal uprisings also occurred in this period. During the traditional time of Shi'i mourning in the month of Muharram, which climaxed in early June of 1963, many mourning processions and clerical sermons took on a highly political character. Khomeini delivered a particularly critical attack on the shah and was promptly arrested. This arrest sparked large demonstrations in Tehran, which were savagely attacked by the security forces. Violent rioting ensued and spread to other cities, with protesters attacking government buildings and assaulting unveiled women. Hundreds of civilians were killed by the security forces, thousands were injured, and hundreds were arrested before the rioting ended several days later. Khomeini remained in

[38]U.S. Embassy, Tehran, "Some Comments on Recent Religious Agitation in Iran," December 29, 1962; Chehabi, "Modernist Shi'ism and Politics," chap. 5.

prison until August 1963. In October 1964 he publicly denounced the Status of Forces Agreement, an arrangement under which U.S. military personnel serving in Iran received certain diplomatic privileges and immunities. He was arrested and sent into exile, first to Turkey and later to Iraq, where he remained until 1978.[39]

The Politics of the Highly Autonomous State, 1964–1977

The year 1963 can be regarded as the one in which a highly autonomous state was finally established in Iran. The modern middle class was greatly weakened by the collapse of the Second National Front, the main political organization that represented this class. The replacement of independent nationalists like Amini and Arsanjani with loyalists and apolitical technocrats and the increasingly personalized and centralized character of the state apparatus further weakened the modern middle class by reducing its role in running the state. The traditional upper class had already lost most of its influence by early 1963 as a result of the shah's control over the Majles and his appointments of Amini and Alam to the premiership. Representatives of the traditional upper class such as Teimur Bakhtiar and the Rashidians had been unsuccessful in ousting Amini and halting the land reform program, which soon essentially destroyed this class. The Iranian bourgeoisie remained weak and subservient to the state, with no significant role in politics. The industrial working class had not been able to exert much influence over the state since the collapse of the Tudeh party and tacitly relied on the now-weak modern middle class. Similarly, traditional middle- and lower-class elements relied on alliances with the traditional upper class or the modern middle class for influence over the state. Consequently, these latter classes had also lost their main sources of influence over the state by the end of 1963.

In the following years the state harshly suppressed all forms of opposition to the shah's regime and it continued to develop institutions and mechanisms to co-opt the modern middle class, the industrial working class, and other key societal groups, undermining support for opposition organizations among these groups. As a result, the organizations and figures that had constituted the main sources of opposition to the shah's

[39]See n. 38 and U.S. Department of State, Bureau of Intelligence and Research, "The Iranian Riots and Their Aftermath, RNA 30," June 26, 1963; U.S. Embassy, Tehran, "Year-End Report on the Political Situation in Iran," December 31, 1963; Rouhollah K. Ramazani, *Iran's Foreign Policy, 1941–1973: A Study of Foreign Policy in Modernizing Nations* (Charlottesville: University Press of Virginia, 1975), 361–63.

regime in the 1950s and early 1960s rapidly disappeared in the mid-1960s.

The harsh repression of 1962 and 1963 and the growing factionalism within the Second National Front had severely disrupted the Mosaddeqist opposition by the fall of 1963. A radical faction consisting of the National Front's student group and younger leaders such as Shahpour Bakhtiar, Dariush Foruhar, and Hedayatollah Matin-Daftari began in late 1963 to criticize Saleh and other National Front moderates, whom they viewed as indecisive and overly conciliatory. Saleh, in turn, held negotiations with Amini to establish a united opposition coalition. Mosaddeq himself joined the dispute in early 1964 by writing several letters criticizing the moderates and supporting the radicals. Saleh soon resigned from the National Front and thereafter remained politically inactive. The radical faction joined with members of the Liberation Movement of Iran and several other groups to establish a new organization, which became known as the Third National Front. After a series of arrests in late 1964 and early 1965, the Third National Front went underground, organizing itself into a network of cells. By early 1966 most its leaders were in prison or were being closely watched by the security forces, and this organization soon became inactive. The leaders of the Liberation Movement remained in prison until 1966, and this organization therefore became inactive (inside Iran) in this period as well. Both the National Front and the Liberation Movement reemerged in 1977, as the first signs of revolutionary unrest began to appear.[40]

Most of the independent nationalists and political opportunists who had been prominent in the 1950s and early 1960s also became politically inactive after 1963. Amini was kept under surveillance by the security forces and repeatedly threatened with arrest; he therefore became inactive. Arsanjani served briefly as ambassador to Italy after his dismissal as minister of agriculture but then returned to Iran and worked quietly as a lawyer until he died (of natural causes) in 1969. Ebtehaj, who had been arrested in late 1961 on corruption charges, was not cleared until early 1964, after which he remained inactive. Many other independent nationalists were co-opted with lucrative positions in the state bureaucracy or the private sector. Baqai remained moderately active and mildly critical of the shah's regime after 1963, but only because SAVAK believed that his

[40]U.S. Embassy, Tehran, , "Recent Developments in the National Front," April 29, 1964; idem, "Semi-Annual Assessment of the Political Situation in Iran," February 4, 1965, 4–5; idem, "Semi-Annual Assessment of the Political Situation in Iran," February 19, 1966, 12; idem, "The State of the Hard-Core Non-Communist Opposition in Iran," April 21, 1969, reprinted in Muslim Students, *Documents from the U.S. Espionage Den* 20:27–39; Mohammadi-Nejad, "Elite-Counterelite Conflict," 142–43.

activities would help divide the opposition. Aramesh served for a time as head of the Plan Organization but was then arrested in 1965 for oppositional activity; he did in a shootout with the police in October 1973 after apparently trying to establish a guerrilla organization. Derakhshesh was arrested several times after being dismissed as minister of education in 1962 but was also given several minor positions in the state bureaucracy; he ceased to be a threat to the regime. Pezeshkpour and the Pan-Iranists remained active and mildly critical of the regime after 1963 but, like Baqai, apparently received state support in order to divide the opposition.[41]

The radical Shi'i clergy were also harshly repressed. Ayatollah Khomeini remained in exile; his associates in Iran such as Ayatollah Hussein Ali Montazari and Hojjat al-Islam Ali Akhbar Hashemi Rafsanjani were repeatedly arrested and imprisoned. Other activist clerics and laymen were repressed as well, including the leaders of the Liberation Movement, the writer and activist Ali Shariati, and Ayatollah Mohammad Reza Saidi, who was apparently tortured to death by the security forces. SAVAK made extensive efforts to penetrate Khomeini's network and other clerical organizations. The state also tried to increase its control over the clergy and undermine its popular support by taking over many Islamic schools, reducing subsidies to clergymen and clerical students, seeking to rationalize and control the clergy's finances through the Religious Endowments Organization, and using the Religion Corps and the Department of Religious Propaganda to try to undermine the clergy's ties to other societal groups. Moreover, the state's social and economic development programs tended to undermine support for the clergy among lower- and middle-class Iranians.[42]

The harsh suppression of the opposition in the 1960s and 1970s had two main consequences. First, by neutralizing the main political organizations through which the modern middle class and other middle and lower class groups could engage in collective political action, it enabled the state to remain highly autonomous vis-à-vis these groups. With the virtual destruction of the traditional upper class and the continued weakness and subservience of the bourgeoisie, this left the state highly autonomous vis-à-vis Iranian society as a whole. Second, the suppression of the established opposition in the mid-1960s fostered the emergence of new opposition

[41]Muslim Students, *Documents from the U.S. Espionage Den* 23:135–39; ibid. 26:40–42, 52, 73–74; Zonis, *Political Elite of Iran*, 60, 67–69, 93; Hubert Otis Johnson III, "Recent Opposition Movements in Iran" (M.A. thesis, University of Utah, 1975), 237–38.

[42]Ervand Abrahamian, *Iran between Two Revolutions* (Princeton, N.J.: Princeton University Press, 1982), 475; interview with a SAVAK official (Chap. 4, n. 62); Akhavi, *Religion and Politics in Contemporary Iran*, 129–43, 159–61.

organizations which were much more radical and used very different tactics in their struggle against the shah's regime. These new organizations were of three types: Marxist and secular Islamic guerrilla groups, student-based groups operating abroad, and underground networks organized by the radical Shi'i clergy.

Of the many guerrilla groups, the most important were the Mojahedin-e Khalq (People's Warriors) and the Cherikha-ye Fedayan-e Khalq (People's Guerrilla Warriors). The Mojahedin-e Khalq was established in 1965 by six recent graduates of Tehran University who had been members of the Liberation Movement and had participated in the unrest of June 1963. Like the leaders of the Liberation Movement, the founders of the Mojahedin shared many of the goals of the Mosaddeqist movement but were deeply religious and articulated these goals in the metaphor of Shi'i Islam. With the 1963 defeat of the Mosaddeqists, the founders of the Mojahedin had concluded that armed struggle was the only way to achieve their goals. The Fedayan-e Khalq was created in 1970 with the merger of two groups that had been formed in the mid-1960s by Tehran University students who had been active in the Tudeh party's youth group, the National Front, and Maleki's Third Force. Its members were Marxist-Leninists who had rejected the Tudeh as nonrevolutionary and Soviet-dominated and had embraced the ideas and tactics of such contemporary Third World revolutionaries as Fidel Castro and Che Guevara. Smaller Marxist and secular-Islamic guerrilla groups also appeared in this period, including a Maoist offshoot of the Tudeh party called the Revolutionary Organization of the Tudeh.[43]

Many student-based Iranian opposition groups were established in Europe and the United States in the 1960s. Students sympathetic to the National Front had taken over the Iranian Students' Association in 1960; and the Tudeh-dominated Confederation of Iranian Students, which had chapters throughout Europe, was taken over by National Front sympathizers and anti-Tudeh Marxists in 1963. The Second National Front had also established affiliates in the United States and Europe in 1962. As in Iran, the Mosaddeqists abroad began to split into moderate and radical factions in the early 1960s, with most of the students gravitating toward the radical faction; this faction, in turn, split into factions with Marxist, non-Marxist, and Islamic tendencies. The Iranian student organizations abroad were extremely active and visible in their opposition to the shah's regime in the 1960s and 1970s and became important mechanisms of recruitment and indoctrination for the opposition.[44] As a result, SAVAK

[43]Abrahamian, *Iran between Two Revolutions*, 480–95.
[44]Chehabi, "Modernist Shi'ism and Politics," 367–75.

greatly increased its activities abroad, trying, with little success, to undermine these organizations.

An important but little-known Iranian opposition group operating abroad in the 1960s and 1970s was a semiclandestine offshoot of the Liberation Movement known as the Liberation Movement of Iran (Abroad). This organization was founded in 1963 by Ali Shariati, Ibrahim Yazdi, and Mostafa Chamran, who were studying in France and the United States at the time. Shariati soon left the organization and returned to Iran, where he later became associated with an influential Islamic educational forum known as the Hosseinieh Ershad. Yazdi and Chamran, however, decided to pursue armed struggle against the shah's regime and went to Egypt in 1964 for guerrilla training, accompanied by a young National Front activist named Sadeq Qotbzadeh. The three left Egypt in 1966 and returned to the United States and Europe to work with the Muslim Students' Association, a small, radical Islamic student organization. Yazdi and Qotbzadeh remained in the United States and Europe, respectively, until the late 1970s, heading the Muslim Students' Association and the Liberation Movement (Abroad) and establishing close ties with the Mojahedin-e Khalq. Chamran moved to Lebanon in 1970, where he became involved with the Shi'i Amal guerrilla group and established contact with Palestinian guerrilla groups. As the Liberation Movement (Abroad) became increasingly radicalized in the mid- and late 1960s, it severed most of its ties with secular groups such as the Iranian Students' Association and the Confederation of Iranian Students and with the founders of its parent organization, the Liberation Movement of Iran. At the same time, its leaders drew much closer to Ayatollah Khomeini.[45]

The most important of the underground networks established by the radical Shi'i clergy in the mid-1960s was the one established by Khomeini from his base in Iraq. It initially consisted of small cells organized by Ayatollahs Mohammad Hussein Beheshti and Morteza Mottahari, who had studied under Khomeini. As Khomeini's influence and circle of students grew, this network expanded accordingly. Khomeini's network refrained almost entirely from engaging in antiregime violence before 1978 and concentrated instead on propaganda, recruitment, and organization. Khomeini maintained close ties with the Liberation Movement (Abroad), even designating Yazdi as his spokesman in the United States. He also publicly praised the Mojahedin-e Khalq in 1972 and thereafter apparently provided it with financial assistance. Many Khomeini followers were apparently sent to Lebanon and Libya in the 1970s for guerrilla training with Amal and other groups. Khomeini also refined the doctrinal founda-

[45]Ibid., 376–83, 404.

tions of his movement, publishing his seminal work *Islamic Government* in 1971. Though well-organized and very effective, Khomeini's network encompassed only a small minority of the Iranian Shi'i clergy. Khomeini often criticized other Shi'i clerics and remained isolated from the mainstream clerical leadership. Another underground clerical network established in the mid-1960s was the Islamic Nations party, led by Sayyid Kazem Bojnurdi, which apparently maintained close ties with Khomeini's network.[46]

The effectiveness of these new opposition groups was shaped by their ideology, their tactics, and especially by the character of their social bases of support. The relatively sophisticated ideology and violent tactics of the guerrilla groups limited their bases of support mainly to students and a few workers, and their attempts to launch violent uprisings against the shah's regime without first developing broader bases of support made it fairly easy for the security forces to inflict great damage on them. The student-based groups operating abroad were quite effective in mobilizing Iranian students against the shah's regime and focusing world attention on human rights abuses in Iran, but their inability to operate effectively inside Iran and establish broader bases of support limited their ability to influence the state or undermine the regime. The ideology espoused by the radical clergy had considerable appeal among Iran's traditional middle class and its growing urban lower class. By keeping a low profile and steadily expanding their network, Khomeini and his associates developed a large base of support among the urban lower class at a time when this class was growing rapidly and becoming increasingly disaffected over Iran's growing economic, social, and cultural problems. Moreover, because the Mosaddeqists and the guerrilla groups had been severely weakened by the late 1970s, many students, workers, and even members of the modern middle class came to support Khomeini. Consequently, although few observers realized it at the time, Khomeini's network had become quite powerful by 1977.

With the radicalization of the opposition and the state's increasingly repressive character, opposition political activity after 1963 became much more violent and was increasingly aimed at overthrowing the shah's regime rather than simply influencing the state's policies. The first manifestation of this new form of political activity was the January 1965 assassination of Prime Minister Hassan Ali Mansur, who had succeeded

[46]Ibid., 415; Amir Taheri, *The Spirit of Allah* (London: Hutchinson, 1985), 149, 155–70, 189; Muslim Students, *Documents from the U.S. Espionage Den* 24:113, 116; Abrahamian, *Iran between Two Revolutions*, 473–79.

Alam in February 1964. Mansur's assassins, who were soon executed, were apparently members of one of the Khomeinist cells established by Beheshti and Mottahari, although they were described at the time as members of the defunct Fedayan-e Islam. In April 1965 a soldier disguised as a member of the Imperial Guard tried to assassinate the shah. The soldier was quickly killed by other guards, and the shah was slightly wounded. In the following months, fourteen Iranians were tried for complicity in the assassination attempt and given sentences ranging from six months' imprisonment to death. Although the political affiliations of the conspirators were never revealed, several had been students in Britain, and the group was described as Maoist, which suggests that they may have been associated with the Confederation of Iranian Students or with an offshoot of the Tudeh party. Fifty-five members of the Islamic Nations party were arrested for plotting an armed uprising in the fall of 1965; they were soon tried and given sentences ranging from three years' imprisonment to death. These arrests greatly weakened this organization, although it quietly reestablished itself in the mid-1970s.[47]

The general climate of repression and the effectiveness of the security forces greatly reduced opposition political activity in the next few years. Scattered student demonstrations occurred in Tehran and other cities in February 1968 to protest a plan to raise tuition. At about the same time, fourteen members of a small Marxist group led by Bizhan Jazani were arrested on charges of belonging to the Tudeh party, plotting against the regime, and trafficking in arms. All fourteen were convicted and given three- to ten-year prison terms. The defendants alleged that they had been tortured before the trial, and several, including Jazani, were eventually "shot while trying to escape" in April 1975. The trial of the Jazani group sparked protests by Iranian students abroad and by groups like the International Association of Democratic Jurists and a committee formed by Jean-Paul Sartre, called the Committee for the Defense of Iranian Political Prisoners. In the following years these and other groups joined with Iranian student groups in Europe and the United States to orchestrate highly visible international criticism of the shah's regime. It was the survivors of the Jazani group that merged with a group of Tehran University students in 1970 to create the Fedayan-e Khalq.[48]

Opposition political activity inside Iran increased sharply in 1970. After an announcement early in the year that bus fares in Tehran would

[47]Taheri, *Spirit of Allah*, 156; Johnson, *Recent Opposition Movements in Iran*, 37–66. The shah later commuted all three death sentences handed out in these incidents.

[48]Johnson, *Recent Opposition Movements in Iran*, 73–89; Abrahamian, *Iran between Two Revolutions*, 484.

soon be increased, Tehran University students organized a bus boycott and a partial closure of the bazaar. Demonstrations and rioting soon broke out, and many demonstrators were beaten and arrested. In May, unknown assailants broke windows and vandalized displays at the headquarters of the Iran-America Society in Tehran to protest a conference being held there for foreign investors. In October an Iran Air flight was hijacked to Baghdad by three Iranians who demanded the release of twenty-one political prisoners, including several members of the Jazani group. Another plane was hijacked in November on a flight from Dubai by six Iranian prisoners and three of their guards. Although these prisoners were described at the time as common criminals, they were apparently members of the Mojahedin-e Khalq. Large demonstrations were held at Tehran University in late November over the scheduling of exams. These demonstrations continued through mid-December and spread to several other campuses; many students were arrested, and Tehran University and another campus were closed and occupied by the security forces. Amnesty International reported that over one thousand political arrests had been made in Iran by the end of 1970. Although it is not entirely clear which groups organized these antiregime activities, the Confederation of Iranian Students, the Jazani group, the Mojahedin-e Khalq, and possibly the National Front appear to have been largely responsible. An attempt to kidnap U.S. ambassador Douglas MacArthur, Jr., in November 1970 was apparently the work of the Revolutionary Organization of the Tudeh.[49]

A much more deadly round of opposition activity began in February 1971, when a large group of Fedayan-e Khalq guerrillas attacked a Gendarmerie post in the town of Siakal in Gilan province, apparently to rescue a comrade being held there. Several guerrillas and members of the security forces were killed in the attack and in subsequent clashes, and thirteen captured guerrillas were executed in March after secret trials. The Fedayan-e Khalq had apparently robbed several banks to finance their activities in the preceding months; and they followed up on the Siakal raid by assassinating Iran's chief military prosecutor, who had presided over the trial of the Jazani group. The security forces then tried to weaken the Fedayan-e Khalq by arresting a large number of students. These arrests provoked large student demonstrations in April 1971, which led the police to occupy Tehran University for three weeks and arrest over five hundred demonstrators. The Fedayan-e Khalq staged a series of bank robberies and bombings in the following months. The Mojahedin-e Khalq simultaneously increased its activities, trying unsuccessfully to kidnap the

[49]Johnson, *Recent Opposition Movements in Iran*, 98–111, 174. The government blamed much of this unrest on Teimur Bakhtiar's network; see ibid., 124.

son of Princess Ashraf in September and to bomb a Tehran power station in October, during the celebration of the coronation of Cyrus the Great, which the shah had organized at the ancient Persian capital of Persepolis. The Fedayan and the Mojahedin tried to disrupt this celebration further by robbing banks, planting bombs, and engaging in gun battles with the security forces in September and October.[50]

Elaborate security measures prevented the guerrillas from attacking the Persepolis celebration itself. Moreover, hundreds (and perhaps thousands) of Iranians were arrested in conjunction with the celebration, including at least 185 members of the Mojahedin-e Khalq, the Fedayan-e Khalq, and the Revolutionary Organization of the Tudeh. The guerrillas arrested during this period were put on trial in early 1972, and at least twenty-eight were executed in the following months. Allegations of torture emerged frequently during the trials, producing a new wave of international criticism. During these trials the Mojahedin and Fedayan began a new round of attacks, which lasted through the summer of 1972: many banks were robbed; dozens of bombings occurred; many more guerrillas were arrested; and several guerrillas and security officers were killed in shootouts, including a police general. At least twenty-eight more guerrillas were executed by the end of 1972.[51]

The arrests and executions of 1971 and 1972 so weakened the Mojahedin-e Khalq and the Fedayan-e Khalq that attacks by these groups thereafter declined. The Iraqi government, however, began to infiltrate saboteurs into Iran's western provinces in this period, resulting in several clashes with the security forces. In a spectacular but isolated incident, a small team of Mojahedin guerrillas assassinated a U.S. Army colonel in June 1973 in Tehran. A plot to kidnap and execute the shah and other members of the royal family was broken up in October 1973, but the political affiliations of those arrested were never revealed. In March 1974, a series of bombings occurred in Tehran and the Fedayan-e Khalq assassinated a SAVAK agent. In addition, a wave of student unrest occurred in February and March of 1973 and scattered labor unrest occurred in September 1974.[52]

After two years of reduced activity, the Mojahedin-e Khalq and Fedayan-e Khalq renewed their violent attacks on the shah's regime in December 1974 by jointly assassinating a member of the security forces. This attack began a two-year period of increased guerrilla activity by these two groups, including further assassinations and many bombings and bank

[50]Ibid., 133–59, 171; Abrahamian, *Iran between Two Revolutions*, 491.
[51]Johnson, *Recent Opposition Movements in Iran*, 159–218.
[52]Ibid., 219–52; Muslim Students, *Documents from the U.S. Espionage Den* 24:108.

robberies. In May 1975 the Mojahedin-e Khalq split into Marxist and Islamic factions. The Marxist faction then carried out a series of spectacular attacks on the shah's regime and assassinations of U.S. targets, including two more U.S. military officers, an Iranian employee of the U.S. embassy, and three U.S. civilian employees of Rockwell International. The Islamic faction remained active as well, bombing a Jewish emigration office in Tehran and robbing a bank in Isfahan. The Fedayan-e Khalq also split into two factions in late 1975, after a minority of its members renounced armed struggle and merged with the Tudeh party.[53]

In response, Iran's security forces launched a major effort to penetrate and destroy the Mojahedin-e Khalq and the Fedayan-e Khalq. In 1975 and 1976 alone, at least thirty guerrillas were executed or "shot while trying to escape" and at least seventy-six more were killed in shootouts with the security forces; many more were arrested and imprisoned.[54] Most of the top leaders of the Mojahedin and Fedayan were killed, and the rank-and-file membership of these groups was decimated. These actions, together with the splits that had occurred in 1975, left both groups seriously weakened by the end of 1976;[55] they did not resume armed attacks until the Iranian revolution began to unfold in 1978. With the apparent destruction of the Mojahedin, the Fedayan, and the other guerrilla groups, the absence of overt political activity by the radical Shi'i clergy, and the continued dormancy of the Mosaddeqists, Iran seemed to be politically stable at the end of 1976.

[53]Abrahamian, *Iran between Two Revolutions*, 488–95; Muslim Students, *Documents from the U.S. Espionage Den* 24:116–17. The Mojahedin also managed to infiltrate an agent into the U.S. embassy in 1975 and acquired the ability to monitor SAVAK radio communications; see Muslim Students, *Documents from the U.S. Espionage Den* 24:114.

[54]These figures were calculated from articles in *New York Times* and *Keesing's Contemporary Archives* for this period.

[55]Muslim Students, *Documents from the U.S. Espionage Den* 24:103–17.

7

The Policies of the Highly Autonomous State

The Iranian state's high degree of autonomy in the 1960s and 1970s enabled it to operate without the kind of societal input that is often provided by such mechanisms as legitimate political parties, popularly elected legislatures, a free press, and local-level political activity. Lacking societal constraint, the state's policies largely reflected the shah's particular priorities rather than society's interests and needs. Those priorities included promoting very rapid economic growth, maintaining tight control over domestic politics, strengthening Iran's military forces, projecting an image of imperial splendor and opulence, promoting Westernization and secularization, and making Iran an important actor in regional and world affairs;[1] the shah showed little interest in reducing poverty and inequality, democratizing the political system, or preserving Iran's traditional customs and institutions. The state's policies were also inevitably shaped by a variety of other factors in this period, including shortages of resources such as capital and skilled manpower, international political and economic conditions, and aspects of Iran's culture and traditions. However, the tremendous increase in world oil prices in the early 1970s and certain other changes sharply reduced the constraints imposed by these factors, giving the shah much more latitude to pursue his priorities. As a result, the divergence between state policy and societal needs grew rapidly, producing increased political unrest and eventually a revolution.

Economic Policy

The state's dominant role in the economy in the 1960s and 1970s gave the shah considerable freedom to pursue his economic priorities, which, as

[1]The shah's priorities are outlined in some detail in Mohammed Reza Shah Pahlavi, *Mission for My Country* (New York: McGraw-Hill, 1961).

well as promoting very rapid industrialization, included generating enough public revenue to finance his ambitious military and public works projects and providing a relatively high standard of living for Iran's upper and middle classes. Reflecting its highly centralized and highly personalized character, the state carried out economic policies in pursuit of these priorities which had little coherence and did not reflect the interests of Iranian society as a whole. As a result, three main kinds of distortions began to emerge in the Iranian economy: imbalances in the growth and productivity of the different sectors, an overly capital-intensive industrial sector, and a very high level of public consumption. These distortions, in turn, produced growing economic problems and an economic crisis in Iran after the oil boom.

Sectoral imbalances in growth and productivity were mainly a consequence of the economic development strategy embodied in the Second through Fifth Development Plans, especially its emphasis on import-substitution industrialization. The great emphasis these plans placed on industrialization, together with the dislocations caused by the land reform program, produced a relatively slow 4.3 percent real growth rate in the agricultural sector in the 1960s and negative real growth in this sector in the 1970s. Agricultural production therefore fell from 29.1 percent of Iran's GDP in 1960 to 19.4 percent in 1970 and only 9.1 percent in 1977, creating a growing imbalance between the agricultural sector and the other sectors of the economy.[2]

Within the industrial sector the state's development efforts focused almost exclusively on modern rather than traditional products, producing stagnation in traditional industries such as carpet weaving and handicrafts. In the modern part of the industrial sector, the strategy of import substitution led the state to focus its development efforts mainly on consumer goods industries. This meant not only that intermediate and capital goods industries were de-emphasized in the state's development plans but also that demand for intermediate and capital goods grew rapidly. Moreover, high tariffs associated with the import-substitution strategy reduced the efficiency of consumer goods industries; and the intermediate goods industries that were established in this period developed considerable excess capacity. In general, the import-substitution strategy reduced competition and weakened interindustry and intersectoral linkages in the Iranian economy, undermining its efficiency and increasing the volume of imports.[3]

[2]These figures are from Imperial Government of Iran, Plan and Budget Organization, *Economic Statistics and Trends of Iran*, 3d ed. (Tehran, 1976), 13–14, 39–40; and Bank Markazi Iran, *Annual Report and Balance Sheet* (Tehran, 1978), 97.

[3]For a good critical evaluation of Iran's import-substitution strategy see Manoucher

The industrialization program also tended to be capital intensive. This meant that fewer investment projects could be financed with a given amount of capital than if labor-intensive techniques had been used. It also generated less employment for skilled and unskilled workers and more employment for managers, engineers, and other white-collar workers, straining Iran's labor resources and fueling social tension.[4]

The rapid growth of public consumption (see Table 12) greatly increased demand for certain factors of production, such as construction materials, technicians, and white-collar workers. High public expenditures on military equipment added to Iran's import bill, both for the military equipment itself and for related services such as training and maintenance. Moreover, because Iran's public consumption expenditures were financed mainly with oil revenues after the early 1960s and accounted for a substantial share of total domestic consumption, they increased the sensitivity of the Iranian economy to fluctuations in the world price of oil.[5]

These distortions caused economic problems even before the oil boom of 1971–74 began. One such problem was the extensive rural-urban migration caused by the relative neglect of agriculture and the lure of employment in the rapidly growing industrial sector. Most rural migrants were unable to find suitable employment and lived in squalid shantytowns, creating an increasingly embittered urban lower class that became the main base of support of the radical Shi'i clergy.

Closely related to this wave of migration was an increase in inequality. The relative neglect of agriculture and rapid economic growth in urban areas produced a growing disparity between rural and urban consumption levels (see Table 17). In urban areas, rapid economic growth, the relative neglect of traditional industries, the capital intensity of modern industry, and the rapid expansion of the public sector generated considerable employment for technicians and white-collar workers but less employment for blue-collar workers. These distortions in the urban labor market, together with the great influx of unskilled rural migrants, produced rapid growth in the incomes of urban middle- and upper-class Iranians but much slower income growth for the urban lower class. The

---

Parvin and Amir N. Zamani, "Political Economy of Growth and Destruction: A Statistical Interpretation of the Iranian Case," *Iranian Studies* 12 (Winter–Spring 1979), 58–67.

[4]See Gail Cook Johnson, *High-Level Manpower in Iran: From Hidden Conflict to Crisis* (New York: Praeger, 1980), chap. 2; and International Labor Office, *Employment and Income Policies for Iran* (Geneva, 1973).

[5]Robert E. Looney, *Economic Origins of the Iranian Revolution* (New York: Pergamon, 1982), 69, 136, 143; Parvin and Zamani, "Political Economy of Growth and Destruction," 66.

share of total urban consumption accruing to the poorest 40 percent of the urban population fell from 13.9 percent to 12.0 percent between 1959 and 1973; the share accruing to the richest 20 percent grew from 51.8 to 55.6 percent; and the share accruing to the remaining (middle) 40 percent declined from 34.3 to 32.5 percent.[6] This growing inequality fueled social tensions and undermined Iran's industrialization program by restricting the size of the domestic market for consumer goods.

The distortions in the Iranian economy also undermined its overall efficiency and made it more dependent on the world economy. High tariffs associated with the import-substitution strategy reduced the competitiveness of Iran's consumer goods industries. Moreover, as Table 18 shows, while import substitution slowed the growth of Iran's consumer goods imports in the 1960s and early 1970s, it produced large increases in intermediate and capital goods imports. Similarly, the relative neglect of agriculture produced a rapid increase in agricultural imports in the late 1960s and early 1970s. These trends indicate that interindustry and intersectoral linkages declined substantially and that Iran's dependence on imports consequently increased. They also led Iran's total merchandise imports to rise even faster than its GDP in the 1960s and early 1970s. The rapid growth of Iran's imports and the much slower growth of its industrial exports indicate that Iran's manufacturing sector was not competitive in world markets. Iran's growing merchandise imports, its growing imports of services, and its inability to broaden its export base produced frequent balance of payments deficits in the 1960s and early 1970s, depleting the state's foreign exchange reserves and forcing it to export more of the country's limited oil resources.

Inflation was another adverse effect of the distortions in the Iranian economy. As measured by changes in the consumer price index, inflation averaged only 2.4 percent annually between 1960 and 1968. Then rapid economic growth, increases in import prices, and the shah's refusal to exercise fiscal or monetary restraint produced a gradual rise in the inflation rate, which averaged 5.6 percent annually between 1968 and 1973.[7]

The efforts of the Organization of Petroleum Exporting Countries (OPEC) in the early 1970s to raise the world price of oil, together with increases in Iran's oil production, raised the Iranian state's oil revenue from $791 million in 1970 to $2.6 billion in 1973, $4.6 billion in 1974, and $17.8 billion in 1975.[8] This tremendous increase in the state's revenue

[6]M. H. Pesaran, "Income Distribution in Iran," in Jane W. Jacqz, ed., *Iran: Past, Present, and Future* (New York: Aspen Institute, 1976), 278.

[7]These figures are from Bank Markazi Iran, *Annual Report and Balance Sheet* (various years). On the causes of inflation see Robert E. Looney, *A Development Strategy for Iran through the 1980s* (New York: Praeger, 1977), chap. 8.

[8]United Nations, *Statistical Yearbook* (New York, various years).

Table 18. Composition of Iran's imports and exports

Year	Merchandise imports		Percentage share				All exports		Services, income, etc. (net imports) (9)	Balance of payments (10)
	Total (1)	Total as % of GDP (2)	Agricultural products (3)	Consumer goods (4)	Intermediate goods (5)	Capital goods (6)	Total (7)	Manufactured goods (8)		
1959	1,537	11.6	10.9	30.2	49.2	20.6	2,256	6.6	1,037	−190
1960	1,550	11.8	12.8	28.6	42.2	24.3	2,314	8.6	1,142	−256
1961	1,469	12.0	12.9	25.5	53.4	21.1	2,409	15.0	1,095	−16
1962	1,363	10.0	n.a.	21.9	57.2	21.0	2,484	13.9	1,238	148
1963	1,241	9.2	10.9	24.2	55.9	20.3	2,878	11.9	1,455	255
1964	1,513	10.6	13.9	23.2	55.0	21.9	2,915	18.2	1,318	113
1965	2,047	12.4	13.2	17.5	57.7	24.8	3,289	14.2	1,522	−252
1966	2,278	12.3	7.1	15.0	57.9	27.1	3,683	19.0	1,751	−317
1967	2,864	13.4	5.1	12.6	59.7	27.7	4,432	43.5	1,931	−339
1968	3,750	15.0	n.a.	11.3	61.7	27.1	5,190	69.9	2,631	−1,176
1969	3,868	12.9	n.a.	10.9	64.0	25.1	5,333	77.1	2,816	−1,341
1970	4,631	14.6	n.a.	12.9	63.7	23.3	6,751	142.7	3,547	−1,416
1971	5,172	13.1	n.a.	11.7	64.8	23.4	9,310	179.0	4,442	−295
1972	6,068	13.5	n.a.	12.9	62.1	25.0	9,288	240.3	4,141	−909
1973	7,154	11.8	n.a.	14.9	60.8	24.2	10,991	189.8	3,555	276
1974	8,019	10.6	14.9	15.4	64.5	20.1	23,598	180.2	1,988	13,555
1975	12,898	17.8	13.7	n.a.	n.a.	n.a.	20,432	145.7	2,808	4,707
1976	13,211	17.2	9.9	17.6	52.6	29.8	19,818	126.2	2,689	3,902
1977	10,794	16.5	11.4	n.a.	n.a.	n.a.	16,614	98.0	2,348	3,466

Sources: Cols. 1, 2, 7, 9, 10: International Monetary Fund, *International Financial Statistical Yearbook, 1983* (Washington, 1983), 280–81; Col. 3: United Nations, *Yearbook of International Trade Statistics*, vol. 1 (New York, various years); Cols. 4–6, 8: Bank Markazi Iran, *Annual Report and Balance Sheet* (Tehran, various years).

Notes: Figures in Cols. 1 and 7–10 are in millions of constant 1975 U.S. dollars (deflated with the GDP deflator). Cols. 3–6 add up to more than 100 percent because agricultural products are also classified as either consumer goods or intermediate goods.

virtually eliminated, at least temporarily, the capital shortages that had previously constrained its economic policy making. Given the shah's extensive personal control over the state apparatus and the absence of an effective opposition, the Iranian state's economic policies therefore increasingly reflected the shah's ambitious priorities rather than society's interests and needs, and the economic distortions that had already begun to emerge grew rapidly.

The immediate consequence of this tremendous increase in oil revenue was a dramatic increase in public spending, which had already become very high by the early 1970s. Public investment and consumption expenditures increased by 130.2 and 104.1 percent, respectively, in real terms between 1970 and 1975. This dramatic increase generated a corresponding increase in private investment, which grew by 115.0 percent in real terms. But although private consumption expenditures grew rapidly in the first two years of the oil boom, mounting inflation outpaced the nominal growth in private consumption expenditures after 1972. Public consumption expenditures therefore grew from 21.3 percent of total consumption in 1970 to an incredible 38.0 percent of the total in 1975 (see Tables 9 and 12).

In an economy where public spending was already very high and where large sectoral imbalances and other distortions had already emerged, this great influx of oil revenue had many adverse effects. The great increase in public and private spending produced a considerable expansion in urban employment and therefore further enhanced rural-urban migration. Moreover, since workers' wages and per capita rural consumption grew much slower than per capita urban consumption in the early and mid-1970s (see Table 17), inequality grew rapidly as well. The high import content of public expenditures, the increased demand for consumer goods and capital goods, and the growing excess demand for agricultural products produced a sharp increase in imports (see Table 18), absorbing much of the new oil revenue and producing tremendous port congestion and other infrastructural bottlenecks. Similarly, increased public and private spending created severe shortages of construction materials, housing, electric power, skilled manpower, and other items. These bottlenecks created tremendous waste and inefficiency; for example, port congestion produced shipping demurrage charges of over one billion dollars in 1974 alone. Much of the state's new oil wealth was spent on projects that brought glamor and prestige but were of little or no economic value, such as advanced military equipment, nuclear power plants, uranium-enriching facilities, a 25 percent share in West Germany's Krupp steel company, and even a foreign aid program. Corruption also flourished, as bottlenecks created costly delays and foreign corporations competed for access to top government officials. Finally, the rapid growth in demand and the waste and inefficiency generated by the oil boom produced a substantial increase in inflation, which averaged 16.7 percent annually between 1973 and 1977.[9]

Many of these problems had been anticipated by Iran's economic planners as the oil boom began, and some measures were taken to avert them. The initial version of the Fifth Development Plan earmarked large expenditures for transportation, electric power, housing, and education. In 1973, Iran's central bank began to raise interest rates and use other monetary measures in a limited effort to reduce inflation. After world oil prices quadrupled in 1973 and early 1974, economists in the Plan Organization urged the shah to restrain public spending, arguing that large increases would create infrastructural bottlenecks and inflation. Although the shah refused to exercise fiscal restraint at this time, he did approve further increases in spending for transportation and housing under the Revised Fifth Development Plan.[10]

As the adverse consequences of the oil boom became more apparent, and as oil revenue began to fall in real terms after 1975, the state was forced to take increasingly drastic action to deal with the emerging economic crisis. An elaborate system of price controls covering 2,236 items was introduced in 1974 to offset the effect of rising prices on consumers; by the end of 1975 this system had been expanded to include some 16,000 items. Subsidies were introduced for many food products and other consumer goods, at a cost of over $650 million in 1974 alone. Taxes and user fees for education, health care, and other public services were reduced or eliminated. The minimum wage was raised by 36 percent in 1974 and by another 42 percent in 1975. A workers' profit-sharing program was introduced in July 1975 which required most private firms to sell 49 percent of their shares to their employees or to the public. Bank reserve requirements and interest rates were raised again in 1975 and 1976. In an official antiprofiteering campaign begun in 1975 to combat inflation, some 31,000 merchants were given jail terms or sentenced to internal exile and 250,000 businesses were fined or closed down. (Most of these measures were later rescinded.) An anticorruption campaign begun in early 1976

[9]Robert Graham, *Iran: The Illusion of Power* (New York: St. Martin's, 1980), chap. 5; Nicholas Cumming-Bruce, *Iran: A MEED Special Report* (London: Middle East Economic Digest, 1977); *New York Times*, December 3, 1974, 69:3, December 24, 1974, 27:5, February 24, 1975, 2:8, March 5, 1975, 1:4, and October 20, 1976, 67:1; Bank Markazi Iran, *Annual Report and Balance Sheet* (various years).

[10]Jahangır Amuzegar, *Iran: An Economic Profile* (Washington: Middle East Institute, 1977), 166–75; Looney, *Economic Origins of the Iranian Revolution*, 185–86; Hossein Razavi and Firouz Vakil, *The Political Environment of Economic Planning in Iran, 1971–1983* (Boulder, Colo.: Westview, 1984), 66–75.

eventually led to the arrest of many top state officials and businessmen. The state began to implement austerity measures in early 1976, halting payments to contractors, canceling several large investment projects, and trimming $3.5 billion from its 1977–78 budget. Incredibly, the state even began to borrow abroad in early 1976, barely two years after the OPEC oil embargo had produced a fivefold increase in its oil revenue.[11]

These measures were too restrained and were begun too late to halt the emerging economic crisis. Rural migrants continued to stream into Iran's major cities in the mid-1970s; Iran's import bill continued to grow; waste and corruption continued to flourish; and inflation continued to rise. Moreover, several of these measures actually exacerbated the economic crisis: price controls and food subsidies produced shortages and further damaged the agricultural sector; and the profit-sharing and anticorruption campaigns and other inflation-fighting measures produced capital flight amounting to two billion dollars in 1976 alone, stifling economic growth.[12] Consequently, while the oil boom had created expectations that an era of great prosperity was imminent, inept state policy making and distortions in the economy produced a serious economic crisis instead, fueling political unrest.

Political, Social, and Cultural Matters

The state's high degree of autonomy also enabled the shah to pursue his own priorities on various political, social, and cultural matters. These priorities included preserving the highly centralized and highly personalized authoritarian regime that had been constructed in the 1950s and early 1960s, maintaining social conditions that would facilitate rapid economic growth, improving the living standards of the upper and middle classes, promoting Western and certain Persian customs and traditions, and deemphasizing the role of Islam in Iran. As with its economic policies, the state's policies on these matters did not reflect the interests and needs of society and helped create growing political unrest in the 1970s.

The shah relied on a combination of repression and co-optation to preserve his authoritarian regime, suppressing all forms of genuine opposition and emasculating Iran's fledgling democratic institutions. Even

[11]Looney, *Economic Origins of the Iranian Revolution*, 187–90, 210–16; Nicholas Gage, "Iran: Making of a Revolution," *New York Times Magazine*, December 17, 1978, 135; *Economist*, August 28, 1976, Survey 22–32; Graham, *Iran*, 98–102, 143, 184; Anthony Parsons, *The Pride and the Fall* (London: Cape, 1984), 81–82.

[12]Looney, *Economic Origins of the Iranian Revolution*, 213–20; Fred Halliday, "The Genesis of the Iranian Revolution," *Third World Quarterly* 1 (October 1979), 8.

within the narrow limits of the shah's authoritarian regime, actions such as the suppression of labor unions and the abrupt elimination of the state-sponsored two-party system ensured that opportunities for political participation were minimal. The increasingly severe repression and the absence of legitimate representative institutions alienated many Iranians, especially among the modern middle class, radicalizing the opposition and creating growing unrest. (See Chapters 5 and 6.)

Growing economic inequality in the 1960s and 1970s created glaring differences between the living standards of the upper and lower classes. Members of the upper class enjoyed very opulent lifestyles, living in beautiful houses in exclusive sections of Tehran, employing many cooks, servants, and maids, traveling frequently to Europe and the United States, and dressing in the finest Western fashions. The opulence of the upper class was most pronounced among members of the royal family, who lived in luxurious palaces and mixed in exclusive social circles in Europe and the United States. Moreover, the shah deliberately cultivated this image of splendor through events such as the 1971 Persepolis celebrations, which reportedly cost one hundred million dollars.[13] With the vast amounts of wealth created by the oil boom, the opulence of the upper class and royal family became even more pronounced in the mid- and late 1970s.

The living standards of the upper class contrasted sharply with those of the urban and rural lower classes. Most measures of health, nutritional, and educational standards in Iran were at or below the average for all underdeveloped countries in 1970 (see Table 8). Although aggregate figures of this kind provide a concrete basis for assessing the degree of poverty in Iran, they do not give a very clear picture of what life was really like for Iran's urban and rural lower classes. A careful analysis of the living conditions of the migrant poor in south Tehran conducted by Farhad Kazemi in the 1970s depicts a life of squalor and desperation. Of 3,780 migrant poor households surveyed, 55.1 percent lived in shacks or hovels, 32.9 percent lived in active or inactive brick kilns, 9.8 percent lived in tents, and a smaller number lived in cemeteries or "cavelike dwellings," including shelters constructed in huge, fetid garbage pits. Construction laborers in Tehran routinely lived at their construction sites, either in makeshift tents or in partly constructed buildings. Few members of the urban lower class had access to electricity, running water, or sanitary sewage facilities. Drug addiction, prostitution, and crime were common in the shantytowns of south Tehran and in other cities.[14] Furthermore, the

[13]*New York Times*, October 12, 1971, 39:2.

[14]Farhad Kazemi, *Poverty and Revolution in Iran* (New York: New York University Press, 1980), chap. 4.

high rate of rural-urban migration suggests that living standards were much worse for the rural lower class. One observer of rural life in Iran in the mid-1970s reported that villagers lived on four or five grams of protein per week and that some picked through horse droppings to retrieve undigested oats.[15]

The sharp contrast between the living standards of the upper and lower classes closely paralleled a growing gap between their values and social customs. The upper class, and the royal family in particular, was widely perceived to be decadent and un-Islamic. Lurid stories circulated about the sexual habits of the shah, his sister Princess Ashraf, and other members of the royal family; and it was well known that members of the royal family and the upper class engaged in opium smoking, gambling, and other sordid activities. Iran's upper class also became increasingly Westernized, as did the modern middle class. Most members of the upper class could speak one or more Western languages and traveled frequently in the West, and many had been educated in Europe or the United States. Contact with the West led many members of the upper class and the modern middle class to adopt habits that clashed sharply with Iran's traditional values and customs, including alcohol consumption, more liberal attitudes toward women, freer sexual practices, Western styles of dress, and preferences for Western or Westernized music and art. At the same time, many members of the upper class and the modern middle class drew away from Islam and even became openly disdainful of the clergy. The shah promoted these decadent and nontraditional values and customs both by example and through specific policies, such as the construction of a lavish casino and resort complex on Kish Island in the Persian Gulf. Moreover, he tried to undermine the role of Islam by emphasizing Iran's pre-Islamic heritage through actions such as the Persepolis celebrations and the replacement of the Islamic calendar with that of the ancient Persians.[16]

One aspect of the new, nontraditional values and social customs of the upper class and royal family which was especially disturbing to many Iranians was the widespread practice and toleration of corruption. Although corruption had existed for centuries in Iran and was certainly not confined to the royal family and upper class, it reached new, intolerably high levels, especially after the oil boom. The shah had always permitted a

[15] *Washington Post*, May 8, 1977, A-14.

[16] Fereydoun Hoveyda, *The Fall of the Shah* (New York: Wyndham, 1979), 31–32, 95–97, 141–142; Marvin Zonis, *The Political Elite of Iran* (Princeton, N.J.: Princeton University Press, 1971), 177, 181. Many of Iran's most gifted writers in the 1960s and 1970s focused extensively on Westernization; see Brad Hanson, "The 'Westoxication' of Iran: Depictions and Reactions of Behrangi, Al-e Ahmad, and Shariati," *International Journal of Middle East Studies* 15 (February 1983), 1–23.

fair amount of corruption among state officials, using it as a means of cooptation, and for years members of the royal family had accepted large commissions on business deals, gained favorable treatment from state agencies for their own businesses, and apparently even engaged in drug trafficking. But with the great influx of oil revenues, corruption became even more widespread: top state officials, members of the royal family, and assorted "influence peddlers" accepted huge commissions and bribes from foreign corporations trying to sell arms or other products in Iran, and many made huge profits in the booming real estate market and in other business activities. One close observer likened this corruption to "a haunch of meat thrown to an army of starving rats."[17]

The decadence, corruption, and Westernized outlook of the upper class and royal family clashed sharply with the values and social customs of the traditional middle and lower classes, creating growing cultural dualism. These latter groups were still deeply religious and very conservative, and they were often isolated from the upper class and the modern middle class by barriers associated with their lack of education and the nature of their occupations and social milieux. This was particularly true of the large numbers of rural migrants who streamed into Iran's cities in the late 1960s and 1970s. The traditional middle and lower classes increasingly regarded the royal family and the upper class as immoral and un-Islamic and blamed the shah and his policies for this moral degeneration. Moreover, the growing gap between the values and social customs of the modern and traditional sectors of society largely paralleled the gap between the living standards of the upper and lower classes, compounding the alienation of the traditional sector. The resulting political unrest was heightened and brought into clearer focus by the radical Shi'i clergy, who had also suffered considerably from the shah's policies.

Foreign Policy

Lacking societal constraint, the Iranian state's foreign policy in the 1960s and 1970s also tended to reflect the shah's priorities rather than society's interests. Iran's foreign policy was, of course, shaped and constrained by various international political factors, especially by the activities of the superpowers in the region and the changing foreign policies of regional actors such as Iraq, Saudi Arabia, Israel, and Egypt. But Iran's

[17]Hoveyda, *Fall of the Shah*, 91–96, 136, 144–45; *New York Times*, February 23, 1976, 1:4; *Le Monde*, March 5, 1972, 18; *Washington Post*, November 19, 1978, A21; U.S. Embassy, Tehran, "Corruption in Iran: A Problem for American Companies," June 20, 1972.

growing military power, the emergence of détente between the two superpowers, and the departure of British military forces from the Persian Gulf in the early 1970s enabled the shah to pursue much more actively his ambition of making Iran a major actor in regional affairs. At the same time, Iran maintained a close relationship with the United States and its allies in the region. Many knowledgeable Iranians regarded the shah's more activist foreign policy and his close relationship with the United States and its regional allies as capitulations to the forces of imperialism, a view that added to the simmering unrest.

Iran's relationship with the United States was the cornerstone of its foreign policy in the 1960s and 1970s. Although the U.S. economic aid program, the close ties between the CIA and SAVAK, and other aspects of the U.S.-Iran cliency relationship had ended or declined substantially by the mid-1960s, the bond between the two countries thereafter remained very strong. The United States continued to provide large amounts of advanced military equipment to Iran, especially after the oil boom, and the two countries continued to carry out joint military maneuvers and other kinds of joint security-oriented activities. The United States was one of Iran's largest trade partners, buying large amounts of Iranian oil and exporting consumer goods and other products to Iran. The two countries also engaged in various kinds of cultural interactions, such as student and artistic exchanges and close media ties. These interactions brought tens of thousands of Americans to Iran, which fostered Westernization and made many Iranians acutely aware of how close the two countries had become.[18]

Iran also maintained fairly close relations with Israel in this period. Iran had established de facto diplomatic relations with Israel in 1950, and Israel had been permitted to open an unofficial liaison office in Tehran in 1957.[19] In addition to their close cooperation on military and intelligence matters, Iran began to sell large amounts of oil to Israel in the 1960s and helped finance construction of the Eilat-Ashkelon oil pipeline, while Israel provided agricultural and disaster relief assistance to Iran. Although both governments tried to keep their relationship as discreet as possible, most knowledgeable Iranians had some awareness of how close the two countries really were. Many Iranians sympathized with the Palestinian people on anti-imperialist or pan-Islamic grounds and therefore deeply resented the shah's willingness to maintain close relations with Israel. Moreover, as the United States drew closer to Israel, many Iranians began to view the

[18]Ali Pasha Saleh, *Cultural Ties between Iran and the United States* (Tehran: n.p., 1976); Iran White Paper, sec. III.G.

[19]On the origins of Iran's relationship with Israel see Avner Yaniv, *Deterrence without the Bomb: The Politics of Israeli Strategy* (Lexington, Mass.: Lexington Books, 1987), 93–95.

relationship between Iran and Israel as a further manifestation of U.S. imperialism in Iran.

After the oil boom and the withdrawal of British military forces from the Persian Gulf, the shah increasingly involved Iran in regional conflicts such as those in Oman and in the Horn of Africa. Many Iranians regarded these actions as further examples of Iran's involvement in U.S. imperialism. Of these regional conflicts, the Dhofar uprising in Oman was particularly alarming to Iranians because Iranian soldiers were fighting and dying in an effort to suppress an uprising by Muslims against a dictatorial monarch who was little more than a British puppet.

The shah tried to counter the impression that he was an instrument of U.S. imperialism by maintaining good relations with the Soviet Union, working hard within OPEC to increase oil prices, becoming active in the nonaligned movement and other neutral forums, and frequently criticizing the United States and the West. Indeed, although it is rarely admitted by critics of the shah, these actions left Iran quite independent of the United States, much to the disappointment of U.S. policy makers.[20] Nevertheless, the popular image of the shah as a U.S. puppet persisted and fueled growing unrest.

The Gathering Storm, 1977–1978

Political unrest had grown substantially in Iran by 1977 as a result of the growing economic, social, and political problems caused by the state's inept and unpopular policies. These problems affected some societal groups much more severely than others, producing considerable differences in the degree of unrest from one group to another. Moreover, the state's repressive and co-optative activities had been directed more intensively at some groups than at others. These differences, as well as differences in group characteristics such as the level of social mobilization and the effectiveness of political organizations, produced considerable variation in the political power of different societal groups. These factors determined not only which groups were to participate in the opposition movement that emerged in the late 1970s but also the relative importance of each group in this movement and thus the movement's fundamental character.

The modern middle class had benefited considerably from rapid economic growth and from many of the state's social and cultural policies, such as its expansion of the educational system and its efforts to promote

[20]See Rouhollah K. Ramazani, *Iran's Foreign Policy, 1941–1973* (Charlottesville: University Press of Virginia, 1975), chaps. 13–16.

Westernization. These benefits co-opted many members of the modern middle class, especially among the technocratic fraction, leaving them fairly content with the status quo. Moreover, the systematic suppression of the Mosaddeqists and the independent nationalists had left much of the modern middle class leaderless, apathetic, and politically inactive. Consequently, despite the tremendous increase in the size of the modern middle class, its level of social mobilization had declined substantially by the late 1970s and it posed less of a threat to the shah's regime than it had in the 1950s and early 1960s.

Nevertheless, many members of the modern middle class remained troubled by the absence of democratic institutions, by the extensive repression and censorship, and by Iran's close relationship with the United States and other Western countries. As repression and censorship became more severe and as inflation and corruption increased in the 1970s, unrest grew further among this class. The leadership of the Mosaddeqist movement, dormant since the collapse of the Third National Front, therefore resumed its political activity in the late 1970s. Those members of the modern middle class who had not succumbed to the co-optative enticements offered by the shah's regime enthusiastically joined the Mosaddeqist leadership in the opposition movement that emerged in 1977, providing one important component of the revolutionary coalition that was eventually to bring down the shah.

Iran's rapidly growing population of high school, college, and university students could expect to benefit handsomely from rapid economic growth and many of the state's social and cultural policies. Yet while many students were co-opted by these enticements, many others were deeply distressed by the absence of democratic institutions, the extensive repression and censorship, the growing inequality, the corruption and decadence of the royal family and upper class, and Iran's close relationship with the United States and Israel. A great deal of unrest therefore existed among Iran's student population. In the 1950s and early 1960s, Iran's students had generally supported the Mosaddeqists. But the weakness and vacillation of the Mosaddeqists and their subsequent suppression by the state had led many students to join or sympathize with the Marxist and secular Islamic guerrilla groups that emerged in the 1960s and early 1970s. Moreover, the activities of the Islamic guerrillas and of Islamic activists like Ali Shariati had led many students to embrace Islam more closely and come under the influence of radical clergymen like ayatollahs Khomeini and Taleqani. The various guerrilla groups and Islamic activists, together with the student organizations operating abroad, generated a very high level of social mobilization among Iranian students and made them a key component in the emerging revolutionary coalition.

Although the industrial working class had benefited somewhat from Iran's rapid economic growth and from some of the state's social and cultural policies, the absence of legitimate labor unions and various other factors had restrained the growth of industrial wages and therefore limited these benefits. Furthermore, while most members of the industrial working class had benefited modestly from the economic boom, many had relatives and friends among the impoverished urban and rural lower classes and therefore nevertheless resented the state's economic policies. The modest economic benefits realized by the industrial working class contrasted sharply with the opulence of the upper class and the royal family. Many members of the industrial working class were also distressed by the repression and the absence of democratic institutions, by growing inflation and corruption, and by Iran's close ties with the United States and other Western countries. The destruction of the Tudeh party and the suppression of legitimate labor unions and other working-class organizations left the industrial working class politically inarticulate and therefore relatively weak. Still, many members of this class joined the growing opposition movement, forming another important component of the revolutionary coalition.

The traditional middle class also benefited from rapid economic growth, but these benefits were partially offset by the declining importance of the bazaar in the Iranian economy and by the neglect of traditional industries in the state's development plans. Moreover, the growing inflation and corruption, higher interest rates, price controls, antiprofiteering drive, and government austerity measures all adversely affected the bazaar merchants and craftsmen who were the core of the traditional middle class. Similarly, although the traditional middle class benefited from social programs such as improvements in education and health care, most of its members opposed the state's efforts to promote secularization and Westernization and deeply resented the decadence of the royal family and the upper class. Many also resented the absence of democratic institutions, the high level of repression and censorship, and the shah's close ties with the United States and Israel. [21]

The urban lower class benefited very little from Iran's rapid economic growth and the state's social and cultural policies. Its members remained impoverished, suffering from slow wage growth, the decline of traditional industries, and the limited availability of social services. Their plight grew worse in the mid- and late 1970s as rural migrants streamed into the cities, food and housing prices soared, and government austerity measures and

[21]For a good discussion of the sources of unrest in the Tehran bazaar see *Le Monde*, May 21–22, 1978, 7, and November 24, 1978, 3.

private capital flight reduced employment opportunities. Many members of the urban lower class were well aware of the vast disparities that existed in Iran and resented them deeply, as they did the growing secularization, Westernization, and corruption. Moreover, the rapid growth of the urban lower class as a result of rural-urban migration, greatly increased its potential political power.[22]

The Shi'i clergy continued to maintain close ties with the traditional middle class and the urban lower class and shared the resentment of these classes toward growing secularization and Westernization, the decadence of the upper class and the royal family, and Iran's close ties with the United States, Israel, and other Western countries. Moreover, with the virtual destruction of the landowning class as a result of the land reform program, the traditional middle class and the urban lower class became the main allies of the Shi'i clergy, which therefore increasingly sympathized with and articulated the views of these classes. The clergy was also greatly angered by the land reform program, by the shah's efforts to improve the status of women, and by his concerted efforts to suppress clerical activism and gain control over the clergy's finances and institutions. Many members of the clergy had begun to oppose the shah's regime in the 1960s, and a small but growing fraction became associated with Khomeini's network or with other radical Islamic groups. An alliance of the traditional middle class, the urban lower class, and the Shi'i clergy therefore became another key component in the revolutionary coalition.[23]

The bourgeoisie benefited greatly from Iran's rapid economic growth, despite the state's dominant role in the economy. Many of its members also profited from the rampant corruption and favored the Westernization promoted by the shah. Consequently, while some members of the bourgeoisie were undoubtedly distressed about the repression and the absence of democratic institutions, and others were presumably concerned about the growth of Westernization and secularization, this class as a whole strongly supported the shah's regime in the 1960s and early 1970s. Nevertheless, growing inflation and the other economic problems that emerged in the mid-1970s increasingly concerned the bourgeoisie, as did the antiprofiteering and anticorruption campaigns, the workers' profit-sharing program, the price control program, and the state's austerity measures and stricter monetary policy. By the late 1970s, many members

[22]On unrest among Iran's urban lower class see Farhad Kazemi, "Urban Migrants and the Revolution," *Iranian Studies* 13 (1980), 257–77.

[23]On clerical unrest and the clergy's alliance with the traditional middle class and the urban lower class see Nikki R. Keddie, *Roots of Revolution* (New Haven, Conn.: Yale University Press, 1981), 239–47.

of the bourgeoisie had become critical of the shah.[24] Although this class still generally supported the shah's regime, it became more ambivalent in this period. The bourgeoisie was not, in any case, powerful enough to serve as an effective base of support for the state.

Finally, Iran's rural lower class remained mired in poverty, benefiting little from the rapid economic growth and the state's social and cultural programs. Despite its grueling poverty and its large size, however, Iran's rural lower class remained too politically unorganized and too isolated to participate significantly in the revolutionary coalition that brought down the shah.

The social base of the opposition movement therefore had four main components: the modern middle class, students, the industrial working class, and a closely knit alliance consisting of the traditional middle class, the urban lower class, and the Shi'i clergy. The opposition movements of the early 1950s and early 1960s had been based essentially on these same four groups, but changes in the structure of society, the differential impact of the state's social and economic policies and its co-optative and repressive efforts, and the ideology and tactics adopted by the main opposition organizations gave the new opposition movement a fundamentally different character. The most important difference was that the radical Shi'i clergy, rather than the Mosaddeqists, came to dominate this movement.

One important reason for the dominance of the radical clergy was the rapid growth of the urban lower class and its increasing frustration over its failure to benefit substantially from the tremendous changes that were occurring in the 1970s. The clergy's long-standing ties to the urban lower class, its own growing frustration, and the charismatic, activist character of the radical clergy enabled it to mobilize much of the urban lower class and rely on this class as its primary base of support.

Another reason was the failure of the Mosaddeqists adequately to mobilize the modern middle class, students, and the industrial working class, which together had comprised their main base of support in the 1950s and early 1960s and which were also growing rapidly and becoming increasingly frustrated in the 1970s. This failure had several causes. First, the state's extensive efforts to repress the Mosaddeqists since 1953 had made it difficult for them to operate. By the late 1970s they had been dormant for over a decade and their support among students, workers, and the traditional middle class had gradually eroded. Although the radical clergy had also been repressed, its secretive character and less

[24]See, e.g., *Iran Trade and Industry*, May 1977, 5–7, October 1977, 8–10, and November 1977, 6–8.

threatening posture spared it from much of the damage inflicted on the Mosaddeqists. Second, the modern middle class had been heavily co-opted, reducing its level of social mobilization and therefore weakening the Mosaddeqists' main base of support. Students, workers, and the traditional middle class had also been co-opted in varying degrees, further weakening the Mosaddeqists. Third, the bitter factionalism that had emerged in the Mosaddeqist movement in the early 1960s and the gradual erosion of its populist character had reduced its popularity among students, workers, and the traditional middle class.

The independent nationalists and guerrilla groups had also been greatly weakened by repression, by the co-optation of their main bases of support, and by the nature of their ideology and tactics. The independent nationalists had never enjoyed much appeal beyond the technocratic fraction of the modern middle class, and their importance in Iranian politics had declined considerably as a result of harassment by the security forces and the co-optation of the modern middle class. Similarly, the appeal of the guerrilla groups had been limited mainly to radical students and a few workers, and their attempts to launch popular uprisings without first developing broader bases of support had made it fairly easy for the security forces to weaken them. Consequently, neither the independent nationalists nor the guerrillas were capable of dominating the opposition movement in the late 1970s.

Although the radical clergy was therefore the strongest member of the revolutionary coalition, its considerable differences with the other members did not prevent it from working closely with them to bring down the shah. The radical clergy, the Mosaddeqists, and the guerrillas shared a strong antipathy toward the shah's regime and wanted either to change it fundamentally or to destroy it altogether; their immediate goals were therefore quite similar. These three opposition factions were also fairly closely linked with one another, especially through the Liberation Movement of Iran and the Liberation Movement of Iran (Abroad), whose leaders had developed close personal ties with the leaders of each opposition faction and held political views that overlapped considerably with those of each faction. Moreover, the radical clergy remained vague about its long-term intentions, leading the Mosaddeqists and the guerrillas to downplay their ideological differences with the radical clergy and eventually even to accept the clergy's de facto leadership. Although these circumstances permitted the three factions to work together to bring down the shah's regime, the strength of the radical clergy enabled it to gain control over the state in the first few years after the shah's demise and drive the Mosaddeqists and the guerrilla groups underground or into exile.

With the apparent destruction of the main guerrilla groups and the absence of overt political activity by the radical Shi'i clergy and the Mosaddeqists, and facing growing criticism abroad about human rights conditions in Iran, the shah in late 1976 began to make clear hints that he was willing to permit a limited amount of political liberalization. In response to these hints, members of the Mosaddeqist opposition and certain other figures began to circulate leaflets and open letters expressing mild criticisms of the shah's regime. The first of these was a long open letter quietly circulated in February 1977 by Ali Asghar Hajj-Sayyid-Javadi which criticized the state's social and economic policies and the absence of democratic institutions. This letter was soon followed by others, expressing similar themes, authored by Mozaffar Baqai, Khalil Azar, and Amir Rahimi. In May 1977 fifty-three lawyers published an open letter to the shah which criticized Iran's judicial system and announced the formation of a special commission to monitor judicial matters. In June 1977 veteran National Front activists Karim Sanjabi, Shahpour Bakhtiar, and Dariush Foruhar published another open letter to the shah which criticized the state's social and economic policies and called for the full implementation of the 1906 constitution. Shortly thereafter, forty prominent writers sent an open letter to Prime Minister Hoveida calling for an end to censorship and a return to constitutional rule.[25]

The shah made no effort to suppress these opposition statements; he even allowed a Tehran magazine to publish a summary of them. He also began to permit official bodies such as the Rastakhiz party and an organization called the Group for the Study of Iranian Problems to debate social and political matters more openly. In July 1977 the shah replaced Prime Minister Hoveida with Jamshid Amuzegar, an able technocrat who was widely regarded as better qualified to solve Iran's growing economic problems. The shah's greater willingness to tolerate dissent led the Mosaddeqists to become increasingly active during the summer and fall of 1977. Organizations such as the Writers' Association, the Group for Free Books and Free Thought, the Iranian Committee for the Defense of Freedom and Human Rights, the National Organization of University Teachers, and the Society of Merchants, Traders, and Craftsmen were established and began to agitate for political reform. More significantly, Sanjabi, Bakhtiar, Foruhar, and several other National Front veterans established an organization called the Union of National Front Forces in the summer of 1977; Ba-

[25]U.S. Embassy, Tehran, "Straws in the Wind: Intellectual and Religious Opposition in Iran," July 25, 1977; Ervand Abrahamian, *Iran between Two Revolutions* (Princeton, N.J.: Princeton University Press, 1982), 501–2.

zargan and his allies revived the Liberation Movement; and a new Mosaddeqist organization called the Radical Movement was established by a group of young intellectuals led by Rahmatollah Moqadam-Maraghehi. These groups became increasingly active in the fall of 1977, holding meetings and rallies and issuing statements. Then in mid-November the shah apparently decided that the trend toward liberalization had gone far enough. Police units and groups of thugs broke up a series of poetry readings and rallies at Aryamehr University in Tehran in late November and early December, injuring and arresting scores of participants.[26]

During the mid-1970s the radical clergy had been agitating against the shah's regime in mosques and religious schools throughout Iran and through the medium of taped sermons prepared by Khomeini in Iraq and smuggled into Iran by special couriers. As unrest grew and became increasingly visible in the fall of 1977, the radical clergy began to play a more active and overt role in fomenting it. Two events, in late 1977 and early 1978, thrust the radical clergy into a position of leadership in the opposition movement. First, Khomeini's son Mostafa died suddenly on October 21. Khomeini's allies organized a series of memorial services for Mostafa in Tehran and other cities which were heavily attended, in part because of widespread rumors that Mostafa had been killed by SAVAK. The large attendance demonstrated that Khomeini's name was still widely known and respected in Iran, despite his many years in exile, and therefore encouraged Khomeini and the radical clergy to step up their criticism of the shah's regime. Second, in response to this growing agitation by the radical clergy, the semiofficial newspaper *Ettela'at* published an article on January 7 that denounced Khomeini as an agent of British colonialism and a native of India (rather than Iran). In response, Khomeini's allies organized large demonstrations in the holy city of Qom. The security forces attacked the demonstrators, killing at least seven and arresting more than one hundred.[27]

During the winter and spring of 1978, more large demonstrations occurred in various cities at regular forty-day intervals, in accordance with the traditional Shi'i practice of mourning for the dead. The first occurred in mid-February, forty days after the Qom riots, in response to a joint call for demonstrations by the radical clergy and the National Front. Demonstrations occurred throughout the country but were most severe in Tabriz, where government buildings, movie theaters, banks, and stores that sold liquor were attacked by clergy-led crowds. Army units occupied Tabriz for several days to put down the unrest, killing at least nine

[26]Abrahamian, *Iran between Two Revolutions*, 503–5; U.S. Embassy, Tehran, "Straws in the Wind"; *F.Y.I.* (Tehran), July 10, 1977, 2–9; *New York Times*, November 26, 1977, 24:1.

[27]Amir Taheri, *The Spirit of Allah* (London: Hutchinson, 1985), chap. 11.

demonstrators and arresting some 650. The next forty-day cycle of demonstrations occurred in late March, when a general strike was held in Tabriz to commemorate the February riots and violent demonstrations occurred in Tehran, Qom, Isfahan, Mashad, and other cities. Similar disturbances arose forty days later, in mid-May, with general strikes in several cities and violent demonstrations throughout the country, resulting in at least fifteen deaths. Opposition activity during this period was led by a coalition of the Mosaddeqist leadership, members of Khomeini's network, and moderate clergymen such as Ayatollah Sayyid Mohammad Kazem Shariatmadari. The participants in these events were mostly high school and college students, clergymen, seminary students, and members of the urban lower class.[28]

The state responded with a mixture of repression and conciliatory gestures. The armed forces, the police, and government-backed thugs suppressed rallies and demonstrations, and SAVAK agents kidnapped and beat two prominent Mosaddeqists and bombed several opposition offices. Opposition leaders were denounced as "Islamic Marxists" and "red and black reactionaries," and some clerical figures were forced into internal exile. But the state also permitted the opposition to operate fairly openly, and it apparently scaled back or discontinued altogether extreme repressive measures such as torture, administrative detention, and the use of military courts for political offenses. The shah also ended the antiprofiteering campaign and other unpopular economic programs; dismissed General Nassiri, the head of SAVAK, and several other top security officials; and tried to placate the clergy by banning sexually explicit films, making a pilgrimage to the shrine of Imam Reza in Mashad, and taking other conciliatory steps.[29]

The opposition remained fairly active after the bloody demonstrations of mid-May, organizing a nationwide general strike in early June and a series of demonstrations in mid-June to commemorate the forty-day anniversary of the May demonstrations. Labor unrest also began to emerge in June, with scattered strikes in Tehran and other cities. The peaceful nature of these activities led many observers to conclude that unrest had begun to subside and that the shah's regime would survive the lingering crisis. This guarded optimism persisted through mid-July, despite further labor unrest and an increasingly vocal Mosaddeqist campaign for political reforms.[30]

[28]Jerrold D. Green, *Revolution in Iran: The Politics of Countermobilization* (New York: Praeger, 1982), 92–94; *New York Times*, February 24, 1978, 10:5, May 13, 1978, 1:4; U.S. Embassy, Tehran, "The Internal Scene," June 1, 1978.

[29]U.S. Embassy, Tehran, "Internal Scene"; Abrahamian, *Iran between Two Revolutions*, 508–9.

[30]Abrahamian, *Iran between Two Revolutions*, 512; John D. Stempel, *Inside the Iranian Revolution* (Bloomington: Indiana University Press, 1981), 104–8.

It was soon clear, however, that the apparent calm of June and early July was merely a temporary respite during which the radical clergy and other opposition groups were reorganizing their forces and developing a strategy for the destruction the shah's regime. The first evidence of this came on July 23, when two days of bloody rioting erupted in Mashad after a prominent clergyman was killed in a routine traffic accident. Violent unrest spread throughout the country in the following weeks, leaving scores dead. This unrest differed from the unrest that had occurred earlier in two important ways: it was led mainly by the radical clergy, with little or no apparent Mosaddeqist involvement; and it was better organized and much more deliberate, with clerical activists and Islamic guerrillas coordinating uprisings in different cities and provoking retaliation by the security forces by shooting at them from the crowds and carrying out a campaign of arson and bombings. The Islamic guerrillas who became active in this period apparently included the reconstituted Fedayan-e Islam and the Islamic Nations party, both led by Khomeini associates, but not the Mojahedin-e Khalq, which remained largely inactive until October 1978. The radical clergy also launched a campaign to promote unrest within the armed forces, which began to undermine the effectiveness of this critical pillar of the shah's regime. This period of growing unrest culminated on August 19, when arsonists set fire to the Rex Theater in Abadan, killing over four hundred people. Although the identity of the arsonists has never been determined, rumors quickly spread throughout the country that the fire had been set by SAVAK agents.[31]

Nationwide unrest followed the Rex Theater fire. In an effort to stem the growing chaos, the shah replaced Prime Minister Amuzegar with Jafar Sharif-Emami, a trusted adviser who had close family and personal ties to certain moderate clergymen. Sharif-Emami quickly dismissed some top state officials (including several alleged Bahai's), released hundreds of political prisoners, dropped the Minister for Women's Affairs from the cabinet, elevated the Religious Endowments Organization to cabinet level, reinstated the Islamic calendar, and closed casinos. The shah also announced that free elections would soon be held, that independent political parties could be established, and that guarantees of free speech and assembly would be enacted; and he authorized Sharif-Emami to negotiate with the opposition. Sharif-Emami permitted the Mosaddeqists to organize large demonstrations in early September in exchange for promises that the demonstrations would be orderly. At the same time, Ayatollah

[31]Stempel, *Inside the Iranian Revolution*, 109–10; *Keesing's Contemporary Archives*, January 5, 1979, 29384–29385; Taheri, *Spirit of Allah*, 189–91; Muslim Students Following the Line of the Imam, *Documents from the U.S. Espionage Den* 24 (Tehran: n.p., n.d.), 114.

Shariatmadari called on the opposition to give Sharif-Emami three months to implement a constitutional regime. These measures did not dampen the growing unrest. Over one hundred thousand demonstrators marched peacefully in Tehran on September 4, and larger demonstrations followed, despite calls for restraint by the moderate opposition. By September 7 the crowds in Tehran numbered over half a million. That evening, martial law was declared and the shah ordered the arrest of several Mosaddeqist leaders. The next day, commando units backed by tanks and helicopter gunships dispersed a relatively small crowd gathered in Jaleh Square in Tehran. In what has come to be known as the Jaleh Square massacre, these units fired directly into the crowds, killing at least eighty-seven demonstrators and wounding hundreds more.[32]

The period of unrest that culminated in the Jaleh Square massacre embodied two important trends. First, the crowds that demonstrated in Tehran in the days before this horrible event were not only much larger than earlier crowds but drew much more heavily on Tehran's urban lower class. Second, and integrally related to this first trend, the failure of the Mosaddeqists and the moderate clergy led by Shariatmadari to maintain control over the crowds that marched in Tehran in early September signaled the ascent of Khomeini and the radical clergy to a position of unparalleled leadership in the revolutionary coalition. During the next two months the radical clergy consolidated its leadership and was therefore able to impose Khomeini's uncompromising position on the other coalition members.

The declaration of martial law in most parts of Iran discouraged the opposition from organizing large demonstrations in the immediate aftermath of the Jaleh Square massacre. Instead, smaller demonstrations and confrontations with the security forces became routine in Tehran and other major cities. In addition, two other forms of opposition activity became widespread. First, the labor unrest that had begun to surface in the summer spread rapidly, making the industrial working class a key participant in the revolution. The most important instance of labor unrest was a strike by oil workers that began in mid-September, gradually drying up Iran's main source of foreign exchange and therefore further weakening the economy. The oil workers were quickly joined by workers in many other major industries, and shorter work stoppages were held in bazaars throughout the country and by state employees and workers in such critical sectors of the economy as telecommunications, banking, and transportation. Second, in September the Fedayan-e Khalq began a series of bloody attacks on police and Gendarmerie stations throughout Iran

[32]Abrahamian, *Iran between Two Revolutions*, 513–16.

which was to continue until the shah was finally overthrown. The Mojahedin-e Khalq also increased its activity, but apparently avoided violence and confined itself primarily to political organizing in loose association with the Mosaddeqists.[33] The labor unrest and Fedayan attacks broadened the scope of antiregime activity and contributed greatly to the chaos that was rapidly engulfing Iran.

The shah continued to respond to the growing crisis with a mixture of repression and conciliation. Under the martial law regulations enacted in early September, the security forces arrested several top opposition leaders and put down strikes and demonstrations, often with considerable force. The shah also persuaded the Iraqi government to deport Khomeini in early October, apparently assuming that he would be less effective if he were farther away from Iran. Khomeini settled in a small town on the outskirts of Paris, where he was soon joined by Ibrahim Yazdi and Sadeq Qotbzadeh of the Liberation Movement of Iran (Abroad) and by Abol-Hassan Bani-Sadr, a Paris-based writer and exile activist whose views were fairly similar to those of the Liberation Movement. The shah also freed many political prisoners, declared an amnesty for exiled opposition members, dismissed or arrested many top government and SAVAK officials, dissolved the Rastakhiz party, and made a variety of other conciliatory gestures. He also began to approach the Mosaddeqists and non-Mosaddeqist opposition figures such as Ali Amini about the possibility of establishing a coalition government that would preserve his position as monarch. Although these measures might well have saved the shah's regime in the summer of 1978, in October they were simply brushed aside by most of the opposition.[34]

Two events in early November appear, in retrospect, to have sealed the fate of the shah's regime. First, Mosaddeqist leaders Sanjabi, Bazargan, and Nasser Minatchi traveled to Paris to try to persuade Khomeini to authorize cooperation with the shah toward establishing an opposition-led government within the framework of the constitution. Khomeini flatly rejected this idea and maneuvered the Mosaddeqist leaders into issuing a joint statement with him on November 6 rejecting any compromise with the shah. This statement ended all hope for a coalition government. Second, waves of clergy- and guerrilla-led mobs swarmed through Tehran in the first week of November, briefly seizing the British embassy and attacking police stations, government buildings, banks, and stores that sold liquor and foreign-made products. The ferocity of these mobs dem-

[33]Muslim Students, *Documents from the U.S. Espionage Den* 24:109–10, 114; Abrahamian, *Iran between Two Revolutions*, 517–18.

[34]Abrahamian, *Iran between Two Revolutions*, 519; Stempel, *Inside the Iranian Revolution*, 124.

onstrated the power of the radical clergy and the failure of martial law and the shah's conciliatory measures to reduce unrest. In response to these events, the shah replaced Sharif-Emami with a military government headed by General Gholam Reza Azhari.[35]

Relative calm prevailed briefly in mid-November, after Azhari arrested National Front leaders Sanjabi and Foruhar and forced most of the striking oil workers to return to work. Azhari also released several hundred political prisoners and ordered the arrest of more than sixty top state officials, including former prime minister Hoveida and former SAVAK chief Nassiri. The shah continued to negotiate secretly through emissaries with non-Mosaddeqists such as Amini and Mohsen Pezeshkpour, with the Mosaddeqists through the Liberation Movement and the Committee for the Defense of Freedom and Human Rights, and even with Sanjabi. The shah offered to let the moderate opposition form a government but insisted that he remain in power as a constitutional monarch with command over the armed forces. The Mosaddeqists rejected this proposition, insisting that the shah leave the country and that a regency council of prominent, nonestablishment figures be created. As these negotiations bogged down, the opposition called for a new round of demonstrations. Nationwide violence in the last ten days of November left over six hundred dead. Oil workers and workers in many other industries went back on strike, bringing the economy to a standstill. Secular and Islamic guerrillas roamed the streets of Tehran and other cities, attacking the security forces and fomenting unrest. Islamic activists seized control of the holy cities of Qom and Mashad and announced the creation of an Islamic republic in Qom. Unrest continued to build in early December, with another seven hundred deaths by December 9. On December 10 and 11, which coincided with the days of Tasua and Ashura, when the martyrdom of Imam Hussein is commemorated, crowds numbering in the millions marched in Tehran and other cities. Violence continued on the following days, and the armed forces began to disintegrate.[36]

In the days after the Ashura demonstrations the shah began to meet directly with opposition figures such as Sanjabi and Amini in an effort to establish a coalition government. He soon invited Gholam Hussein Sadiqi, a cabinet minister under Mosaddeq who had been politically inactive since the early 1960s, to form a government. When this effort collapsed, the shah turned to Shahpour Bakhtiar, a leading figure in the National Front who had broken with his colleagues over the issue of

[35]Stempel, *Inside the Iranian Revolution*, 130–32. Emissaries of Shariatmadari made a similar trip to Paris in mid-November to try to persuade Khomeini to compromise but were also rebuffed; see ibid., 147.

[36]Ibid., 139–51; *Keesing's Contemporary Archives*, July 27, 1979, 29737–29738.

establishing an alliance with Khomeini. Bakhtiar agreed to form a government if the shah would leave the country, dissolve SAVAK, release all remaining political prisoners, and meet several other conditions. Having exhausted every alternative, and with the country engulfed in an increasingly violent revolution, the shah was forced to agree. Bakhtiar was named prime minister on December 30, 1978, leading the National Front immediately to expel him. He spent the next several days assembling a cabinet and a regency council to take over the shah's duties. The Bakhtiar government was formally presented to the Majles on January 11 and immediately denounced by Khomeini. On January 16 the shah and his entourage flew to Egypt for "an extended vacation," signaling the end of the Pahlavi dynasty and the destruction of the U.S. client state in Iran.[37]

[37]Ibid., 29740–29741; Chapour Bakhtiar, *Ma Fidélité* (Paris: Albin, 1982), 119–31; *New York Times*, January 17, 1979, 1:8.

Conclusion

This book has argued that the U.S.-Iran cliency relationship established in 1953 acted as an important exogenous structural determinant of Iranian domestic politics by strengthening the state and enabling it to become highly autonomous by the mid-1960s—despite changes in Iran's mode of production which had created a large modern middle class and industrial working class by this time. The modern middle class had been the most prominent actor in Iranian politics in the first half of the twentieth century, working with the industrial working class and other groups through organizations such as the constitutional movement, the Tudeh party, and the National Front to increase its influence over the state. When Mosaddeq was named prime minister in 1951, the modern middle class seemed poised to establish hegemony over the state. Moreover, it continued to grow in the following decades and probably would have succeeded if exogenous structural factors had not intervened. The creation of a highly autonomous state not only interrupted this process but actually reversed it, facilitating the co-optation of much of the modern middle class and virtually destroying the political organizations that represented it.

The state's high degree of autonomy enabled it to carry out policies that increasingly diverged from society's interests, creating growing political unrest. The huge increase in world oil prices and other changes in the early 1970s temporarily eliminated the capital shortages and certain other factors that had constrained state policy-making. The divergence between the state's policies and society's interests therefore became even larger, creating severe economic and social crises. Iran's modern middle class, industrial working class, urban lower class, and student population all grew rapidly and became increasingly restive about these crises, creating the social base for a revolutionary movement. Thus by enabling the state to become highly autonomous, the U.S.-Iran cliency relationship helped bring about the 1978–79 revolution.

Although this book has focused mainly on the domestic political effects of cliency, Iran's rapidly growing oil revenue also contributed to the state's autonomy (see Chapter 5). However, there are several reasons to believe that cliency was a more important determinant of state autonomy than oil revenue. First, cliency affected the state's autonomy mainly in the decade that began with the 1953 coup, when the shah was in the process of constructing a highly autonomous state. By contrast, it was only in the mid-1960s, *after* such a state had been established, that Iran's oil revenue became large enough to affect the state's autonomy by expanding its revenue base and fostering rapid economic growth. Second, by promoting rapid economic growth, oil revenue contributed to the sharp increase in the size and hence the political power of the modern middle class, industrial working class, urban lower class, and student population, the main groups that carried out the revolution. Consequently, although oil revenue helped increase the state's autonomy in the short term, it also undermined it in the long term by strengthening these groups.

Finally, cliency also had a much more direct effect than oil revenue on the characteristics and capabilities of the state and society that affected state autonomy. The U.S.-instigated coup and the emergency U.S. assistance given to the post-coup government greatly weakened the National Front and the Tudeh party, undermining the political power of the modern middle class and other societal groups. The subsequent U.S. economic aid program facilitated rapid economic growth and many of the social reforms that served as mechanisms of co-optation. The U.S. security assistance programs vastly improved the state's repressive capabilities. By contrast, although oil revenue enhanced the state's co-optative capabilities by increasing its revenue base and generating rapid economic growth, it did not directly affect the characteristics of the state apparatus itself.

Two other points must be emphasized here. First, it should be clear that a delay of roughly a decade occurred between the establishment of the cliency relationship and the emergence of a highly autonomous state. This delay was due to the inevitable difficulties the shah encountered in neutralizing the National Front, the traditional upper class, and other sources of opposition and to the relatively slow pace at which state institutions such as the security forces and the economics and planning ministries were modernized with U.S. assistance. Similarly, there was a delay of roughly fifteen years between the establishment of a highly autonomous state and its collapse in early 1979. This delay was due to the slow buildup of popular resentment and to the slow pace at which this resentment was transformed into effective opposition political activity.

Second, the 1978–79 revolution was not an inevitable consequence of the state's high degree of autonomy. For one thing, if oil prices had not increased sharply in the early 1970s, capital shortages might well have prevented the shah from carrying out some of the inept and unpopular policies that precipitated the revolution. Moreover, although the state's high degree of autonomy enabled the shah to carry out these policies, it certainly did not compel him to do so; and once some of the adverse consequences of these policies became apparent, state autonomy did not prevent him from acting more quickly to avert the emerging crises. Finally, the tactics that the shah, opposition leaders, and even U.S. policy makers pursued as revolutionary unrest grew in 1978 helped determine the outcome of this unrest. The shah's illness, Khomeini's charismatic personality, and the preoccupation of U.S. policy makers with the Camp David negotiations strongly affected the tactics pursued by these actors and therefore contributed to the success of the revolution. Thus the state's high degree of autonomy did not directly cause the revolution; rather, it created conditions that were conducive to revolution.

The ideas developed in this book have important implications for the study of Third World politics and for the conduct of U.S. foreign policy. Since cliency relationships are most common in strategically important regions of the world such as Central America, Eastern Europe, the northern tier of the Middle East, east Asia, and Southeast Asia, these ideas should be most applicable to countries located in these regions. Although it is not possible to carry out a detailed comparative analysis here, these ideas should be especially applicable to the strong clients and some of the moderately important and weak clients identified in Table 2. Indeed, one would be hard pressed to explain post–World War II domestic politics in countries like Nicaragua, Panama, Cuba, Czechoslovakia, Poland, Mongolia, North and South Korea, the Vietnams, and the Philippines without taking into account their cliency relationships with the superpowers. Each of these countries has had a very strong state, and most experienced considerable domestic unrest while they were involved in cliency relationships.

More generally, an important underlying theme of this book has been that international politics can have a considerable impact on domestic politics. In addition to cliency relationships, international political phenomena such as war,[1] the threat of war,[2] foreign subversion,[3] and foreign

[1]See esp. Charles Tilly, *Coercion, Capital, and European States, AD 990–1990* (Cambridge, Mass.: Basil Blackwell, 1990); and the studies reviewed in Peter Gourevitch, "The International System and Regime Formation," *Comparative Politics* 10 (April 1978), 419–38.

[2]Ellen Kay Trimberger, *Revolution from Above* (New Brunswick, N.J.: Transaction Books, 1978).

[3]Andrew M. Scott, *The Revolution in Statecraft: Informal Penetration* (New York: Random House, 1965).

political and military domination[4] can have important domestic political consequences. This focus on the domestic effects of international political phenomena differs substantially from that of the most prominent paradigms for studying Third World politics—modernization theory and dependency theory—which emphasize the effects of domestic and international economic factors. A focus on international political phenomena appears to be particularly suitable for studying the domestic politics of countries located in strategically important regions of the world. Nevertheless, economic factors still have important domestic political consequences in such countries. Studies that focus on the domestic impact of international political phenomena must therefore consider how these phenomena interact with economic factors in affecting a country's domestic politics.

The Iranian revolution clearly had very damaging consequences for U.S. national security. Its most immediate consequence was the elimination of an important U.S. ally that had served as a buffer between the Soviet Union and the Persian Gulf, acted as a surrogate for the United States in the Middle East and elsewhere, and provided the United States with bases for critically important electronic listening posts aimed at the Soviet Union. Another immediate consequence was a tremendous increase in world oil prices, which produced a severe worldwide recession. Once the postrevolutionary regime had been established, radical Islamic movements inspired and often backed by the new regime emerged throughout the Islamic world and began to threaten pro-American regimes in Tunisia, Egypt, the Israeli-occupied territories, Lebanon, Saudi Arabia, Kuwait, Bahrain, Pakistan, Malaysia, and elsewhere. Finally, the fall of the shah's regime and the subsequent hostage crisis seriously undermined U.S. prestige and influence in the Middle East, making it more difficult for the United States to pursue its regional interests.

These damaging consequences of the revolution illustrate the basic paradox of cliency relationships mentioned in the first chapter of this book: although cliency relationships are generally intended to promote political stability in client countries, they may instead promote instability in the long run by enabling client states to become so autonomous that they generate popular unrest. Indeed, in light of the tremendous problems created by the Iranian revolution and by similar crises in U.S. client countries such as South Vietnam and Nicaragua, one can argue that the problem of managing cliency relationships has emerged as one of the greatest challenges to U.S. national security in the post-World War II era.

[4]Christopher D. Jones, *Soviet Influence in Eastern Europe* (New York: Praeger, 1981); Hamza Alavi, "The State in Post-Colonial Societies: Pakistan and Bangladesh," *New Left Review* 74 (July–August 1972), 59–82.

The United States appears to have four options for dealing with the problem of popular unrest in client countries. First, in what would amount to a return to isolationism, the United States could simply withdraw from its existing cliency relationships and refrain from establishing new ones. This approach would certainly obviate the problem, but it might well bring about the rapid collapse of vitally important client states, such as those in Egypt, Turkey, and the Philippines, and it would greatly undermine U.S. influence over other former clients. Moreover, because cliency relationships have come to play such a vital role in U.S. global strategy, this approach would necessitate a fundamental restructuring of the entire U.S. national security posture: the United States would be forced to develop alternatives to the vast network of alliances, military bases, and intelligence-gathering installations made possible by cliency relationships, a daunting prospect at best. While such a restructuring would be welcomed by many critics of U.S. foreign policy, U.S. policy makers would clearly oppose it.

Second, the United States could attempt to deal with popular unrest in client countries by further enhancing the repressive capabilities of the corresponding client states or, in extreme cases, by undertaking overt or covert interventions on behalf of these states. This approach was, of course, the basic strategy followed by the United States in the 1950s and 1960s. Although this approach has often been successful in the short term, it has produced several spectacular failures in the long term, most notably in South Vietnam. The problem with this approach is not only that it fails to address the underlying causes of popular unrest but that it may, in fact, exacerbate this unrest by further increasing the client state's autonomy. Moreover, with the growing concern in the United States today about human rights and democratization in the Third World, political pressures have made this approach much less attractive to U.S. policy makers, as was demonstrated in the cases of the Philippines and South Korea in the mid-1980s.

A third option is to try to reduce the intensity of certain cliency relationships or perhaps phase them out altogether by engaging in negotiations with the Soviet Union aimed at mutual disengagement in particular regions of the world. If matched by appropriate Soviet concessions, negotiations of this kind could reduce or eliminate the autonomy-enhancing effects of cliency and therefore gradually reduce this particular source of popular unrest without adversely affecting U.S. security interests. The climate of U.S.-Soviet relations in the early 1990s suggests that this approach holds considerable promise.

Fourth, the United States could try to conduct its cliency relationships in ways that do not promote high levels of state autonomy. This could be done in at least two ways. First, by using cliency instruments such as economic aid and security assistance more judiciously, it may be possible to strengthen a client state's military apparatus and promote political stability without greatly increasing the client state's autonomy. For example, security assistance programs can be tailored to strengthen the war-fighting capabilities of the client's security forces rather than their ability to repress domestic unrest; and training programs for military, police, and intelligence personnel can be designed to emphasize the importance of democratic institutions, human rights, civilian rule, and civic action. Similarly, by placing greater emphasis on project aid than on budgetary assistance, economic aid programs can be structured to maximize the benefits realized by the recipient population and to minimize the state's ability to use aid as a mechanism of co-optation. Second, depending on the dynamics of a particular cliency relationship, the patron may be in a position to exert considerable influence over the client state. If so, the patron can use this influence to reduce the client state's autonomy by encouraging it to increase opportunities for popular political participation, as the United States did to some extent in Iran in the late 1950s and early 1960s.

Options three and four appear to hold some promise, but they clearly have practical limits. Even if the United States and the Soviet Union can successfully negotiate mutual withdrawals from certain regions, they will probably reserve the right to maintain cliency relationships with countries located near their borders and with countries that are of special interest to them, as Israel is to the United States. Moreover, because the United States has many other adversaries in the world today (such as Cuba, Libya, Syria, Vietnam, North Korea, and potentially even China), U.S. global strategy is likely to involve continued reliance on cliency relationships. And while the United States may have considerable latitude in some cases to tailor a cliency relationship in ways that minimize its autonomy-enhancing effects or to pressure a client state to expand opportunities for political participation, there are inevitably situations in which this cannot be done. It therefore seems unavoidable that the United States, and presumably other major powers as well, will continue to rely on cliency relationships to advance their national interests. If so, then cliency will continue to affect the domestic politics of strategically important countries and therefore pose vexing problems for policy makers in patron countries.

Selected Bibliography

Abrahamian, Ervand. "Oriental Despotism: The Case of Qajar Iran." *International Journal of Middle East Studies* 5 (January 1974), 3–31.

——. *Iran between Two Revolutions*. Princeton, N.J.: Princeton University Press, 1982.

Acheson, Dean. *Present at the Creation*. New York: Norton, 1969.

Akhavi, Shahrough. *Religion and Politics in Contemporary Iran: Clergy-State Relations in the Pahlavi Period*. Albany: State University of New York Press, 1980.

Alavi, Hamza. "The State in Post-Colonial Societies: Pakistan and Bangladesh." *New Left Review* 74 (July–August 1972), 59–82.

Alexander, Yonah, and Allan Nanes, eds., *The United States and Iran: A Documentary History*. Washington: University Publications of America, 1980.

Amnesty International. *Annual Report, 1974–1975*. London, 1975.

——. *Amnesty International Briefing: Iran*. London, 1976.

Amuzegar, Jahangir. *Technical Assistance in Theory and Practice: The Case of Iran*. New York: Praeger, 1966.

——. *Iran: An Economic Profile*. Washington: Middle East Institute, 1977.

Arjomand, Said Amir. *The Shadow of God and the Hidden Imam*. Chicago: University of Chicago Press, 1984.

Ashraf, Ahmad. "Historical Obstacles to the Development of a Bourgeoisie in Iran." In M. A. Cook, ed., *Studies in the Economic History of the Middle East*, 308–32. London: Oxford University Press, 1970.

——. "Iran: Imperialism, Class, and Modernization from Above." Ph.D. diss., New School for Social Research, 1971.

Ashraf, Ahmad, and H. Hekmat. "Merchants and Artisans and the Development Processes of Ninteenth-Century Iran." In A. L. Udovitch, ed., *The Islamic Middle East, 700–1900: Studies in Economic and Social History*, 725–50. Princeton, N.J.: Darwin, 1981.

Azimi, Fakhreddin. "The Reconciliation of Politics and Ethics, Nationalism and Democracy: An Overview of the Political Career of Dr. Muhammad Musaddiq." In James A. Bill and William Roger Louis, eds., *Musaddiq, Iranian Nationalism, and Oil*, 47–68. Austin: University of Texas Press, 1988.

Bakhtiar, Chapour *Ma fidélité*. Paris: Albin, 1982.
Baldwin, George B. *Planning and Development in Iran*. Baltimore: Johns Hopkins University Press, 1967.
Bamford, James. *The Puzzle Palace*. Boston: Houghton Mifflin, 1982.
Banani, Amin. *The Modernization of Iran, 1921–1941*. Stanford, Calif.: Stanford University Press, 1961.
Bank Markazi Iran. *Annual Report and Balance Sheet*. Tehran, various years.
Baraheni, Reza. *The Crowned Cannibals*. New York: Random House, Vintage, 1977.
——. "The Perils of Publishing." *Index on Censorship* 7, (September–October 1978), 12–17.
Beck, Lois. *The Qashqa'i of Iran*. New Haven, Conn.: Yale University Press, 1986.
Behnam, Djamchid, and Mehdi Amani. *La population de L'Iran*. Paris: CICRED, 1974.
Benedick, Richard Elliot. *Industrial Finance in Iran*. Boston: Harvard University, Graduate School of Business Administration, 1964.
Bharier, Julian. *Economic Development in Iran, 1900–1970*. London: Oxford University Press, 1971.
Bill, James Alban. *The Politics of Iran: Groups, Classes, and Modernization*. Columbus, Ohio: Charles E. Merrill, 1972.
——. *The Eagle and the Lion: The Tragedy of American-Iranian Relations*. New Haven, Conn.: Yale University Press, 1988.
Binder, Leonard. *Iran: Political Development in a Changing Society*. Berkeley and Los Angeles: University of California Press, 1962.
Block, Fred. "The Ruling Class Does Not Rule: Notes on the Marxist Theory of the State." *Socialist Revolution* 7 (May–June 1977), 6–28.
Browne, Edward G. *The Persian Revolution of 1905–1909*. London: Cass, 1966.
Brzezinski, Zbigniew. *The Soviet Bloc*. Cambridge: Harvard University Press, 1976.
Butler, William J., and Georges Levasseur. *Human Rights and the Legal System in Iran*. Geneva: International Commission of Jurists, 1976.
Campbell, John C. *Defense of the Middle East: Problems of American Policy*. Rev. ed. New York: Praeger, 1960.
Carnoy, Martin. *The State and Political Theory*. Princeton, N.J.: Princeton University Press, 1984.
Chehabi, Houchang Esfandiar. "Modernist Shi'ism and Politics: Liberation Movement of Iran." Ph.D. diss., Yale University, 1986.
Chubin, Shahram, and Sepehr Zabih. *The Foreign Relations of Iran*. (Berkeley and Los Angeles: University of California Press, 1974).
Citibank. *Investment Guide to Iran*. New York, n.d.
Clawson, Patrick, and Cyrus Sassanpour. "Adjustment to a Foreign Exchange Shock: Iran, 1951–1953." *International Journal of Middle East Studies* 19 (May 1987), 1–22.
Committee against Repression in Iran. *Iran: The Shah's Empire of Repression*. London, 1976.
Confederation of Iranian Students. *Documents on the Pahlavi Reign of Terror*. 3 vols. Frankfurt, 1971.
Confederation of Iranian Students (National Union). *Documents on Iranian Secret Police, SAVAK*. N.p., 1976.
Cottam, Richard W. *Nationalism in Iran*. Pittsburgh: University of Pittsburgh Press, 1979.

Croziat, Victor J. "Imperial Iranian Gendarmerie." *Marine Corps Gazette*, October 1975, 28–31.

Cumming-Bruce, Nicholas. *Iran: A MEED Special Report*. London: Middle East Economic Digest, 1977.

Curzon, George N. *Persia and the Persian Question*. London: Cass, 1966.

Dahl, Robert A. *Who Governs?* New Haven, Conn.: Yale University Press, 1961.

Diba, Farhad. *Mohammad Mossadegh: A Political Biography*. London: Croom Helm, 1986.

Dix, Robert H. "Populism: Authoritarian and Democratic." *Latin American Research Review* 20 (1985), 29–52.

Editors. "How the CIA Turns Foreign Students into Traitors." *Ramparts*, April 1967.

Eisenstadt, S. N., and Rene Lemarchand, eds., *Political Clientelism, Patronage, and Development*. Beverly Hills, Calif.: Sage, 1981.

Elwell-Sutton, L. P. "Political Parties in Iran, 1941–1948." *Middle East Journal* 3 (January 1949), 45–62.

——. *Persian Oil: A Study in Power Politics*. London: Lawrence and Wishart, 1955.

Etzold, Thomas H., and John Lewis Gaddis, eds., *Containment: Documents on American Policy and Strategy, 1945–1950*. New York: Columbia University Press, 1980.

Faroughy, Ahmad, and Jean-Loup Reverier. *L'Iran contre le chah*. Paris: Simoen, 1979.

Fesharaki, Fereidun. *Development of the Iranian Oil Industy: International and Domestic Aspects*. New York: Praeger, 1976.

Gaddis, John Lewis. *Strategies of Containment*. New York: Oxford University Press, 1982.

Gage, Nicholas. "Iran: Making of a Revolution." *New York Times Magazine*, December 17, 1978.

Garthwaite, Gene R. *Khans and Shahs: A Documentary Analysis of the Bakhtiyari in Iran*. Cambridge: Cambridge University Press, 1983.

Gasiorowski, Mark J. "Dependency and Cliency in Latin America." *Journal of Inter-American Studies and World Affairs* 28 (Fall 1986), 47–65.

——. "The 1953 *Coup d'Etat* in Iran." *International Journal of Middle East Studies* 19 (August 1987), 261–86.

Gasiorowski, Mark J., and Seung-hyun Baek. "International Cliency Relationships and Client States in East Asia." *Pacific Focus* 2 (Fall 1987), 113–43.

Ghareeb, Edmund. *The Kurdish Question in Iraq*. Syracuse, N.Y.: Syracuse University Press, 1981.

Godson Roy. ed., *Intelligence Requirements for the 1980's. No. 4, Covert Action*. Washington: National Strategic Information Center, 1981.

Graham, Robert. *Iran: The Illusion of Power*. New York: St. Martin's, 1980.

Green, Jerrold D. *Revolution in Iran: The Politics of Countermobilization*. New York: Praeger, 1982.

Hale, W. M. and Julian Bharier. "CENTO, R.C.D. and the Northern Tier: A Political and Economic Appraisal." *Middle Eastern Studies* 8 (May 1972), 217–26.

Halliday, Fred. *Arabia without Sultans*. New York: Random House, Vintage, 1975.

Hamilton, Nora. *The Limits of State Autonomy: Post-revolutionary Mexico*. Princeton, N.J.: Princeton University Press, 1982.

Hammond, Paul Y. "NSC-68: Prologue to Rearmament." In Warner R. Schilling, Paul Y. Hammond, and Glen H. Snyder, eds., *Strategy, Politics, and Defense Budgets*, 267–378. New York: Columbia University Press, 1962.
Hanson, Brad. "The 'Westoxication' of Iran: Depictions and Reactions of Behrangi, Al-e Ahmad, and Shariati." *International Journal of Middle East Studies* 15 (February 1983), 1–23.
Harkness, Richard, and Gladys Harkness. "The Mysterious Doings of CIA." *Saturday Evening Post*, November 6, 1954, 66–68.
Heikel, Mohamed. *Iran: The Untold Story*. New York: Pantheon, 1981.
Herz Martin F., ed. *Contacts with the Opposition*. Washington: Georgetown University Institute for the Study of Diplomacy, 1979.
Hooglund, Eric. *Land and Revolution in Iran, 1960–1980*. (Austin: University of Texas Press, 1982.
Hoveyda, Fereydoun. *The Fall of the Shah*. New York: Wyndham, 1979.
Hulbert, Mark. *Interlock*. New York: Richardson and Snyder, 1982.
Huntington, Samuel P., and Joan M. Nelson. *No Easy Choice: Political Participation in Developing Countries*. Cambridge: Harvard University Press, 1976.
Imperial Government of Iran, Plan and Budget Organization. *Economic Statistics and Trends of Iran. 3d ed.* Tehran, 1976.
International Labor Office. *Employment and Income Policies for Iran*. Geneva, 1973.
International Monetary Fund. *International Financial Statistics, 1983 Yearbook*. Washington, 1983.
Iran Committee. *Torture and Resistance in Iran*. London, 1978.
Issawi, Charles, ed. *The Economic History of Iran, 1800–1914* Chicago: Univerity of Chicago Press, 1971.
Johnson, Gail Cook. *High-Level Manpower in Iran: From Hidden Conflict to Crisis*. New York: Praeger, 1980.
Johnson, Hubert Otis III. "Recent Opposition Movements in Iran." M.A. thesis, University of Utah, 1975.
Katouzian, Homa. *The Political Economy of Modern Iran: Despotism and Pseudo-Modernism, 1926–1979*, New York: New York University Press, 1981.
——. "Oil Boycott and the Political Economy: Musaddiq and the Strategy of Non-oil Economics." In James A. Bill and William Roger Louis, eds., *Musaddiq, Iranian Nationalism, and Oil*, 203–27. Austin: University of Texas Press, 1988.
Katzenstein, Peter J. "International Relations and Domestic Structures: Foreign Economic Policies of Advanced Industrial States." *International Organization* 30 (Winter 1976), 1–46.
——. "Conclusion: Domestic Structures and Strategies of Foreign Economic Policy." In Peter J. Katzenstein, ed., *Between Power and Plenty: Foreign Economic Policies of Advanced Industrial States*, 323–32. Madison: University of Wisconsin Press, 1978).
Kaufman, Burton I. *The Oil Cartel Case: A Documentary Study of Antitrust Activity in the Cold War Era*. Westport, Conn: Greenwood, 1978.
Kazemi, Farhad. *Poverty and Revolution in Iran*. New York: New York University Press, 1980.
——. "The Military and Politics in Iran: The Uneasy Symbiosis." In Elie Kedourie and Sylvia G. Haim, eds., *Toward a Modern Iran*, 217–40. London: Cass, 1980.
——. "Urban Migrants and the Revolution." *Iranian Studies* 13 (1980), 257–77.
——. "The Feda'iyan-e Islam: Fanaticism, Politics, and Terror." In Said Amir

Arjomand, ed., *From Nationalism to Revolutionary Islam*, 158–76. Albany: State University of New York Press, 1984.

Kazemi, Farhad, and Ervand Abrahamian. "The Nonrevolutionary Peasantry of Modern Iran." *Iranian Studies* 11 (1978), 259–304.

Kazemzadeh, Firuz. *Russia and Britain in Persia, 1864–1914*. New Haven, Conn.: Yale University Press, 1968.

Keddie, Nikki R. *Roots of Revolution: An Interpretive History of Modern Iran*. New Haven, Conn.: Yale University Press, 1981.

——, "The Origins of the Religious-Radical Alliance in Iran." In Nikki R. Keddie ed. *Iran: Religion, Politics, and Society*, 53–65. London: Cass, 1980.

Keddie, Nikki, and Mark J. Gasiorowski, eds. *Neither East nor West: Iran, the Soviet Union, and the United States*. New Haven, Conn.: Yale University Press, 1990.

Keohane, Robert O. "The Big Influence of Small Allies." *Foreign Policy* 2 (Spring 1971), 161–82.

Klare, Michael T. *Supplying Repression*. New York: Field Foundation, 1977.

Knorr, Klaus. *The Power of Nations*. New York: Basic Books, 1975.

Krasner, Stephen D. *Defending the National Interest*. Princeton, N.J.: Princeton University Press, 1978.

Kuniholm, Bruce Robellet. *The Origins of the Cold War in the Near East*. Princeton, N.J.: Princeton University Press, 1980.

Ladjevardi, Habib. *Labor Unions and Autocracy in Iran*. Syracuse, N.Y.: Syracuse University Press, 1985.

——. "Constitutional Government and Reform under Musaddiq." In James A. Bill and William Roger Louis, eds., *Musaddiq, Iranian Nationalism, and Oil*, 69–90. Austin: University of Texas Press, 1988.

Lambton, Ann K. S. *Landlord and Peasant in Persia*. London: Oxford University Press, 1953.

Lenczowski, George. *Russia and the West in Iran, 1918–1948: A Study in Big-Power Rivalry*. Ithaca, N.Y.: Cornell University Press, 1949.

Linz, Juan J. "Totalitarian and Authoritarian Regimes." In Fred I. Greenstein and Nelson W. Polsby, eds., *Handbook of Political Science*, Vol. 3, 175–411. Reading, Mass.: Addison-Wesley, 1975.

Looney, Robert E. *A Development Strategy for Iran through the 1980s*. New York: Praeger, 1977.

——. *Economic Origins of the Iranian Revolution*. New York: Pergamon, 1982.

Louis, William Roger. *The British Empire in the Middle East, 1945–1951*. Oxford: Clarendon, 1984.

Love, Kennett. "The American Role in the Pahlavi Restoration on 19 August 1953." Allen Dulles Papers, Princeton University Library, 1960.

Lowi, Theodore J. *The End of Liberalism: Ideology, Policy, and the Crisis of Public Authority*. New York: Norton, 1969.

Lytle, Mark Hamilton. *The Origins of the Iranian-American Alliance, 1941–1953*. New York: Holmes and Meier, 1987.

Macridis, Roy C. *Modern Political Regimes*. Boston: Little, Brown, 1986.

Mahdavy, Hossein. "Patterns and Problems of Economic Development in Rentier States: The Case of Iran," in M. A. Cook, ed., *Studies in the Economic History of the Middle East*, 428–67. London: Oxford University Press, 1970.

Miliband, Ralph. *The State in Capitalist Society*. New York: Basic Books, 1969.

Mills, C. Wright. *The Power Elite*. New York: Oxford University Press, 1957.

Moghadam, Val. "Oil, the State, and Limits to Autonomy: The Iranian Case." *Arab Studies Quarterly* 10 (1987), 225–38.

Mohammadi-Nejad, Hassan. "Elite-Counterelite Conflict and the Development of a Revolutionary Movement." Ph.D. diss., Southern Illinois University, 1970.

Moore, Barrington. *Social Origins of Dictatorship and Democracy: Lord and Peasant in the Making of the Modern World*. Boston: Beacon, 1966.

Motter, T. Vail. *United States Army in World War II: The Middle East Theater, the Persian Corridor, and Aid to Russia* (Washington: Department of the Army, Office of the Chief of Military History, 1952.

Muslim Students Following the Line of the Imam. *Documents from the U.S. Espionage Den*. Tehran: N.p., n.d.

National Front of Iran (operating abroad). "A Portion of the Secrets of the Security Organization (SAVAK)," May 1971.

Nelson, Joan M. *Aid, Influence, and Foreign Policy*. New York: Macmillan, 1968.

Nobari, Ali-Reza. *Iran Erupts*. (Stanford, Calif.: Iran-America Documentation Group, 1978.

Nordlinger, Eric. *On the Autonomy of the Democratic State*. Cambridge: Harvard University Press, 1981.

Oney, Earnest R. "The Eyes and Ears of the Shah." *Intelligence Quarterly* 1 (February 1986), 1–3.

Pahlavi, Ashraf (Princess). *Faces in a Mirror*. Englewood Cliffs, N.J.: Prentice-Hall, 1980.

Pahlavi, Mohammed Reza. *Mission for My Country*. New York: McGraw-Hill, 1961.

——. *Answer to History*. New York: Stein and Day, 1980.

Parsons, Anthony. *The Pride and the Fall*. London: Cape, 1984.

Parvin, Manoucher, and Amir N. Zamani. "Political Economy of Growth and Destruction: A Statistical Interpretation of the Iranian Case." *Iranian Studies* 12 (Winter–Spring 1979), 43–78.

Pesaran, M. H. "Income Distribution in Iran." In Jane W. Jacqz, ed., *Iran: Past, Present, and Future*, New York: Aspen Institute, 1976.

Plan Organization, Iranian Statistical Centre. *National Census of Population and Housing*. Vol. 168. Tehran, 1968.

Plan and Budget Organization, Statistical Centre of Iran. *National Census of Population and Housing, Total Country*. Tehran, 1976.

Plate, Thomas, and Andrea Darvi. *Secret Police: The Inside Story of a Network of Terror*. New York: Doubleday, 1981.

Poulantzas, Nicos *Political Power and Social Classes*. London: New Left, 1973.

——. *Fascism and Dictatorship*. London: New Left, 1974.

Rafizadeh, Mansur. *Witness: From the Shah to the Secret Arms Deal*. New York: Morrow, 1987.

Ramazani, Rouhollah K. *The Foreign Policy of Iran: A Developing Nation in World Affairs, 1500–1941*. Charlottesville: University Press of Virginia, 1966.

——. *Iran's Foreign Policy, 1941–1973: A Study of Foreign Policy in Modernizing Nations*. Charlottesville: University Press of Virginia, 1975.

Razavi, Hossein, and Firouz Vakil. *The Political Environment of Economic Planning in Iran, 1971–1983*. Boulder, Colo.: Westview, 1984.

Razi, Gholam Hossein "The Press and Political Institutions in Iran: A Content Analysis of Ettela'at and Keyhan." *Middle East Journal*, Vol. 22 (Autumn 1968), 463–74.

Richard, Yann. "Ayatollah Kashani: Precursor of the Islamic Republic?" In Nikki R. Keddie, ed., *Religion and Politics in Iran: Shi'ism from Quietism to Revolution*, 101–24. New Haven, Conn.: Yale University Press, 1983.

Ricks, Thomas M. "U.S. Military Missions to Iran, 1943–1978: The Political Economy of Military Assistance." *Iranian Studies* 12 (Summer–Autumn 1979), 168–77.

Roosevelt, Archie Jr. "The Kurdish Republic of Mahabad." *Middle East Journal* 1 (July 1947), 247–69.

Roosevelt, Kermit. *Countercoup*. New York: McGraw-Hill, 1979.

Rossow, Robert Jr. "The Battle of Azerbaijan." *Middle East Journal* 10 (Winter 1956), 17–32.

Rubin, Barry. *Paved with Good Intentions*. New York: Oxford University Press, 1980.

Saleh, Ali Pasha. *Cultural Ties between Iran and the United States*. Tehran: N.p., 1976.

Schmitter, Phillippe C. "Still the Century of Corporatism?" *Review of Politics* 36 (1974), 85–131.

Scott, Andrew M. "Nonintervention and Conditional Intervention." *Journal of International Affairs* 22 (1968), 208–16.

Sheikholeslami, A. Reza. "The Patrimonial Structure of Iranian Bureaucracy in the Late Nineteenth Century." *Iranian Studies* 11, (1978), 199–258.

Shoemaker, Christopher C., and John Spanier. *Patron-Client State Relationships: Multilateral Crises in the Nuclear Age*. New York: Praeger, 1984.

Shuster, W. Morgan. *The Strangling of Persia*. London: T. Fisher Unwin, 1912.

Sick, Gary. *All Fall Down: America's Tragic Encounter with Iran*. (New York: Random House, 1985.

Singer, Marshall R. *Weak States in a World of Powers: The Dynamics of International Relationships*. New York: Free Press, 1972.

Skocpol, Theda. *States and Social Revolutions*. Cambridge: Cambridge University Press, 1979.

——. "Political Response to Capitalist Crisis: Neo-Marxist Theories of the State and the Case of the New Deal." *Politics and Society* 10 (1980), 155–201.

——. "Rentier State and Shi'a Islam in the Iranian Revolution." *Theory and Society* 11 (May 1982), 265–83.

——. "Bringing the State Back In: Strategies of Analysis in Current Research." In Peter B. Evans, Dietrich Rueschemeyer, and Theda Skocpol, eds., *Bringing the State Back In*, 3–37. Cambridge: Cambridge University Press, 1985.

Snyder, Glen H. "The 'New Look' of 1953." In Warner R. Schilling, Paul Y. Hammond, and Glen H. Snyder, eds., *Strategy, Politics, and Defense Budgets*, 379–524. New York: Columbia University Press, 1962.

Stempel, John D. *Inside the Iranian Revolution*. Bloomington: Indiana University Press, 1981.

Stepan, Alfred *The State and Society: Peru in Comparative Perspective*. Princeton N.J.: Princeton University Press, 1978.

Sullivan, William H. *Mission to Iran*. New York: Norton, 1981.

Taheri, Amir. *The Spirit of Allah*. London: Hutchinson, 1985.

Tahir-Kheli, Shirin. "Proxies and Allies: The Case of Iran and Pakistan." *Orbis* 24 (Summer 1980), 339–52.

Trimberger, Ellen Kay, *Revolution from Above*. New Brunswick, N.J.: Transaction Books, 1978.

Triska, Jan F. ed., *Dominant Powers and Subordiante States: The United States in Latin America and the Soviet Union in Eastern Europe*. Durham, N.C.: Duke University Press, 1986.

Truman, David B. *The Governmental Process*. New York: Knopf, 1951.

United Nations. *Statistical Yearbook*. New York, various years.

U.S. Agency for International Development. *U.S. Overseas Loans and Grants: Series of Yearly Data*. Vols. 1–5. Washington, 1985.

U.S. Department of Defense, Defense Security Assistance Agency. *Fiscal Year Series, 1980*. Washington, 1980.

De Villiers, Gérard. *S.A.S. contre C.I.A.*. Paris: Plon, 1965.

Walton, Thomas. "Economic Development and Revolutionary Upheavals in Iran." *Cambridge Journal of Economics* 4 (September 1980), 271–302.

Warne, William E. *Mission for Peace: Point 4 in Iran*. Indianapolis: Bobbs-Merrill, 1956.

Weber, Max. *Economy and Society*. New York: Bedminster, 1968.

Whitehead, Laurence. "International Aspects of Democratization." In Guillermo A. O'Donnell, Phillippe C. Schmitter, and Laurence Whitehead, eds., *Transitions from Authoritarian Rule: Comparative Perspectives*, 3–46. Baltimore: Johns Hopkins University Press, 1986.

Wilber, Donald N. *Riza Shah Pahlavi: The Resurrection and Reconstruction of Iran*. Hicksville, N.Y.: Exposition, 1975.

——. *Adventures in the Middle East: Excursions and Incursions*. Princetion, N.J.: Darwin, 1986.

Woodhouse, Christopher Montague. *Something Ventured*. St. Albans, Hert. Granada, 1982.

World Bank. *World Tables. 3d ed. Vol. 2*. Baltimore: Johns Hopkins University Press, 1983.

Yaniv, Avner. *Deterrence without the Bomb: The Politics of Israeli Strategy*. Lexington, Mass.: Lexington Books, 1987.

Yeselson, Abraham. *United States–Persian Diplomatic Relations, 1883–1921*. New Brunswick, N.J.: Rutgers University Press, 1956.

Young, T. Cuyler. "The Social Support of Current Iranian Policy." *Middle East Journal* 6 (Spring 1952), 125–43.

Zabih, Sepehr. *The Communist Movement in Iran*. Berkeley and Los Angeles: University of California Press, 1966.

Zonis, Marvin. *The Political Elite of Iran*. Princeton, N.J.: Princeton University Press, 1971.

Index

Library of Congress Cataloging-in-Publication Data

Gasiorowski, Mark J., 1954-
U.S. foreign policy and the shah: building a client state in Iran / Mark Joseph Gasiorowski.
p. cm.
Includes bibliographical references and index.
ISBN 0–8014–2412–7 (cloth : alk. paper)
1. United States—Foreign relations—Iran. 2. Iran—Foreign relations—United States.
3. Iran—Politics and government—1941–1979. I. Title.
E183.8.I55G37 1991
327.73055—dc20 90–55919